LIBRARY OF NEW TESTAMENT STUDIES

675

formerly the Journal for the Study of the New Testament Supplement series

Editor
Chris Keith

Editorial Board
Dale C. Allison, Lynn H. Cohick, R. Alan Culpepper, Craig A. Evans, Jennifer Eyl, Robert Fowler, Simon J. Gathercole, Juan Hernández Jr., John S. Kloppenborg, Michael Labahn, Matthew V. Novenson, Love L. Sechrest, Robert Wall, Catrin H. Williams, Brittany E. Wilson

Purifying the Consciousness in Hebrews

Cult, Defilement and the Perpetual Heavenly Blood of Jesus

Joshua D. A. Bloor

t&tclark
LONDON • NEW YORK • OXFORD • NEW DELHI • SYDNEY

T&T CLARK
Bloomsbury Publishing Plc
50 Bedford Square, London, WC1B 3DP, UK
1385 Broadway, New York, NY 10018, USA
29 Earlsfort Terrace, Dublin 2, Ireland

BLOOMSBURY, T&T CLARK and the T&T Clark logo are trademarks of
Bloomsbury Publishing Plc

First published in Great Britain 2023
This paperback edition published 2024

Copyright © Joshua D. A. Bloor, 2023

Joshua D. A. Bloor has asserted his right under the Copyright,
Designs and Patents Act, 1988, to be identified as Author of this work.

For legal purposes the Acknowledgements on p. x constitute an
extension of this copyright page.

All rights reserved. No part of this publication may be reproduced or transmitted
in any form or by any means, electronic or mechanical, including photocopying,
recording, or any information storage or retrieval system, without prior
permission in writing from the publishers.

Bloomsbury Publishing Plc does not have any control over, or responsibility for, any
third-party websites referred to or in this book. All internet addresses given in
this book were correct at the time of going to press. The author and publisher
regret any inconvenience caused if addresses have changed or sites have
ceased to exist, but can accept no responsibility for any such changes.

A catalogue record for this book is available from the British Library.

A catalog record for this book is available from the Library of Congress.

ISBN: HB: 978-0-5677-0810-6
PB: 978-0-5677-0814-4
ePDF: 978-0-5677-0811-3
eBook: 978-0-5677-0813-7

Series: Library of New Testament Studies, volume 675
ISSN 2513-8790

Typeset by RefineCatch Limited, Bungay, Suffolk

To find out more about our authors and books visit www.bloomsbury.com
and sign up for our newsletters.

Contents

List of tables	ix
Acknowledgements	x
List of abbreviations	xi

1 Introduction 1
   1.1 The statement of the problem 2
   1.2 The situation of the recipients 3
   1.3 Συνείδησις: An overview 6
      1.3.1 An interpretative history 6
      1.3.2 Ancient Greek origins 9
      1.3.3 The Jewish Scriptures 10
      1.3.4 Philo 11
      1.3.5 Josephus 13
      1.3.6 New Testament 13
   1.4 Συνείδησις in Hebrews 14
      1.4.1 Defining συνείδησις in Hebrews scholarship 14
      1.4.2 The application of συνείδησις in Hebrews 16
   1.5 Methodological approach 22
   1.6 Outline of the study 26

Part One The defiled consciousness

2 Cosmic defilement: The cultic context of defilement 31
   2.1 Introduction 31
   2.2 The present problem 31
   2.3 Defilement in the cultic sphere 33
      2.3.1 Dorian Gray and impurity in the cultic sphere 33
      2.3.2 Moral and ritual impurity 35
      2.3.3 The reality of defilement 37
   2.4 The heavenly tabernacle in Hebrews 39
      2.4.1 Hebrews and cosmology 39
      2.4.2 Construing the architecture of the heavenly tabernacle 41
      2.4.3 Earthly and heavenly tabernacle terminology 42

	2.4.4	The absence of temple terminology	43
	2.4.5	The 'sketch' and 'foreshadow'	45
2.5	Defilement in Hebrews		48
	2.5.1	Introducing sin in Hebrews	48
	2.5.2	Moral and ritual impurity?	48
	2.5.3	Sin as conscious defilement (συνείδησις) in Hebrews	49
	2.5.4	'Dead works'	50
	2.5.5	Types of sin? Unintentional/intentional sin	51
	2.5.6	Defiled heavenly tabernacle	53
2.6	The effects of a defiled συνείδησις		55
	2.6.1	Restricted access	55
	2.6.2	The stain, dread and timidity of defilement	55
	2.6.3	Apostasy, rebellion and the wilderness motif	56
2.7	Conclusion		58

Part Two Purifying the consciousness: Cosmic purgation

3 Navigating Hebrews' sacrificial argumentation: Yom Kippur and Jesus' earthly and heavenly achievements — 61
- 3.1 Introduction — 61
- 3.2 Navigating scholarship — 61
  - 3.2.1 Critiquing Moffitt — 64
  - 3.2.2 Mitigating Moffitt — 65
  - 3.2.3 Kerygma and allowing Hebrews to speak — 66
- 3.3 Yom Kippur and Hebrews — 67
  - 3.3.1 Yom Kippur — 67
  - 3.3.2 Yom Kippur in Hebrews — 68
  - 3.3.3 An overarching Yom Kippur hermeneutic — 69
  - 3.3.4 The problem with 'atonement' — 71
- 3.4 A death that redeems (Heb. 9.11-17) — 73
  - 3.4.1 Having obtained an eternal redemption (Heb. 9.11-14) — 73
  - 3.4.2 Death and redemption (Heb. 9.15-17) — 75
  - 3.4.3 The paschal lamb who redeems (Heb. 2.14-15) — 76
- 3.5 Not to offer himself again and again (Heb. 9.24-8) — 79
  - 3.5.1 He offered himself (Heb. 9.24-6) — 79
  - 3.5.2 He was offered up (Heb. 9.27-8) — 80
  - 3.5.3 Offered up on earth in order to bear away the sins of many in heaven (Heb. 9.24-8) — 80

	3.6	An offering of obedience and a heavenly offering (Heb. 10.5-14)	83
		3.6.1 The sacrificial life of Jesus (Heb. 10.5-10)	84
		3.6.2 Jesus' personal offering? (Heb. 5.1-10; 7.26-8)	86
		3.6.3 Made holy by Jesus' earthly offering (Heb. 2.5-11; 10.5-10)	88
		3.6.4 The sacrificial offering of Jesus (Heb. 10.11-14)	89
	3.7	Conclusion	90
4	How much more the blood of Christ? Ritual, perfection and the finality of purgation		93
	4.1	Introduction	93
	4.2	Purifying the heavenly tabernacle	93
		4.2.1 Entering with blood	93
		4.2.2 Purifying the heavenly tabernacle (Heb. 1.3; 2.17; 9.23)	94
	4.3	The drama of sacrifice: Purifying the consciousness	98
		4.3.1 An internal–external/συνείδησις–σάρξ purification contrast?	98
		4.3.2 Σάρξ	99
		4.3.3 Earthly regulations/purifications	102
		4.3.4 The drama of ritual	104
		4.3.5 Levitical אשם and the consciousness of sin	105
	4.4	How much more? Perfection and the finality of purgation	109
		4.4.1 Perfection and purification	109
		4.4.2 Qualitative purgation (Heb. 9.13-14; 10.1-4)	111
		4.4.3 Without αἱματεκχυσία there is no ἄφεσις (Heb. 9.22)	113
		4.4.4 Washing and sprinkling (Heb. 10.22)	118
	4.5	Conclusion	120

Part Three   Assurance and the purified consciousness

5	Divine help, assurance and perpetual blood		125
	5.1	Introduction	125
	5.2	Becoming the enthroned high priest	125
		5.2.1 The eternal Son (Heb. 1.1-14)	126
		5.2.2 The narrative of the enthroned Son (Heb. 2.5-9)	127
		5.2.3 A high priest, like Melchizedek (Heb. 5.1-10; 7:1–28)	130
	5.3	Divine help	132
		5.3.1 Holiness, fighting temptation and post-baptismal sin	133
		5.3.2 The Father helps the Son (Heb. 5.7-8)	134
		5.3.3 Helping the descendants of Abraham (Heb. 2.16-18)	135

	5.3.4	Mercy and grace to help in time of need (Heb. 4.14-16)	137
	5.3.5	He makes intercession for them (Heb. 7.25)	138
	5.3.6	Divine help, approach and entering the rest	139
5.4	The perpetual assurance of Jesus and his heavenly blood offering		141
	5.4.1	Jesus as guarantor	141
	5.4.2	Jesus as mediator	142
	5.4.3	Perpetual heavenly blood	143
		5.4.3.1 The nature of Jesus' heavenly offering	144
		5.4.3.2 The substance of Jesus' heavenly offering	145
		5.4.3.3 What does Jesus' heavenly blood represent?	146
	5.4.4	Blood that is speaking (Heb. 11.4; 12.24)	148
	5.4.5	Purifying the consciousness: Confidence, assurance and amnesia	150
5.5	Conclusion		151
6	**Conclusion**		**153**
6.1	Summary		153
6.2	Contributions		155
6.3	Limitations and further research		157
6.4	Pastoral implications for the contemporary church		157

Bibliography	159
Ancient index	193
Author index	209
Subject index	213

Tables

1. Earthly and heavenly terminology in Hebrews and Platonism — 16
2. The priestly system — 34
3. Earthly–heavenly contrast (Heb. 9.24-8) — 81
4. By means of his flesh (Heb. 10.20) — 100
5. Renderings for 'δικαιώματα σαρκὸς' (9.10) and 'σαρκὸς καθαρότητα' (9.13) — 102

Acknowledgements

The following monograph is a light revision of my PhD thesis which was submitted to the University of Manchester in the spring of 2021. Attached to each section of this work are countless joyful memories over the course of six and a half years. I remember where I was sitting and who was making the teas, as I wrote and rewrote different portions. It has been a wonderful journey. Thank you to the University of Manchester, the Nazarene Theological College and to Dr Peter Rae, for helping me obtain extra time to access resources and complete this thesis throughout the COVID-19 pandemic.

I am thankful for the feedback and for the opportunity to have presented papers in Edinburgh, Maynooth, Manchester and Reutlingen. Dr James Sedlacek, Dr Nick Moore and Dr Madison Pierce read my work at different stages and gave helpful feedback. I am grateful for the support of Dr David Moffitt and for distributing his work. The Didsbury Lectures at NTC continue to stimulate my thinking, although the four nights on Hebrews from Professors Dr Philip and Dr Loveday Alexander has had the most personal impact. I am thankful for their support. My examiners, Dr Samuel Hildebrandt and Prof Loveday Alexander, engaged with my work in a detailed and encouraging manner. People who have encouraged me since my Masters include Dr Geordan Hammond, Prof Peter Oakes and Dr Joseph Wood. The research community has provided a place of solidarity and support. Dr Mi-Ja Wi, Dr Ezekiel Shibemba, Dr James Sedlacek and Dr Andrew Pottenger spent the majority of time with me on campus. The conversations over coffee, our Greek reading group and our long trips to the BNTC; thank you for sharing these times with me. I am indebted to Richard and the whole of King's Church for cheering me on and helping me to grow.

To my wonderful supervisors. Dr Kent Brower's 2012 Biblical Studies MA class sparked an early interest in Hebrews. Thank you for helping me to – in your own words – 'kill my grammatical darlings'. I fear I will continue to yield to these. Dr Svetlana Khobnya, my pastoral polyglot, thank you for being my number one supporter and for overseeing this research project from the beginning, for always asking me how *I* am, before you ask how my research is going.

Thank you to my family and especially my dad, who read my thesis in a single day. To the Perkins, your friendship and continued celebration of my achievements will always be treasured. Thank you, Dave, for attending my many papers (I hope you enjoyed the buffets at least). Kleo, our loyal cat, who has sat by my side as I studied hard. To my wife and high-school sweetheart, Charlotte. You have always been with me and you have always believed in me (even when I doubted myself). To our daughter, Iris, thank you for being born three weeks *after* my Viva! Your constant smile and beaming joy acts as a daily reminder of God's love for us.

Abbreviations

Primary sources

1 Clem.	1 Clement
1 En.	1 (Ethiopic) Enoch
1 Macc.	1 Maccabees
1QM	War Scroll
1QS	Community Rule / Manuel of Discipline
11Q13	Melchizedek
2 Bar.	2 (Syriac) Baruch
2 En.	2 (Slavonic) Enoch
3 Bar.	3 (Greek) Baruch
3 En.	3 (Hebrew) Enoch
4 Macc	4 Maccabees
4Q400	Songs of the Sabbath Sacrifice
4Q504	Words of the Luminaries
4QFlor	Florilegium
Abr.	De Abrahamo
Anab.	Anabasis
Ant.	Antiquities of the Jews
Apion.	Against Apion
Asc. Isa.	Ascension of Isaiah
Ass. Mos.	Assumption of Moses
Bar.	Baruch
Barn.	Barnabas
CD	Damascus Document
Cher.	De cherubim
Conf.	Confessions
Conf. Ling.	De confusione linguarum
Congr.	De congressu eruditionis gratia
Dec.	De decalogo
Det. Pot. Ins.	Quod deterius potiori insidiari soleat
Deus Imm.	Quod Deus sit immutabilis
Did.	Didache
Ebr.	De ebrietate
Ep.	Epistulae morales
Eq.	Equites
Flacc.	Against Flaccus
Gen. Rab.	Genesis Rabbah
Her.	Quis rerum divinarum heres sit
Hermas, Vis.	Hermas, Vision
Hist.	Historiae

Jdt.	Judith
Jos.	*De Josepho*
Josh. Asen.	*Joseph and Asenath*
Jub.	*Jubilees*
LAB	*Liber Antiquitatum Biblicarum*
Leg. All.	*Legum allegoriae*
Leg. Gai.	*Legatio ad Gaium*
Midr.	Midrash
Op. Mund.	*De opificio mundi*
Orest.	*Orestes*
Pesaḥ.	*Pesahim*
Poet.	*Poetics*
Poster. C.	*De posteritate Caini*
Praem. Poen.	*De praemiis et poenis*
Prob.	*Quod omnis probus liber sit*
Pss. Sol.	*Psalms of Solomon*
Qidd.	*Qiddushin*
Rep.	*Republic*
Rhet.	*Rhetoric*
Sanh.	*Sanhedrin*
Sera	*De sera numinis vindicta*
Sir.	Sirach
Spec. Leg.	*De specialibus legibus*
T. Dan	*Testament of Dan*
T. Levi	*Testament of Levi*
Test. XII Patr.	*Testaments of the Twelve Patriarchs*
Thesm.	*Thesmophoriazusae*
Tob.	Tobit
Virt.	*De virtutibus*
Vit. Apoll.	*Vita Apollonii*
Vit. Mos.	*De vita Mosis*
War	*Jewish War*
Wis.	Wisdom of Solomon

Secondary sources

AB	Anchor Bible
ABD	*Anchor Bible Dictionary*. Edited by David Noel Freedman. 6 vols. New York: Doubleday, 1992.
AC	*Acta Classica*
AGJU	Arbeiten zur Geschichte des antiken Judentums und des Urchristentums
ALGHJ	Arbeiten zur Literatur und Geschichte des hellenistischen Judentums
AM	Abhandlungen zur Moraltheologie
AOTC	Abingdon Old Testament Commentaries

BBR	*Bulletin for Biblical Research*
BBRSup	Bulletin for Biblical Research Supplement
BDAG	Danker, Frederick W., Walter Bauer, William F. Arndt and F. Wilbur Gingrich. *Greek-English Lexicon of the New Testament and Other Early Christian Literature*. 3rd edn. Chicago: University of Chicago Press, 2000 (Danker-Bauer-Arndt-Gingrich).
BDF	Blass, Friedrich, Albert Debrunner and Robert W. Funk. *A Greek Grammar of the New Testament and Other Early Christian Literature*. Chicago: University of Chicago Press, 1961.
BBTL	Bibliotheca Ephemeridum Theologicarum Lovaniensium
BHS	*Biblia Hebraica Stuttgartensia*
Bib	*Biblica*
BibInt	Biblical Interpretation Series
BJS	Brown Judaic Studies
BNT	Die Botschaft des Neuen Testaments
BR	*Biblical Research*
BSac	*Bibliotheca Sacra*
BST	Basel Studies of Theology
BT	*The Bible Translator*
BTS	Biblical Tools and Studies
BU	Biblische Untersuchungen
BZ	*Biblische Zeitschrift*
BZNW	Beihefte zur Zeitschrift für die neutestamentliche Wissenschaft
CBQ	*Catholic Biblical Quarterly*
CBQMS	Catholic Biblical Quarterly Monograph Series
CJ	*Concordia Journal*
CJT	*Canadian Journal of Theology*
ConBNT	Coniectanea Biblica: New Testament Series
CQS	Companion to the Qumran Scrolls
CurBR	*Currents in Biblical Research*
DCH	*Dictionary of Classical Hebrew*. Edited by David J. A. Clines. 9 vols. Sheffield: Sheffield Phoenix Press, 1993–2014.
DCLY	Deuterocanonical and Cognate Literature Yearbook
DDD	*Dictionary of Deities and Demons in the Bible*. Edited by Karel van der Toorn, Bob Becking and Pieter W. van der Horst. Leiden: Brill, 1995. 2nd rev. edn. Grand Rapids: Eerdmans, 1999.
DHR	Dynamics in the History of Religions
EBib	*Etudes bibliques*
EBC	Earth Bible Commentary
EBR	*Encyclopedia of the Bible and Its Reception*. Edited by Hans-Josef Klauck et al. Berlin: de Gruyter, 2009–.
ECC	Eerdmans Critical Commentary
EDEJ	*The Eerdmans Dictionary of Early Judaism*. Edited by John J. Collins and Daniel C. Harlow. Grand Rapids: Eerdmans, 2010.

EdF	Erträge der Forschung
EDNT	*Exegetical Dictionary of the New Testament*. Edited by Horst Balz and Gerhard Schneider. 3 vols. Grand Rapids: Eerdmans, 1990–3.
EGGNT	Exegetical Guide to the Greek New Testament
EKKNT	Evangelisch-katholischer Kommentar zum Neuen Testament
EncJud	*Encyclopedia Judaica*. Edited by Fred Skolnik and Michael Berenbaum. 2nd edn. 22 vols. Detroit: Macmillan Reference USA, 2007.
EvQ	*Evangelical Quarterly*
ExpTim	*Expository Times*
FAT	Forschungen zum Alten Testament
FB	Forschung zur Bibel
FRLANT	Forschungen zur Religion und Literatur des Alten und Neuen Testaments
GELS	*A Greek-English Lexicon of the Septuagint*. Takamitsu Muraoka. Leuven: Peeters, 2009.
GOTR	*Greek Orthodox Theological Review*
HA	*History and Anthropology*
HALOT	Koehler, L., W. Baumgartner and J. J. Stamm. *The Hebrew and Aramaic Lexicon of the Old Testament*. Translated and edited under the supervision of M. E. J. Richardson. 2 vols. Leiden: Brill, 2001.
HBM	Hebrew Bible Monographs
HBT	*Horizons in Biblical Theology*
HNT	Handbuch zum Neuen Testament
HTR	*Harvard Theological Review*
ICC	International Critical Commentary
IDBSup	*Interpreter's Dictionary of the Bible: Supplementary Volume*. Edited by Keith Crim. Nashville: Abingdon, 1976.
Int	*Interpretation*
ITQ	*Irish Theological Quarterly*
JAJSup	Journal of Ancient Judaism Supplements
JBL	*Journal of Biblical Literature*
JETS	*Journal of the Evangelical Theological Society*
JLRS	*Journal of Law, Religion and State*
JNES	*Journal of Near Eastern Studies*
JPSTC	JPS Torah Commentary
JSJSup	Supplements to the Journal for the Study of Judaism
JSNT	*Journal for the Study of the New Testament*
JSNTSup	Journal for the Study of the New Testament Supplement Series
JSOT	*Journal for the Study of the Old Testament*
JSOTSup	Journal for the Study of the Old Testament Supplement Series
JTI	*Journal of Theological Interpretation*
JTS	*Journal of Theological Studies*
KC	Kerux Commentaries
KEK	Kritisch-exegetischer Kommentar über das Neue Testament (Meyer-Kommentar)

KNT	Kommentar zum Neuen Testament
L&N	Louw, Johannes P., and Eugene A. Nida, eds. *Greek-English Lexicon of the New Testament: Based on Semantic Domains*. 2nd edn. New York: United Bible Societies, 1989.
LHBOTS	The Library of Hebrew Bible/Old Testament Studies
LNTS	The Library of New Testament Studies
LCL	Loeb Classical Library
LQHR	*London Quarterly and Holborn Review*
LSJ	Liddell, Henry George, Robert Scott, Henry Stuart Jones. *A Greek-English Lexicon: With a Revised Supplement*. 9th edn. Oxford: Clarendon, 1996.
ModChm	*The Modern Churchman*
MTS	Münchener Theologische Studien
NA²⁸	*Novum Testamentum Graece*, Nestle-Aland, 28th edn.
NAC	New American Commentary
NBBC	New Beacon Bible Commentary
Neot	*Neotestamentica*
NICNT	New International Commentary on the New Testament
NIDB	*New Interpreter's Dictionary of the Bible*. Edited by Katharine Doob Sakenfeld. 5 vols. Nashville: Abingdon, 2006–9.
NIDNTTE	*New International Dictionary of New Testament Theology and Exegesis*. Edited by Moisés Silva. 5 vols. 2nd edn. Grand Rapids: Zondervan, 2014.
NIGTC	New International Greek Testament Commentary
NIVAP	NIV Application Commentary
NovT	*Novum Testamentum*
NovTSup	Supplements to Novum Testamentum
NSBT	New Studies in Biblical Theology
NTL	New Testament Library
NTS	*New Testament Studies*
Numen	*Numen: International Review for the History of Religions*
OBO	Orbis Biblicus et Orientalis
OTE	*Old Testament Essays*
ÖTK	Ökumenischer Taschenbuch-Kommentar
OTM	Oxford Theological Monographs
PRSt	*Perspectives in Religious Studies*
RB	*Revue biblique*
RBS	Resources for Biblical Study
RC	*Religion Compass*
RE	*Realenzyklopädie für protestantische Theologie und Kirche*. Edited by Albert Hauck. 24 vols. 1896–1913.
RGG	*Religion in Geschichte und Gegenwart*. Edited by Hans Dieter Betz. 4th edn. Tübingen: Mohr Siebeck, 1998–2007.
RMP	*Rheinisches Museum für Philologie*
RNT	Regensburger Neues Testament
RS	Rhetorica Semitica

RSR	*Recherches de science religieuse*
ResQ	*Restoration Quarterly*
RevScRel	*Revue des sciences religieuses*
SBG	Studies in Biblical Greek
SBJT	Southern Baptist Journal of Theology
SBL	Society of Biblical Literature
SBLDS	Society of Biblical Literature Dissertation Series
SBLMS	Society of Biblical Literature Monograph Series
SBT	Studies in Biblical Theology
SJLA	Studies in Judaism in Late Antiquity
SJT	*Scottish Journal of Theology*
SK	*Skrif en kerk*
SNTSMS	Society for New Testament Studies Monograph Series
SP	Sacra Pagina
SPCK	Society for Promoting Christian Knowledge
SPhilo	*Studia Philonica*
StBibLit	Studies in Biblical Literature
TB	*Théologie biblique*
TBN	Themes in Biblical Narrative
TDNT	*Theological Dictionary of the New Testament*
TDOT	*Theological Dictionary of the Old Testament*
TJ	*Trinity Journal*
TLG	*Thesaurus Linguae Graecae: Canon of Greek Authors and Works.* Edited by Luci Berkowitz and Karl A. Squitier. 3rd edn. New York: Oxford University Press, 1990.
TLNT	*Theological Lexicon of the New Testament.* Ceslas Spicq. Translated and edited by James D. Ernest. 3 vols. Peabody, MA: Hendrickson, 1994.
TOTC	Tyndale Old Testament Commentaries
TSK	*Theologische Studien und Kritiken*
TynBul	*Tyndale Bulletin*
VE	*Vox Evangelica*
VT	*Vetus Testamentum*
WAWSup	Writings from the Ancient World Supplement Series
WBC	Word Biblical Commentary
WMANT	Wissenschaftliche Monographien zum Alten und Neuen Testament
WTJ	*Westminster Theological Journal*
WUNT	Wissenschaftliche Untersuchungen zum Neuen Testament
ZNW	*Zeitschrift für die neutestamentliche Wissenschaft und die Kunde der älteren Kirche*

Other

2TP	Second Temple Period
ANE	Ancient Near Eastern

GNT	Greek New Testament
H	Holiness Code
HB	Hebrew Bible
LXX	Septuagint
MSS	Manuscripts
MT	Masoretic Text
NC	New Covenant
NT	New Testament
OC	Old Covenant
P	Priestly Source

1

Introduction

Over the last decade or so much has been written concerning the sacrificial cult in Hebrews.[1] This surge of interest has focused extensively on understanding and locating Jesus' sacrificial offering, especially as it relates to his earthly life and heavenly ascension. Nevertheless, little attention has been devoted to understanding the role of the recipients within this sacrificial ritual. Why does the author of Hebrews choose to

---

[1] To name a few (but see §3.2), David M. Moffitt, 'Jesus' Sacrifice and the Mosaic Logic of Hebrews' New-Covenant Theology', in *Understanding the Jewish Roots of Christianity: Biblical, Theological, and Historical Essays on the Relationship between Christianity and Judaism*, ed. G. R. McDermott (Bellingham, WA: Lexham Press, 2021), 51–68; 'Jesus as Interceding High Priest and Sacrifice in Hebrews: A Response to Nicholas Moore', *JSNT* 42.4 (2020): 545–52; 'It is Not Finished: Jesus' Perpetual Atoning Work as the Heavenly High Priest in Hebrews', in *So Great a Salvation: A Dialogue on the Atonement in Hebrews*, ed. George H. Guthrie, Cynthia L. Westfall and Jon C. Laansma, LNTS 516 (London: Bloomsbury T&T Clark, 2019), 257–75; 'Jesus' Heavenly Sacrifice in Early Christian Reception of Hebrews: A Survey', *JTS* 68.1 (2017): 46–71; 'Serving in the Tabernacle in Heaven: Sacred Space, Jesus's High-Priestly Sacrifice, and Hebrews' Analogical Theology', in *Hebrews in Contexts*, ed. G. Gelardini and H. Attridge, AGJU 91 (Leiden: Brill, 2016), 259–79; 'Blood, Life, and Atonement: Reassessing Hebrews' Christological Appropriation of Yom Kippur', in *The Day of Atonement: Its Interpretations in Early Jewish and Christian Traditions*, ed. Thomas Hieke and Tobias Nicklas, TBN 15 (Leiden: Brill, 2012), 211–24; *Atonement and the Logic of Resurrection in the Epistle to the Hebrews*, NovTSup 141 (Leiden: Brill, 2011), esp. 215–303; Nicholas J. Moore, 'Sacrifice, Session and Intercession: The End of Christ's Offering in Hebrews', *JSNT* 42.4 (2020): 521–41; '"Vaine Repeticions"? Re-evaluating Regular Levitical Sacrifices in Hebrews 9:1-14', in *Son, Sacrifice, and Great Shepherd*, ed. Eric F. Mason and David M. Moffitt, WUNT 2.510 (Tübingen: Mohr Siebeck, 2020), 115–34; *Repetition in Hebrews: Plurality and Singularity in the Letter to the Hebrews, Its Ancient Context, and the Early Church*, WUNT 2.388 (Tübingen: Mohr Siebeck, 2015), 149–57, 166–88; Benjamin J. Ribbens, 'The Sacrifice God Desired: Psalm 40.6-8 in Hebrews 10', *NTS* 67.2 (2021): 284–304; 'The Positive Functions of Levitical Sacrifice in Hebrews', *Son*, 95–113; 'Ascension and Atonement: The Significance of Post-Reformation, Reformed Responses to Socinians for Contemporary Atonement Debates in Hebrews', *WTJ* 80.1 (2018): 1–23; *Levitical Sacrifice and Heavenly Cult in Hebrews*, BZNW 222 (Berlin: de Gruyter, 2016), 83–148; Simon J. Joseph, '"In the Days of His Flesh, He Offered Up Prayers": Reimagining the Sacrifice(s) of Jesus in the Letter to the Hebrews', *JBL* 140.2 (2021): 207–27; Robert B. Jamieson, *Jesus' Death and Heavenly Offering in Hebrews*, SNTSMS 160 (Cambridge: Cambridge University Press, 2019), esp. 9–12, 23–70; 'When and Where Did Jesus Offer Himself? A Taxonomy of Recent Scholarship on Hebrews', *CurBR* 15.3 (2017): 338–68; William R. G. Loader, 'Revisiting High Priesthood Christology in Hebrews', *ZNW* 109.2 (2018): 235–83; Philip Church, *Hebrews and the Temple: Attitudes to the Temple in Second Temple Judaism and in Hebrews*, NovTSup 171 (Leiden: Brill, 2017), 412–32; Michael Kibbe, 'Is It Finished? When Did It Start? Hebrews, Priesthood, and Atonement in Biblical, Systematic, and Historical Perspective', *JTS* 65.1 (2014): 25–61; Scott D. Mackie, *Eschatology and Exhortation in the Epistle of the Hebrews*, WUNT 2.223 (Tübingen: Mohr Siebeck, 2007), 95–6, 172–81; Georg Gäbel,

make his prime sacrificial comparison – 'how much more' (πόσῳ μᾶλλον)² – with respect to the purging of the recipients' consciousness³ (συνείδησις) from sin (Heb. 9.14; cf. 9.9, 10.2, 22)? What exactly is the συνείδησις and why does Hebrews innovatively announce its purification? What is the connection between blood purgation and the consciousness of sin? Why is sin and not people spoken of as needing to be 'purified' (1.3; 9.14, 22, 23; 10.2), 'removed' (9.26), 'done away with' (10.11), 'taken away' (10.4) and 'sprinkled' clean (10.22)? What significance does a heavenly tabernacle play amidst all of this and why does it supposedly require purging (cf. 1.3; 9.23)? What does Levitical sacrifice say regarding the role of 'consciousness' within sacrificial ritual? How is the dominance of cultic language in Hebrews to be understood, especially as it relates to defilement and purgation? In short, if recent scholarship has asked and continues to ask, 'when', 'where' and even 'what' Jesus offered, the purpose of this study is to ask *why* a heavenly blood offering is so significant for Hebrews with respect to the recipients' consciousness of sin?

In this chapter, the statement of the problem will be introduced, as well as the justification for this study. The situation of the recipients will be explored, before turning to a diachronic analysis of συνείδησις. From here a working definition of this term will be suggested and a survey of how Hebrews scholarship has understood and applied the motif of συνείδησις will be examined. The methodological approach will be established and the chapter will end with an outline of the study.

1.1 The statement of the problem

In the initial stages of this research, the motif of a defiled and subsequently purged συνείδησις appeared significant yet lacked scholarly engagement. The term seemed misunderstood and underappreciated, with a thorough study being absent.[4] Across Hebrews scholarship a diversity of interpretation can also be witnessed. For some, συνείδησις evokes a Platonic worldview denoting an unseen world; for others, συνείδησις is just another way of speaking about heaven. Many view the purging of the συνείδησις as *the* distinctive difference between Levitical sacrifices and Christ's

---

Die Kulttheologie des Hebräerbriefes: Eine exegetisch-religionsgeschichtliche Studie, WUNT 2.212 (Tübingen: Mohr Siebeck, 2006), esp. 3–16, 292–5, 411–12; Ekkehard W. Stegemann and Wolfgang Stegemann, 'Does the Cultic Language in Hebrews Represent Sacrificial Metaphors? Reflections on Some Basic Problems', in *Hebrews: Contemporary Methods – New Insights*, ed. Gabriella Gelardini, BibInt 75 (Leiden: Brill, 2005), 13–23; Christian A. Eberhart, 'Characteristics of Sacrificial Metaphors in Hebrews', *Hebrews: Contemporary Methods*, 37–64; Richard D. Nelson, 'He Offered Himself: Sacrifice in Hebrews', *Int* 57.3 (2003): 251–65.

[2] All translations of the GNT (NA²⁸) are my own.
[3] This will be the general rendering for συνείδησις throughout this study. See my reasoning (§1.4).
[4] Studies that exist are either brief or do not explore συνείδησις with reference to Jesus' heavenly offering. See especially Barnabas Lindars SSF, *The Theology of the Letters to the Hebrews* (Cambridge: Cambridge University Press, 1991), 1–15; G. S. Selby, 'The Meaning and Function of Συνείδησις in Hebrews 9 and 10', *ResQ* 28.3 (1986): 145–54; C. A. Pierce, *Conscience in the New Testament: A Study of Syneidesis in the New Testament*, SBT 15 (London: SCM, 1955), 99–103. Of course, scholars engage with συνείδησις (§1.4), yet no major study has been devoted to this motif in Hebrews.

sacrifice. The former can 'only' purify externally, whereas the latter purges inwardly (the συνείδησις). References to συνείδησις are frequently viewed as synonymous with other terms in the epistle, such as the 'heart', 'soul' or 'mind'. Scholars are divided over what 'purifying the συνείδησις' denotes, with 'forgiveness', 'redemption' and 'justification' all suggested possibilities. This cluster of ideas will be examined in more detail below (§1.4).

Not only is a better lexical understanding required, but an exploration into the significance of this motif within Hebrews' sacrificial argumentation is lacking. How does this motif relate to Jesus' earthly and heavenly achievements? Why is it, as will be argued, that only Jesus' heavenly offering can purge the consciousness of sin? Much can be learnt from Philo and other Greek writers about this concept, but how might Levitical sacrificial ritual inform Hebrews? For instance, scholars often unequivocally state that Levitical sacrifices did nothing with respect to one's consciousness, but Hebrews never explicitly makes this claim (see §4.3.5, §4.4.2). Instead, the problem, as will be argued throughout, is that sacrificial ritual *did* deal with the issue of συνείδησις, yet the recipients' own inherited kerygma could not. At this point it will be helpful to turn to the situation of the recipients, since this will help to ground some key assumptions for this study.

1.2 The situation of the recipients

The situation of the recipients in Hebrews remains elusive.[5] Some have suggested that this elusiveness is because Hebrews is just a theological exposition, devoid of any pastoral or ethical concerns.[6] Nonetheless, it is generally accepted that Hebrews was written to a community of believers by someone who not only shared a personal connection with the recipients[7] but who felt compelled to compose this letter for a specific reason. Bryan Dyer helpfully outlines seven possible reasons for provoking the writing of Hebrews.[8] While none of these viewpoints are mutually exclusive, out of these hypotheses the most compelling and related to this study is the notion that the recipients were potentially relapsing into Judaism, although 'relapsing' might not be the

---

[5] This section and §2.2 will make assumptions and arguments about the situation, purpose and dating of Hebrews. Theories concerning the authorship and destination do not impact this study greatly. For helpful overviews, see Patrick Gray and Amy Peeler, *Hebrews: An Introduction and Study Guide* (London: Bloomsbury T&T Clark, 2020), 1–16; Gareth Lee Cockerill, *The Epistle to the Hebrews*, NICNT (Grand Rapids: Eerdmans, 2012), 1–41; David A. deSilva, *Perseverance in Gratitude: A Socio-Rhetorical Commentary on the Epistle 'to the Hebrews'* (Grand Rapids: Eerdmans, 2000), 1–39.

[6] Pamela M. Eisenbaum, 'Locating Hebrews within the Literary Landscape of Christian Origins', *Hebrews: Contemporary Methods*, 213–37; Jon M. Isaak, *Situating the Letter to the Hebrews in Early Christian History*, SBEC 53 (Lewiston, NY: Mellen, 2002), 153–8.

[7] Throughout his commentary Cockerill refers to the author of Hebrews as the 'Pastor' of the community, pointing to various instances where the author is invested in the past, present and future state of the recipients, *Hebrews*, 2–41.

[8] Bryan R. Dyer, *Suffering in the Face of Death: The Epistle to the Hebrews and Its Context of Situation*, LNTS 568 (London: Bloomsbury T&T Clark, 2017), 25–46. Dyer leans more towards the 'threat of persecution' theory and links this with the 'fear of death' and 'suffering'. Mackie is also helpful here, *Eschatology*, 9–17.

most helpful term.[9] This viewpoint is often associated with the work of Barnabas Lindars, who views Hebrews as written before 70 CE.[10] The next chapter will explore the text of Hebrews more closely, its tabernacle terminology and how this might inform the date it was written (§2.2). Presently, the work of Lindars will be renewed and critiqued, with a nuanced viewpoint suggested in order to move this hypothesis forward.[11]

'Consciousness of sin', according to Lindars, 'is the crucial issue'[12] in Hebrews. The recipients were grounded in the basic kerygma of early Christian proclamation, that is, 'Christ died for our sins' (1 Cor. 15.3). However, they found no assurance when it came to post-baptismal sin and consequently, they were experiencing a 'misery of the consciousness of sin'.[13] Lindars observes:

> Their [the recipients'] baptism gave assurance of forgiveness of the sins of their former life. They simply assumed that they would remain in a state of grace until the parousia. But as time passed, some of them at least began to be oppressed by renewed consciousness of sin, and the gospel as they had received it appeared not to allow for it. We can imagine that the leaders took a pastoral concern . . . and tried hard to persuade them that Christ's sacrifice covers the present as well as the past . . . On the other hand they knew from their Jewish past that atonement for sin is constantly attended to in Jewish liturgy. The return to the Jewish community thus offered a practical way of coping with a problem which was deeply felt and not adequately provided for in the Christian teaching which they had received.[14]

In short, the message of Christ dying for past sins eclipsed any message of Christ dying for present or post-baptismal sin. The recipients 'have a real and distressing problem of conscience. They need to *feel* that they are forgiven.'[15] They are 'smitten with a consciousness of sin for which they can find no relief without some practical method of atonement with God'.[16] The only way to solve their consciousness of sin was to leave their current community in search of a ceremonial solution, something against which

---

[9] 'Returning' might be preferable to 'relapse'. Some advocates of this view are Church, *Temple*, 17–18; Ben Witherington III, *Letters and Homilies for Jewish Christians: A Socio-Rhetorical Commentary on Hebrews, James and Jude* (Downers Grove, IL: InterVarsity Press, 2007), 26; Lindars, *Hebrews*, 1–15; F. F. Bruce, *The Epistle to the Hebrews*, rev. edn, NICNT (Grand Rapids: Eerdmans, 1990), 7; C. Spicq, *L'Épître aux Hébreux*, 2 vols, EBib (Paris: Gabalda, 1952–3), 1:228–9.

[10] Lindars, *Hebrews*, 20.

[11] This viewpoint has its flaws. Bruce raises concerns about equating a return to Judaism with apostasy and alienation from God, *Hebrews*, 5–6. The possibility that the recipients had a choice between two well defined religious communities raises the 'parting of the ways' debate. James D. G. Dunn writes, '[f]or Hebrews and a Judaism still focussed on the Temple and its cult the ways had parted', 121 (emphasis his own), *The Partings of the Ways between Christianity and Judaism and their Significance for the Character of Christianity*, 2nd edn (London: SCM, 2006), 115–21. Richard Hays is helpful, '"Here We Have No Lasting City": New Covenantalism in Hebrews', *The Epistle to the Hebrews and Christian Theology*, ed. Richard Bauckham et al. (Grand Rapids: Eerdmans, 2009), 151–73.

[12] Lindars, *Hebrews*, 88.

[13] Lindars, *Hebrews*, 103.

[14] Lindars, *Hebrews*, 13–14.

[15] Lindars, *Hebrews*, 14.

[16] Lindars, *Hebrews*, 88 (emphasis his own).

Hebrews was quick to warn them (Heb. 10.25).[17] For Lindars, Hebrews is a rhetorical letter aimed at convincing the community to remain by reminding them of the assurance that Jesus' death brings.

Lindars picks up on a motif that is widely neglected and misunderstood in Hebrews scholarship: the consciousness of sin. By starting with this motif Lindars displays the relevance of Hebrews' sacrificial discourse for the recipients' present situation. Nonetheless, Lindars' assessment contains weaknesses and contradictions. First, he notes that ritual practices, and the recipients' temptation to return to these practices, do not solve the issue of consciousness of sin. Yet, Lindars argues that rituals like Yom Kippur[18] *do* significantly help individuals to psychologically deal with the presence of sin.[19] Second, Lindars' discussion concerning the relationship between the OC and the NC with respect to the consciousness of sin requires further examination. What exactly is the tension between, what Georg Gäbel calls, the 'divine foundations and the shortcomings of the cult on earth'?[20]

Third, Lindars affirms that the 'wound of the consciousness of sin is healed'[21] when the recipients participate in Christian practices that strengthen fellowship with God and reassure the recipients of Christ's atoning work:

> There is no need for specific ceremonies of purification, because all that is necessary for atonement has been done by Jesus. On the other hand those whose consciences are wounded by the sense of sin should remember that the atoning sacrifice of Christ is the central theme of Christian worship ... Thus, instead of being enticed away from the Christian assembly, the readers should redouble their efforts to participate fully in worship, and indeed in all aspects of Christian life. In this way they will regain full confidence, and the debilitating sense of a stain on the conscience, creating a barrier to open relationship with God, will be removed.[22]

Lindars' assessment appears undecided. He concludes that the Christian community had overemphasized the message of Christ dying for past sins, which fueled their consciousness of sin. At the same time Lindars affirms that if the recipients continually reflect on Jesus' sacrificial death, then their consciousness of sin will be healed. Consequently, Lindars *does* affirm ritual, at least within their own Christian community. It remains unclear as to why the recipients would search elsewhere for a solution to their defiled συνείδησις if they were part of a community that presumably celebrated the death of Christ. Lindars is right to unearth this vital motif in Hebrews, although his analysis leaves many unanswered questions.

---

[17] Lindars sees 10.25 as evidence that the Christian assembly was being neglected in favour of the benefit received from synagogue meetings and Jewish customs, 'Hebrews and the Second Temple', in *Templum Amicitiae: Essays on the Second Temple Presented to Ernst Bammel*, ed. William Horbury, JSNTSup 48 (Sheffield: JSOT Press, 1991), 410–33.
[18] 'Yom Kippur' and the 'Day of Atonement' will be used synonymously henceforth.
[19] Lindars, *Hebrews*, 85.
[20] Georg Gäbel, '"You Don't Have Permission to Access This Site": The Tabernacle Description in Hebrews 9:1-5 and Its Function in Context', *Son*, 174.
[21] Lindars, *Hebrews*, 105.
[22] Lindars, *Hebrews*, 117.

If Lindars' assessment is reassessed in the light of recent Hebrews scholarship – regarding Jesus' heavenly offering – then the problem of the consciousness of sin can be solved. Rather than focusing on Jesus' death as the solution, this study will argue that Jesus' death was unable to offer purification for the consciousness (§2.2, §3.2.3, §3.4.1).[23] The temptation to leave their Christian community in search of a sacrificial solution to the problem of συνείδησις is evidence that ritual *does* work, or at least individuals felt it was a solution to their problem. Thus, Hebrews widens the conversation of defilement and purgation on a cosmic level, arguing that Jesus' heavenly blood offering is now where and how the consciousness of sin is purged (§3.7, §4.2, §4.3, §4.4). Additionally, Jesus' heavenly blood is perpetual and as a result, offers perpetual assurance concerning the consciousness of sin (§5.4).

1.3 Συνείδησις: An overview[24]

The purpose of this study is not to outline a diachronic survey of συνείδησις outside of Hebrews. Rather, its aim is to understand, conceptually, the 'consciousness of sin' and its role within Hebrews' cultic argumentation. Nonetheless, while 'parallelomania'[25] and the limitations of etymology in biblical lexicography are warnings to be heeded,[26] the interpretative history of συνείδησις will supply a helpful background for understanding Hebrews' own innovative usage of the term.

1.3.1 An interpretative history

The interpretation of the substantive, συνείδησις, has undergone an interesting yet complicated journey.[27] There is dispute concerning the earliest occurrence,[28] although

---

[23] Lindars rules out a heavenly offering, *Hebrews*, 94.
[24] 'Conscience' is an exhaustive cross-disciplinary topic, overlapping across philosophy, ethics, psychology and social science. Some may contend that conscience is as old as humankind itself, Otto Seel, 'Zur Vorgeschichte des Gewissens-begriffes, im altgriechischen Denken', in *Festschrift Franz Dornseiff zum 65. Geburtstag*, ed. H. Kusch (Leipzig: VEB Bibliographisches Institut, 1953), 291–319. Others have attributed Greek thought – namely Euripides – to the birth of 'conscience', Bruno Snell, *The Discovery of the Mind: The Greek Origins of European Thought*, trans. T. G. Rosenmeyer (Cambridge: Harvard University Press, 1953), 163.
[25] This term is adopted from Samuel Sandmel's Presidential address at the 1961 SBL Conference, 'Parallelomania', *JBL* 81 (1962): 1–13.
[26] See James Barr's landmark work, particularly his critique of Kittel, *The Semantics of Biblical Language* (Oxford: Oxford University Press, 1961), 206–67.
[27] For comprehensive overviews see Philip R. Bosman, *Conscience in Philo and Paul: A Conceptual History of the synoida Word Group*, WUNT 2.166 (Tübingen: Mohr Siebeck, 2003), 16–48; Anthony C. Thiselton, *The First Epistle to the Corinthians: A Commentary on the Greek Text*, NIGTC (Grand Rapids: Eerdmans, 2000), 640–4; H. J. Eckstein, *Der Begriff Syneidesis bei Paulus: Eine neutestamentlich-exegetische Untersuchung zum 'Gewissensbegriff'*, WUNT 2.10 (Tübingen: Mohr Siebeck, 1983), 4–12, 35–49; R. Jewett, *Paul's Anthropological Terms: A Study of Their Use in Conflict Settings* (Leiden: Brill, 1971), 402–46, 458–60; Christian Maurer, 'σύνοιδα, κτλ.', *TDNT* 7:898–919; Johannes Stelzenberger, *Syneidesis im Neuen Testament* (Paderborn: F. Schöningh, 1961); Pierce, *Conscience*, 21–53.
[28] The *TLG* includes quotations and fragments from Stobaeus, Aesop, Isocrates, Hippocrates, Menander, Chrysippus, Diodorus Siculus and Dionysius of Halicarnassus. Bosman views these with 'circumspection', with dating and glosses raising doubt over authenticity, *Conscience*, 60, 61–7.

some scholars view a fragment attested to Democritus as the earliest occurrence of the Ionic term.[29] It is not until the first and second centuries CE that συνείδησις finds prominence, especially in the NT and other early Christian writings.[30] The first major development of the term came with Jerome's Latin translation of the NT, when he traded συνείδησις for the Latin *conscientia*.[31] This was a 'fatal' decision and the 'first step in the decline'[32] of the term according to Claude Pierce, namely, because it blended the meaning of two very similar yet different notions.[33] By the mediaeval and early modern periods *conscientia* became understood as the 'God conscience' (*conscientia Dei*) or 'God's voice' (*vox Dei*). *Conscientia* denoted a natural inclination towards good, as well as an innate capacity to distinguish between good and evil.[34] It was a 'religious organ', an 'antenna into the divine sphere'.[35] It was neither safe nor right, as Martin Luther famously exclaimed, to go against *conscientia*.[36]

This was the consensus until the historical-critical period, which dominated German scholarship in the nineteenth century, when 'more accurate interpretations [of συνείδησις] began to emerge'.[37] For instance, Franz Delitzsch insisted that συνείδησις should be interpreted as a witness of the human consciousness, not as an internal guide, because it is 'vollends falsch, das Gewissen die Stimme Gottes des Erlösers zu nennen'.[38] Martin Kähler set a strong precedent when he argued that τὸ συνειδός and

---

[29] For the fragment, see H. A. Diels, *Die Fragmente der Vorsokratiker: Griechisch und Deutsch von Hermann Diels*, 3 vols, 9th edn (Berlin: Weidmannsche Verlagsbuchhandlung, 1959-60), 2:206-7. For acceptance, see Bosman, *Conscience*, 59-60; Don E. Marietta, 'Conscience in Greek Stoicism', *Numen* 17.3 (1970): 176-87; Maurer, *TDNT* 7:902.

[30] The writings of Clement of Rome, Clement of Alexandria, Ignatius, Irenaeus, Justin Martyr and Polycarp reveal wide usage of the term. Additionally, references to an 'evil' συνείδησις are evident in other writers, *Barn.* 19.12 (cf. 1.4); *Did.* 4.14; Hermas, *Vis.* 28.4. See also *Test. XII Patr.* 4.3-4.

[31] It is not the purpose or scope of this study to examine the Latin development of *conscientia* and its relationship (if any) with συνείδησις (see n. 43). As a stand-alone term *conscientia* occurs prominently in the younger Seneca, Quintilian and Cicero. Eckstein offers a thorough survey of these usages, *Syneidesis*, 80-104. Peter Schönlein is the main proponent for *conscientia* preceding συνείδησις, 'Zur Entstehung eines Gewissensbegriffes bei Griechen und Römern', *RMP* 112.4 (1969): esp. 300-3. Marietta, among others, points to the Democritus fragment as evidence for συνείδησις preceding *conscientia*, 'Conscience', 178. As Bosman writes, '[w]e have to accept that whatever its meaning, the Greek lexeme was in existence before *conscientia* ... Thus, it has to be accepted that either the words developed independently or that the Romans borrowed their word from the Greeks', *Conscience*, 75, also 71-5, 184-5.

[32] Pierce, *Conscience*, 118.

[33] Pierce, *Conscience*, 114-15, 129.

[34] To complicate matters further in the twelfth century συνείδησις was misspelled as συντήρησις in the margin of Jermone's Ezekiel commentary, leading to συντήρησις (spelt '*synderesis*' or '*synteresis*') developing its own meaning, different from but connected with *conscientia*. The *synderesis* became associated with an innate natural law, while *conscientia* was the ability to carry this out. See A. Schinkel, *Conscience and Conscientious Objections* (Amsterdam: Pallas Publications, 2007), 137-54, 172-4; Bosman, *Conscience*, 17-19; R. J. Smith, *Conscience and Catholicism: The Nature and Function of Conscience in Contemporary Roman Catholic Moral Theology* (University Press of America: Oxford, 1998), 5-10; E. Wolf, 'Gewissen', *RGG* 2:1555-7.

[35] Bosman, *Conscience*, 17.

[36] See M. G. Baylor, *Action and Person: Conscience in the Late Scholasticism and the Young Luther* (Brill: Leiden, 1977), 1-2.

[37] Jewett, *Anthropological*, 404.

[38] 'It is completely wrong to call the conscience the voice of God the Saviour', Franz Delitzsch, *System der biblischen Psychologie* (Leipzig: Dörffling und Franke, 1855), 104. All German translations are my own.

the verbal form, σύνοιδα, provided a strong interpretative foundation for the NT use of συνείδησις.[39] Over the last century the NT study of συνείδησις has only increased,[40] with the focus primarily on the Pauline corpus. The first major study came when Pierce sought to distinguish between ancient and modern understandings of συνείδησις through nine distinct categories.[41] A key conclusion for Pierce was that συνείδησις refers specifically to an individual's past behaviour, causing that individual discomfort or pain.[42] A weakness of Pierce's work is its blasé dismissal of a Stoic influence on συνείδησις, something he labels as a 'fallacy'.[43]

Johannes Stelzenberger also focused on the diverse nature of συνείδησις yet goes to the extreme of defining each unique usage in the NT.[44] Like Robert Jewett,[45] he is unable to find a single definition for συνείδησις in Paul. Stelzenberger concludes that συνείδησις should never be rendered with the typical 'Gewissen' since the modern term has little, if any, commonality with the ancient concept. Christian Maurer set an important precedent when he began his article exploring the reflexive phrase 'σύνοιδα ἐμαυτῷ' leading to his overall evaluation of the NT usage of συνείδησις.[46] For Maurer, it is Philo who contributed significantly towards the notion of a 'moral conscience',[47] 'assessing and condemning acts already committed'[48] and not in decision making.

---

[39] M. Kähler, 'Gewissen', in *RE* 6:646–54.
[40] To name a few, M. R. Crawford, '"Confessing God from a Good Conscience": I Peter 3:21 and Early Christian Baptismal Theology', *JTS* 67.1 (2016): 23–37; Richard Sorabji, *Moral Conscience Through the Ages: Fifth Century BCE to the Present* (Oxford: Oxford University Press, 2014), esp. 11–36, 216–18; M. Silva, 'συνείδησις', in *NIDNTTE* 4:402–6; Stuart P. Chalmers, *Conscience in Content: Historical and Existential Perspectives* (Bern: Peter Lang, 2013); Schinkel, *Conscience*, 137–54; Thiselton, *Corinthians*, 640–4; Bosman, *Conscience*; '"Why Conscience Makes Cowards of us all": a Classical Perspective', *AC* 40 (1997): 63–75; G. Lüdemann, 'Συνείδησις', in *EDNT* 3:301–3; P. W. Gooch, 'Conscience in 1 Corinthians 8 and 10', *NTS* 33.2 (1987): 244–54; Selby, 'Συνείδησις', 145–54; M. Espy, 'Paul's "Robust Conscience" Reexamined', *NTS* 31.2 (1985): 161–88; Eckstein, *Syneidesis*; R. A. Horsley, 'Consciousness and Freedom among the Corinthians: 1 Corinthians 8–10', *CBQ* 40.4 (1978): 574–89; C. Spicq, *Notes de lexicographie néo-testamentaire*, 2 vols, OBO 22.2 (Fribourg; Göttingen: Éditions Universitaires, Vandenhoeck & Ruprecht, 1978), 2:852–8; 'La conscience dans le NT', *RB* 47 (1938): 50–80; Jewett, *Anthropological*, 402–46; Marietta, 'Conscience', 176–87; Maurer, *TDNT* 7:898–919; Schönlein, 'Entstehung', 289–305; M. Thrall, 'The Pauline use of συνείδησις', *NTS* 14.1 (1967): 118–25; C. S. Lewis, *Studies in Words*, 2nd edn (Cambridge: Cambridge University Press, 1967), 181–213; A. C. Bouquet, 'Numinous Uneasiness', *ModChm* 9 (1966), 203–9; J. K. Stendahl, 'The Apostle Paul and the Introspective Conscience of the West', *HTR* 56.3 (1963): 118–25; Johannes Stelzenberger, *Syneidesis, Conscientia, Gewissen: Studie zum Bedeutungswandel eines moraltheologischen Begriffes*, AM 5 (Paderborn: F. Schöningh, 1963), 23–66; *Syneidesis im Neuen Testament*; N. H. G. Robinson, *Christ and Conscience* (London: James Nisbet, 1956); Wolf, 'Gewissen'; Pierce, *Conscience*; Seel, 'Vorgeschichte', *Festschrift*, 291–319; R. A. Congdon, 'The Doctrine of Conscience', *BSac* 102 (1945): 226–32; H. Osborne, 'Συνείδησις', *JTS* 32.126 (1931): 167–79.
[41] Pierce, *Conscience*, 12.
[42] Pierce, *Conscience*, 45, 50.
[43] Pierce, *Conscience*, 13–20. Pierce is partially right, συνείδησις is not a 'divine voice' or knowledge of a natural law, but it is wrong to dismiss Stoic influence on NT thought, see J. N. Sevenster's critique of Pierce, *Paul and Seneca*, NovTSup 4 (Leiden: Brill, 1961), 84–92. The Roman Stoics probably did not develop a 'theory' of conscience, but they nonetheless embraced a popular term (συνείδησις) in their continued use of *conscientia*, rightly Schinkel, *Conscience*, 162; Marietta, 'Conscience', 185–7.
[44] Stelzenberger, *Syneidesis im Neuen Testament*, 42–3.
[45] Jewett, *Anthropological*, 415.
[46] Maurer, *TDNT* 7:899–902.
[47] Maurer, *TDNT* 7:900.
[48] Maurer, *TDNT* 7:904.

While the HB has no lexical equivalent for συνείδησις, H. J. Eckstein, like Maurer,[49] understood συνείδησις to find meaning with the OT understanding of the heart (לב).[50] For Eckstein, συνείδησις is a unified term,[51] but like לב its meaning is broad, including 'knowing', decision making, human will and emotion.[52]

Recently broader works devoted to conscience have been published by Anders Schinkel and Richard Sorabji.[53] Yet the most recent and critical remains Philip Bosman's work, *Conscience in Philo and Paul*, a work yet to be outmatched. Bosman's detailed philological study covers the ancient Greek origins of the σύνοιδα word group, before categorizing Philo's use of σύνοιδα/τὸ συνειδός/συνείδησις. From here Bosman surveys Paul's use of σύνοιδα/συνείδησις. Bosman draws an impressive range of similarities between Paul and Philo,[54] yet notes that while Philo interprets τὸ συνειδός as a potentially divine aspect, Paul understands συνείδησις mainly as an anthropological term, similar in nature to an OT understanding of the 'inner man',[55] functioning as an 'inner monitor'[56] of moral conduct (Rom. 2.15; 9.1; 13.1-7; 1 Cor. 4.1-5) and an 'inner court of law'.[57]

1.3.2 Ancient Greek origins

The ancient Greek culture is often labelled as being primarily concerned with shame and honour, as opposed to guilt.[58] Moral infringements posed an external threat resulting in public shame, 'inner disharmony ... relate[d] directly to social vulnerability',[59] since one's self-perception was tied to the οἶκος/πόλις.[60] However, following the devastating Peloponnesian war, 'the seeds of individualism were allowed to germinate and the inner world of the human psyche was afforded more and more interest'.[61] Thus, while συνείδησις and τὸ συνειδός were sparse in the years prior to the first century BCE,[62] σύνεσις (Attic ξύνεσις) – from συνίημι – the verbal form (σύνοιδα),

---

[49] Maurer, *TDNT* 7:908-10.
[50] Eckstein, *Syneidesis*, 12. All translations of the MT (*BHS*) are my own.
[51] Eckstein, *Syneidesis*, 311.
[52] Eckstein, *Syneidesis*, 311-14.
[53] Schinkel, *Conscience*, 137-54; Sorabji, *Conscience*, 11-36.
[54] Bosman, *Conscience*, 175-90, 264-75.
[55] Bosman, *Conscience*, 283.
[56] Bosman, *Conscience*, 265-7.
[57] Bosman, *Conscience*, 270-1.
[58] This is of course an oversimplification; however, Bosman argues that the absence of σύνοιδα and the reflexive (σύνοιδα ἐμαυτῷ) in Homer is due to the general theme of avoiding shame, as well as attributing irrational impulses to external causes, *Conscience*, 87-9. Contra R. T. Wallis, who views the Homeric notion of αἰδώς as denoting conscience, 'The Idea of Conscience in Philo of Alexandria', in *Two Treatises of Philo of Alexandria: A Commentary on De Gigantibus and Quod Deus sit Immutabilis*, BJS 25 (Chico, CA: Scholars Press, 1983), 207-8.
[59] Bosman, *Conscience*, 78, also 80-100. This is expressed in Plato's *Republic*, where the ψυχή is contrasted with the πόλις, *Rep.* 2.368d-9a.
[60] If the soul experienced inner turmoil the individual became weak and socially shameful, impacting the overall πόλις. The incentive for obeying rules set by the πόλις was largely due to avoiding shame upon one's family and city, Bosman, *Conscience*, 84-6.
[61] Bosman, *Conscience*, 90.
[62] See n. 28.

the reflexive (σύνοιδα ἐμαυτῷ) and the infinitive (συνειδέναι) are all evident in the 'golden age' of fifth century Athens and onwards. The reflexive (σύνοιδα ἐμαυτῷ) is indicative of a shared knowledge of something, or of someone. While knowing one has done wrong does not always assume negative self-judgement (Xenophon, *Anab.* 1.3.10), negative self-judgement is the common understanding of the phrase (Aristophanes, *Eq.* 184; *Thesm.* 476–7).[63]

An often-cited occurrence of both σύνεσις and σύνοιδα comes from Euripides. After killing his own mother, Orestes is tormented by madness and the Furies. When Menelaus asks Orestes what is wrong with him, Orestes replies: 'understanding: the awareness that I have done dreadful things' (ἡ σύνεσις, ὅτι σύνοιδα δείν' εἰργασμένος, Euripides, *Orest.* 396).[64] Elsewhere, Plutarch reflects that everyone who does wrong 'is held fast in the toils of justice; he has snapped up in an instant the sweetness of his iniquity, like a bait, but with the barbs of τὸ συνειδός embedded in his vitals and paying for his crime. He, like a stricken tunny, churns the sea' (Plutarch, *Sera* 554.10). Finally, in an account of Euripides' Orestes, Philostratus states that one's 'σύνεσις' is what destroys a person, 'when they realize that they have done evil'. It was the σύνεσις that invoked Orestes' visions. If one does evil, σύνεσις:

> [W]ill not allow him to look another in the eye, or speak with a free tongue. It drives him from sanctuaries and from prayer, not allowing him to raise his hands to any image, but restraining him when he does so, as the laws restrain those who contravene them. It drives him from all company, and terrifies him as he sleeps ... σύνεσις will condemn me whether the people I visit know me or not.
>
> Philostratus, *Vit. Apoll.* 7.14

The use of συνείδησις was rare in ancient Greek literature, but the implementation of σύνεσις and the σύνοιδα word group reveals the presence of a 'conscience concept' at work. This, as will become evident, was not so dissimilar to the preferred NT term, συνείδησις.

1.3.3 The Jewish Scriptures

It is frequently observed that there is no equivalent for συνείδησις in the HB,[65] although there are numerous places where a conceptually 'guilty conscience' can be observed (Gen. 3.7-13; 42.21; 1 Sam. 24.5; 25.31; 2 Sam. 24.10; Pss. 24.4; 51.10). These instances have led scholars to find a correlation between συνείδησις and לב.[66] Additionally, the notion of a 'pure heart' (לב טהור, cf. Ps. 51.10) is read as synonymous with a 'good/pure

---

[63] Equally one is able to be unaware of anything wrong committed in the past (Polybius, *Hist.* 4.86.5).
[64] Bosman argues that Euripides (*Orest.* 397; cf. *Orest.* 1524) is further proof of a modern gloss forced on an ancient text that possessed no technical term for 'conscience', 68–9, also 49–60, esp. 56–60. Contra Sorabji, *Conscience*, 15–30; Wallis, 'Conscience', *Treatises*, 207–8.
[65] Lüdemann, *EDNT* 3:301; Stelzenberger, *Syneidesis im Neuen Testament*, 37.
[66] H. J. Fabry, 'לב', in *TDOT* 7:399–437, esp. 426; H. J. Klauck, 'Accuser, Judge and Paraclete – on Conscience in Philo of Alexandria', *SK* 20.1 (1999): 107–18, esp. 114. The notion of an 'evil' and 'good' inclination (Gen. 6.5; 8.21) is a possible connection too, Maurer, *TDNT* 7:910.

conscience/consciousness' (καλός/καθαρός τὸ συνειδός/συνείδησις).[67] But a 'good conscience' does not negate a 'pure heart'. In Hebrews a 'καλὴν συνείδησιν' (Heb. 13.18) and a 'καθαροῦ τοῦ συνειδότος' in Philo (*Leg. Gai.* 165; *Praem. Poen.* 84; *Prob.* 99; *Spec. Leg.* 1.203–4) and Josephus (*War* 1.453)[68] denotes the lack of negative knowledge affirmed in a positive manner.[69] It does not imply good knowledge but the lack of bad or evil knowledge. While לב hosts diverse meanings, the problem occurs when Greek texts, like Hebrews, employ a range of terms supplementary to συνείδησις, such as the soul (ψυχή), spirit (πνεῦμα), mind (διάνοια) and heart (καρδία). The LXX sheds little light too. The reflexive 'σύνοιδα ἐμαυτῷ' occurs only once (Job 27.6),[70] derived from the inner man (לבב) or heart, whereas συνείδησις occurs just twice (Eccl. 10.20; Wis. 17.10).[71] The LXX renders the Ecclesiastes passage from knowledge (מדע) associating συνείδησις with a cognitive nuance.

1.3.4 Philo

Philo employs the term συνείδησις less than Hebrews, but when he does, it is consistently rendered 'consciousness' with reference to sin/misdeeds.[72] The reflexive phrase (σύνοιδα ἐμαυτῷ) denotes negative judgement towards oneself and is found just three times.[73] Yet it is Philo's preference for the participle (τὸ συνειδός) which is noteworthy, employing it thirty-two times, with other supplementary terminology adding further nuances.[74] The dominating metaphors for Philo's conception of τὸ συνειδός are the forensic descriptors he employs. It is described as a judge (δικαστής, *Deus Imm.* 128) established in the soul to convict (ἔλεγχος, *Deus Imm.* 126; *Ebr.* 125; *Op. Mund.* 128; *Prob.* 149).[75] It functions as a lawcourt (δικαστήριον, *Flacc.* 7) with an active accuser (κατήγορος, *Dec.* 87). While the σύνοιδα word group was employed prior to Philo, he is innovative in his depiction of τὸ συνειδός as an inner lawcourt.[76] Moreover, for Philo, the judgement provided through τὸ συνειδός might be construed as the retribution of God, or divine vengeance (δίκη).[77]

Additionally, τὸ συνειδός shares a connection with the mind (νοῦς) acting as a witness (μάρτυς, *Poster. C.* 59) and being described as internally painful and terrifying

---

[67] Klauck, 'Accuser', 114; Eckstein, *Syneidesis*, 124; Maurer, *TDNT* 7:909–10.
[68] Also 'ἀγαθὸν τὸ συνειδὸς' in *War* 2.582.
[69] Bosman, *Conscience*, 116.
[70] Cf. Lev. 5.1 for 'σύνοιδα'.
[71] Possibly three, Sir. 42.18 א.
[72] There are three certain uses here, *Det. Pot. Ins.* 146; *Spec. Leg.* 2.49; *Virt.* 124, with the disputed *Quaestiones in Exodum* fragment providing a possible fourth occurrence, see TLG and F. Petit, *Quaestiones in Genesim et in Exodum. Fragmenta Graeca* (Paris: Éditions du Cerf, 1978), 305–6.
[73] *Her.* 6; *Leg. Gai.* 341; *Prob.* 124.
[74] The verbal substantive τὸ συνειδός does not occur in the GNT and is rare in early Christian literature. There are many reasons why Philo preferred the Attic form, possibly just for elegance.
[75] The positive aspect of ἔλεγχος as *proving* something to be right is evident in Heb. 11.1. However, Philo implies the negative sense expressing 'strong disapproval'. So 'reproach' or 'correction' are the given senses of the term, see BDAG 315. Philo employs ἐλέγχω too (*Conf. Ling.* 121).
[76] Bosman, *Conscience*, 184–5.
[77] Bosman, *Conscience*, 189–90.

(*Dec.* 86-7; *Jos.* 196-7; *Spec. Leg.* 4.6, 40). Even though one 'simulates a smile' the 'consciousness of wrongdoing' (συνειδήσει τῶν ἀδικημάτων) 'torments' and 'depresses' the soul (*Spec. Leg.* 2.49). Another important corresponding term is 'boldness' or 'freedom to speak' (παρρησία).[78] The one who offers sacrifices can place his hands on the sacrificial animal and speak with παρρησία, since he has a 'καθαροῦ τοῦ συνειδότος' (*Spec. Leg.* 1.203-4), that is, he is unaware of any sinful act. Abraham is able to speak to God with παρρησία because he knows within himself that he has done nothing wrong ('ἠδικηκότι μὲν ἑαυτῷ μηδὲν συνειδῇ', *Her.* 6).

Philo's allegorical readings might be stylistically different from Hebrews, yet both include τὸ συνειδός/συνείδησις within their cultic discussions. In his retelling of the guilt-reparation offering in Lev. 6.4-7 (5.23-6 MT), Philo recites the priestly text closely, but adds an intriguing innovation when he contrasts external judgement (ἔλεγχος) with internal judgement (ἔλεγχος). Philo essentially says that you can escape the external judgement (ἔλεγχος) of others, but one is unable to escape 'being convicted inwardly by conscience' (ἔνδον ὑπὸ τοῦ συνειδότος ἐλεγχθείς, *Spec. Leg.* 1.235; cf. *Spec. Leg.* 4.6). Philo helps to show here how an inward realization of guilt plays an important role in the sacrificial cult. Elsewhere Philo discusses the laws on leprosy (Lev. 13-14) with regards to unintentional and intentional sins (*Deus Imm.* 122-35). For Philo, an involuntary sin is evident through the absence of an accusing τὸ συνειδός; however, an intentional sin awakens the inner judgement of τὸ συνειδός (*Deus Imm.* 128-9). Also, τὸ συνειδός relies on an internal divine rational (λόγος) which works alongside τὸ συνειδός within the soul (ψυχή) to detect and punish immorality. Thus, in Philo, 'rationality is a precondition for culpability or guilt'[79] (*Deus Imm.* 128-9; *Det. Pot. Ins.* 146).

An intriguing feature in Philo is that he differentiates between sacrificial offerings that purge the soul (ψυχή) and washings that cleanse the body (*Spec. Leg.* 1.257-8). Yet for Philo the focus appears to be ethical. Time must be spent choosing the right animal (*Spec. Leg.* 1.259-60) and so the mind (διάνοια) is purged, not by blood, but by wisdom's teaching and the contemplative nature of the worshipper (*Spec. Leg.* 1.269). This is also the case in *Her.* 6-7, where loyalty and purity from sin is juxtaposed with παρρησία and knowing no wrong. Therefore, unlike Hebrews, τὸ συνειδός in Philo does not need purifying, since it accompanies individuals in order to affirm or congratulate their moral achievements.[80]

---

[78] Esp. *Her.* 5-7. Also, Josephus, *Ant.* 13.316. See Alan Mitchell's helpful discussion, 'Holding on to Confidence: παρρησία in Hebrews', in *Friendship, Flattery, and Frankness of Speech*, ed. John T. Fitzgerald, NovTSup 82 (Leiden: Brill, 1996), 203-26; Bosman, 'Conscience', 63-75.

[79] Bosman, *Conscience*, 146.

[80] Rightly Martin Karrer, *Der Brief an die Hebräer*, 2 vols, ÖTK 20 (Gütersloh: Gütersloher Verlagshaus, 2002-8), 2:150. Hebrews' discussion regarding a purged συνείδησις via a sacrificial offering is unique, rightly Sebastian Fuhrmann, *Vergeben und Vergessen: Christologie und Neuer Bund im Hebräerbrief*, WMANT 113 (Neukirchen-Vluyn: Neukirchener Verlag, 2007), 97; Herbert Braun, *An die Hebräer*, HNT 14 (Tübingen: Mohr Siebeck, 1984), 262. Contra Erich Grässer, who claims that a pure heart is Jewish whereas a purified συνείδησις is Hellenistic and typical of Philo, *An die Hebräer*, 3 vols, EKKNT 17 (Zurich: Benziger, 1990-7), 137. Nor is Hebrews describing a noble manner of living when he refers to a 'καλὴν συνείδησιν' (13.18), so Philip A. Davies Jr., *The Place of Paideia in Hebrews' Moral Thought*, WUNT 2.475 (Tübingen: Mohr Siebeck, 2018), 115; Karrer, *Hebräer*, 2:150.

Philo's employment of 'conscience' is diverse and, as will be observed shortly, distinctly different from Hebrews. His limited use of συνείδησις is consistently rendered as 'consciousness', yet his more dominant employment of τὸ συνειδός might be rendered as 'conscience', since it refers to an inner judge who reproaches one's conduct/deeds. Nonetheless, the concept evolves throughout his writings, becoming 'neutral' and almost divine, being associated more and more with the soul.[81]

1.3.5 Josephus

Josephus' employment of συνείδησις and τὸ συνειδός is modest in comparison to Philo but reveals some important observations. Both τὸ συνειδός (*Ant.* 3.13; *War* 3.501) and συνείδησις (*Ant.* 16.103) can have a general sense of 'consciousness', as well as being qualified in a negative[82] and positive sense.[83] Similar to Philo, Josephus describes τὸ συνειδός as an active agent that 'haunts' individuals concerning their past deeds (*Ant.* 2.25–6; 13.414; 16.212; *War* 4.189); their 'consciousness' will 'strike the mind' (*Ant.* 13.316). Like Philo, one does not need to rely on others to convict, since their own τὸ συνειδός is their 'judge' (*Ant.* 1.209; 3.320; 4.285–6) and 'witness' (*Apion.* 2.218); παρρησία is the opposite of a convicting τὸ συνειδός (*Ant.* 2.52; cf. Heb. 10.19-22). Earlier (§1.3.3) it was suggested that a 'guilty conscience' might be observed conceptually in Gen. 3.7-13. Interestingly, when Josephus describes Adam hiding from God in the garden he is said to have been 'silent', unable to speak and lacking παρρησία.[84] The reason for this is because of Adam's 'evil conscience' (συνειδότι πονηρῷ, *Ant.* 1.48), a consequence of his sin.

1.3.6 New Testament

By NT times συνείδησις had established itself as the favourable term, occurring thirty times.[85] Most notably there are no occurrences in the Synoptics or Fourth Gospel, with the majority occurring in the Corinthian correspondence. The συνείδησις can be weak (ἀσθενής) if one's knowledge and criteria for judgement is underdeveloped (1 Cor. 8.7, 10, 12; cf. Tit. 1.15),[86] as well as endorsing actions through the Spirit (Rom. 9.1; cf. 2.15; 2 Cor. 1.12). Individuals are supposed to subject themselves to συνείδησις (Rom. 13.5; 1 Cor. 10.25, 27, 28, 29 (x2); 2 Cor. 4.2; 5.11; 2 Tim. 1.3) because it will monitor and

---

[81] Bosman, *Conscience*, 182–3.
[82] 'Συνειδήσει τῶν εἰργασμένων' (Josephus, *War* 4.193–4).
[83] Note the prior discussion (§1.3.3) concerning a 'good' τὸ συνειδός (Josephus, *War* 1.453; 2.582).
[84] Being silent and unable to speak is often an outward sign of a guilty conscience (Josephus, *Ant.* 16.102–3).
[85] John 8.9 in the *Textus Receptus* adds that the woman's accusers were 'reproved by συνείδησις' (ὑπὸ τῆς συνειδήσεως ἐλεγχόμενοι). The verbal form σύνοιδα occurs twice, Acts 5.2; 1 Cor. 4.4.
[86] In a similar manner to Hebrews, Paul describes the συνείδησις as being stained (μολύνω, 1 Cor. 8.7), but unlike Hebrews, says nothing about the συνείδησις being purified. In this passage (1 Cor. 8.7-13) συνείδησις is not equal to knowledge (γνῶσις), contra Joseph A. Fitzmyer, *First Corinthians: A New Translation with Introduction and Commentary*, AB 32 (New Haven: Yale University Press, 2008), 344. If this was so, the 'strong' could have simply informed the 'weak' with their superior γνῶσις, rightly Bosman, *Conscience*, 209–13.

register all behaviour that is not good.⁸⁷ One uniting factor in recent explorations of συνείδησις in the NT – especially as it relates to Paul – is that 'conscience' remains a weak translation for the majority of scholars, with 'consciousness' or 'self-awareness' being argued as the preferred rendering in some contexts.⁸⁸ This is because συνείδησις as a stand-alone term can be neutral (cf. 1 Pet. 2.19) unless it is accompanied by other qualifying terms (Acts 23.1; 24.16; 1 Tim. 1.5, 19; 3.9; 4.2; 1 Pet. 3.16, 21).

1.4 Συνείδησις in Hebrews

In turning to Hebrews' use of συνείδησις (Heb. 9.9, 14; 10.2, 22; 13.18) it is important to establish a working definition of the term, as well as categorizing the various ways in which the term has been incorporated across Hebrews scholarship.

1.4.1 Defining συνείδησις in Hebrews

Some argue that συνείδησις is a key term for Hebrews⁸⁹ while others dismiss it as irrelevant or unimportant.⁹⁰ Typically commentators are quick to define the term as 'awareness' or 'consciousness' – often of 'sin' – but they and translators render the term frequently as 'conscience'.⁹¹ The lack of research into Hebrews' use of συνείδησις is probably due to the fact that the term is 'arguably the most complex anthropological term in the NT'.⁹² Nevertheless, there remains a wealth of diverse descriptors used by scholars in attempting to describe συνείδησις in Hebrews. For instance, Delitzsch defines συνείδησις as one's 'own inward consciousness of his [of her] relation to God'.⁹³ For James Moffatt it is one's 'inner personality'.⁹⁴ Hermann defines συνείδησις as pressurizing people ('bedrängt').⁹⁵ Elsewhere it is labelled as 'the individual's personal

---

⁸⁷ Bosman, *Conscience*, 264.
⁸⁸ Horsley, 'Consciousness', 574–89; Gooch, 'Corinthians', 252; Thiselton, *Corinthians*, 640–4.
⁸⁹ See n. 4.
⁹⁰ Chalmers disregards Hebrews' use of συνείδησις, arguing that its use is irrelevant and 'inconsistent', *Conscience*, 40–1. Similarly, Michel Coune states that in more 'Jewish' styled texts the term is absent, 'Le Problème des Idolothytes et l'Éducation de la Syneidêsis', *RSR* 51 (1963): 497–534, 497 n. 2.
⁹¹ BDAG 967–8 categorizes between 'consciousness' (Heb. 10.2) and 'moral consciousness' or 'conscience' (9.9, 14; 10.22; 13.18). However, there is no reason why the term should be understood as having different renderings in Hebrews. Hebrews 10.2 might be an objective genitive but this does not explain why 9.14 or 10.22 should not be translated as 'consciousness', rightly Harold W. Attridge, *Hebrews: A Commentary on the Epistle to the* Hebrews, Hermeneia (Minneapolis: Fortress Press, 1989), 288.
⁹² Mackie, *Eschatology*, 190.
⁹³ Franz Delitzsch, *Commentary on the Epistle to the Hebrews*, 2 vols, trans. Thomas L. Kingsbury, 3rd edn (Edinburgh: T&T Clark, 1886–7), 2:98. To purge the συνείδησις from dead works means to relieve 'the mind from that shameful burden of a sense of impurity and alienation', 98.
⁹⁴ James Moffatt, *A Critical and Exegetical Commentary on the Epistle to the Hebrews*, ICC 40 (Edinburgh: T&T Clark, 1924), 124.
⁹⁵ Markus-Liborius Hermann, *Die "hermeneutische Stunde" des Hebräerbriefes: Schriftauslegung in Spannungsfeldern* (Freiburg im Breisgau: Herder, 2013), 321.

cognizance of sin',[96] and the 'faculty of moral consciousness in human beings'.[97] There is a tendency to interpret the term as an active agent, a moral indicator, which helps an individual decide right from wrong via an internal moral law.[98] Here 'conscience' would be a suitable translation.

Rather than viewing συνείδησις as a positive active moral agent, many read it as a passive term, registering only that which is negative, or sinful.[99] In Philo the cult validates one's conscience, but in Hebrews the cult 'hinterfragt den Kultteilnehmer'.[100] Thus, 'consciousness [of sin]' may be a helpful rendering for this sense. According to Marie Isaacs, the 'author uses συνείδησις not in the sense of some neutral moral geiger counter, registering both right and wrong, but as a negative indicator, registering only what is reprehensible'.[101] When Hebrews speaks of a 'consciousness of evil' (συνειδήσεως πονηρᾶς, 10.22), Isaacs argues that συνείδησις is not 'to be re-educated but done away with'.[102] Further, '[f]or our author, the person without a conscience is not someone who is unprincipled, but one who has no inner accuser'.[103] Isaacs suggests 'guilt' rather than 'conscience' as the rendering in Hebrews.[104]

Similarly, Lindars notes that συνείδησις 'does not denote a moral law within the mind, telling one what one ought or ought not to do. It is rather knowledge within oneself of the moral status of one's own actions, whether good or bad, usually the latter.'[105] William Johnsson's insights are worth quoting in full:

> [Σ]υνείδησις concerns only the sense of 'wrong'; it is not involved in decision making but in 'remembering' or 'consciousness'; and it is collective: the community, not the individual, is in view. It seems to us, therefore, that it would be wise for students of these chapters to eliminate all talk of 'conscience' as they discuss the argumentation.[106]

---

[96] Selby, 'Συνείδησις', 145.
[97] Kevin L. Anderson, *Hebrews: A Commentary in the Wesleyan Tradition*, NBBC (Kansas City: Beacon Hill Press, 2013), 245.
[98] David deSilva for instance argues that '[c]onscience is a person's internal moral faculty, the resource by which a person discerns right from wrong', *Perseverance*, 300. See also Chalmers, *Conscience*, 40–1; Helen Costigane, 'A History of the Western Idea of Conscience', in *Conscience in World Religions*, ed. Jayne Hoose (Notre Dame: University of Notre Dame Press, 1999), 3–20; Selby, 'Συνείδησις', 145; Coune, 'Problème', 497 n. 2.
[99] Pierce places each occurrence of συνείδησις in Hebrews into certain categories. Hebrews 9.9 is MBA, 9.14 and 10.22 are MBNorm, 10.2 is MBNeg and 13.18 is MBNeg/MPG. See his explanation of these categories, *Conscience*, 23–8.
[100] '[The cult] questions the cult-participant', Karrer, *Hebräer*, 2:150.
[101] Marie E. Isaacs, *Sacred Space: An Approach to the Theology of the Epistle to the Hebrews*, JSNTSup 73 (Sheffield: JSOT Press, 1992), 98. Throughout Hebrews, as Selby states, 'there is no indication of the conscience as a positive moral or ethical guide for one's life', 'Συνείδησις', 147.
[102] Isaacs, *Sacred*, 98.
[103] Isaacs, *Sacred*, 98.
[104] Isaacs, *Sacred*, 98. Hence why Heb. 10.22 speaks of an evil conscience, that is, a consciousness of one's evil deeds.
[105] Lindars, *Hebrews*, 88. See also David G. Peterson, *Hebrews and Perfection: An Examination of the Concept of Perfection in the 'Epistle to the Hebrews'*, SNTSMS 47 (Cambridge: Cambridge University Press, 1982), 135.
[106] William G. Johnsson, 'Defilement and Purgation in the Book of Hebrews' (PhD diss., Vanderbilt University, 1973), 284–5.

Johnsson's analysis is important here as it positions the συνείδησις not as an active accuser or something alerting negative morality, but more psychological, something that simply *remembers* faults. In this sense συνείδησις is not a convicting judge, but one's memories might conjure up these feelings of inner judgement[107] acting as an 'impediment to worshipping God'[108] and causing the believer to be 'painfully aware of his sinfulness'.[109] On the basis of the data examined so far (and later discussions §2.5.3, §4.3.5), συνείδησις will be referred to in this study as 'consciousness'. Since συνείδησις is typically negative in Hebrews, συνείδησις might also be referred to as 'consciousness of sin'. This extends to the 'consciousness of defilement', with sin *behaving* like defilement (§2.3, §2.5, §2.6).

1.4.2 The application of συνείδησις in Hebrews scholarship

There are four dominant ways in which scholars have interpreted and facilitated συνείδησις within Hebrews' argumentation. The first is the *Platonic inference* of συνείδησις. Since the seventeenth-century Hebrews has been read through the lenses of Middle Platonism[110] due to its similarities with Philo. As a contemporary of Hebrews, Philo critiqued animal sacrifice and alongside other influential philosophies such as Stoicism and Epicureanism, he focused on the inner life of the rational soul, the mind and the λόγος. True and superior worship, for Philo, consisted of internal approaches through the mind and the divine senses,[111] with τὸ συνειδός a component of the soul (*Op. Mund.* 128).[112] Table 1 shows how typical Platonic terms might be mapped beside

Table 1 Earthly and heavenly terminology in Hebrews and Platonism

	Hebrews			Platonism		
ἀληθινός	τύπος		εἰκών	παράδειγμα	ἀρχέτυπος	ἀληθής
True	Pattern		Image	Paradigm	Archetype	Real
	συνείδησις				νοῦς	
	Consciousness				Mind	
	σάρξ				σάρξ	
	Flesh				Flesh	
ὑπόδειγμα	ἀντίτυπος	σκιά		μίμημα	σκιά	εἰκών
Representation	Antitype	Shadow		Copy	Shadow	Image

[107] Similarly, William L. Lane, *Hebrews*, 2 vols, WBC 47A–B (Dallas: Word, 1991), 2:225.
[108] Selby, 'Συνείδησις', 148.
[109] Selby, 'Συνείδησις', 148.
[110] 'Platonism' and 'Middle Platonism' are used interchangeably for simplicity, although the latter represents a later development and alteration. See Ronald Williamson's rebuttel, *Philo and the Epistle to the Hebrews*, ALGHJ 4 (Leiden: Brill, 1970).
[111] *Dec.* 41; *Det. Pot. Ins.* 20, 21, 107; *Spec. Leg.* 1.294; *Vit. Mos.* 2.81–3, 107.
[112] Bosman, *Conscience*, 183.

Hebrews. The chart contrasts the earthly 'unseen' realm – the shadowy 'copy' – with the 'true' heavenly realities.[113]

The defiled συνείδησις is interpreted as barring access to true worship and the heavenly realities, whereas a purged συνείδησις enables true inner worship and access into the unseen realm.[114] Earthly sacrifices could only cleanse the flesh (σάρξ) because σάρξ belongs to the human side of existence (cf. Heb. 9.13-14). But the blood of Christ purifies the συνείδησις since it belongs to 'the heavenly side of human existence',[115] leading to a more internal ethical and moral form of worship.[116] As James Thompson notes:

> This contrast between 'flesh' and 'conscience' suggests two dimensions of human existence corresponding to the earthly and heavenly tabernacles ... The earthly side of human existence can be cleansed with material offerings, while the whole person requires a superior sacrifice. *Syneidēsis* refers to the 'consciousness' (10:2-4), which can be cleansed only by the entrance of Christ into the heavenly world (cf. 10:22). Thus the argument assumes not only that material sacrifices have been superseded but also that they are fundamentally ineffective.[117]

Thompson's main innovation is that συνείδησις possesses an eternal and ontological identification with the heavenly realm and therefore slots naturally into Middle Platonic philosophy.[118]

The positives of this viewpoint are that the heavenly dimension is given larger scope in Hebrews' soteriological pronouncements (since Middle Platonism is concerned with an earthly–heavenly dualism). Nonetheless, the heavenly realm can only ever be soteriologically significant because Jesus 'entered' it, not because he purged it; since purging the heavenly realm is unthinkable in a Platonic worldview.[119] The argument

---

[113] Craig R. Koester, *Hebrews: A New Translation with Introduction and Commentary*, AB 36 (New York: Doubleday, 2001), 98. See also Knut Backhaus who views Christ's offering as impacting the spiritual realm, which he labels as the internal centre of believers (συνείδησις), *Der Hebräerbrief*, RNT (Regensburg: Friedrich Pustet, 2009), 323.

[114] Koester, *Hebrews*, 100.

[115] James W. Thompson, *Hebrews*, Paideia (Grand Rapids: Baker Academic, 2008), 187. See also 'Middle Platonism', in *Reading the Epistle to the Hebrews: A Resource for Students*, ed. Eric F. Mason and Kevin B. McCruden, RBS 66 (Atlanta: SBL, 2011), 42; Sidney G. Sowers, *The Hermeneutics of Philo and Hebrews: A Comparison of the Interpretation of the Old Testament in Philo Judaeus and the Epistle to the Hebrews*, BST 1 (Richmond, VA: John Knox, 1965), 101–3; F. J. Schierse, *Verheissung und Heilsvollendung: Zur theologischen Grundfrage des Hebräerbriefes*, MTS 9 (Munich: Karl Zink, 1955), 119.

[116] Witherington, *Letters*, 270; Luke Timothy Johnson, *Hebrews: A Commentary*, NTL (Louisville: Westminster John Knox, 2006), 27, 238; James W. Thompson, *The Beginnings of Christian Philosophy: The Epistle to the Hebrews*, CBQMS 13 (Washington: The Catholic Biblical Association of America, 1982), 109–15.

[117] Thompson, *Hebrews*, 185 (emphasis his own).

[118] Backhaus draws on the popular Seneca citation (*Ep.* 41.1) and sees the Holy Spirit as playing a key role in discerning the συνείδησις – the internal centre of believers, *Hebräerbrief*, 323. This does not explain why or how the συνείδησις requires purification.

[119] Aelred Cody, *Heavenly Sanctuary and Liturgy in the Epistle to the Hebrews: The Achievement of Salvation in the Epistle's Perspectives* (St. Meinrad, IN: Grail, 1960), 179–80; Thompson, *Hebrews*, 185.

that the σάρξ–συνείδησις contrast in Hebrews optimizes the earthly–heavenly Platonic contrast seems inconsistent with Hebrews' positive view of σάρξ (§4.3.2, §4.3.3). Additionally, the extent to which συνείδησις links ontologically with the heavenly realm in Hebrews has its problems, namely, if the συνείδησις is 'heavenly', how is it that it can become defiled and purged within the assumed worldview?[120] The purging of the συνείδησις in Hebrews is an innovative phenomenon and a departure from authors like Philo who describe the συνείδησις/τὸ συνειδός alongside forensic terminology commending or condemning an ethical life. Thus, when Hebrews speaks of a 'good consciousness' (καλὴν συνείδησιν, Heb. 13.18) some understand this as a reference to an inner 'ethos'.[121] This will be discussed in more detail later (§2.4.1); for now it is sufficient to say that Hebrews suits the worldview of Jewish eschatology more so than Platonic dualism,[122] since the blessings of the age to come are being experienced by believers now (1.2; 2.5; 6.5; 12.22).[123]

Second, there is the *cultic earthly–heavenly contrast*. This viewpoint is like the first but focuses specifically on the cosmic cultic issues of defilement and purgation rather than Platonic ideals. It is not that the σάρξ is bad, or that humanity requires an interior form of worship, but that the status of the audience's earthly embodiment is entangled in the status of the heavenly tabernacle.[124] While a defiled heavenly tabernacle would be unthinkable in a Platonic worldview, it is a very real possibility here. Since cultic offerings took place on earth, they were ineffective. However, because Jesus offered himself in the heavenly tabernacle and purged the συνείδησις,[125] a connection can be made between the cleansing of the heavenly tabernacle and the cleansing of the συνείδησις.[126]

In line with other notable eschatological texts (Ezek. 36.25-7; 1QS IV, 20-2) Gäbel asserts that Jesus' heavenly self-offering has brought about an eschatological purgation whereby the interiority of the worshippers is now purified.[127] Earthly events relate to the purification of the σάρξ and heavenly events relate to the purification of the συνείδησις[128] and so a correspondence between the συνείδησις and the heavenly

---

[120] Graham Hughes is right to question this, '[b]ut if the conscience or "spiritual" part of man is not wholly good, even less can it be said that his flesh is wholly evil', *Hebrews and Hermeneutics: The Epistle to the Hebrews as a New Testament Example of Biblical Interpretation*, SNTSMS 36 (Cambridge: Cambridge University Press, 1979), 42.

[121] deSilva, *Perseverance*, 509.

[122] Technically both of these worldviews believe in temporal dualism. See Philip Alexander, 'The Dualism of Heaven and Earth in Early Jewish Literature and Its Implications', in *Light Against Darkness: Dualism in Ancient Mediterranean Religion and the Contemporary World*, ed. Bennie H. Reynolds III et al., JAJS 2 (Göttingen: Vandenhoeck & Ruprecht, 2011), 169–85.

[123] Cody writes: 'Hebrews has drawn much of its terminology, philosophical thought, and literary expression from Alexandrian Judaism if not from Philo himself, but [it can be argued] that the substance of its temple theme is closer to the Palestinian Rabbinic literature and to the Jewish apocalypses', *Heavenly*, 36. This comment reflects the tensions in Cody's work, see n. 131.

[124] Gäbel, *Kulttheologie*, 131, 208, 320, 378, 380, 385, 411–12 n. 349. See also Lane, *Hebrews*, 2:246–7; Johnsson, 'Defilement', 329–41.

[125] Ribbens, *Levitical*, 190.

[126] See my later discussion (§4.2.2).

[127] Gäbel, *Kulttheologie*, 379.

[128] Gäbel, *Kulttheologie*, 422–4.

tabernacle can be observed: 'Das Gewissen ist dem himmlischen Heiligtum zugeordnet'.[129]

Therefore, although Jesus is the offeror and offering, it is the location of these salvific acts that is significant. As Aelred Cody notes:

> One sanctuary and its liturgy cannot in itself and of itself be better able to purify the inner man, the spiritual, or axiologically celestial man, than another. The difference must be made by the systems to which they belong. If one liturgy belongs to a terrestrial system, its validity will remain terrestrial. But if another liturgy, another action, belongs to a celestial system because it has been constituted in a system which belongs to the immediacy of God's activity and of God's dynamic presence, it will have a celestial and divine validity.[130]

As Cody stresses, as earthly inhabitants, the recipients are directly impacted by heavenly events because heavenly events are enduring.[131]

The first viewpoint above separates earthly and heavenly realities, but this second view brings them closer;[132] more significantly, it promotes a positive view of the cult by viewing the earthly worshippers as becoming part of an enduring heavenly cult.[133] Nevertheless, this view does not adequately explore *why* or *how* Jesus' heavenly offering corresponds to the συνείδησις and why Jesus' death and earthly life might not. A connection is acknowledged between the heavenly tabernacle and the συνείδησις but this view lacks an explanation and a link with the Levitical framework. The question as to why the συνείδησις required purging, or what this looks like practically, is left unexplored. Finally, it is firmly maintained, as with all these viewpoints, that the συνείδησις was unable to be purged under the OC.

Third is the *internal-external cultic contrast*. This understands the problem in terms of the efficaciousness of the earthly cult. The location of Jesus' offering is a secondary issue; what really matters is the offeror, Jesus, who has come to do away with the cult by his superior offering. Within this nuance it is Jesus' (often earthly)[134] offering that is simply more effective than Levitical sacrifices, which were too weak to offer internal purification.[135] Consequently, scholars speak of Jesus obtaining a 'deeper

---

[129] 'Conscience is assigned to the heavenly sanctuary', Gäbel, *Kulttheologie*, 424.
[130] Cody, *Heavenly*, 154–5.
[131] Cody is difficult to pin down as he reads Hebrews from a Platonic vantage point yet is convinced of the cultic reality of defilement and purgation in relation to the heavenly realm, *Heavenly*, 36, 154–5, 168–202.
[132] Thus, for Gäbel a purified συνείδησις is obtained on earth via one's baptism, *Kulttheologie*, 388, 401. So too Spicq, *Hébreux*, 2:317. For my critique of this view see §4.4.4. See also Moore's helpful observations, *Repetition*, 191.
[133] Jared C. Calaway, *The Sabbath and the Sanctuary: Access to God in the Letter to the Hebrews and its Priestly Context*, WUNT 2.349 (Tübingen: Mohr Siebeck, 2013), 157; Gäbel, *Kulttheologie*, 424.
[134] Some do link a heavenly offering with internal purification, see Jamieson, *Death*, 63, 163; Calaway, *Sabbath*, 113, 147; Gäbel, *Kulttheologie*, 282, 292, 374–92. Cf. Ribbens, *Levitical*, 190.
[135] Guido Telscher, *Opfer aus Barmherzigkeit: Hebr 9,11–28 im Kontext biblischer Sühnetheologie*, FB 112 (Würzburg: Echter, 2007), 259–60; Hermut Löhr, 'Anthropologie und Eschatologie im Hebräerbrief: Bemerkungen zum theologischen Interesse einer frühchristlichen Schrift', in *Eschatologie und Schöpfung: Festschrift für Erich Gräßer zum siebzigsten Geburtstag*, ed. Martin Evang, Helmut Merklein and Michael Wolter, BZNW 89 (Berlin: de Gruyter, 1997), 182–3.

purification',[136] one that 'reaches beyond the body to the depths of human interiority'.[137] Jesus' offering took place on the cross but impacted the 'spiritual realm' and so purified the συνείδησις, understood here as the internal life of the worshippers.[138] Central to this efficaciousness is the belief that Levitical sacrifices dealt exclusively with external (σάρξ) purification, whereas Jesus' superior offering purges internally (συνείδησις).[139]

A general criticism of this view is that it interprets one of Hebrews' key juxtapositions (Heb. 9.13-14) as a contrast between the purgation obtained by the Levitical cult (σάρξ) and the purgation obtained by Jesus (συνείδησις). This presents a negative contrast which views OC offerings as inferior, outward and unable to purify or deal with the συνείδησις. This hermeneutic fails to take into account the present situation of the recipients and ignores the inner psychological impact of sacrificial ritual. Promoters of this view often render σάρξ as 'fleshy' or 'outwardly', which has a decisive impact on how purification is understood.

---

[136] Philip E. Hughes, *A Commentary on the Epistle to the Hebrews* (Grand Rapids: Eerdmans, 1977), 324. Also, Thomas R. Schreiner, *Commentary on Hebrews*, BTCP (Nashville: B&H, 2015), 264; Cockerill, *Hebrews*, 431; Andrew T. Lincoln, *Hebrews: A Guide* (London: T&T Clark, 2006), 29; Bruce, *Hebrews*, xii, 31; Selby, 'Συνείδησις', 147; Pierce, *Conscience*, 101.

[137] Johnson, *Hebrews*, 27.

[138] H. Orton Wiley, *The Epistle to the Hebrews*, rev. edn (Kansas City: Beacon Hill, 1984), 266–8; Alexander Nairne, *The Epistle of Priesthood: Studies in the Epistle to the Hebrews* (Edinburgh: T&T Clark, 1913), 364.

[139] R. Hollis Gause, *Hebrews*, Pentecostal Commentary Series 7 (Leiden: Brill, 2022), 221; Herbert W. Bateman IV and Steven W. Smith, *Hebrews: A Commentary for Biblical Preaching and Teaching*, Kerux Commentaries (Grand Rapids: Kregel, 2021), 249–53; A. C. Heidel, *Das glaubende Gottesvolk: Der Hebräerbrief in israeltheologischer Perspektive*, WUNT 2.540 (Tübingen: Mohr Siebeck, 2020), 90; Dana M. Harris, *Hebrews*, EGGNT (Nashville: B&H, 2019), 226; Jamieson, *Death*, 63, 162; David M. Moffitt, 'Weak and Useless? Purity, the Mosaic Law, and Perfection in Hebrews', in *Law and Lawlessness in Early Judaism and Early Christianity*, ed. David Lincicum, Ruth Sheridan and Charles M. Stang, WUNT 420 (Tübingen: Mohr Siebeck, 2019), 89–90; Joachim Ringleben, *Wort und Geschichte: Kleine Theologie des Hebräerbriefes* (Göttingen: Vandenhoeck & Ruprecht, 2019), 146; Christian Rose, *Der Hebräerbrief*, BNT (Göttingen: Vandenhoeck & Ruprecht, 2019), 140; Davies, *Paideia*, 75 n. 160; David A. Brondos, *Jesus' Death in New Testament Thought*, 2 vols (Mexico City: Comunidad Teológica de México, 2018), 2:1011; Ole J. Filtvedt, *The Identity of God's People and the Paradox of Hebrews*, WUNT 2.400 (Tübingen: Mohr Siebeck, 2015), 182–3; Schreiner, *Hebrews*, 269; A. Vanhoye, *The Letter to the Hebrews: A New Commentary*, trans. Leo Arnold (Mahwah, NJ: Paulist Press, 2015), 150; *A Different Priest: The Epistle to the Hebrews*, RS (Miami, FL: Convivium, 2011), 287; Anderson, *Hebrews*, 250; Cockerill, *Hebrews*, 385, 397; Backhaus, *Hebräerbrief*, 310–11; Thompson, *Hebrews*, 185–8; *Beginnings*, 103–15; Alan C. Mitchell, *Hebrews*, SP 13 (Collegeville, MN: Liturgical Press, 2007), 184; Kenneth L. Schenck, *Cosmology and Eschatology in Hebrews: The Settings of the Sacrifice*, SNTSMS 143 (Cambridge: Cambridge University Press, 2007), 133–9; Telscher, *Opfer*, 258–60; Gäbel, *Kulttheologie*, 282, 292, 374–92; Johnson, *Hebrews*, 238; Robert P. Gordon, *Hebrews* (Sheffield: Sheffield Academic, 2000), 26–7, 118, 139; Victor C. Pfitzner, *Hebrews*, ANTC (Nashville: Abingdon, 1997), 129; Paul Ellingworth, *The Epistle to the Hebrews: A Commentary on the Greek Text*, NIGTC (Grand Rapids: Eerdmans, 1993), 442–4, 453–4; Grässer, *Hebräer*, 2:139; Lane, *Hebrews*, 2:239; Samuel Bénétreau, *L'Épître aux Hébreux*, 2 vols (Vaux-sur-Seine: Édifac, 1989–90), 2:95; Bruce, *Hebrews*, 201–7; Attridge, *Hebrews*, 250; H. A. Montefiore, *Commentary on the Epistle to the Hebrews* (London: A&C Black, 1964), 164; Franz Laub, *Bekenntnis und Auslegung: Die paränetische Funktion der Christologie im Hebraërbrief*, BU 15 (Regensburg: Pustet, 1980), 193–5, 199; Otto Michel, *Der Brief an die Hebräer*, 12th edn, KEK 13 (Göttingen: Vandenhoeck & Ruprecht, 1966), 313. Spicq, *Hébreux*, 2:317; Moffatt, *Hebrews*, 118–19; Brooke F. Westcott, *The Epistle to the Hebrews: The Greek Text with Notes and Essays*, 3rd edn (London: Macmillan, 1920), 255–63; Delitzsch, *Hebrews*, 2:98.

Fourth, there is the *democratization* of συνείδησις. This is an extension of the above viewpoints, except that these scholars understand συνείδησις as synonymous with other terms which the author uses to denote interiority (ψυχή, πνεῦμα, διάνοια, καρδία).[140] As a result συνείδησις is broadened; it is another way of speaking about the 'heart'[141] or the 'soul'.[142] The result of this is that purgation through Jesus' blood refers to a broad internal cleansing, not exclusive to the συνείδησις. As Philip Church notes, in contrasting the purification of the σάρξ with the συνείδησις (Heb. 9.13-14) the 'author is using familiar cultic terminology to refer to inward (heart) and outward (body) and therefore comprehensive, cleansing to support the exhortation to approach the presence of God'.[143] This broadening of συνείδησις is often linked by scholars to the Jer. 31 citation in Hebrews which speaks of laws written/put on the καρδία/διάνοια (Heb. 8.8-13; 10.16-17).[144] A cleansed συνείδησις 'fits God's promise to write his laws upon the "mind" (dianoia), which is synonymous with the "heart" (8:10; 10:16)'.[145] As Harold Attridge writes, 'the perfection of conscience, which involves primarily its "cleansings" from the burden of guilt, is the way in which the Jer[emiah] prophecy of a new covenant written on the heart is fulfilled'.[146] Thus, the 'purification of the conscience brings about the "new heart"'.[147] Like the heart, the συνείδησις thinks, wills, believes and decides.[148]

This viewpoint is particularly hazardous as it reduces the significance of συνείδησις for Hebrews. Treating συνείδησις as 'just another interior term' undermines the author's argument and reduces the soteriological possibility of a purified συνείδησις and why this might be of particular significance for Hebrews. As a result, these issues will need to be explored in more detail (§4.4.3, §4.4.4).

Some further additional commonalities link these four viewpoints together. For instance, while Hebrews uses the language of 'purification' and 'perfection' in relation to the συνείδησις, many scholars supplement the notion of the 'forgiveness of sins',[149]

---

[140] Gause, *Hebrews*, 153, 198; Moffitt, *Atonement*, 200, 211; Mitchell, *Hebrews*, 23; Gäbel, *Kulttheologie*, 380, 386–7, 400; Koester, *Hebrews*, 100, 399; Richard W. Johnson, *Going Outside the Camp: The Sociological Function of the Levitical Critique in the Epistle to the Hebrews*, JSNTSup 109 (Sheffield: Sheffield Academic, 2001), 104–7; Ellingworth, *Hebrews*, 442; Grässer, *Hebräer*, 2:137; Attridge, *Hebrews*, 242; Peterson, *Perfection*, 135.

[141] Douglas W. Kennard, *A Biblical Theology of Hebrews* (Eugene, OR: Wipf & Stock, 2018), 105; Cockerill, *Hebrews*, 385, 401; Mackie, *Eschatology*, 191, 191 n. 83; Bénétreau, *Hébreux*, 2:82; Stelzenberger, *Syneidesis im Neuen Testament*, 94–5.

[142] Bruce, *Hebrews*, 218.

[143] Church, *Temple*, 387.

[144] Harris, *Hebrews*, 204; Mitchell, *Hebrews*, 23; Stegemann and Stegemann, 'Cultic', *Hebrews: Contemporary Methods*, 21.

[145] Koester, *Hebrews*, 100, also 399.

[146] Attridge, *Hebrews*, 242.

[147] Peterson, *Perfection*, 5.

[148] Harris, *Hebrews*, 275; Bénétreau, *Hébreux*, 2:82; Mathias Rissi, *Die Theologie des Hebräerbriefs: Ihre Verankerung in der Situation des Verfassers und seiner Leser*, WUNT 41 (Tübingen: Mohr Siebeck, 1987), 94.

[149] Ringleben, *Wort*, 147; Davies, *Paideia*, 92; Adriani M. Rodriques, *Toward a Priestly Christology: A Hermeneutical Study of Christ's Priesthood* (Lanham, MD: Lexington Books/Fortress Academic, 2018), 139; Kennard, *Hebrews*, 132; Moore, *Repetition*, 210–11; David L. Allen, *Hebrews*, NAC 35 (Nashville: B&H, 2010), 515; deSilva, *Perseverance*, 307; Gordon, *Hebrews*, 181; Ellingworth, *Hebrews*, 442; Wiley, *Hebrews*, 267; Peterson, *Perfection*, 136, 249, 203; Spicq, *Hébreux*, 2:259; Moffatt, *Hebrews*, 125.

'redemption', or both.[150] As Schreiner writes, 'the conscience must be cleansed by the blood of Christ for sinners to be forgiven'.[151] As argued later (§4.4.3), adding the notion of 'forgiveness' is not only a foreign entity in Hebrews, but a distraction from the real problem of consciousness of sin (§1.2, §2.2). There also appears to be confusion around 'perfection' and 'purification' language with respect to συνείδησις (9.9, 14; 10.2, 22). Scholars either view the two terms as synonymous[152] or they assume that because Levitical offerings could not bring about perfection, this presupposes an inability to purify the συνείδησις.[153] This will also be addressed in subsequent chapters (§4.4.1, §4.4.2).

1.5 Methodological approach

'Knowledge of the world that produced Hebrews is not yet knowledge of the world of Hebrews.'[154] This remark from L. T. Johnson indicates that historical objectivity remains a hurdle in approaching Hebrews. While no single methodological approach will ever be satisfactory, this present study will explore two: intertextuality and ritual theory.

'Intertextuality' has been widely accepted within NT studies. At the same time it has been criticized as 'fuzzy'[155] and confusing. From a NT perspective it might be broadly interpreted as the general engagement and incorporation of the HB and LXX within the NT.[156] The use of the OT in the NT has witnessed a surge of interest in recent years.[157] After all, 'Christianity did not spring out of a vacuum', as Steve Moyise notes, 'but is in direct continuity with the religion enshrined in what Christians now call the Old Testament'.[158] Richard Hays' seminal work, *Echoes of Scripture in the Letters of Paul*,

---

[150] Ribbens, *Levitical*, 194–5. Grässer goes as far as to compare the purging of the συνείδησις to justification, *Hebräer*, 2:138–9.
[151] Schreiner, *Hebrews*, 272 n. 443.
[152] Gäbel, *Kulttheologie*, 378; Isaacs, *Sacred*, 101–2.
[153] Matthew C. Easter, *Faith and the Faithfulness of Jesus in Hebrews*, SNTSMS 160 (Cambridge: Cambridge University Press, 2014), 48.
[154] Luke Timothy Johnson, 'The Scriptural World of Hebrews', *Int* 57.3 (2003): 238.
[155] See G. K. Beale's comments, *Handbook on the New Testament Use of the Old Testament: Exegesis and Interpretation* (Grand Rapids: Baker Academic, 2012), 39–40; Paul Foster, 'Echoes without Resonance: Critiquing Certain Aspects of Recent Scholarly Trends in the Study of the Jewish Scriptures in the New Testament', *JSNT* 38.1 (2015): 96–111. Stanley E. Porter discourages the use of intertextuality as 'unnecessary', 'The Use of the Old Testament in the New Testament: A Brief Comment on Method and Terminology', in *Early Christian Interpretation of the Scriptures of Israel: Investigations and Proposals*, ed. Craig A. Evans and James A. Sanders (Sheffield: Sheffield Academic Press, 1997), 84 n. 17. Porter certainly has a point; scholars need to be clearer in what they mean when they speak of 'intertextuality'. See N. T. Wright's helpful defence and engagement with these issues, 'Pictures, Stories, and the Cross: Where Do the Echoes Lead?', *JTI* 11.1 (2017): 49–68.
[156] Like other NT writers Hebrews appears reliant on some form of Greek translation of the HB. Rahlf's Greek text will be the assumed default text, but I make no assumptions as to the text the author of Hebrews engaged with. In this study I will draw on the LXX but also the MT, especially when discussing key and contentious terms and passages relating to the sacrificial cult.
[157] See David M. Allen's helpful summary, 'Introduction: The Study of the Use of the Old Testament in the New', *JSNT* 38.1 (2015): 3–16. This article is part of a wider periodical volume in the *JSNT* devoted to this topic. C. H. Dodd might be regarded as the father of this discipline, *According to the Scriptures: The Sub-Structure of New Testament Theology* (London: Nisbet, 1952).
[158] Steve Moyise, *The Old Testament in the New: An Introduction* (London: Continuum, 2001), 1.

further introduced the notion of an 'intertextual echo'.[159] While cited scriptural references and allusions are considered as 'obvious intertextual references',[160] an 'echo' is often subtle, unconscious and lacking in authorial intent. Although small, within its native 'echo chamber' it reverberates and becomes audible for its intended audience. Moyise describes it helpfully when he notes: '[a] popular game show on television required contestants to guess the title of a piece of music from its opening bars. Sometimes, the winner managed this from just two notes. Similarly, not many words are necessary to evoke Israel's Passover or Exile'.[161] Intertextuality also involves inner biblical exegesis,[162] with authors often seeking to address problems or issues in biblical texts.[163] The role of the author was 'not to discern what the text meant in the past but what it means today',[164] since these texts were 'living traditions, regularly updated to apply to new situations'.[165]

If Hebrews is the 'Cinderella' of NT studies, it 'might be called the "Queen" when it comes to the use of the OT in the NT'.[166] Unmistakably, Hebrews 'interacts with the Jewish Scriptures perhaps more than any other book in the New Testament',[167] with recent studies in Hebrews scholarship displaying a keen interest.[168] This study will

---

[159] Richard B. Hays, *Echoes of Scripture in the Letters of Paul* (New Haven: Yale University Press, 1989), 18–29. See also *Reading with the Grain of Scripture* (Grand Rapids: Eerdmans, 2020); *Echoes of Scripture in the Gospels* (Waco: Baylor University, 2016); *Reading Backwards: Figural Christology and the Fourfold Gospel Witness* (London: SPCK, 2015); *The Conversion of the Imagination: Paul as Interpreter of Israel's Scripture* (Cambridge: Eerdmans, 2005), esp. 34–45.

[160] Hays, *Echoes*, 29.

[161] Steve Moyise, 'Intertextuality and the Study of the Old Testament in the New Testament', in *The Old Testament in the New Testament: Essays in Honour of J. L. North*, ed. Steve Moyise, JSNTSup 189 (Sheffield: Sheffield Academic Press, 2000), 19.

[162] I take this term from Michael Fishbane's influential work, *Biblical Interpretation in Ancient Israel* (Oxford: Clarendon, 1985) where he states, 'inner-biblical exegesis starts with the received Scripture and moves forward to the interpretations based on it', 7. As part of his criticism of the term 'intertextuality', Beale suggests replacing this term with 'inner-biblical exegesis' or 'inner-biblical allusion', *Handbook*, 40.

[163] Susan E. Docherty, 'Crossing Testamentary Borders: Methodological Insights for OT/NT Study from Contemporary Hebrew Bible Scholarship', in *Methodology in the Use of the Old Testament in the New: Context and Criteria*, ed. David Allen and Steve Smith, LNTS 597 (London: Bloomsbury T&T Clark, 2019), 11–23.

[164] Moyise, *Old Testament*, 4.

[165] Moyise, *Old Testament*, 4.

[166] George H. Guthrie, 'Hebrews', in *Commentary on the New Testament Use of the Old Testament*, ed. G. K. Beale and D. A. Carson (Grand Rapids: Baker Academic, 2007), 919.

[167] Kenneth L. Schenck, 'Shadows and Realities', in *Exploring Intertextuality: Diverse Strategies for New Testament Interpretation of Texts*, ed. B. J. Oropeza and Steve Moyise (Eugene, OR: Wipf & Stock, 2016), 81. Yet it remains unclear exactly how many times Hebrews directly cites the OT, with some scholars suggesting as many as fifty-two. See Guthrie's chapter, 'Hebrews', *Commentary*, 919–95, as well as Mark Cooper's helpful piece, where he argues for nineteen clear quotations, notwithstanding allusions and intertexts, 'To Quote or Not to Quote? Categorizing Quotations in the Epistle to the Hebrews', *JSNT* 44.3 (2022): 452–68.

[168] Recent significant studies include Susan E. Docherty, 'The Use of the Old Testament in Hebrews Chapter 13 and Its Bearing on the Question of the Integrity of the Epistle', *Son*, 207–18; 'Composite Citations and Conflation of Scriptural Narratives in Hebrews', in *Composite Citations in Antiquity: Volume 2: New Testament Uses*, ed. S. A. Adams and S. M. Ehorn, LNTS 593 (London: Bloomsbury T&T Clark, 2018), 190–208; 'The Text Form of the OT Citations in Hebrews Chapter 1 and the Implications for the Study of the Septuagint', *NTS* 55.3 (2009): 355–65; *The Use of the Old Testament*

explore Hebrews' citations (§2.4.5, §2.6.3), allusions (§2.3, §3.3.2, §3.4.3, §4.2, §5.4.3.3) and intertextual echoes (§4.3.5) with the Jewish Scriptures. In particular, Hebrews' engagement with sacrificial texts is part of the author's own reconstruction and retelling of important ritual narratives – what Gary Anderson labels as the 'scripturalization of the cult'.[169] Therefore, this work will seek to uncover corresponding motifs between OT sacrificial texts and Hebrews, such as Yom Kippur and other rituals (§3.3.2). Engaging with these narratives allows key terms such as 'atonement' and 'redemption' to be examined.

Secondly, reading Hebrews as a powerful 'ritual' text will play a significant role in this study. With no biblical lexical correspondent, 'ritual' is difficult to define.[170] Michael Hundley defines ritual as 'meaningfully interacting with God … [through] activities that elicit the response of God'.[171] Consequently, 'ritual serves as a bridge between two worlds, the human and divine. When these two worlds intersect, transformation inevitably occurs, as God, the wholly other, becomes accessible in the here and now'.[172] Linked to ritual is the notion of defilement and subsequent purgation. These terms are not only essential for understanding the social environment and formation of early Judaism and Christianity, but they continue to impact contemporary society across diverse cultures.[173] Previous scholarship interpreted defilement as a primitive evolutionary concept, denoting the idea of the 'taboo',[174] but Mary Douglas' landmark

---

in Hebrews, WUNT 2.260 (Tübingen: Mohr Siebeck, 2009); Jared Compton, *Psalm 110 and the Logic of Hebrews*, LNTS 537 (London: Bloomsbury T&T Clark, 2015); Georg Walser, *Old Testament Quotations in Hebrews*, WUNT 2.356 (Tübingen: Mohr Siebeck, 2013); David M. Allen, 'Why Bother Going Outside?: The Use of the Old Testament in Heb 13:10-16', in *The Scriptures of Israel in Jewish and Christian Tradition: Essays in Honour of Maarten J. J. Menken*, ed. Bart J. Koet, Steve Moyise and Joseph Verheyden, NovTSup 148 (Leiden: Brill, 2013), 239–52; *Deuteronomy and Exhortation in Hebrews: A Study in Narrative Re-representation*, WUNT 2.238 (Tübingen: Mohr Siebeck, 2008); King L. She, *The Use of Exodus in Hebrews*, StBibLit 142 (New York: Peter Lang, 2011); Dirk J. Human and Gert J. Steyn, eds, *Psalms and Hebrews: Studies in Reception*, LHBOTS 527 (London: T&T Clark, 2010); George H. Guthrie, 'Hebrews', Commentary, 919–95; 'Hebrews' Use of the Old Testament: Recent Trends in Research', *CurBR* 1.2 (2003): 271–94; Harold W. Attridge, 'The Psalms in Hebrews', in *The Psalms in the New Testament*, ed. Steve Moyise and Maarten J. J. Menken (London: T&T Clark, 2004), 197–212; Radu Gheorghita, *The Role of the Septuagint in Hebrews: An Investigation of its Influence with Special Consideration to the Use of Hab 2:3-4 in Heb 10:37-38*, WUNT 2.160 (Tübingen: Mohr Siebeck, 2003); Johnson, 'Scriptural', 237–50.

[169] Gary A. Anderson, 'Sacrifice and Sacrificial Offerings (OT)', *ABD* 5:870–86, esp. 882–6.

[170] See Catherine M. Bell's discussion in her seminal work, *Ritual Theory, Ritual Practice* (Oxford: Oxford University Press, 1992), 19–29.

[171] Michael B. Hundley, *Keeping Heaven on Earth: Safeguarding the Divine Presence in the Priestly Tabernacle*, FAT 2.50 (Tübingen: Mohr Siebeck, 2011), 20.

[172] Hundley, *Heaven*, 21. See Roy E. Gane for a helpful summary, *Cult and Character: Purification Offerings, Day of Atonement, and Theodicy* (Winona Lake, IN: Eisenbrauns, 2005), 3–24.

[173] Wil Rogan, 'Purity in Early Judaism: Current Issues and Questions', *CurBR* 16.3 (2018): 309–39; Moshe Blidstein, *Purity, Community, and Ritual in Early Christian Literature* (Oxford: Oxford University Press, 2017), 3–17, 18–58; Robbie Duschinsky, 'Recognizing Secular Defilement: Douglas, Durkheim and Housework', *HA* 25.5 (2014): 553–70; Christian Frevel and Christophe Nihan, 'Introduction', in *Purity and the Forming of Religious Traditions in the Ancient Mediterranean World and Ancient Judaism*, ed. Christian Frevel and Christophe Nihan, DHR 3 (Leiden: Brill, 2013), 1–46; E. J. Warren, *Cleansing the Cosmos: A Biblical Model for Conceptualizing and Counteracting Evil* (Eugene, OR: Wipf & Stock, 2012), 127–42; 143–59; Hannah K. Harrington, 'Clean and Unclean', *NIDB* 1:681–9.

[174] William R. Smith, *Lectures on the Religion of the Semites* (Edinburgh: A&C Black, 1889).

work, *Purity and Danger*, dispelled this notion. Douglas showed that impurity and purity were not distinguished out of fear or ignorance, but demonstrated a rational process culminating in boundaries that helped societies to self-protect from outside pollution.[175] Defilement and its relation to ritual were not simply primitive issues, but contemporary matters too.[176] Douglas writes that 'our ideas of dirt also express symbolic systems and that the difference between pollution behaviour in one part of the world and another is only a matter of detail'.[177] Douglas further notes that '[w]here there is dirt there is system. Dirt is the by-product of a systematic ordering and classification of matter'.[178] Thus, '[w]here there is no differentiation there is no defilement'.[179]

Typically, Hebrews' discussion around sacrifice and ritual is understood by scholars as either a condemnation of ritual under the OC,[180] or, as an example of metaphorical or creative symbolism that theologizes the text of Hebrews.[181] Instead, ritual and categories of defilement and purgation are real and present concerns for Hebrews. Johnsson is particularly helpful here:

> It seems impossible to escape the conclusion that the cultic language of Hebrews was not merely some momentary illustration to be picked up and cast aside quickly in favour of the 'real' meaning. No: the cult furnishes the vehicle for the most profound reflections of the writer. That is, the *auctor ad Hebraeos* apparently thought in cultic categories.[182]

Therefore, the cult is 'fulfilled not abrogated',[183] a foreshadowing reality that finds its ongoing realization in the perpetual heavenly blood offering of Christ (§5.4.3, §5.4.4). Hebrews scholarship has successfully exposed the dangers of overemphasizing the importance of slaughter, but it does not need to fall into the trap of isolating sacrifice from ritual as well.[184] Throughout this study, reading Hebrews' sacrificial argumentation through the lenses of ritual will be vital (§2.3, §2.5, §2.6, §3.3, §4.3.4, §5.4).

---

[175] Mary Douglas, *Purity and Danger: An Analysis of Concepts of Pollution and Taboo* (London: Routledge, 1966). See also *Natural Symbols: Explorations in Cosmology* (London: Routledge, 1996). It is important to note that *Natural Symbols* displays a deviation from some of Douglas' assertions in *Purity and Danger*. See Robbie Duschinsky, Simone Schnall and Daniel H Weiss, eds, *Purity and Danger Now: New Perspectives* (London: Routledge, 2016).
[176] Douglas, *Purity*, 8-35, 36-47. See also Yitzhaq Feder, *Purity and Pollution in the Hebrew Bible: From Embodied Experience to Moral Metaphor* (Cambridge: Cambridge University Press, 2022), 1-21.
[177] Douglas, *Purity*, 43.
[178] Douglas, *Purity*, 44.
[179] Douglas, *Purity*, 198.
[180] If Hebrews condemns OC sacrifices as useless then the author 'must' be contradicting himself, see A. J. M. Wedderburn, 'Sawing Off the Branches: Theologizing Dangerously Ad Hebraeos', *JTS* 56.2 (2005): 393-414. Hebrews is not 'sawing off branches'. Wedderburn's conclusions are generally debunked, see Filtvedt, *Identity*, 106-7; Moore, *Repetition*, 13-14, 16-17.
[181] Stegemann and Stegemann, 'Cultic', *Hebrews: Contemporary Methods*, 15. See my discussion in §3.2.
[182] Johnsson, 'Defilement', 11 (emphasis his own). Similarly, as Moore notes, '[Hebrews] uses cultic categories because it believes they are indicative of the nature of reality ... they tell us something about how the world truly is', *Repetition*, 17.
[183] G. B. Caird, 'The Exegetical Method of the Epistle to the Hebrews', *CJT* 5.1 (1959): 46.
[184] Richard D. Nelson sees these two as harmful starting points, *Raising Up a Faithful Priest: Community and Priesthood in Biblical Theology* (Louisville: Westminster John Knox, 1993), 55.

1.6 Outline of the study

This study is in three parts. Part One ('The Defiled Consciousness') and Chapter 2 will suggest that grounding Hebrews within OT cultic thought is essential for a better understanding of the epistle. The significance of defilement within its cultic setting will be examined, with the relationship between sin, defilement and the tabernacle being addressed. From here, Hebrews' tabernacle terminology will be analysed. It will be argued that Hebrews' language is both spatial and horizontal; the heavenly tabernacle was foreshowed by the earthly realities. These discussions are essential for the entirety of this study, since they will map out Hebrews' conception of the heavenly tabernacle. The final part of Chapter 2 will focus on sin as defilement and its relation to the problem of συνείδησις. Sin is a multifaceted concept in Hebrews, but sin as *conscious* defilement is a significant motif. In agreement with Jacob Milgrom's 'aerial miasma', it will be proposed that sin and defilement in Hebrews stretch to the heavens. The general effects of a defiled συνείδησις will then be examined, paving the way for the second part of this study.

Part Two ('Purifying the Consciousness: Cosmic Purgation'), Chapters 3 and 4, will assess Hebrews' cultic argumentation and the solution to a defiled συνείδησις. Chapter 3 will engage with the recent developments regarding Hebrews' sacrificial argumentation. While Yom Kippur is an important ritual for Hebrews, an overarching Yom Kippur hermeneutic hinders the richness of Hebrews' soteriological pronouncements. Instead, it will be contended that Hebrews purposefully distinguishes between what Jesus achieves on earth and what he achieves in heaven. Jesus' earthly life of obedience, culminating in death, constitutes his own personal offering – for himself and for his followers. It enacts a NC, redeems and makes people holy; it deals with the objective issues of sin. But only Jesus' heavenly blood offering can purge the συνείδησις and deal with the ongoing subjective consciousness of sin.

Chapter 4 will examine the purification of the συνείδησις. It will argue that sacrifice cannot be emptied of its ritual impact. The importance of blood and the purification of the heavenly tabernacle will be the starting point. The majority of Chapter 4 will be devoted to understanding Hebrews' concept of cultic purification. It will argue against the common συνείδησις–σάρξ/internal–external purification contrast. Σάρξ denotes the 'earthly' or 'human' aspect of existence and so the contrast is an earthly–heavenly one, with a subsequent cultic blood contrast implied. Furthermore, the Levitical concept of אשם provides an important conceptual link for interpreting Hebrews' concept of συνείδησις. It was not that the earthly cult could not purge the consciousness, but that it lacked a qualitative type of purgation, that is 'perfection'. Earthly offerings required repetition, whereas Jesus' heavenly blood offering was offered once perpetually.

Part Three ('Assurance and the Purified Consciousness') and Chapter 5 will engage with debates concerning the nature of Jesus' heavenly blood offering, with specific focus on how this relates to συνείδησις. Questions around Jesus' heavenly priestly ministry and how this relates to his session will be explored. The ongoing discussion concerning the 'once-for-all' or 'perpetual' nature of Jesus' heavenly offering will be observed. Psalm 110.1 and the act of Jesus 'sitting down' does not indicate a finished sacrificial work; it is a celebration of the Son and the crowning achievement of his earthly life of obedience. From this seated stature Jesus functions as a high priest who offers 'divine help' for his followers in their own perseverance; this is not linked with atonement or purgation. Jesus' roles as guarantor and meditator offer 'assurance' of the continued benefits of the NC. Additionally, Jesus' heavenly blood functions as a separate entity, offering perpetual assurance regarding purgation and the consciousness of sin. This blood is speaking and through it, the recipients are assured of their confidence in approaching the heavenly realities, being granted confidence, boldness and sacrificial amnesia.

Finally, Chapter 6 will conclude by summarizing the contributions and limitations of this study. It will offer some pastoral implications for the contemporary church with reference to the problem of συνείδησις, suggesting that further research is warranted concerning the 'consciousness of sin' and contemporary discussions around mental health.

Part One

The defiled consciousness

2

Cosmic defilement: The cultic context of defilement

2.1 Introduction

The purpose of this chapter is to explore how Hebrews understands the nature of defilement,[1] how it functions and how it affects people within a cultic framework. This chapter will lay the foundation for later chapters by establishing a particular understanding of the heavenly tabernacle and its relationship with defilement. To achieve this, this chapter will be structured into four stages. First, defilement in the cultic sphere will be introduced. This part will discuss the role of sin and defilement in its priestly conception, especially as it relates to the sanctuary. Second, the cultic context of defilement in Hebrews will be explored. This section will address significant questions concerning how Hebrews understands the heavenly and earthly tabernacles, as well as the role of the Second Temple. Third, defilement in Hebrews will be explored, and fourth, the effects of defilement. Both these sections will focus specifically on the defiled συνείδησις as well as the defiled heavenly tabernacle. Defilement and specifically *conscious* defilement is a central problem in Hebrews. This chapter will pave the way for subsequent chapters which focus on how this problem is to be solved. To begin, the discussion will be anchored in what will be referred to throughout as the 'present problem'.

2.2 The present problem

It is important to begin this chapter by asking how the problem of συνείδησις impacts the recipients in their current situation. Hebrews describes the recipients as existing within an interim period. For instance, the cultic regulations of the first covenant are referred to as wearing away and about to disappear (Heb. 1.10-11; 8.13) yet the inauguration of the 'new covenant' (διαθήκης καινῆς) and Christ's heavenly cultic ministry (9.11-14)[2] are simultaneously underway. This is expressed especially in Heb. 9.1-10. After describing the earthly priest's entrance into the tabernacle and the regulations (9.1-7) Hebrews draws on the revelation of the Holy Spirit to decipher

---

[1] The terms 'defilement' and 'impurity' will be used synonymously henceforth.
[2] Gäbel, *Kulttheologie*, 280, 485; Koester, *Hebrews*, 398; Peterson, *Perfection*, 133.

additional meaning. What the Spirit reveals is that the way into the heavenly sanctuary[3] has yet to be disclosed while the first tabernacle 'has standing' (ἐχούσης στάσιν, 9.8). The phrase 'ἐχούσης στάσιν' is best understood as a reference to the functioning legality of the earthly tabernacle, as opposed to the physical standing of the structure.[4] In other words, the Second Temple might still be physically standing but because Christ now functions as a high priest in the heavenly tabernacle the earthly cult's legal standing has expired (cf. 13.10).

The dating of Hebrews continues to be a contentious issue. The discussion around the earthly cult is spoken of in the present tense (9.1-10; 10.1-4; 13.10) and this is further contrasted with Jesus' offering in the past tense (10.11-12). This and the question concerning the cessation of present offerings (10.1-4) has led some to view Hebrews as written before 70 CE.[5] Alternatively, a later dating is possible with the recipients still able to partake in a localized Yom Kippur ceremony in certain social settings.[6]

Nonetheless, given the author's discussion concerning 'the present time' (τὸν καιρὸν τὸν ἐνεστηκότα) and the 'time of correction'[7] (καιροῦ διορθώσεως, 9.9-10), a date before 70 CE is likely. The recipients live in this 'present time' where the earthly cult is described as a type (παραβολή)[8] which the Spirit reveals as pointing beyond itself (9.9) to the inauguration of the 'true tent' (8.2) and Christ's heavenly cultic ministry.[9] The

---

[3] The genitive of direction ('τὴν τῶν ἁγίων ὁδόν', 9.7) indicates that a heavenly sanctuary is an obvious referent, see Harris, *Hebrews*, 216; Daniel B. Wallace, *Greek Grammar Beyond the Basics: An Exegetical Syntax of the New Testament* (Grand Rapids: Zondervan, 1996), 100-1; BDF §166.

[4] Rightly Gäbel, 'Permission', *Son*, 140-1; Harris, *Hebrews*, 216; Ribbens, *Levitical*, 166; Backhaus, *Hebräerbrief*, 310; Attridge, *Hebrews*, 240-1. It lost its status when Christ entered the heavenly sanctuary, not when the earthly temple was destroyed.

[5] For a pre-70 CE reading, see Joseph, 'Days of His Flesh', 209, 227; Church, *Temple*, 14-15; Gäbel, *Kulttheologie*, 484; D. A. Hagner, *Encountering the Book of Hebrews: An Exposition* (Grand Rapids: Baker Academic, 2002), 111; deSilva, *Perseverance*, 20-3; Ellingworth, *Hebrews*, 29-33; Lane, *Hebrews*, 1:lxii-lxvi; Lindars, *Hebrews*, 20; Bruce, *Hebrews*, 20-2, 236. While Josephus (*Ant.* 3.102-87, 224-57; *Apion.* 2.77, 193-8) and Clement (*1 Clem.* 41.2) employ the present tense when writing after the destruction of the temple (cf. m. *Qidd.* 1.8), unlike Hebrews, they are not describing the end of the cult. The destruction of the temple would have been gold dust for Hebrews' argumentation, see Church, *Temple*, 14-16. For a post-70 CE reading see Kenneth L. Schenck, *A New Perspective on Hebrews: Rethinking the Parting of the Ways* (Lanham: Fortress Academic, 2019), 100-17; Mitchell, *Hebrews*, 7-11; G. Gelardini, *Verhärtet eure Herzen nicht: der Hebräer, eine Synagogenhomilie zu Tischa be-Aw* (Leiden: Brill, 2007), 107-27; Isaacs, *Sacred*, 41-5. Some affirm that accuracy in dating is not possible, see Koester, *Hebrews*, 50-4; Attridge, *Hebrews*, 6-9.

[6] Hebrews' assertion that the community *have* a high priest of their own (Heb. 8.1) might have increased their social identity in the light of a destroyed temple, Steven Muir, 'Social Identity in the Epistle to the Hebrews', in *T&T Clark Handbook of Social Identity in the New Testament*, ed. J. B. Tucker and C. A. Baker (London: Bloomsbury T&T Clark, 2014), 425-39.

[7] Or the 'time of the new order', BDAG 251. This does not mean that the author is only ever referring to the earthly cult, since he includes the wilderness tabernacle in his discussions (§2.4.5).

[8] BDAG 759. The παραβολή is a model pointing beyond itself to a fuller realization (cf. Heb. 11.19); it draws the old and new closer and states that there is something in the old to be learnt about the new. The old *illustrates* the new, see Angela Rascher, *Schriftauslegung und Christologie im Hebräerbrief*, BZNW 153 (Berlin: de Gruyter, 2007), 153-61; Steve Stanley, 'Hebrews 9:6-10: The 'Parable' of the Tabernacle', *NovT* 37.4 (1995): 389-99. 'Πρώτης σκηνῆς' is the likely antecedent for the relative 'ἥτις' (Heb. 9.8-9), rightly Ellingworth, *Hebrews*, 439; Attridge, *Hebrews*, 241. Contra Bruce, *Hebrews*, 195 n. 60.

[9] While 'πρώτης σκηνῆς' is given a spatial sense earlier (Heb. 9.2, 6) a temporal sense is required in 9.8, displaying the author's linguistic flexibility. Opting for a spatial/temporal sense does not diminish the author's overall argumentation, so Church, *Temple*, 414-15; Ribbens, *Levitical*, 165-6.

continual function of the earthly cult and its participants must give way to the 'time of correction'. The heavenly cult is not a replacement of the earthly cult but brings it to its *telos*.[10] In a sense, the 'present time' and the 'time of correction' (9.9-10) refer to the same thing,[11] since the exaltation of Christ in these last days (1.1-3) places the recipients in an overlap of the ages.[12] The definitive problem with this 'present time' and the earthly cult is the inability 'to perfect the worshipper [in reference to] the consciousness'[13] (κατὰ συνείδησιν τελειῶσαι τὸν λατρεύοντα, 9.9).

This present time lacks perfection (7.11, 19; 9.9-10; 10.1) and the ability to bring about total purgation (§4.4.1, §4.4.2). Although gifts and sacrifices are presently offered under the earthly cult (10.1-4) they deal only with 'food and drink and various baptisms' (9.10) – 'earthly regulations' (δικαιώματα σαρκός, 9.10) until the 'time of correction' (§4.3.3). Put simply, Hebrews understands the earthly cult and heavenly cult as coexisting, with the earthly cult being stripped of its authority and legality since the heavenly cult is now in operation and the earthly cult is wearing away.

2.3 Defilement in the cultic sphere

As noted already (§1.5), Hebrews is embedded in the cultic and priestly categories of defilement and purgation, with the study of purity–impurity being vital in understanding both the social environment and the scriptural formation of early Judaism and Christianity. Douglas' work revealed that these very categories are present in our own society; yet Douglas left some questions unanswered. For instance, what is meant by terms such as 'sin' or 'impurity'? Are these concepts synonymous, analogous or distinct? Are there different forms of defilement? Is all defilement sinful? What role does symbolism and metaphor play in understanding these concepts? In short, how can our own postmodern cognizance comprehend the conceptual world of these terms as they appear in their initial Pentateuchal context and subsequently in Hebrews? Before turning to Hebrews, it will be beneficial to introduce the categories of sin and defilement as they are conceptualized in the priestly corpus.

2.3.1 Dorian Gray and impurity in the cultic sphere

Leviticus 10.10 underpins the essence of the purity–impurity system. YHWH instructs Aaron to distinguish 'between the holy and the common, and between the unclean

---

[10] Church, *Temple*, 18.
[11] Church, *Temple*, 415.
[12] The Jewish understanding of the 'present age' (עולם הוה) and the 'age to come' (עולם הבא) may well be present here, see Delitzsch, *Hebrews*, 2:69.
[13] I agree with Peterson: 'it is not strictly the conscience that is perfected ... [the] one who would draw near to God, is perfected "in relation to conscience" (κατὰ συνείδησιν). One's relationship with God cannot be perfected until conscience is cleansed from guilt', *Perfection*, 136. See Harold J. Greenlee, *An Exegetical Summary of Hebrews*, 2nd edn (Dallas: Summer Institute of Linguistics, 2008), 306–7; Wallace, *Grammar*, 377.

and the clean' (בין הקדש ובין החל ובין הטמא ובין הטהור).¹⁴ Table 2 outlines this visually.¹⁵ Persons and objects are defined by four possible states: holy, common, pure and impure. Two of these can exist simultaneously (pure things can be holy or common, common things can be pure or impure). The holy cannot come into contact with the impure. Instead, these two categories are dynamic. They both seek to extend their influence and control over the other two categories – the common and the pure.

Within these categories the tabernacle and its status are fundamental. Sin and defilement, however, counteract the cult's purpose to 'safeguard the divine presence in the tabernacle'.¹⁶ Although it is home to divine habitation, the tabernacle is prone to contamination and when this happens the people are restricted from participating in the cult.¹⁷ Defilement is a hinderance to cultic participation.¹⁸ The result is that 'the contagious power of impurity has an unavoidable impact on the pure space ... every transgression, be it physical or metaphorical, endangers the state of purity ... as purity is the precondition for a proper cult, a sacred space is accordingly disqualified or impaired for valid cultic actions by defilement'.¹⁹ In order to approach the divine through the cult, individuals require a certain level of purity.²⁰ Purging the tabernacle purges the people and the divine presence is able to remain, with the relationship between the Lord and his people being restored.²¹

In an article in 1976, Jacob Milgrom creatively drew upon Oscar Wilde's short novel *The Picture of Dorian Gray*²² in order to illustrate the relationship between sin and the

Table 2 The priestly system

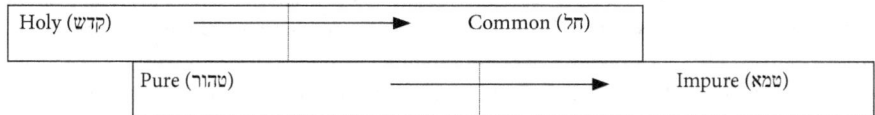

---

14. One might also read this as a distinction between what stays *inside* the tent of meeting and what stays *outside*, see Liane M. Feldman, *The Story of Sacrifice: Ritual and Narrative in the Priestly Source*, FAT 141 (Tübingen: Mohr Siebeck, 2020), 114–16.
15. This is adopted from Jacob Milgrom's diagram, 'The Dynamics of Purity in the Priestly System', in *Purity and Holiness: The Heritage of Leviticus*, ed. Marcel Poorthuis and Joshua J. Schwartz (Leiden: Brill, 2000), 29; *Leviticus 1–16: A New Translation with Introduction and Commentary*, AB 3 (New York: Doubleday, 1991), 732.
16. Hundley, *Keeping*, 2–3. Milgrom often cites Ezekiel to promote this idea, *Leviticus 1–16*, 258, 982; 'Israel's Sanctuary: The Priestly "Picture of Dorian Gray"', *RB* 83.3 (1976): 390–9. Cf. Ezek. 5.11; 8.6; 10.3-5, 18-19; 11.22; 23.38-9; 24.21; 44.7.
17. Impurity is not tantamount with that which causes impurity – these simply produce impurity. See Baruch J. Schwartz, 'The Bearing of Sin in the Priestly Literature', in *Pomegranates and Golden Bells: Studies in Biblical, Jewish, and Near Eastern Ritual, Law, and Literature in Honour of Jacob Milgrom*, ed. David P. Wright, David Noel Freedman and Avi Hurvitz (Winona Lake, IN: Eisenbrauns, 1995), 5. Also Baruch A. Levine, *In the Presence of the Lord: A Study of Cult and Some Cultic Terms in Ancient Israel*, SJLA 5 (Leiden: Brill, 1974), 75–7.
18. Frevel and Nihan, 'Introduction', *Purity*, 15.
19. Frevel and Nihan, 'Introduction', *Purity*, 16.
20. Philip Peter Jenson, *Graded Holiness: A Key to the Priestly Conception of the World*, JSOTSup 106 (Sheffield: JSOT Press, 1992), 89–93.
21. James A. Greenberg, *A New Look at Atonement in Leviticus: The Meaning and Purpose of Kipper Revisited*, BBRSup 23 (Winona Lake, IN: Eisenbrauns, 2019), 51–62, 189–93; Hundley, *Keeping*, 1–15, 39–43, 53–93. See §4.2.2.
22. Milgrom, 'Sanctuary', 390–9.

tabernacle. In Wilde's novel a man named Dorian Gray wished that his painted portrait would age and erode instead of himself. While embracing a life of hedonism, murder and deceit, Dorian's wish comes true; he escapes the erosion of time. However, although he remains youthful and ageless, to Dorian's surprise his painted portrait starts to age and erode. The book concludes with an angry Dorian, who stabs his aged portrait, leading unfortunately to his own death. For Milgrom, just as Dorian's reckless and sensual living was reflected in his portrait, the sin of Israel is reflected in the pollution of the sanctuary.

Milgrom further describes this reality as an 'aerial miasma'[23] – a threatening force that pervades and penetrates both people and objects, being drawn automatically to the inner sanctuary. This 'miasma' motif continues to be advanced and critiqued by scholars.[24] Examples of sin defiling the inner sanctum are evident (Lev. 16.16, 19; 20.3; 21.23; Num. 19.20). One particular instance is the death of Aaron's two sons, Nadab and Abihu (Lev. 10.2). As priests themselves they offered strange (זר) fire and were consumed (10.1-2). Interestingly, their deaths did not prevent the ongoing consequences of their sin. Instead, the whole house of Israel was told to mourn (which assumes they became defiled by mourning)[25] and their defiling corpses remained (10.4-5), leading to the pollution of the Most Holy Place, and setting the context for Yom Kippur (16.1-34).[26] This example reveals the deepening and lingering effect of sin, even after the perpetrator has died. In this specific case, the bodies of Nadab and Abihu act as a reminder of sin, with this lingering repercussion leading to the pollution of the sanctuary.

2.3.2 Moral and ritual impurity

Jonathan Klawans' distinction between 'ritual' and 'moral' impurity has shaped much of the conversations around sin and impurity in recent times.[27] Too often, as Klawans

---

[23] Milgrom, *Leviticus 1–16*, 270; 'Rationale for Cultic Law: The Case of Impurity', *Semeia* 45 (1989): 103–9; 'Atonement in the OT', *IDBSup* (1976): 79; Milgrom, 'Sanctuary', 394–5.

[24] Milgrom's views initially represented a shift in traditional scholarship. Instead of viewing the sanctuary as the medium for expiation with God, as was typical, Milgrom interpreted the sanctuary as collecting and, through sacrifice, removing defilement. Many scholars continue to advance Milgrom's writings and the 'miasma' motif, see Gane, *Cult*, 144–51; Jonathan Klawans, *Impurity and Sin in Ancient Judaism* (Oxford: Oxford University Press, 2000), 26; David P. Wright, 'The Spectrum of Priestly Impurity', in *Priesthood and Cult in Ancient Israel*, ed. Gary A. Anderson and Saul M. Olyan, JSOTSup 125 (Sheffield: JSOT Press, 1991), 161–64; Baruch A. Levine, *Leviticus*, JPSTC (Philadelphia: Jewish Publication Society, 1989), 136–7. For a critique see Greenberg, *Atonement*, 30–4, 52–5, 154–6.

[25] Nobuyoshi Kiuchi, *The Purification Offering in the Priestly Literature: Its Meaning and Function*, JSOTSup 56 (Sheffield: JSOT Press, 1987), 71.

[26] R.J. Barry IV, 'The Two Goats: A Christian Yom Kippur Soteriology' (PhD diss., Marquette University, 2017), 176–7.

[27] Klawans, *Impurity*, 22–31. Prior to Klawans other scholars differentiated between types of impurities. David P. Wright differentiated between 'tolerated' and 'prohibited', 'Clean and Unclean (OT)', *ABD* 6:729–42; 'Spectrum', 150–81; 'Two Types of Impurity in the Priestly Writings of the Bible', *Koroth* 9 (1988): 180–93; *The Disposal of Impurity: Elimination Rites in the Bible and in Hittite and Mesopotamian Literature*, SBLDS 101 (Atlanta: Scholars Press, 1987), 85, 283–4. Tikva Frymer-Kensky differentiated between 'contagious pollutions' and 'danger beliefs', 'Pollution, Purification,

writes, 'scholars assume that defilement and sin are identical or closely related'.[28] 'Ritual' impurity for Klawans involves the list of impurities mentioned in Lev. 11–15 and Num. 19. Those who are ritually impure are banned from participating in ritual activity since they are a defiling threat to others. Sprinkling, sacrifices, washings and bathings deal with 'ritual' impurity. Ritual impurity is not necessarily sinful, but 'moral' impurity is. Klawans acknowledges that the term 'moral' impurity is 'imperfect',[29] being 'best understood as a potent force unleashed by certain sinful human actions. The force unleashed defiles the sinner, the sanctuary and the land, even though the sinner is not ritually impure and does not ritually defile.'[30]

Despite its continual influence, Klawans' work has had its criticisms,[31] namely, that the terms 'moral' and 'ritual' do not appear in the Hebrew text. His assertion that moral impurity leads to a long-lasting impurity (affecting sinner and land) while ritual impurity has brief ramifications is criticized based on texts like Num. 35.33, which shows that the land can be purified from homicide if the assailant's blood is spilled on the ground. Following Klawans' ritual–moral hypothesis, others have sought to find an alternate solution for understanding sin and impurity.[32] Thomas Kazen defines impurity, not in moral terms, but as a general category of 'disgust',[33] describing impurity as 'inner' and 'outer'.[34] Mila Ginsburskaya suggests 'physical impurity' and 'sin–impurity' as two viable alternatives.[35] Jay Sklar distinguishes between 'sin' and 'impurity' and divides the later into minor and major impurities.[36]

---

and Purgation in Biblical Israel', in *The Word of the Lord Shall Go Forth: Essays in Honour of David Noel Freedman in Celebration of his Sixtieth Birthday*, ed. Carol L. Meyers and M. O'Connor (Winona Lake, IN: Eisenbrauns, 1983), 399–410. Danger beliefs refer to the threat of punishment, while contagious pollutions refer to the two levels of severity, dictated by the longevity of the defilement, esp. 404, 407–9. David Zvi Hoffmann referred to 'bodily' impurities and more 'moral' types of impurities, *Das Buch Leviticus*, 2 vols (Berlin: M. Poppelauer, 1905–6), 2:303–5. Adolph Büchler differentiated between 'Levitical' and 'moral' impurity, *Studies in Sin and Atonement in the Rabbinic Literature of the First Century* (New York: Ktav, 1928).

[28] Klawans, *Impurity*, 3.
[29] Klawans, *Impurity*, 26.
[30] Klawans, *Impurity*, 26.
[31] See Feder, *Purity and Pollution*, 97, 183; Hannah K. Harrington, *The Purity and Sanctuary of the Body in Second Temple Judaism* (Göttingen: Vandenhoeck & Ruprecht, 2019), 24–35, esp. 28–9; T. M. Lemos, 'Where There Is Dirt, Is There System? Revisiting Biblical Purity Constructions', *JSOT* 37.3 (2013): 265–94; Thomas Kazen, *Jesus and the Purity Halakhah: Was Jesus Indifferent to Impurity?*, ConBNT 30 (Winona Lake, IN: Eisenbrauns, 2010), 219–20.
[32] For other hypotheses that precede Klawans' work, see n. 27. See Gane's helpful discussion too, *Cult*, 198–213.
[33] Thomas Kazen, 'Dirt and Disgust: Body and Morality in Biblical Purity Laws', in *Perspectives on Purity and Purification in the Bible*, ed. Baruch J. Schwartz et al., LHBOTS 474 (New York: T&T Clark, 2008), 43–64; *Emotions in Biblical Law: A Cognitive Science Approach* (Sheffield: Sheffield Phoenix Press, 2011), 46. In his *Issues of Impurity in Early Judaism*, ConBNT 45 (Winona Lake, IN: Eisenbrauns, 2010), Kazen argues for three emotions connected with the experience of impurity: disgust, fear and justice, 13. I agree here with Wil Rogan concerning Kazen's psycho-biological approach to understanding Israelite purity, in that it 'too quickly passes over Israel's self-understanding', 'Purity', 316.
[34] Kazan, *Jesus*, 208, 216–20.
[35] Mila Ginsburskaya, 'Purity and Impurity in the Hebrew Bible', in *Purity: Essays in Bible and Theology*, ed. Andrew Brower Latz and Arseny Ermakov (Eugene, OR: Wipf & Stock, 2014), 4. 'Physical' impurity (impurity that does not involve breaking God's commandments) is preferred instead of 'ritual' impurity. Both of these distinctions are further defined by minor and major impurities.
[36] Jay Sklar, 'Sin and Impurity: Atoned or Purified? Yes!', *Perspectives on Purity*, 26; *Sin, Impurity, Sacrifice, Atonement: The Priestly Conceptions*, HBM 2 (Sheffield: Sheffield Phoenix, 2005), 128.

While Milgrom engages with Klawans' ritual–moral distinction, he never adopted it in his lifetime, refusing to place parameters on a text that, he claims, does not possess a consistent categorization of sin and impurity.[37] There is some merit in Klawans' distinction, but one should be cautious of reducing a group of texts into singular categories. Tracy Lemos instead encourages scholars to 'move away from a synchronic approach ... to a more historicized perspective assessing how different authors and different communities made use of purity constructions, and also manipulated these constructions in different contexts and as a response to different historical situations'.[38]

2.3.3 The reality of defilement

Scholars continue to debate the 'reality' or 'literality' of defilement in cultic texts. What does it mean to label something as 'impure'? Jacob Neusner argues that 'sin' and 'impurity', as terms,

> [A]re not hygienic categories and do not refer to observable cleanliness or dirtiness. The words refer to a status in respect to contact with a source of impurity and the completion of acts of purification from that impurity. If you touch a reptile, you may not be dirty, but you are unclean. If you undergo a ritual immersion, you may not be free of dirt, but you are clean. A corpse can make you unclean, though it may not make you dirty. A rite of purification involving the sprinkling of water mixed with the ashes of a red heifer probably will not remove a great deal of dirt, but it will remove the impurity.[39]

For Neusner, our terms – whether one employs 'impurity', 'defilement' or 'uncleanness' – denote a semantic field which points back to a status of being. They are not to be understood as descriptive and observable realities, but as subjective and conscious states of defilement.

On the other hand, Klawans argues that the 'dichotomy between literal and metaphorical language is not very helpful when it comes to understanding the differences between ritual and moral impurity'.[40] In his view, scholars who label 'sin' and 'impurity' as metaphorical empty those terms of their literal meaning.[41] Thus, '[w]hat this boils down to is that when purity language is used metaphorically, then no real defilement or purification is actually taking place'.[42] For Klawans, Neusner's understanding of sin and impurity as a metaphor and Douglas' understanding of sin

---

[37] Jacob Milgrom, 'Systemic Differences in the Priestly Corpus: A Response to Jonathan Klawans', *RB* 112.3 (2005): 321–9.
[38] Lemos, 'Where', 292. Lemos is right '[ultimately] making a distinction between purity and impurity was an important part of life throughout ancient Israel', 289.
[39] Jacob Neusner, *The Idea of Purity in Ancient Judaism: The Haskell Lectures, 1972–1973*, SJLA 1 (Leiden: Brill, 1973), 1.
[40] Klawans, *Impurity*, 32.
[41] Klawans, *Impurity*, 33.
[42] Klawans, *Impurity*, 33.

and impurity as symbolism are both unsatisfactory and do not leave the reader with a clear explanation of the relationship between sin and impurity and their impact.[43]

The problem with Klawans' analysis is that distinguishing between 'real' and 'literal' is not always helpful. Just because something is metaphoric, it does not mean it is not 'real'.[44] Lakoff and Johnson in their seminal work, *Metaphors We Live By*, remind us that metaphors are not mere poetic imaginations but are 'pervasive in everyday life, not just in language but in thought and action'.[45] Thus, 'it is impossible to understand sin', as Anderson notes, 'without attending carefully to the metaphors in which these concepts are embedded'.[46] Whereas previous scholarship sought to understand sin through a lexical or theological approach,[47] in recent years scholars have turned to the surrounding biblical metaphors in order to understand the conceptualization of sin.[48]

For instance, Lev. 24.15 states that whoever curses his God will bear (נשׂא) his own sin. This common idiom imagines sin as a burden which is carried by the sinner and 'conveys a sense of ongoing culpability for the offender through the image of bearing a heavy object'.[49] This example shows that metaphors consist of, as Ricœur notes, intersecting 'semantic fields' or a 'network of interactions'.[50] Subsequently, readers are supposed to pay close attention to the tapestry of language employed by various authors in describing the concept of 'sin'. The prime metaphor discussed so far is sin as defilement. It is not that sin is equal to defilement but that sin *behaves* like defilement.[51] Contrary to Klawans, when the effects of defilement are described as metaphorical for sin, this does not empty sin of its literal meaning, but further describes the reality of sin. It is through metaphorical language where 'words and images are given on loan to abstract ideas like "sin" so that we might discuss what is unspeakable'.[52] Therefore, 'sin',

---

[43] Klawans, *Impurity*, 11. Klawans' later work adds clarity, 'Methodology and Ideology in the Study of Priestly Ritual', *Perspectives on Purity*, 84–95. See also Yitzhaq Feder, 'Contagion and Cognition: Bodily Experience and the Conceptualization of Pollution (ṭum'ah) in the Hebrew Bible', *JNES* 72 (2013): 151–67.

[44] Thomas Kazen, 'The Role of Disgust in Priestly Purity Law: Insights from Conceptual Metaphor and Blending Theories', *JLRS* 3.1 (2014): 68.

[45] George Lakoff and Mark Johnson, *Metaphors We Live By* (Chicago: University of Chicago Press, 2003), 3. See esp. 3–9.

[46] Gary Anderson, *Sin: A History* (New Haven: Yale University Press, 2009), 4.

[47] There are numerous terms for describing 'sin' in the HB, see E. Lipinski, 'Sin', *EncJud* 18:621–4. Most discussions concern the verbs 'to sin' (חטא), 'to transgress, rebel' (פשׁע) and the noun 'iniquity' (עון). See S. Lyonnet and L. Sabourin, *Sin, Redemption, and Sacrifice: A Biblical and Patristic Study* (Rome: Biblical Institute, 1970), 12–23. For a summary of scholarship see Joseph C. P. Lam, 'The Concept of Sin in the Hebrew Bible', *RC* 12 (2018): e12260.

[48] Judith V. Stack, *Metaphor and the Portrayal of the Cause(s) of Sin and Evil in the Gospel of Matthew*, BibInt 182 (Leiden: Brill, 2020), 1–26; Lesley R. DiFransico, *Washing Away Sin: An Analysis of the Metaphor in the Hebrew Bible and its Influence*, BTS 23 (Leuven: Peeters, 2016); Joseph C. P. Lam, *Patterns of Sin in the Hebrew Bible: Metaphor, Culture, and the Making of a Religious Concept* (Oxford: Oxford University Press, 2016); Schwartz, 'Bearing', *Pomegranates*, 3–22.

[49] Lam, *Sin*, 5.

[50] Paul Ricœur, *The Rule of Metaphor: Multi-disciplinary Studies of the Creation of Meaning in Language*, trans. Robert Czerny (Toronto: University of Toronto Press, 1975), 98. See Janet M. Soskice, who describes metaphor as one thing suggestive of another, *Metaphor and Religious Language* (Oxford: Clarendon, 1985), 15.

[51] Sklar, 'Sin and Impurity', *Perspectives on Purity*, 23–4; Schwartz, 'Bearing', *Pomegranates*, 7.

[52] Barry, 'Two Goats', 177.

as Richard Barry states, 'creates a "something".[53] Although defilement can be said to be 'invisible', it is 'believed to be quite real; though amorphous, it is substantive'.[54] Now that a foundation has been laid for the cultic categories of sin and defilement, Hebrews' use of tabernacle imagery will now be examined.

2.4 The heavenly tabernacle in Hebrews

The author of Hebrews is greatly invested in the motif of the tabernacle. From the beginning (Heb. 1.3) all the way through to the end of the epistle (13.10-11) the tabernacle plays a vital role. It is the place where the ultimate act of purgation takes place (1.3; 2.17; 9.12-14, 23, 26, 28; 10.12-14) and where Christ is now seated (1.3-4; 4.14; 6.19-20; 7.26; 8.1-2; 9.12, 24; 10.12-14, 19-21; 12.2). More pertinent for this chapter is the significant connection shared between defilement and the tabernacle. Yet, Hebrews' employment of tabernacle terminology is not straightforward and continues to divide scholars, especially in relation to the Second Temple. As a result, this section will not only aid the discussion concerning defilement but it will lay a foundation for understanding Hebrews' conception of the earthly and heavenly tabernacles for subsequent chapters.

2.4.1 Hebrews and cosmology

Hebrews never defines its worldview but cosmological concepts permeate the epistle.[55] The suspected similarities with Philo have already been noted (§1.4.2).[56] Ceslas Spicq's list of parallels between Philo and Hebrews cemented a Middle Platonic hermeneutic.[57] The discovery of the scrolls at Qumran dented Spicq's suspicions and gave way to a fresh background that eclipsed a previous Platonic reading. C. K. Barrett was instrumental in helping to pave the way for a Jewish apocalyptic hermeneutic.[58] Some wish to turn the clocks back[59] to a 'pre-Barrett'[60]

---

[53] Barry, 'Two Goats', 176.
[54] Schwartz, 'Bearing', *Pomegranates*, 5.
[55] Edward Adams, 'The Cosmology of Hebrews', *Hebrews*, 138. R. J. McKelvey argues for a hybrid of influences, *Pioneer and Priest: Jesus Christ in the Epistle to the Hebrews* (Eugene, OR: Wipf & Stock, 2013), 86–7.
[56] For a helpful summary see Stefan N. Svendsen, *Allegory Transformed: The Appropriation of Philonic Hermeneutics in the Letter to the Hebrews*, WUNT 2.269 (Tübingen: Mohr Siebeck, 2009), 55–68; L. D. Hurst, *The Epistle to the Hebrews: Its Background of Thought*, SNTSMS 65 (Cambridge: Cambridge University Press, 1990), 8–42, 134–45.
[57] Spicq, *Hébreux*, 1:72–6; 'Le philonisme de l'Épître aux Hébreux', *RB* 56 (1949): 212–42.
[58] C. K. Barrett, 'The Eschatology of the Epistle to the Hebrews', in *The Background of the New Testament and its Eschatology*, ed. W. D. Davies and D. Daube (Cambridge: Cambridge University Press, 1956), 363–93.
[59] Thompson, 'Middle Platonism', *Reading Hebrews*, 31–52; *Hebrews*, 21–4; *Beginnings*, 10; Johnson, *Hebrews*, 12–15; Gregory E. Sterling, 'Ontology versus Eschatology: Tensions between Author and Community in Hebrews', *SPhilo* 13 (2001): 190–211; Lala K. K. Dey, *The Intermediary World and Patterns of Perfection in Philo and Hebrews*, SBLDS 25 (Missoula: Scholars Press, 1975), 68–72. For a harmonized cosmology see George W. MacRae, 'Heavenly Temple and Eschatology in the Letter to the Hebrews', *Semeia* 12 (1978): 179–99.
[60] Hurst, *Hebrews*, 10.

era, but modern scholarship has arrived at a majority consensus that now welcomes a Jewish apocalyptic worldview.[61]

The intellectual terminology employed by Hebrews suggests that the author was versed in philosophical categories like that of Philo.[62] At the same time the content of Hebrews suggests a typical Jewish eschatology. Both these worldviews affirm temporal dualism yet Jewish thinking has an 'all-important modification: some of the blessings of the age to come are already being experienced by believers at the close of the present age'.[63] The opening verses state that God now speaks in these 'last days' (Heb. 1.2), assuming a two-age spectrum. The author speaks of a 'coming world' (2.5), a 'coming city' (13.14) and a heavenly city that Abraham eagerly awaited (11.10). The earthly habitual world is a place where Christ lived (1.6; 4.15; 10.5) before passing through to the heavenly tabernacle (4.14-16; 6.19-20; 9.11-12, 24; 10.20-1). Furthermore, Jesus' body (σῶμα) and flesh (σάρξ) are not viewed as inferior but are a positive aspect of his earthly life of obedience (§3.6.1, §4.3.2).

The habitual and heavenly worlds are not contrasted negatively but both have been accessed and passed through by Christ, with the earthly realm still awaiting his return (9.28).[64] Hebrews goes on to make the point that the recipients have already arrived at Mount Zion, the heavenly city of the living God (12.22), since Christ has already entered on their behalf (6.20). The recipients 'share' in Christ (3.14) and in a heavenly calling (3.1) having tasted of the 'powers of the age to come' (δυνάμεις ... μέλλοντος αἰῶνος, 6.5). Additionally, Hebrews' emphasis on spatial language and entering/

---

[61] To name a few: Jihye Lee, *A Jewish Apocalyptic Framework of Eschatology in the Epistle to the Hebrews: Protology and Eschatology as Background*, LNTS 662 (London: Bloomsbury T&T Clark, 2021), 99–126, 127–45, 147–52; Grant Macaskill, 'Hebrews 8-10 and Apocalyptic Theology in the New Testament', *Son*, 79–93; Ringleben, *Wort*, 93–118; Church, *Temple*, 434; Ribbens, *Levitical*, 85–8; Moore, *Repetition*, 12–14; David M. Moffitt, 'Perseverance, Purity, and Identity: Exploring Hebrews' Eschatological Worldview, Ethics, and In-Group Bias', in *Sensitivity to Outsiders: Exploring the Dynamic Relationship between Mission and Ethics in the New Testament and Early Christianity*, ed. Jacobus (Kobus) Kok, Tobias Nicklas, Dieter T. Roth and Christopher M. Hays, WUNT 2.364 (Tübingen: Mohr Siebeck, 2014), 362; *Atonement*, 223; Calaway, *Sabbath*, 2–11; Jody A. Barnard, 'Ronald Williamson and the Background of Hebrews', *ExpTim* 124.10 (2013): 469–79; *The Mysticism of Hebrews: Exploring the Role of Jewish Apocalyptic Mysticism in the Epistle to the Hebrews*, WUNT 2.331 (Tübingen: Mohr Siebeck, 2012); Scott D. Mackie, 'Ancient Jewish Mystical Motifs in Hebrews Theology of Access and Entry Exhortations', *NTS* 58.1 (2012): 88–104; 'Heavenly Sanctuary Mysticism in the Epistle to the Hebrews', *JTS* 62.1 (2011): 77–117; Eric F. Mason, '"Sit at My Right Hand": Enthronement and the Heavenly Sanctuary in Hebrews', in *A Teacher for All Generations: Essays in Honour of James C. VanderKam*, ed. Eric F. Mason et al., JSJSup 2.153 (Leiden: Brill, 2012), 901–16; *'You Are a Priest Forever': Second Temple Jewish Messianism and the Priestly Christology of the Epistle to the Hebrews*, STDJ 74 (Leiden: Brill, 2008); Gäbel, *Kulttheologie*, 121–7; Rissi, *Theologie*, 125–30; Otfried Hofius, *Der Vorhang vor dem Thron Gottes: Eine exegetisch-religionsgeschichtliche Untersuchung zu Hebräer 6,19f und 10,19f*, WUNT 14 (Tübingen: Mohr Siebeck, 1972), 49. Some suggest that Platonism is antithetical with Christian belief, Mackie, *Eschatology*, 83–104; Hurst, *Hebrews*, 38–42. Ronald Williamson notes that 'Plato's ideal world is not a heaven that could be entered by Jesus', 'Platonism and Hebrews', *SJT* 16.4 (1963): 419.

[62] Mason, 'Sit', *Teacher*, 907–8; *Priest*, 38.

[63] Larry L. Helyer, 'Apocalypticism', in *The World of the New Testaments: Cultural, Social, and Historical Contexts*, ed. Joel Green and L. M. McDonald (Grand Rapids: Baker, 2013), 256.

[64] Alexander, 'Dualism', *Light*, 169–85. Lee's employment of Gunkel's *Urzeit-Endzeit* is an appropriate hermeneutic for reading Hebrews' eschatology, *Jewish Apocalyptic Framework*, 147–52.

approaching from 'one sphere (the earthly) to another (the heavenly)'[65] is not only a present soteriological reality but an eschatological statement. Craig Koester is particularly helpful when he states that, 'Hebrews operates with both categories, yet it fits neatly into neither category ... Rather than focusing on traditions that might lie behind the text, we can compare Hebrews to Platonic and apocalyptic patterns in order to sharpen the way we perceive the constellations of ideas within the text.'[66] One aspect which situates Hebrews within an apocalyptic worldview is its focus on the heavenly tabernacle and the eschatological city of God, as explored below.

2.4.2 Construing the architecture of the heavenly tabernacle[67]

Within Hebrews the imagery of both the earthly and the heavenly tabernacle provides the prime stage for discussing defilement.[68] Just as the earthly temple was not an alien concept for Hebrews, neither was the heavenly temple, with the concept of a heavenly temple being prevalent throughout the ANE and the 2TP.[69] Regarding Hebrews, some scholars understand the heavenly tabernacle as spoken of metaphorically.[70] Some also understand the heavenly tabernacle as a cosmic extension,[71] that is, the cosmos *is* a temple, with the earth and the heavens representing different parts of this cosmic temple. Whether Hebrews speaks of a multi-tiered heaven (οὐρανός) is not clear. Certain texts refer to tiers of heaven,[72] but Hebrews' knowledge of these texts is uncertain.[73] The use of the singular (Heb. 9.24; 11.12; 12.26) and plural forms (1.10; 4.14; 7.26; 8.1; 9.23; 12.23, 25) of οὐρανός do not present definite conclusions.[74] On this basis, Hermut

---

[65] Isaacs, *Sacred*, 57–8.
[66] Koester, *Hebrews*, 98.
[67] Heavenly tabernacle language occurs throughout Hebrews, although the prime discussions take place within two passages (8.1-6; 9.1-28), see Mason, 'Sit', *Teacher*, 908.
[68] See Church, *Temple*, 433–4; Barnard, *Mysticism*, 88–118; Thomas Keene, 'Heaven is a Tent: The Tabernacle as an Eschatological Metaphor in the Epistle to the Hebrews' (PhD diss., Westminster Theological Seminary, 2010), 13–45; Gäbel, *Kulttheologie*, 112–30, 241–2; Cody, *Heavenly*, 9–46; Schierse, *Verheissung*, 26–59.
[69] See *T. Levi* 2.5-9; 3.1-8; *1 En.* 14; 71.5; *3 En.* 1.7; *3 Bar.* 11; 14; 4Q403 1 I, 41-6. Although the latter describes a very 'complex structure', Philip Alexander, *The Mystical Texts: Songs of the Sabbath Sacrifice and Related Manuscripts*, CQS 7 (London: T&T Clark, 2006), 30. See OT texts too (Ps. 78.69; Isa. 6.1-9; Jer. 17.12). Also, Calaway, *Sabbath*, 122–3; G. K. Beale, *The Temple and the Church's Mission*, NSBT 17 (Downers Grove, IL: InterVarsity Press, 2004), 31–2, 51–2.
[70] Kenneth L. Schenck, 'An Archaeology of Hebrews' Tabernacle Imagery', *Hebrews in Contexts*, 240–5; Craig R. Koester, *The Dwelling of God: The Tabernacle in the Old Testament, Intertestamental Jewish Literature, and the New Testament*, CBQMS 22 (Washington, DC: Catholic Biblical Association of America, 1989), 174–81; Cody, *Heavenly*, 18. Metaphorical-literal terminology is not always helpful, see Barnard, *Mysticism*, 104–8. Moffitt is helpful, 'Serving', *Hebrews in Contexts*, 259–79.
[71] Schenck, 'Archaeology', *Hebrews in Contexts*, 251; *Cosmology*, 151–4; Gäbel, *Kulttheologie*, 473–80; Isaacs, *Sacred*, 86.
[72] Texts such as *T. Levi* 2.5-9 speak of entering the 'first heaven' before arriving at the second 'more lustrous' heaven, with Rabbinic texts referring to seven chambers in heaven (Midr. Gen. Rab. 19.7) and the second book of Enoch referring to 'ten' heavens (*2 En.* 22.1-10). See n. 69.
[73] Apart from Paul's mention of a 'third' heaven (2 Cor. 12.2) the first century offers little in terms of a widespread understanding of a multi-tiered heaven, see Jonathan T. Pennington, *Heaven and Earth in the Gospel of Matthew*, NovTSup 141 (Leiden: Brill, 2007), 99–103.
[74] See Barnard, *Mysticism*, 60–2. Rissi argues for 'lower' and 'higher' heavens in Hebrews, *Theologie*, 36, cf. Heb. 7.26; *Ascen. Isa.* 7–10; 11.22-3.

Löhr concludes, '[o]b der auctor ad Hebraeos an ein Heiligtum im Himmel oder an den Himmel als Heiligtum denkt, ist nicht sicher zu entscheiden'.[75] Nevertheless, there does remain much warrant for understanding the heavenly tabernacle as mirroring the earthly tabernacle in design. This is observed through the language Hebrews employs (§2.4.3) and in the scriptural citations (§2.4.5).

2.4.3 Earthly and heavenly tabernacle terminology

In attempting to piece together the earthly and heavenly tabernacles, two key terms dominate Hebrews: σκηνή and τὰ ἅγια. When Hebrews discusses the entire earthly tabernacle, the term σκηνή is used.[76] It is described predicatively as an 'earthly' (κοσμικός, Heb. 9.1) 'hand-made' (χειροποίητος, 9.24) tabernacle which Moses erected (8.5; 9.2). When speaking of the heavenly tabernacle, σκηνή is again employed (8.2; 9.11), except this tabernacle is 'true' (ἀληθινός, 8.2) and not 'earthly'. It is the 'greater and more perfect tent' (μείζονος καὶ τελειοτέρας σκηνῆς, 9.11). To confuse matters, Hebrews also uses σκηνή to refer to both the earthly Holy Place and the earthly Holy of Holies (9.1-8). However, when σκηνή is employed an additional term accompanies the context to specify what is meant. For instance, the ordinal 'first' (πρῶτος) accompanies σκηνή to clarify that the 'first' part of the earthly tabernacle (Holy Place) is being referred to (9.2, 6), with the 'second' (δεύτερος) referring to the earthly Holy of Holies (9.7), although 'πρώτης σκηνῆς' in 9.8 describes the earthly tabernacle as a whole.[77]

A major disagreement in scholarship concerns how the plural term τὰ ἅγια is rendered. Some prefer to translate τὰ ἅγια as 'sanctuary',[78] others favour 'Holy of

---

[75] 'Whether the *auctor ad Hebraeos* thinks of a sanctuary in heaven or of heaven as a sanctuary cannot be decided with certainty', Hermut Löhr, 'Thronversammlung und preisender Tempel. Beobachtungen am himmlischen Heiligtum im Hebräerbrief und in den Sabbatopferliedern aus Qumran', in *Königsherrschaft Gottes und himmlischer Kult: im Judentum, Urchristentum und in der hellenistischen Welt*, ed. Martin Hengel and Anna Maria Schwemer, WUNT 55 (Tübingen: Mohr Siebeck, 1991), 190.

[76] The singular adjective 'ἅγιον' is used once as a substantive to refer to the earthly tabernacle (Heb. 9.1).

[77] It is clear that the 'first' and 'second' parts of the earthly tabernacle are being described in Heb. 9.1-3; the problem is when Hebrews refers to the 'first tent' (9.6, 8) and then simply just the 'second' (δεύτερος, 9.7). This has led to roughly two interpretations. First (1), those who understand 'πρώτην σκηνήν' (9.6, 8) as the entire earthly tabernacle and δεύτερος as the heavenly tabernacle, Schreiner, *Hebrews*, 262; Moffitt, *Atonement*, 224–5; Barnard, *Mysticism*, 91–2; Isaacs, *Sacred*, 42; Bruce, *Hebrews*, 208; Peterson, *Perfection*, 133; Michel, *Hebräer*, 307; Spicq, *Hébreux*, 2:254. Second (2), those who interpret 'πρώτην σκηνήν' as the earthly Holy Place, and δεύτερος as the heavenly Holy of Holies, Harris, *Hebrews*, 218–19; Church, *Temple*, 413–15; Cockerill, *Hebrews*, 381–2; Schenck, *Cosmology*, 149–50; Gäbel, *Kulttheologie*, 280–1; Ellingworth, *Hebrews*, 437–8; Lane, *Hebrews*, 2:216; Eduard Riggenbach, *Der Brief an die Hebräer*, 3rd edn, KNT 24 (Wuppertal: Brockhaus, 1987), 249; N. H. Young, 'The Gospel According to Hebrews 9', *NTS* 27.2 (1981): 200. As Delitzsch notes, 'the point is not the contrast between the two parts of the sanctuary, but the division between them', *Hebrews*, 2:67.

[78] Cockerill, *Hebrews*, 354; Ellingworth, *Hebrews*, 402; Lane, *Hebrews*, 1:200–1; H.F. Weiss, *Der Brief an die Hebräer*, 15th edn, KEK 13 (Göttingen: Vandenhoeck & Ruprecht, 1991), 433; Koester, *Dwelling*, 156; Spicq, *Hébreux*, 2:234.

Holies'.⁷⁹ It is clear contextually that ἅγια (9.2) refers to the Holy Place, yet it is debated as to the exact meaning elsewhere (9.3, 8, 12, 24, 25; 10.19; 13.11) especially in 8.2, where ἅγια is used alongside σκηνή.⁸⁰ The question here is whether Hebrews comprehends the heavenly tabernacle to contain both the Holy Place and the Holy of Holies or simply just the latter.⁸¹ For those who understand the heavenly tabernacle to contain *only* the Holy of Holies, the term 'sanctuary' is used in place for τὰ ἅγια, whereas 'Holy of Holies' is employed by those who understand heaven to mirror the earthly two-part tabernacle – although the Day of Atonement typology (9.12, 25) suggests 'Holy of Holies' for τὰ ἅγια.

Hebrews never mentions the heavenly Holy Place but this does not mean that the author does not believe in its existence. Jesus is spoken of as passing through the heavenly tabernacle and through the 'curtain' (καταπέτασμα, 6.19; 9.3; 10.20)⁸² implying a Holy Place and a Holy of Holies within heaven. The recipients' understanding of the earthly tabernacle could 'inform their understanding of the heavenly sanctuary'.⁸³ Also, when Hebrews says that Christ 'did not enter a hand-made tabernacle' but 'into heaven itself' (9.24), this might imply that heaven is a tabernacle. The absence of a heavenly Holy Place could be an example of Hebrews not wanting to be over-detailed (9.5), choosing instead to focus on key aspects of his argument such as the heavenly Holy of Holies, since this is where the act of purgation occurs.⁸⁴

2.4.4 The absence of temple terminology

Following the analysis of tabernacle terminology, it is significant that Hebrews never mentions the term 'temple' (ναός/ἱερόν), nor is the temple understood as embodied through the people of God.⁸⁵ Some view the absence of temple terminology as a purposeful attack on the integrity of the Second Temple. Hebrews is simply joining in with other writers who criticized animal sacrifices (Philo, *Det. Pot. Ins.* 21.107; *Vit. Mos.* 2.81) and depicted the temple as defiled and unfit for use (*Barn.* 16.1-10; 1QS VIII, 4-10; 4QFlo I, 2-7).⁸⁶ Other scholars argue that whenever tabernacle terminology is

---

[79] Ribbens, *Levitical*, 104–8; Barnard, *Mysticism*, 93; Moffitt, *Atonement*, 223–4; Mackie, *Eschatology*, 165; Grässer, *Hebräer*, 2:83; Attridge, *Hebrews*, 218; Hofius, *Vorhang*, 59–60.
[80] Some see ἅγια and σκηνή as acting epexegetically, Cockerill, *Hebrews*, 354; Cody, *Heavenly*, 164–5; Braun, *Hebräer*, 433.
[81] Cockerill, *Hebrews*, 355; Schenck, 'Archaeology', *Hebrews in Contexts*, 248–9. However, the insertion of πάντα suggests that Moses was to make *everything* according to the τύπος (§2.4.5).
[82] Otfried Hofius, 'Das "erste" und das "zweite" Zelt: Ein Beitrag zur Auslegung von Hbr 9 1–10', *ZNW* 61.3 (1970): 271–7. Hofius notes that Hebrews' reliance on Exod. 25 (Heb. 8.5) reveals that the writer is aware that the earthly tent consisted of two sections, being made clear by the second curtain (9.3). See §4.3.2 for more on the 'curtain' in Hebrews.
[83] Ribbens, *Levitical*, 110.
[84] Although see Gäbel's important observations with respect to Heb. 9.1-5, 'Permission', *Son*, 135–74, esp. 144–7.
[85] 1 Cor. 3.16-17 is the prime Pauline reference, see Michael Newton's helpful chapter, *The Concept of Purity at Qumran and in the Letters of Paul*, SNTSMS 53 (Cambridge: Cambridge University Press, 2005), 52–78. Contra A. Vanhoye, who sees Jesus as the temple, *A Perfect Priest: Studies in the Letter to the Hebrews*, ed. trans. Nicholas J. Moore and Richard J. Ounsworth, WUNT 2.477 (Tübingen: Mohr Siebeck, 2018), 138–41, 145–6.
[86] For a general summary of these various perspectives see Church, *Temple*, 16–18.

read 'it was the temple that the author of Hebrews had in mind'.[87] Steve Motyer notes that the temple does not appear in Hebrews so that the 'profound message of the letter *about the temple* may actually be heard in its scriptural depth, and not be rejected out of hand'.[88] Arguing from a post-70 CE viewpoint, Schenck notes that '[t]he destruction of the temple ... becomes the underlying assumption of the entire argument. It becomes the given that does not have to be mentioned.'[89] Church is right though, 'Hebrews was not written in a vacuum'.[90] No one doubts the author's knowledge of the Second Temple – whether existing or destroyed – but if Hebrews was a grievance against current temple administration one might expect to see temple terminology or an equally clearer critique. Church claims there is no temple terminology because in the HB there are 'no text[s] referring to the divine design of either Solomon's temple or indeed the second temple'.[91] This is unconvincing and does not explain why an author so linguistically equipped avoids ναός or ἱερόν, especially if, as Church claims, Hebrews is speaking of the Second Temple.

It is not that Hebrews is critical of the temple, Jerusalem, the land, or the present earthly sacrificial cult, but the author recognizes that these things were always meant to point towards something that was to come. In a way, Hebrews does take the focus away from the land, to a future land 'of promise' (Heb. 11.9), a 'rest' which awaits the people of God (4.8-9). So too, Jerusalem is not spoken of as an 'earthly city', but a 'heavenly city' (12.22), one that cannot perish (13.14). The Second Temple and the first existed within the author's peripheral view, yet Hebrews chooses tabernacle terminology due to a reliance on the HB and for the purpose of taking the recipients back to where it all began – Moses' vision on Mount Sinai (8.1-6), discussed below. This vision is of further significance since Moses was granted temporary insight into the heavenly tabernacle which Hebrews is now describing.[92] This approach essentially undercuts current temple politics,[93] but allows Hebrews to acknowledge indirectly that the earthly cult in the light of Christ and the heavenly tabernacle is wearing away (1.10-11; 8.13). Gäbel is right, the earthly and heavenly tabernacle discussion highlights both the community's ambivalence and critique of what he calls their 'cultic history'.[94]

---

[87] McKelvey, *Pioneer*, 77.
[88] Steve Motyer, 'The Temple in Hebrews: Is It There?', in *Heaven on Earth: The Temple in Biblical Theology*, ed. T. Desmond Alexander and Simon Gathercole (Carlisle: Paternoster, 2004), 189 (emphasis his own). So too Lindars, 'Temple', *Templum*, 417.
[89] Schenck, *New Perspective*, 105. Also, Eyal Regev, *The Temple in Early Christianity: Experiencing the Sacred* (New Haven: Yale University Press, 2019), 283.
[90] Church, *Temple*, 16.
[91] Church, *Temple*, 405.
[92] I would not go as far as Peter Walker, who argues that Hebrews has no interest in what is happening 'on the ground' in Jerusalem, that is, the physical temple, 'A Place for Hebrews? Contexts for a First-Century Sermon', in *The Letter to the Hebrews: Critical Readings*, ed. Scott D. Mackie (London: T&T Clark, 2018), 382.
[93] Regev, *Temple*, 253–4; Walker, 'Place', *Critical Readings*, 376–88.
[94] Gäbel, 'Permission', *Son*, 157.

2.4.5 The 'sketch' and 'foreshadow'

Hebrews 8.1-6 points to a tabernacle construction in heaven, interrelating and corresponding to the earthly tabernacle.[95] Jesus is described seated in heaven as a minister in the true tent (Heb. 8.2) while the earthly priests minister in a 'sketch and foreshadow' (ὑποδείγματι καὶ σκιᾷ) of the heavenly tabernacle (ἐπουράνιος, 8.5a).[96] Hebrews then cites Exod. 25.40, noting that Moses was warned to 'make everything according to the pattern (τύπος) that was shown to you on the mountain' (ποιήσεις πάντα κατὰ τὸν τύπον τὸν δειχθέντα σοι ἐν τῷ ὄρει, Heb. 8.5b).[97] At this point Hebrews makes no 'claims of any new revelation about the heavenly tabernacle'[98] but merely establishes itself upon scriptural tradition. This verse might be read as describing the Second Temple (8.5a) and then the wilderness tabernacle (8.5b). The result is that Hebrews is contrasting the wilderness tabernacle with the heavenly one, mentioned a few verses before (8.2). Church and Hurst instead see 8.5 as a reference to the Second Temple and the heavenly tabernacle, further suggesting a polemic against the earthly temple.[99] This is a difficult interpretation to accept, since a citation of Exod. 25.40 would suggest that the wilderness tabernacle is being described.[100] To further understand the nature of the heavenly tabernacle and how it relates to both the wilderness tabernacle and the Second Temple, three terms need to be explored from Heb. 8.5: ὑπόδειγμα, σκιά and τύπος.

Regarding ὑπόδειγμα and σκιά, typically both terms are rendered 'copy' and 'shadow'.[101] The consequence of this translation adds significantly to the supposed Platonic influence of Hebrews, with 'copy' and 'shadow' suggesting a vertical and spatial contrast between the inferior earthly shadows and the heavenly superior archetypes. 'Shadow' (σκιά) in particular is understood by some as a reference to Plato's 'Allegory of the Cave'.[102] Thus, it was 'die platonische Ideenlehre, vielleicht auch in populär-philosophischer Ausprägung, [die] diese Wortwahl geprägt [hat]'.[103] Reading ὑπόδειγμα

---

[95] See William G. Johnsson, 'The Heavenly Sanctuary – Figurative or Real?', in *Issues in the Book of Hebrews*, ed. Frank L. Holbrook (Silver Spring, MD: Biblical Research Institute, 1989), 35–51. Also, Barnard, *Mysticism*, 95–118; Schenck, *Cosmology*, 165–8, 171–3, for a summary of these discussions.

[96] 'Heavenly things' (τῶν ἐπουρανίων) refer to the tabernacle and all its paraphernalia, rightly Delitzsch, *Hebrews*, 2:31. Contra Church, *Temple*, 409–10, 424–5, who sees the 'heavenly things' as the 'better promises' obtained through Jesus' death. This appears to be a difficult argument to maintain, when Heb. 8.5 (and 9.23) imply a reference to the heavenly tabernacle.

[97] The inclusion of πάντα is one of the noticeable differences when compared with the LXX, although Exod. 25.8 includes πάντα. Philo also includes πάντα with Exod. 25.40 (*Vit. Mos.* 2.26–44) possibly suggesting a common textual tradition, though uncertainty surrounds Hebrews' *Vorlage*, see Gert J. Steyn, *A Quest for the Assumed LXX Vorlage of the Explicit Quotations in Hebrews*, FRLANT 234 (Göttingen: Vandenhoeck & Ruprecht, 2001), 236–47.

[98] Mayjee Philip, *Leviticus in Hebrews: A Transtextual Analysis of the Tabernacle Theme in the Letter to the Hebrews* (Frankfurt: Peter Lang, 2011), 56. See esp. 47–62.

[99] Church, *Temple*, 404–5; Hurst, *Hebrews*, 15.

[100] Contra Church, *Temple*, 405.

[101] Ellingworth, *Hebrews*, 406–8; Lane, *Hebrews*, 1:206; Attridge, *Hebrews*, 219–20; Cody, *Heavenly*, 80; Spicq, *Hébreux*, 2:236; Westcott, *Hebrews*, 218–19.

[102] Dunn, *Parting*, 115; Rascher, *Schriftauslegung*, 161–6.

[103] 'The Platonic doctrine of ideas, perhaps also in a popular philosophical form, [which has] coined this choice of words', Rascher, *Schriftauslegung*, 163.

as 'copy' was famously dented by Hurst, who noted that nowhere in Greek literature does ὑπόδειγμα denote 'copy'.[104] If Hebrews had hoped to introduce a Platonic reading the unmistakable Platonic term παράδειγμα (pattern), instead of ὑπόδειγμα,[105] might have been included.[106] Since the function of the earthly tabernacle involved a close proximity and intermingling with heaven – being a home for the divine presence of God – then a positive relationship between the two tabernacles might be assumed in Hebrews, instead of a possible inferior earthly tabernacle that is merely a 'copy' and 'shadow'.[107]

Instead of understanding ὑπόδειγμα and σκιά as acting spatially, some propose a horizontal reading,[108] with ὑπόδειγμα suggesting a 'sketch' or an 'outline' for something that will come along in the future.[109] Thus, σκιά denotes 'foreshadowing',[110] since this is the manner it is used elsewhere (Heb. 10.1). Church chooses to understand both ὑπόδειγμα and σκιά as a hendiadys, combining both terms to form the idea of a 'symbolic foreshadowing',[111] resulting in the relationship between the two tabernacles being understood temporally rather than spatially.[112] Similarly, Christ's heavenly offering was not intended to mimic Levitical sacrifices, but instead, Levitical sacrifices foreshadowed Christ's final sacrifice.[113] Likewise, these 'sketches' and 'outlines' point more towards future events than existing structures,[114] towards a city which God, the architect, would build himself (11.10).

---

[104] Lincoln D. Hurst initially made this comment in an article, 'How Platonic are Heb. viii.5 and ix.23f?', *JTS* 34.1 (1983): 157. Some draw on Aquila's literal translation of 'likeness' in Deut. 4.17 and Ezek. 8.10 to support the use of 'copy', see Attridge, *Hebrews*, 219 n. 41; Robert B. Jamieson, 'Hebrews 9.23: Cult Inauguration, Yom Kippur and the Cleansing of the Heavenly Tabernacle', *NTS* 62.4 (2016): 571. This however, points to the rarity of such an occurrence, not the overwhelming presence. See N. F. Marcos, *The Septuagint in Context: Introduction to the Greek Version of the Bible* (Leiden: Brill, 2000), 109–22.

[105] Philo never uses ὑπόδειγμα in reference to the tabernacle/temple, rightly Church, *Temple*, 408. Moore states that παράδειγμα not only means 'copy' but is 'nearly synonymous' with ὑπόδειγμα, *Repetition*, 151. But παράδειγμα is never given the sense of 'copy' but 'example', see LSJ 1307–8. BDAG has no entry for παράδειγμα. See Moore's interaction with Church and others, '"The True Tabernacle" of Hebrews 8:2 Future Dwelling with People or Heavenly Dwelling Place?', *TynBul* 72 (2021): 49–71.

[106] It is uncertain if or why Hebrews would avoid παράδειγμα, with the term being used twice in Exod. 25.9. Instead, Hebrews chooses a similar term in τύπος (Exod. 25.40). Calaway, *Sabbath*, 106; Schenck, *Cosmology*, 84; Williamson, *Philo*, 112–13, all suggest it was a purposeful avoidance of a typically technical Platonic term. Contra W. Eisele, *Ein unerschütterliches Reich: Die mittelplatonische Umformung des Parusiegedankens im Hebräerbrief*, BZNW 16 (Berlin: de Gruyter, 2003), 375–80; Spicq, *Hébreux*, 1:72–6. Hebrews avoids many Platonic terms, see Barnard, *Mysticism*, 95; Gäbel, *Kulttheologie*, 112–17. Church is possibly correct in that Hebrews avoids using παράδειγμα, since this term means 'pattern' in Exod. 25.9, but 25.40 uses τύπος, *Temple*, 406 n. 172.

[107] Rightly Ribbens, *Levitical*, 112; Moore, *Repetition*, 11–14; Alexander, 'Dualism', *Light*, 169–85; Gäbel, *Kulttheologie*, 241.

[108] Vanhoye, *Perfect*, 130; Church, *Temple*, 409; Cockerill, *Hebrews*, 259–60; Hurst, *Hebrews*, 13–17.

[109] BDAG 1037. The second rendering is 'outline', 'sketch' or 'symbol' for Heb. 8.5 but never 'copy'. For Heb. 4.11 the initial sense is 'example', 'model' or 'pattern'.

[110] BDAG 929–30. Here the third sense given for Heb. 8.5 is a mere representation of something, such as a 'shadow'.

[111] Church, *Temple*, 409.

[112] Mackie, *Eschatology*, 161–2.

[113] Koester, *Hebrews*, 427.

[114] Schenck reads ὑποδείγματι καὶ σκιᾷ as a 'shadowy illustration', *New Perspective*, 98; *Cosmology*, 166. See also Calaway, *Sabbath*, 105; Hurst, *Hebrews*, 17; Peterson, *Perfection*, 131. Moffatt has 'shadowy outline', *Hebrews*, 105. Contra Jamieson, *Death*, 56.

Probably the most significant question is, what exactly did Moses see? Or, how is τύπος supposed to be interpreted? Richard Davidson gives three options. Either the τύπος was a hollow mould (of the heavenly sanctuary), the heavenly sanctuary itself (which becomes the model), or both.[115] It is important to note that the τύπος is not the ὑπόδειγμα.[116] Even if τύπος is rendered as a 'pattern' or 'blueprint',[117] this does not negate whether a heavenly sanctuary was already in existence, since Moses was only shown a τύπος, not heaven itself. Additionally, the ἀντίτυπος (9.24) is not the antithesis of τύπος but is likely synonymous with ὑπόδειγμα.[118] When all of this is brought together, it seems as if Moses was shown a 'pattern' (τύπος) of the future eschatological heavenly tabernacle and was instructed to build an earthly tabernacle (ὑπόδειγμα/ἀντίτυπος) to foreshadow/prefigure this. It is not possible to assert whether a heavenly sanctuary was already in existence; nevertheless, the τύπος points forward towards what will come with Christ.

Scholars remain polarized over spatial and temporal readings, but a middle way is possible. The presence of a pre-existent tabernacle/temple in heaven is both common in the HB and the literature of the 2TP,[119] where it was not just Moses who caught a glimpse but Adam and Abraham too (*2 Bar.* 4.3-7). Conversely, other passages envisage future heavenly temples (Ezek. 40-8; Rev. 21-2). When reading Heb. 8.1-6 it is helpful to remember that it is not a contrast between Philo and Hebrews[120] or the earthly and heavenly tabernacles.[121] The heart of 8.1-6 is *foreshadowing*. All that precedes Christ points towards him. At the same time a spatial reading is possible since the initial purpose of the earthly tabernacle was to create a heavenly point of reference (initial vertical purpose). Yet, this initial vertical purpose is simultaneously horizontal since its very existence was not a means to an end but was intended to prefigure an eschatological tabernacle.[122]

---

[115] R. M. Davidson, *Typology in Scripture: A Study of Hermeneutical Typos Structures* (Berrien Springs, MI: Andrews University, 1981), 361-2. For a detailed study of τύπος see 119-32.

[116] 'Moses did not build a τύπος; he built a tabernacle based on a τύπος', Church, *Temple*, 426 n. 248.

[117] BDAG 1019-20 sees τύπος as a 'pattern' or 'design', cf. Acts 7.44. The initial sense is of a mark made resulting from a blow, BDAG 1019. According to Philo, the 'τύπος τοῦ παραδείγματος' was 'stamped on Moses' mind' (ἐνεσφραγίζετο τῇ διανοίᾳ, *Vit. Mos.* 2.26). The Hebrew 'pattern' (תבנית) appears twice in Exod. 25.9 (παράδειγμα, LXX) while τύπος (Exod. 25.40) and 'form' (εἶδος, Exod. 26.30) are used elsewhere. It is used in 1 Chron. 28.12, 19, when speaking of the 'plan' to build the temple. F. Laub, '"Ein für allemal hineingegangen in das Allerheiligste" (Hebr 9,12) – Zum Verständnis des Kreuzestodes im Hebraërbrief', *BZ* 35.1 (1991): 71. Moses was not shown a heavenly tabernacle but a blueprint of the heavenly tabernacle.

[118] Contra Ringleben, *Wort*, 155; Moore, *Repetition*, 152. Rightly Vanhoye, *Perfect*, 129-30; Church, *Temple*, 427; BDAG 90-1. As Davidson notes, '[t]he ἀντίτυπος denotes the OT reality, and the τύπος denotes the NT heavenly reality which the OT institution foreshadowed', *Typology*, 361.

[119] See my n. 69.

[120] Rightly Hermut Löhr, '"Umriß" und "Schatten". Bemerkungen zur Zitierung von Ex 25,40 in Hebr. 8', *ZNW* 84 (1993): 232.

[121] So, Ribbens, *Levitical*, 110-12.

[122] Similarly, Gäbel, 'Permission', *Son*, 140; *Kulttheologie*, 242-4.

2.5 Defilement in Hebrews

Having established both the background of defilement as well as Hebrews' contextual stage for defilement (the heavenly tabernacle), the final step is to calculate the ramifications of defilement within Hebrews. How does sin and defilement relate to the problem of συνείδησις and how does this impact the heavenly tabernacle?

2.5.1 Introducing sin in Hebrews

The purpose of Hebrews is not to present a systematic hamartiology.[123] Instead, through drawing on OT texts and employing rich and distinctive terminology a diverse picture of sin is drawn. The term sin (ἁμαρτία) is favoured by the author,[124] but he is not limited by it.[125] Sin is personified; it is deceitful (ἀπάτη, Heb. 3.13) and besetting (εὐπερίστατος, 12.1).[126] Sin is further understood as unrighteousness (ἀδικία, 8.12), a transgression (παράβασις, 2.2; 9.15), rebellion (παραπικρασμός, 3.8, 15; παραπικραίνω, 3.16), 'dead works' (νεκρῶν ἔργων, 6.1; 9.14) and disobedience (παρακοή, 2.2). People sin because of unfaithfulness (ἀπιστία, 3.12, 19), unbelief (ἀπείθεια, 4.6, 11)[127] and the 'the hardening of hearts' (σκληρύνητε τὰς καρδίας, 3.8, 15; 4.7). The community must be careful not to drift away (παραρρέω, 2.1) or become sluggish (νωθρός, 5.11; 6.12), to shrink back (ὑποστολή, 10.39) or to grow weary (κάμνω) and faint-hearted (ἐκλύω, 12.3).[128] They must not neglect to meet together (10.25) nor should they throw away their confidence (10.35).[129] Sin is multifaceted in Hebrews but the 'consciousness of sin' remains a significant and overriding nuance (§2.5.3).

2.5.2 Moral and ritual impurity?

Klawans' contentious ritual–moral distinction was discussed above, but does it fit into Hebrews' discourse? In his brief glance at Hebrews Klawans argues that it does.[130] Yet, such a clear distinction is never expressed in Hebrews[131] and little is said concerning what Klawans might consider as 'ritual' purification (cf. Heb. 6.2; 9.10; 10.22).[132] Hebrews' tripartite mention of 'food, drink and various baptisms' (9.10) may signal

---

[123] Rightly Hermut Löhr, *Umkehr und Sünde im Hebräerbrief*, BZNW 73 (Berlin: de Gruyter, 1994), 135.
[124] The term is used twenty-five times in Hebrews, both in the plural (Heb. 1.3; 2.17; 5.1, 3; 7.27; 8.12; 9.28; 10.2, 3, 4, 11, 12, 17; 26) but less so in the singular (3.13; 4.15; 9.26, 28; 10.6, 8, 18; 11.25; 12.1, 4; 13.11).
[125] Löhr, *Umkehr*, 11–68. See also, ἁμαρτάνω (Heb. 3.17; 10.26) and ἁμαρτωλός (7.26; 12.3).
[126] See n. 63 in §5.3.1.
[127] See ἀπειθέω (Heb. 3.18; 11.31).
[128] The extent to which 'inhospitality' or being 'sluggish of hearing' should be labelled as 'sin' needs further consideration, rightly Löhr, *Umkehr*, 134, contra Easter, *Faith*, 47–8.
[129] Individual sins are sparse (Heb. 12.15-16; 13.4-5).
[130] Klawans, *Impurity*, 155–6. So too Moffitt, 'Weak and Useless? Purity, the Mosaic Law, and Perfection in Hebrews', *Lawlessness*, 89–103.
[131] Rightly Davies, *Paideia*, 224–7; Gäbel, *Kulttheologie*, 385–92, esp. 412–13.
[132] I do not see Heb. 10.22 as a reference to baptism (§4.4.4).

a parallel with Paul's discussions concerning food (Rom. 14; 1 Cor. 8; Col. 2.16-23)[133] although it is likely that this tripartite phrase is a general reference to the earthly cult (§4.3.3). Unlike Paul, these are not dominant themes in Hebrews. If Heb. 9.10-14 is read as an internal–external purification contrast, as is often the case (§1.4.2, §4.3.1), then this further lends to the idea of ritual–moral impurity. This internal–external model is argued against extensively later (§4.3.2, §4.3.3, §4.3.4, §4.3.5). Philip Davies appropriately states that Hebrews 'seems less interested on the whole with physical purifications on the part of his audience than the purification of their consciences, as the emphasis lies consistently with the problem of sin'.[134] Purification rites and rituals may have been an important part in dealing with the consciousness for the recipients[135] (§1.2) but a ritual–moral distinction remains evasive in Hebrews. Hebrews' concern is dealing with the *consciousness* of sin.

2.5.3 Sin as conscious defilement (συνείδησις) in Hebrews

While terms related to defilement are minimal in Hebrews,[136] the concern for purification (Heb. 1.3; 9.9-14, 22-3, 26, 28; 10.12-14, 19-22) automatically denotes the problem of defilement and further confirms that the author understands defilement to be synonymous with the effects of sin. The prime issue facing the recipients is that the present functioning earthly cult is unable to deal with the problem of συνείδησις (9.9, 14; 10.2, 22; §1.2, §2.2). The recipients' consciousness of sin has left them in a state of conscious defilement; in being conscious of their sins, they are subsequently conscious of their impure state. Thus, 'sin' in this sense is not necessarily a direct offense towards God that needs to be removed but the recipients' own subjective awareness of sin which appears to be the problem.

This is best explained in Heb. 10.1-4 which states that the present earthly cult is a 'foreshadow' (σκιά) of the 'good things to come' which are being experienced in the present.[137] If the earthly cult's perpetual sacrifices could bring about perfection then the worshippers would have no 'consciousness of sin' (συνείδησιν ἁμαρτιῶν) since 'they would have been purged once-for-all' (ἅπαξ κεκαθαρισμένους, 10.2) – the perfect participle being placed at the end for emphasis.[138] This contrary-to-fact condition is completed by the statement: 'but in these [sacrifices] [there is] a reminder of sin annually' (ἀλλ' ἐν αὐταῖς ἀνάμνησις ἁμαρτιῶν κατ' ἐνιαυτόν, 10.3).[139]

It is important to highlight Hebrews' flexibility and further nuances regarding συνείδησις here. While συνείδησις stands alone in some places (9.9, 14), it is given further meaning in this passage by the surrounding terms (cf. 10.22; 13.18):

---

[133] Gordon, *Hebrews*, 119; Delitzsch, *Hebrews*, 2:73.
[134] Davies, *Paideia*, 226.
[135] Karrer, *Hebräer*, 2:150, 156-7.
[136] Significant terms include 'to defile' (κοινόω, Heb. 9.13), 'common/defiled' (κοινός, 10.29) and 'undefiled' (ἀμίαντος, 13.4). Elsewhere Hebrews speaks of a 'root of bitterness' which can grow and 'defile' (μιαίνω) many (12.15, cf. Lev. 21.15).
[137] Harris, *Hebrews*, 252; Attridge, *Hebrews*, 269; Lane, *Hebrews*, 2:259.
[138] Harris, *Hebrews*, 254; Cockerill, *Hebrews*, 430.
[139] Support for a eucharistic reference here is minimal, see Ellingworth, *Hebrews*, 495-6.

10.2 ἐπεὶ οὐκ ἂν ἐπαύσαντο προσφερόμεναι διὰ τὸ μηδεμίαν ἔχειν ἔτι <u>συνείδησιν ἁμαρτιῶν</u> τοὺς λατρεύοντας ἅπαξ κεκαθαρισμένους
10.3 ἀλλ᾽ ἐν αὐταῖς <u>ἀνάμνησις ἁμαρτιῶν</u> κατ᾽ ἐνιαυτόν
10.4 ἀδύνατον γὰρ αἷμα ταύρων καὶ τράγων ἀφαιρεῖν <u>ἁμαρτίας</u>

For instance, συνείδησις is further defined as a συνείδησιν ἁμαρτιῶν 'consciousness of sin' (10.2). Rather than repeating this definition, the author chooses to rephrase it as a 'reminder of sin' (ἀνάμνησις ἁμαρτιῶν) a verse later (10.3). This important addition of 'remembrance' (ἀνάμνησις) further implies that συνείδησις denotes a psychological awareness of past sin. The συνείδησις is not only a present consciousness of sin (10.2) but also refers to the memory of sin (10.3). By Heb. 10.4, συνείδησις is simply referred to indirectly as 'sins' (ἁμαρτίας). By associating the consciousness of sin with both a 'reminder of sin' and then 'sins', the author broadens the notion of συνείδησις to other terms, phrases and passages within the epistle. Later sections will advance this discussion in more detail (§4.3, §4.4); for now, it is enough to acknowledge the nature of συνείδησις in relation to defilement.

2.5.4 'Dead works'

Connected to συνείδησις is the presence of 'dead works' (νεκρῶν ἔργων) which point once more towards defilement. Hebrews speaks of God's works (1.10; 3.9; 4.3, 4, 10), the communities' good works (6.10; 10.24; 13.21), but on two occasions (6.1; 9.14) Hebrews refers to 'dead works'. The importance of this latter phrase is dismissed by some,[140] but it remains unique to Hebrews and adds significantly to understanding defilement; coupling 'death' with 'works' is suggestive of cultic defilement.

'Dead works' appears initially in Heb. 6.1. Here the recipients are exhorted to move on towards perfection (τελειότης) while leaving behind the basic teachings of Christ – repentance 'from dead works' (ἀπό νεκρῶν ἔργων).[141] The mention of 'dead works' alongside faith (πίστις) towards God (6.1) forms a possible parallel with James' assertion that πίστις by itself 'if it has no works, is dead' (ἐὰν μὴ ἔχῃ ἔργα, νεκρά ἐστιν, Jas 2.17, 26). Thus, 'dead works' are viewed as 'works of unbelief' (cf. Heb. 3.12, 19).[142] Still, Hebrews' emphasis on repentance 'from dead works' (6.1) suggests that 'dead works' should be interpreted as past sins, not types of faith.[143]

Hebrews 6.1 concerns repentance, but the second occurrence centres around the cult. It states that the blood of Christ will purify 'our consciousness from dead works to serve the living God' (τὴν συνείδησιν ἡμῶν ἀπὸ νεκρῶν ἔργων εἰς τὸ λατρεύειν θεῷ ζῶντι, 9.14). Reading 'dead works' as a reference to the Pauline 'works of the law'[144] has minimal support. Lane's assertion that 'dead works' is a reference to OT external cultic

---

[140] Johnson states that finding an adequate definition for 'dead works' is 'not required' and 'inappropriate', *Hebrews*, 159.
[141] Aligning 'dead works' with idolatry through the occurrence of νεκρός (cf. Wis. 15.17) appears a stretch, see Cockerill, *Hebrews*, 401; deSilva, *Perseverance*, 216–17, 307.
[142] Cockerill, *Hebrews*, 265.
[143] Harris, *Hebrews*, 132; Ellingworth, *Hebrews*, 314, 458.
[144] Westcott, *Hebrews*, 145–6.

regulations[145] has received harsh criticism.[146] Cockerill instead concludes that 'dead works' refer not to 'the rituals of the old covenant but to the sin from which those rituals could not cleanse'.[147] In a sense both Lane and Cockerill might be right. The Levitical cult's inability to purge totally the συνείδησις reinforces and further highlights the consciousness of sin (10.2-3). As a result, 'dead works' may well refer directly to sins, but indirectly they may refer to the earthly cultic practices which attempted to remove the consciousness of sin but instead exacerbated the problem.

Whether 'dead works' refer to specific sins or not, the presence of purgation (καθαρίζω, 9.14) implies that 'dead works' are an impure state resulting in defilement. These works are *dead* (an impure state) and are placed in direct contrast with being able to approach the *living* God (a pure state) (9.13-14). Hence, 'dead works' prevent the ability to worship the living God and function as subjective and objective forms of defilement. As Lane notes, 'the phrase [νεκρῶν ἔργων] reflects a concept of sin as defilement that is inimical to the approach to the living God'.[148] What is often passed over by commentators is the correlation between the phrase 'νεκρῶν ἔργων' and συνείδησις (9.14). These 'dead works' are not simply past events but remain presently within the recipients' consciousness.

In reflecting on 'dead works' in 6.1 and 9.14 it appears that both uses have separate functions.[149] The first concerns repentance from 'dead works', which should be read as a human response – a conscious turning away from sin (6.1). It is a foundational requirement to enter into the Christian community. The second occurrence concerns conscious defilement – the consciousness of sin – and is a separate additional work of Christ, dealt with via his heavenly blood offering (§3.7, §4.2, §4.5). Furthermore, 'dead works' in 6.1, if unrepented from, are to be viewed as active rebellion. However, 'dead works' in 9.14 refer to works from which the addresses have already repented from, yet continue to impact the believer with respect to συνείδησις. The 'dead works' in 9.14 do not necessarily separate God from believers, but believers from God, since they exist within the consciousness culminating in dread and lack of confidence to approach. The dual occurrence of 'dead works' in both 6.1 and 9.14 reveals that sin can be repented from (6.1) but only the blood of Christ can purge the memory of sin (9.14).

2.5.5 Types of sin? Unintentional/intentional sin

Scholars are divided over whether Hebrews observes the priestly distinction[150] between sinning 'unintentionally' (בשגגה) and 'with a high-hand' (ביד רמה).[151] Sinning unintentionally

---

[145] Lane, *Hebrews*, 1:140; 2:240. See also Gäbel, *Kulttheologie*, 379.
[146] deSilva, *Perseverance*, 216–17, 307.
[147] Cockerill, *Hebrews*, 401. But again, Hebrews is not talking about cleansing the heart here but cleansing the consciousness.
[148] Lane, *Hebrews*, 2:240.
[149] Contra Mitchell, *Hebrews*, 184.
[150] It is more accurate to speak of two types of deliberate sins (non-defiant/deliberate and defiant/high-handed), see Gane, *Cult*, 202–13.
[151] See Lev. 4.2, 13, 22, 27; 5.18; Num. 15.22-31. Also, Ellingworth, *Hebrews*, 276; Robert P. Gordon, 'Better Promises: Two Passages in Hebrews against the Background of the Old Testament Cultus', *Templum*, 446–7.

can consist of breaking a known or unknown law unintentionally, or as Roy Gane describes it, as 'unwittingly driving the wrong way down a one-way street'.[152] These are not the same as rebellious sins, which are differentiated elsewhere (Num. 15.22-31). A particular discussion point in Hebrews (cf. §3.6.2) is where earthly priests are spoken of as those who can deal gently with the ignorant (ἀγνοέω) and wayward (πλανάω), since they themselves are subject to weakness (Heb. 5.2). Both ἀγνοέω and πλανάω are often read as hendiadys,[153] that is, 'people go astray through ignorance'. However, πλανάω is used in Heb. 3.10 via Ps. 95 (94 LXX) to describe the wilderness generation who are always 'going astray in [their] hearts' (πλανῶνται τῇ καρδίᾳ, Heb. 3.10, cf. 11.38). Hebrews immediately applies this to those with an 'evil, unbelieving heart that turns away from the living God' (3.12).[154] Additionally, ἀγνοέω has the sense of 'being unaware of sin'[155] and is used alongside ἀκουσίως adverbially to denote sinning 'unintentionally' in the LXX (Lev. 4.13; 5.18; Num. 5.11).[156]

Secondly, Hebrews states that earthly priests offer blood for themselves but also for sins committed 'unintentionally' (ἀγνόημα, Heb. 9.7), literally, 'without knowledge' (α-γινώσκω).[157] Some scholars dispel ἀγνόημα as a technical term for differentiating between types of sins and instead understand ἀγνόημα as synonymous with ἁμαρτία.[158] They argue that since the context is Yom Kippur, ἀγνόημα must refer to all sins and not just unintentional sins, since 'all sins' were atoned for on Yom Kippur (Lev. 16.16, 21).[159] If Hebrews wished to refer to 'all sins' in 9.7, then the plural form of ἁμαρτία would have been expected. Hebrews 9.7 is most likely a reference to Yom Kippur (§3.3.2), yet it can be argued that ἀγνόημα is deliberately employed here as a technical term for 'unintentional sin'.[160] Scholars doubt this, as it could be read as limiting the efficaciousness of Yom Kippur to only 'unintentional sins' and might additionally reflect later Jewish traditions which limited Yom Kippur to unintentional sins.[161] However, by mentioning 'unintentional sins' in 9.7, the author may have been wanting to invoke the daily sacrifices of Lev. 4–5 and additionally the issue of 'guilt' and 'consciousness of sin' (cf. §4.3.5). This is plausible, since Hebrews mentions daily offerings elsewhere (Heb. 7.27; 10.11).

---

[152] Roy E. Gane, *Leviticus, Numbers*, NIVAC (Grand Rapids: Zondervan, 2004), 98.
[153] Harris, *Hebrews*, 117; Ribbens, *Levitical*, 204; Cockerill, *Hebrews*, 234; Löhr, *Umkehr*, 40–1, 52; Issacs, *Sacred*, 93; Bruce, *Hebrews*, 120; Attridge, *Hebrews*, 144.
[154] Intentionality, but also a general sense of 'erring', frames the Hebrew term, תעה, used in Ps. 95.10, see *HALOT* 1766–7.
[155] BDAG gives Heb. 5.2 the fourth sense here of sinning unintentionally, 13.
[156] For a thorough treatment see Löhr, *Umkehr*, 33–5.
[157] A NT *hapax legomenon* used rarely in the LXX (Gen. 43.12; Jdt. 5.20; Tob. 3.3; 1 Macc. 13.39; Sir. 23.2; 51.19).
[158] Ribbens, *Levitical*, 202–5; Weiss, *Hebräer*, 255.
[159] All sins were purged from the sanctuary, but defiant sins are still unaccounted for, see Greenberg, *Atonement*, 30; Gane, *Cult*, 276–7.
[160] Rightly Ellingworth, *Hebrews*, 435–6; Attridge, *Hebrews*, 239; Montefiore, *Hebrews*, 148; Spicq, *Hébreux*, 2:253; Delitzsch, *Hebrews*, 1:230.
[161] See m. *Yoma* 8.9. Having said this, Leviticus is clear that provision for atonement is restricted to those who sin unintentionally (ἀκουσίως), see Lev. 4.1-2, 12, 22, 27; 5.14-15.

Hebrews 10.26 sheds further light here when it refers to those who sin willingly (ἑκουσίως)[162] having already received 'knowledge of the truth' (ἐπίγνωσιν τῆς ἀληθείας).[163] For these there remains no sacrifice for sins. The nature of ἑκουσίως shows contempt for God and is a conscious calculated intention to not only sin but to refuse to return.[164] As Lane notes, this intentional persistence in sin 'removes a person from the sphere of grace'.[165] Hebrews possibly finds agreement with OT texts that restrict atonement to those who commit apostasy, since the perpetrator refuses atonement (Num. 15.22-31).[166] The result is that when Heb. 5.2, 9.7 and 10.26 are read together, a possible threefold distinction for sin is visible: unintentional (ἀγνόημα), intentional/explicable (πλανάω) and high-handed/inexplicable (ἑκουσίως). This distinction emphasizes the severity of sin and the irreversible reality of apostasy – with sacrifice unable to provide recompense (Heb. 6.4-8; 10.26-7). While ἑκουσίως might be considered 'high-handed' and linked with apostasy, πλανάω may refer to a general wandering or deliberate, but not 'defiant', sin, since priests are said to deal gently with this aspect of sin (5.2).[167] Finally, Hebrews is not only concerned with the consciousness of sin but with the consciousness of unconscious sin. The burden of unintentional, or unconscious, sin is not often considered in Hebrews scholarship.[168] This and the notion of Levitical אָשָׁם will be explored in more detail later (§4.3.5).

2.5.6 Defiled heavenly tabernacle

The interrelatedness of earth and heaven is opaque to modern minds. The heavens are conceived of as far away and concealed, when in reality humankind and the cosmos are bound together.[169] The same is true of defilement, as Johnsson notes, '[t]he modern mind is quite at home with the thought of the transmissibility of "infection" from one person to another, or from animals to persons. But the idea of an "infected" ("leprous"!) house boggles the mind – how much more an "infected" cosmos!'[170] As well as portraying humanity as susceptible to defilement, Hebrews applies the same logic to the heavenly tabernacle by speaking of its need for purification. The prime place for this is Heb. 9.23, although it is implied elsewhere (cf. 1.3; 2.17) as discussed later (§4.2.2). The unavoidable aspect of 9.23 is that Hebrews is attaching defilement, and the subsequent need for purification, to the heavens.

---

[162] See 1 Pet. 5.2 for the only other use of ἑκουσίως in the NT.
[163] It is unlikely that ἐπίγνωσις is significantly different in meaning to γινώσκω (BDAG 369), contra Lane, *Hebrews*, 2:292.
[164] BDAG 307.
[165] Lane, *Hebrews*, 2:292.
[166] Contra Ribbens, *Levitical*, 205.
[167] Again, there should be a distinction between types of deliberate sins (see n. 150), where פשע likely denotes deliberate, but not inexplicable sin, Gane, *Cult*, 294–8. Thus, ἑκουσίως may well denote the inexplicable 'high-handed' (ביד רמה) sins, which Hebrews says do not receive sacrifice and lead to apostasy.
[168] Karrer, *Hebräer*, 2:158.
[169] Johnsson, 'Defilement', 132–44, 178–93, 331–2, 414, 430.
[170] Johnsson, 'Defilement', 138.

Grammatically this verse contains the common contrasting construction of both particles, μὲν and δὲ. After noting the importance of blood application for the removal of sins in the previous verse, 9.23 states that it was necessary for the sketches (ὑποδείγμα) of these heavenly things to be purified, 'but the heavenly things [require] better sacrifices' (δὲ τὰ ἐπουράνια κρείττοσιν θυσίαις)[171] The purification of heavenly things is a challenging concept to imagine and as a result scholars interpret this verse in various ways (§4.2.2). Additionally, the rhetorical use of 'exchange' (ὑπαλλαγή, 9.23) – the transfer of qualities from one thing to another – suggests that Hebrews is attaching human defilement to heaven.[172] In essence 9.22-3 expresses inadvertently that since human sin defiled the earthly tabernacle and needed blood application in order to remove sin (9.22), in the same way the heavenly sanctuary, which has been defiled by sin, needed to be purified by Christ's blood (9.23) so that people could partake in heavenly worship.[173]

Hebrews 9.23 points towards a cosmic interpretation of defilement, displaying that the author conceives of defilement as both a subjective and objective reality; it not only impacts the people of God but extends beyond the earthly realm and towards the heavenly sphere. This further echoes and confirms that Hebrews interprets the impact of defilement in a similar manner to Milgrom's 'aerial miasma' (§2.3.1). The sanctuary can be defiled due to sins which occurred from a distance.[174] For instance, a person who touches a corpse and does not cleanse themselves defiles the sanctuary (Num. 19.13, 20).[175] Consequently, keeping oneself clean is imperative for restoring order and preventing the defiling of the tabernacle (Lev. 16.16; 20.3; 21.23). Hebrews' conception of a defiled heavenly tabernacle can be read as a 'miasma' like event that connects the status of the people of God with the status of the heavenly tabernacle.[176] The pollution of the heavens (Heb. 9.23) reveals that human sin extends beyond the individual. The defiled individual 'upsets the ordering of society and the cosmos. That is, the polluted one is also the polluter.'[177] The defiled individual, or the 'polluter', disrupts the cosmic order and is what Douglas labelled a 'doubly wicked object',[178] since this person is not merely impure, but is now contagious and a danger to others as well. For Hebrews then, defilement is not limited to humans but extends and connects to the heavenly tabernacle.

---

[171] The plural here is not a reference to Christ's 'multiple sacrifices' but confirmation that his sacrifice is superior to the many sacrifices of the OC and finds its plurality with the nearby pronoun (τούτοις).
[172] Koester, *Hebrews*, 421.
[173] Gäbel, *Kulttheologie*, 424.
[174] Gane, *Cult*, 144.
[175] As Gane notes, 'the evil that defiles the sanctuary when it occurs is not the physical ritual impurity of corpse contamination itself but the moral fault of wantonly neglecting to remedy the impurity', *Cult*, 144.
[176] Lane is useful here, *Hebrews*, 2:247. See also Anderson, *Hebrews*, 254.
[177] Johnsson, 'Defilement', 189.
[178] Douglas, *Purity*, 172.

2.6 The effects of a defiled συνείδησις

This final section will explore further the defiled συνείδησις and its effects. It will suggest that a defiled συνείδησις denotes the motifs of a 'stain', 'dread' and 'timidity'. A general consequence of a defiled συνείδησις is both 'restricted access' and apostasy.

2.6.1 Restricted access

The impact of defilement results in restricted access to God's presence. This is evident in the cultic dynamic. Defilement impacts the individual and the community, but more importantly it alienates people from participating in the cultus, leading to separation from God. Jenson notes that the architecture of the tabernacle itself comprises of a spatial dimension with 'various zones separated by distinct boundaries'.[179] A certain level of purity is required to enable access. Within Hebrews this same spatial dimension is observed and adhered to, with the author careful to note the regulations (δικαιώματα) under the earthly cult (Heb. 9.1). Under these regulations only the high priest, having been purified himself, can go into the second part of the tabernacle annually (9.7). As noted previously sin and impurity are significant problems because they counteract the purpose of the cult, which is to protect God's presence so that it may remain with his people (§2.3.1, §2.3.3). The contagious nature of impurity disrupts this ideal and prevents access to God and his presence. In Hebrews, the purification of the συνείδησις is met with an exhortation to approach (9.14; 10.19-22). A defiled συνείδησις therefore, bars access. Yet this is mostly subjective. It is the recipients' consciousness of sin that causes them to *feel* unable to approach.

2.6.2 The stain, dread and timidity of defilement

The defiled συνείδησις also functions under the idea of sin as a stain. The language of purging (καθαρίζω, 9.14; 10.2) and sprinkling clean (ῥαντίζω, 10.22) the συνείδησις indicates the notion of a blot or stain that needs to be removed. Stains are not easy to remove, with prophetic texts likening the defilement of sin with stained clothing (Isa. 1.18-20; Jer. 2.22).[180] For instance, Jeremiah notes that although the people attempt to wash themselves with lye and much soap, the stain (κηλιδόω) of their unrighteousness remains (Jer. 2.22). Stains point to past sin, but they also point to the present guilt which past sins continue to evoke. In Hebrews especially it is the consciousness of sin that is representative of a stain. The memory and subsequent awareness of sin lingers as an impure stain. Only one who is without blemish (ἄμωμος) is able to remove the blemish of sin (Heb. 9.14).

Linked to stain is dread. According to Lam, '[s]tains elicit dread, not evaluation – our need for their elimination stems not as much from a process of conscious deliberation as from an instinctual preference for purity, homogeneity, and cleanness'.[181]

---

[179] Jenson, *Graded*, 89.
[180] Lam, *Sin*, 181. See 179–206 for an overview of sin as a 'stain' in the HB.
[181] Lam, *Sin*, 180.

The '[d]read of the impure' for Ricœur is 'in the background of all our feelings and all our behaviour relating to fault ... With defilement we enter into the reign of Terror.'[182] Since συνείδησις is knowledge of present defilement, this automatically culminates in a sense of 'dread' and results in the fear of judgement. Hebrews notes that every transgression (παράβασις) or disobedience (παρακοή) receives a 'just penalty' (ἔνδικος μισθαποδοσία, 2.2). God's wrath was displayed against those who rebelled and whose bodies fell in the wilderness (3.17). Moreover, nothing in all creation is hidden from God, but all is laid bare before him, to whom we must give an account (4.13).[183] Furthermore, wilful (ἑκουσίως) sin – while knowing the truth – results in a fearful prospect of judgement, with sacrifices providing no leeway (10.26-7). Perverting the law of Moses and trampling on the blood of the Son leads to severe punishment (10.28-9). Consciousness of sin results in dread, indeed, it is a fearful thing to fall into the 'hands of the living God' (10.31). Finally, since confidence or 'boldness to speak' (παρρησία) is aligned with a purified συνείδησις (10.19) then timidity and feelings of guilt and shame[184] is a further characteristic of dread in relation to a defiled συνείδησις.[185]

2.6.3 Apostasy, rebellion and the wilderness motif

The greatest threat facing the recipients is the possibility of leaving their community. The present problem of συνείδησις has caused them to consider whether a return to a more familiar Jewish ceremonial context might solve the persistent problem of συνείδησις (§1.2, §2.2).[186] As a result the tone of Hebrews appears stern in certain places (Heb. 2.1-4; 3.7–4.11; 5.11–6.12; 10.26-39; 12.14-29),[187] with the author warning them of the consequences of leaving the community. In order to underline the severity Hebrews draws on, arguably, the ultimate act of rebellion – the wilderness generation and their subsequent inability to enter the 'rest' (κατάπαυσις, 3.7–4.11).[188] The wilderness motif

---

[182] Paul Ricœur, *The Symbolism of Evil*, trans. Emerson Buchanan (New York: Harper & Row Publishers, 1967), 25.
[183] The awkward clause 'πρὸς ὃν ἡμῖν ὁ λόγος' might be intended as a pun concerning God's 'word' (4.12) and our 'word' of account (4.13), Harris, *Hebrews*, 107.
[184] It is unhelpful to *strictly* contrast 'guilt' and 'shame' and to claim, as E. R. Dodds famously did, that guilt overtook shame as a social category, *The Greeks and the Irrational* (Berkeley: University of California Press, 1966). DeSilva's study is thorough and helps to highlight the social concerns relating to 'shame' within Hebrews. However, I differ with his conclusions in viewing the purged συνείδησις as gaining social prestige, as well as viewing Jesus' sacrifice as restoring favour between God and humankind, *Despising Shame: Honour Discourse and Community Maintenance in the Epistle to the Hebrews*, SBLDS 152 (Atlanta: Scholars Press, 1995), 341–7. Christ is high priest not a patron; the defiled συνείδησις denotes guilt and restricted access towards God. Hebrews says that purging the συνείδησις results in access (9.14; 10.19-22) *not* in greater social prestige.
[185] This is certainly the case for Josephus (*Ant.* 1.48). See my discussion in §1.3.5.
[186] Rightly Lindars, *Hebrews*, 14, 66, 88; 'The Rhetorical Structure of Hebrews', *NTS* 35.3 (1989): 382–406.
[187] It is not the purpose of this study to address the theological/soteriological viewpoints concerning these five warning passages. For a summary see Herbert W. Bateman IV ed., *Four Views on the Warning Passages in Hebrews* (Grand Rapids: Kregel, 2007).
[188] The latter will be addressed in more detail later (§5.3.6).

is an important narrative in the story of God's people, being understood and applied by writers for a variety of heuristic purposes.¹⁸⁹ The wilderness generation and the recipients act as characters in a story, as the author blends rhetoric and narrative.¹⁹⁰ For Käsemann, Hebrews employs the wilderness motif to depict the Christian life as a desert wandering experience,¹⁹¹ a state believers remain in until they enter a post-mortem κατάπαυσις.¹⁹²

The problem with Käsemann's analysis is that 'there is no actual reference to the people of Israel as wanderers [in Hebrews]'.¹⁹³ Instead, Hebrews' focus is not on *wandering* in a desert but on failing to inherit the land, that is, the κατάπαυσις.¹⁹⁴ This is evident through employing Ps. 95 (94 LXX)¹⁹⁵ (Heb. 3.7-11, 15; 4.3, 5, 7), a Psalm which focuses on the disobedience of the wilderness generation at Kadesh-Barnea (Num. 13–14). The forty years of wandering is a tragic example (ὑπόδειγμα, Heb. 4.11), a fate to be avoided not imitated. Hebrews' innovative insertion of διό into the Psalm citation (Heb. 3.10) underlines this by placing God's anger after their disobedience and not during the forty years as the Psalm indicates.¹⁹⁶ The author immediately applies the

---

¹⁸⁹ While some employed this narrative positively (Exod. 16.35; Deut. 2.7; Neh. 9.21; Pss. 105.27-45; 136.36; Hos. 2.10-23; Jn 6; Philo, *Dec.* 2–17), Hebrews employs it as a warning to not imitate (cf. Ezek. 20.1-31; Num. 14.33-4; 32.13; Pss. 78.5-67; 106.6-33; Acts 7; 1 Cor. 10.1-13; *4 Ezra* 14.29-30; CD 3.7-9, 12-13). For some, Moses was prevented from entering the land, not out of punishment but through God's mercy so that Moses would not have to experience the people breaking God's law and rebelling (*LAB* 19.6-7). This motif of corruption occurring when the people enter the land is assumed elsewhere too (*Jub.* 50.4).

¹⁹⁰ The recipients are a continuation of the wilderness generation, see Cockerill, *Hebrews*, 154 n. 4; Madison N. Pierce, 'Hebrews 3:7-4:11 and the Spirit's Speech to the Community', in *Muted Voices of the New Testament: Readings in the Catholic Epistles and Hebrews*, ed. Katherine M. Hockey, Madison N. Pierce and Francis Watson, LNTS 565 (London: Bloomsbury T&T Clark, 2017), 182.

¹⁹¹ 'Wandering' not 'pilgrimage' – a key distinction made by William G. Johnsson, 'The Pilgrimage Motif in the Book of Hebrews', *JBL* 97.2 (1978): 239–51.

¹⁹² Ernst Käsemann, *The Wandering People of God: An Investigation of the Letter to the Hebrews*, trans. Roy A. Harrisville and Irving L. Sandberg (Minneapolis: Augsburg Publishing House, 1984), 44–54.

¹⁹³ Johnsson, 'Pilgrimage', 240.

¹⁹⁴ Davies, *Paideia*, 47–63; G. Lee, *Today When you Hear his Voice: Scripture, the Covenants, and the People of God* (Grand Rapids: Eerdmans, 2016), 128–42; Gäbel, *Kulttheologie*, 427; Cockerill, *Hebrews*, 153; Jon Laansma, *'I Will Give You Rest': The 'Rest' Motif in the New Testament with Special Reference to Mt 11 and Heb 3-4*, WUNT 2.98 (Tübingen: Mohr Siebeck, 1997), 262–4; Peter E. Enns, 'Creation and Re-creation: Psalm 95 and Its Interpretation in Hebrews 3:1–4:13', *WTJ* 55.2 (1993): 255–80; Erich Grässer, 'Das Wandernde Gottesvolk: Zum Basismotiv des Hebräerbriefes', *ZNW* 77 (1986): 167–9; Harold W. Attridge, '"Let Us Strive to Enter That Rest": The Logic of Hebrews 4:1–11', *HTR* 73 (1980): 279–88; Otfried Hofius, *Katapausis: Die Vorstellung vom endzeitlichen Ruheort im Hebräerbrief*, WUNT 11 (Tübingen: Mohr Siebeck, 1970), 117–39.

¹⁹⁵ For helpful discussions around Ps. 95, see Robert G. Rayburn II, *'Yesterday, Today and Forever': The Narrative World of Ψ 94 [Ps 95] as a Hermeneutical Key to Hebrews* (Berlin: Peter Lang, 2019), 111–17, 119–66; Gert J. Steyn, 'The Reception of Psalm 95(94): 7-11 in Hebrews 3–4', *Psalms and Hebrews*, 194–228; Christian Frevel, 'σήμερον – Understanding Psalm 95 Within, and Without, Hebrews', *Psalms and Hebrews*, 165–93; David M. Allen, 'More Than Just Numbers: Deuteronomic Influence in Hebrews 3:7–4:11', *TynBul* 58.1 (2007): 129–49.

¹⁹⁶ Susan Docherty, 'Recent Interpretation of Hebrews Chapters 3–4: Critical Issues and Scholarly Trends', *ITJ* 81.4 (2016): 389; Enns, 'Creation', 273–4. Since Heb. 3.10 and 3.17 view the forty years differently, some have suggested two forty-year periods, see Bruce, *Hebrews*, 99, or two views on a single forty-year period, see Koester, *Hebrews*, 256; Ellingworth, *Hebrews*, 232.

Psalm in a midrashic manner,[197] warning them to not have an 'evil unbelieving heart' (καρδία πονηρὰ ἀπιστίας, 3.12).[198] Consequently, sin and rebellion are described as internal desires, a choice rather than a human disposition.[199] For Hebrews, one of the possible consequences of a defiled συνείδησις is apostasy. The temptation to return to previous ritualistic practices displays the vulnerable state of the community. Hebrews' stern warnings reveal this fragility. The author's desire is that they would remain together in their gathering and in their perseverance (10.25).

2.7 Conclusion

This chapter has sought to demonstrate the centrality of defilement and a defiled συνείδησις within Hebrews' cultic argumentation. From the analysis a few conclusions arose. First, the consciousness of sin is a present problem unfulfilled by the earthly cult (§2.2). Second, the dialogue surrounding the earthly tabernacle functions as a foreshadowing of the heavenly tabernacle which Christ now inhabits. Moses was told to construct a ὑπόδειγμα and σκιά – a sketch and foreshadow which pointed towards an eschatological heavenly tabernacle (§2.4.5). Third, defilement is experienced on a communal and cosmic level. OT cultic defilement provides the necessary background for understanding sin and defilement in Hebrews; sin and the sanctuary are intertwined. In Hebrews, consciousness of sin and conscious defilement is a significant issue (§2.5.3). Central to defilement is the problem of συνείδησις and Hebrews' insistence on purging it (9.14; 10.2, 22). The consciousness of sin is further described as 'dead works', a 'reminder' or 'remembrance' of sin and simply as 'sin' (§2.5.3, §2.5.4). A fundamental part of defiled humanity is one's consciousness of defilement (συνείδησις). The defilement of the heavenly tabernacle is also a problem, leading to the conclusion that, just as human sin polluted the tabernacle in Leviticus (§2.3.1, §2.3.3), Hebrews also understands sin to be intrinsically linked to the status of the heavenly tabernacle (§2.5.6).

Fourth, the general effects of a defiled συνείδησις were defined as a 'stain', 'dread' and 'timidity'. Restricted access was another important consequence, with potential apostasy posing a more severe threat. Now that the present problem of συνείδησις has been addressed, the second part of this study will examine *how* the sacrificial argumentation of Hebrews seeks to solve the issue of συνείδησις.

---

[197] See Daniel E. Kim, 'Jewish and Christian Theology from the Hebrew Bible: The Concept of Rest and Temple in the Targumim, Hebrews, and the Old Testament', *Hebrews in Contexts*, 31–46; Docherty, *Old Testament*, 186–9.
[198] Or a 'heart evil with reference to unbelief', Wallace, *Grammar*, 128; Löhr, *Umkehr*, 96–7.
[199] In terms of whether Hebrews is referring to the rabbinic יצר הרע see Bruce, *Hebrews*, 66 n. 60.

Part Two

Purifying the consciousness: Cosmic purgation

3

Navigating Hebrews' sacrificial argumentation: Yom Kippur and Jesus' earthly and heavenly achievements

3.1 Introduction

The previous chapter prioritized the problems of cultic defilement in Hebrews and especially a defiled συνείδησις. This chapter will begin to explore Hebrews' sacrificial solution to these problems. First, the scholarship surrounding Hebrews' cultic argumentation will be engaged and critiqued. Second, Yom Kippur and 'atonement' will be addressed. While Yom Kippur is key for understanding the heavenly offering of Christ, a harmonious overarching Yom Kippur hermeneutic is not apparent. This leads to the third part, where three contentious passages relating to Jesus' offering[1] will be discussed (Heb. 9.11-17, 24-8; 10.5-14). It will be argued that the author is deliberatively selective concerning OT typology in order to distinguish between what Jesus achieves on earth (objectively in relation to sin) and what he achieves in heaven (subjectively in relation to the consciousness of sin). This chapter will confirm the foundational assumption (§1.2, §2.2) that Jesus' death *cannot* deal with the consciousness of sin; only his heavenly blood offering can.

3.2 Navigating scholarship

The last decade or so has seen a growth of literature seeking to understand what is now commonly referred to as Hebrews' 'sacrificial logic'.[2] Traditionally the sacrificial language in Hebrews is interpreted by most scholarship as a metaphorical and

---

[1] The terms 'offering', 'self-offering' and 'sacrifice' denote cultic terminology often associated with Jesus' heavenly offering, but are also as a reference to Jesus' earthly sacrificial life of obedience (§3.6.1, §3.6.2). 'Sacrifice' is not a reference to death but is used in a similar manner to 'offering'/'self-offering'.
[2] For a detailed dilution of scholarship into further nuanced camps see Jamieson, *Death*, esp. 23–70; 'When and Where', 342–54. Jamieson compares the first two viewpoints in the following way: '[u]nlike View 1, for View 2 Jesus' "entry" to the heavenly sanctuary does not refer to an event subsequent to the cross but instead metaphorically expounds the significance of the cross', 347. However, both these views (and maybe the others too) are 'metaphorical'. After all, the cultic language Hebrews draws upon (in Jamieson's first view) to interpret the death of Christ has no actual historical reality.

theological explanation for Jesus' death.³ As Caird stated, '[t]he language of sacrifice is metaphorical when used of the death of Christ. Literally, the death of Christ was no sacrifice, but a criminal execution, regarded by the one side as a political necessity and by the other as a miscarriage of justice.'⁴ Cultic phrases such as 'blood' or 'sprinkling' are viewed as a metaphorical reference for the historical death of Jesus.⁵ While no one claims that Jesus' historical death was an exact re-enactment of the Yom Kippur ritual,⁶ it is understood that Hebrews employs sacrificial metaphors by transferring language from one semantic sphere (the sacrificial cult) to another sphere (the historical death of Jesus).⁷ The motif of the 'blood of Christ' is a good example. Lane notes that whenever Hebrews speaks of Jesus' blood it is not referring to the, 'material substance but to the action of Christ who offered himself to God [on earth]'.⁸ Likewise, 'there is no real suggestion of a heavenly blood-ritual', as Lindars notes, when Hebrews speaks of Christ's blood 'he simply means Christ's death'.⁹

As a result, the cultic passages in Hebrews are perceived as metaphorical in order to shape a 'theological understanding of the death of Christ'¹⁰ since 'heaven is no place for historical events'.¹¹ Heaven is merely a finishing line, with all the essential work accomplished on earth.¹²

Alternatively, some understand Jesus' sacrifice as a 'simultaneous offering'. They do accept that cultic language is transferred to Jesus' earthly death, but when Jesus offers himself on earth, they posit that the same offering is being performed in heaven –

---

³ Hebrews employs metaphor (2.1; 3.4, 8; 4.12; 5.12-14; 6.7-9; 12.29; 13.20) but in relation to sacrifice it is an 'analogical' metaphor, or a 'homoeomorphic' metaphor, see Soskice, *Metaphor*, 101–3.
⁴ G. B. Caird, *The Language and Imagery of the Bible* (London: Duckworth, 1980), 157.
⁵ Gause, *Hebrews*, 205, 229; Bateman and Smith, *Hebrews*, 249–53; Schenck, *New Perspective*, 84; Ringleben, *Wort*, 147–8; Harris, *Hebrews*, 260; Brondos, *Death*, 2:965–1042; Vanhoye, *Perfect*, 148; Loader, 'Revisiting', esp. 276–9; Lukas Stolz, *Der Höhepunkt des Hebräerbriefs Hebräer 12,18-29 und seine Bedeutung für die Struktur und die Theologie des Hebräerbriefs*, WUNT 2.263 (Tübingen: Mohr Siebeck, 2018), 236–43; Church, *Hebrews*, 412–32; S. Finlan, *Sacrifice and Atonement: Psychological Motives and Biblical Patterns* (Minneapolis: Fortress Press, 2016), 10–11; Filtvedt, *Identity*, 158–9; Fleming Rutledge, *The Crucifixion: Understanding the Death of Jesus Christ* (Grand Rapids: Eerdmans, 2015), 234–83; Schreiner, *Hebrews*, 267–72, 300–7; Cockerill, *Hebrews*, 394–7; Christopher A. Richardson, *Pioneer and Perfecter of Faith: Jesus' Faith as the Climax of Israel's History in the Epistle to the Hebrews*, WUNT 2.338 (Tübingen: Mohr Siebeck, 2012), 36–43; Witherington, *Letters*, 271; Stegemann and Stegemann, 'Cultic', *Hebrews: Contemporary Methods*, 13–23; Telscher, *Opfer*, 257–60; Koester, *Hebrews*, 427; Ellingworth, *Hebrews*, 70, 452–8; Weiss, *Hebräer*, 467; Lane, *Hebrews*, 2:94, 249; Bruce, *Hebrews*, 213–16; Rissi, *Theologie*, 99.
⁶ Stegemann and Stegemann, 'Cultic', *Hebrews: Contemporary Methods*, 15.
⁷ This is what Aristotle saw at the heart of metaphor (μεταφορά) – the transference of language from one sphere to another, *Rhet.* 1411b; *Poet.* 1457b. See Colin Gunton, *The Actuality of Atonement: A Study of Metaphor, Rationality and the Christian Tradition* (London: T&T Clark, 1988), 122.
⁸ Lane, *Hebrews*, 2:240.
⁹ Lindars, *Hebrews*, 2. Also, Vanhoye, *Perfect*, 148. The linguistic distinction between 'synecdoche' and 'metonymy' is worth highlighting, see Lakoff and Johnson, *Metaphors*, 35–40. Metonymy is employed by some to explain Jesus' death, see Rutledge, *Crucifixion*, 234–40; Jamieson, *Death*, 159–68, 176; Bateman and Smith, *Hebrews*, 249. See later sections too (§3.2.1, §5.3, §5.4.3.2, §5.4.3.3).
¹⁰ Stegemann and Stegemann, 'Cultic', *Hebrews: Contemporary Methods*, 15.
¹¹ Stegemann and Stegemann, 'Cultic', *Hebrews: Contemporary Methods*, 15.
¹² Schreiner, *Hebrews*, 268 n. 432; Cockerill, *Hebrews*, 393–4; Laub, *Bekenntnis*, 205.

'zugleich'.[13] Or, comparably, some suggest that when Jesus died he ascended by his spirit, leading him to assume a bodily form in heaven.[14] These conclusions are held by a minority of scholars and fail to address the role of the resurrection,[15] or 'take time and space seriously'.[16]

In 2011 the publication of David M. Moffitt's book, *Atonement and the Logic of Resurrection in the Epistle to the Hebrews* marked a significant contribution in the history of Hebrews scholarship.[17] Rather than transferring cultic language exclusively to Jesus' historical death, Moffitt argued that Jesus' death, resurrection and heavenly ascension mirrored the Yom Kippur ritual. Jesus' earthly death paralleled the slaughtered victim; likewise, Jesus' heavenly entrance paralleled the Levitical priests' blood manipulation in the Holy of Holies. Atonement, therefore, was not accomplished in Jesus' death, but in heaven, where Jesus presented his perfected resurrected body to the Father. As Moffitt writes:

> Jesus' death on the cross is not the place or the primary means of atonement for the author of Hebrews ... [atonement occurred] not when Jesus was crucified, but after he was resurrected and ascended into heaven. There he presented himself alive and incorruptible before God. Just as Yom Kippur does not focus on the slaughter of the victim, but the presentation of its blood – that is, its life – before God.[18]

For Moffitt, the *logic* of Levitical sacrifice is intended to inform Hebrews' logic of Jesus' sacrifice. Just as the death of the animal does not atone, but its blood when presented in the Holy of Holies, so too Jesus' death does not atone, but only his offering in heaven. Moffitt argues that all references to Jesus' death in Hebrews are never associated with cultic language, but are focused on his earthly suffering, which he argues acts as a motivational tool for the recipients' own perseverance. Cultic language is only applied once Jesus enters heaven to offer himself.[19] A handful of scholars have put forward similar arguments in preceding articles and monographs,[20] but Moffitt was

---

[13] 'At the same time', Helmut Feld, *Der Hebräerbrief*, EdF 228 (Darmstadt: Wissenschaftliche Buchgesellschaft, 1985), 77. Also Thomas Knöppler, *Sühne im Neuen Testament: Studien zum urchristlichen Verständnis der Heilsbedeutung des Todes Jesu*, WMANT 88 (Neukirchener-Vluyn: Neukirchener Verlag, 2001), 199–200; Attridge, *Hebrews*, 251; Ulrich Luck, 'Himmlisches und irdisches Geschehen im Hebräerbrief: Ein Beitrag zum Problem des "historischen Jesus" im Urchristentum', *NovT* 6 (1963): 209.
[14] Hofius, *Katapausis*, 180–1. See also Laub, *Bekenntnis*, 199.
[15] Loader, 'Revisiting', 276. See Moffitt for criticisms here, *Atonement*, 19, 38–43.
[16] Loader, 'Revisiting', 274.
[17] Moffitt, *Atonement*, esp. 219–20, 269–81, 292–3.
[18] Moffitt, 'Blood', *Atonement*, 211–12; *Atonement*, 218–19.
[19] Moffitt, *Atonement*, 219–20.
[20] Mackie, *Eschatology*, 95–6, 172–81; Gäbel, *Kulttheologie*, 3–16, 292–5, 411–12; Nelson, 'Offered', esp. 254–5; Young, 'Gospel', esp. 208; 'The Impact of the Jewish Day of Atonement upon the Thought of the New Testament' (PhD diss., University of Manchester, 1973), 194–242; Johnsson, 'Defilement', 303; Walter E. Brooks, 'The Perpetuity of Christ's Sacrifice in the Epistle to the Hebrews', *JBL* 89.2 (1970): esp. 208–10; J. H. Davies, 'The Heavenly Work of Christ in Hebrews', in *Studia Evangelica. Vol. IV. Papers presented to the Third International Congress on New Testament Studies held at Christ Church, Oxford, 1965. Part I: The New Testament Scriptures*, ed. F. L. Cross (Berlin: Akademie-Verlag, 1968), 384–7. For further references see Jamieson, *Death*, 9–12.

the first in English scholarship[21] to dedicate his doctoral work to addressing the issue head-on.

3.2.1 Critiquing Moffitt

Following Moffitt's book, a flurry of publications in journal and monograph form reacted to his analysis with both agreement[22] and critique.[23] Perhaps predictably, most of the criticism surrounded Moffitt shifting the location of atonement from Jesus' death to the heavenly tabernacle. Responding to Moffitt, Loader states that scholars must 'view with caution any suggestion that the author [of Hebrews] diminishes the significance of Jesus' death or sees it primarily as preparatory'.[24] Loader affirms this, since:

> He was not the first to use cultic metaphor to describe Christ's death and its benefits. We cannot simply cite cultic understandings of blood as representing life, as it does in Old Testament and Jewish tradition, and ignore what the author must have been familiar with from his Christian tradition of referring to Jesus' death and its benefits by referring to his blood.[25]

For Loader, it is 'quite difficult to imagine that in one breath he sees Jesus' death as all important and in another he reduces it to a preliminary undertaking for a heavenly act'.[26]

Interpreters of Hebrews, therefore, must reconcile the ideas of emerging Christianity as displayed in other NT texts.

Robert Jamieson provides a current and detailed dialogue with Moffitt's work. Jamieson seeks to ascribe soteriological significance to both Jesus' death and heavenly offering, concluding that when Jesus offers his blood in heaven, he is offering the life he gave in his death.[27] Moffitt argued that references to 'blood' primarily denoted Jesus' resurrected life offered to God in heaven, but Jamieson argues to the contrary. Blood is the 'metonym' for Jesus' death; it is the life given in death as an exchange. Thus, 'Jesus' death constitutes sacrificial material he offers to God in heaven'.[28] This echoes Gäbel, who interprets Jesus' earthly life and death as corresponding to his heavenly self-offering.

---

[21] Gäbel's *Kulttheologie* is thorough and essential. Similarly to Moffitt, Gäbel notes that 'Das Heilswerk Christi ist nicht von irdischer, sondern von überlegen-himmlischer Art', *Kulttheologie*, 309.

[22] See Regev, *Temple*, 282.

[23] Michael Kibbe, in his review of Moffitt's book, writes that he finds it 'unfortunate that Moffitt makes no reference to pre-modern Christian readings of Hebrews', *Themelios* 37.1 (2012): 69–70. Moffitt, in responding to this, rightly notes that his book is 'not a study in the reception history of Hebrews', 'Heavenly Sacrifice', 48 n. 3. See Kibbe's article, 'Is It Finished? When Did It Start? Hebrews, Priesthood, and Atonement in Biblical, Systematic, and Historical Perspective', *JTS* 65 (2014): 25–61. Also, Jean-René Moret, 'Le rôle du concept de purification dans l'Épître aux Hébreux: une réaction à quelques propositions de David M. Moffitt', *NTS* 62.2 (2016): 289–307. See Jamieson's helpful conclusions, *Death*, 180–6.

[24] Loader, 'Revisiting', 253.

[25] Loader, 'Revisiting', 250–1.

[26] Loader, 'Revisiting', 253.

[27] Jamieson, *Death*, 127–79, esp. 166–8.

[28] Jamieson, *Death*, 176.

Jesus' earthly life and death are what Gäbel describes as the 'Inhalt seines himmlischen Opfers'.[29] Prior to this, other scholars have similarly described Jesus' heavenly offering as a 'presentation' of his earthly death.[30] If Jamieson views Jesus' heavenly offering as containing that which Jesus offered on earth, then the question must be asked as to why a heavenly offering was required? By viewing blood as a metonym for Jesus' death, the role of blood in Hebrews loses its distinctive purgative purpose. This is enough to say at present; Jamieson's work will be engaged with in greater detail in what follows.[31]

3.2.2 Mitigating Moffitt

Rather than critiquing Moffitt, many play down the ramifications of his conclusions.[32] Michael Kibbe argues that Moffitt is essentially a rehashed Faustus Socinus,[33] who put forth a similar 'sequence'[34] argument in his sixteenth-century polemics. While Socinus shares similarities with Moffitt, there are fundamental deviations. Unlike Moffitt, Socinus nowhere states that the blood of Christ, which is brought into the heavenly Holy of Holies, brings atonement.[35] Furthermore, Moffitt has since shown that these so-called 'sequence' readings precede Socinus.[36] While Moffitt might not follow in the order of Socinus, Benjamin Ribbens, like Kibbe, plays down Moffitt's conclusions. For Ribbens it is 'unclear why Moffitt's work caused such a backlash when other scholars had previously affirmed similar positions'.[37] In fact the contrary is true. The reason Moffitt's work caused such a backlash is because the vast majority of scholars did *not* affirm a similar position.

Ribbens sees Moffitt's work as *deliberately* provocative, and so risks being misconstrued.[38] In short, Ribbens appears to want to mitigate and standardize Moffitt's views so that they suit the framework of 'conservative evangelical scholars'.[39] Ribbens places Moffitt with other 'sequence' approaches, which Ribbens defines as 'each part of the sequence of Christ's death, resurrection, and ascension ... [being] essential to Christ's atoning work'.[40] Yet Moffitt frequently states that the death of Jesus does not atone.[41] Attempts to mitigate Moffitt are likely due to Ribbens being cautious of the

---

[29] 'Content of his heavenly offering', Gäbel, *Kulttheologie*, 473, 474.
[30] See Karrer, *Hebräer*, 2:155; Delitzsch, *Hebrews*, 2:129; Hughes, 'Part II', 197.
[31] Additionally, Moore's recent critique of Moffitt will be addressed in Chapter 5.
[32] See especially Ribbens, 'Ascension', 2–3 n. 4.
[33] Kibbe, 'Finished', 27.
[34] I avoid popular phrases in Hebrews scholarship such as 'sequence approach', 'sequential reading' and the description of Jesus' death as 'preparatory', since they only polarize scholarship when the situation is more complex.
[35] See Ribbens, who states, 'the position that Christ brought blood into heaven is not a "Socinian" position, even though it has been labelled as such', 'Ascension', 17, 18–19.
[36] Moffitt notes that a 'sequential interpretation ... was not the innovation of Socinus, but has ancient roots in the exegetical traditions of early Christianity', 'Heavenly Sacrifice', 50.
[37] Ribbens, 'Ascension', 2–3 n. 4.
[38] Ribbens, 'Ascension', 2–3 n. 4.
[39] Ribbens states, '[i]f the debate is couched in this *either* cross *or* ascension manner, ascension will lose out amongst conservative evangelical scholars who uphold evangelical crucicentrism', 'Ascension', 20 n. 101 (emphasis his own).
[40] Ribbens, 'Ascension', 2 (emphasis own).
[41] Moffitt, *Atonement*, 292. See also, 283–5, 290, 292, 294–5; 'Blood', *Atonement*, 211–12.

death of Jesus being 'diminished'.[42] Ribbens warns of a potential scholarly 'divide between [Jesus'] death and ascension' and he encourages scholars to begin to see 'the vital nature of both in atonement'.[43] However, what if the exegetical conclusions do not associate atonement with Jesus' death? The temptation following Moffitt's book has been to categorize scholars into two camps: those who understand the cultic language in Hebrews to refer to the death of Jesus; and those who understand Jesus' sacrifice as a process, beginning on earth and culminating in heaven.[44] In reality, the situation is far more complex.[45] Moffitt may be criticized for assuming that locating 'atonement' was one of Hebrews' concerns, when the act of 'atonement' is arguably absent (§3.3.4, §4.2.2).

3.2.3 Kerygma and allowing Hebrews to speak

Despite their own differences, Ribbens, Loader, Jamieson and others share one thing in common: they all appear to approach Hebrews' sacrificial argumentation in the hope of finding common ground with what Paul or other NT authors have to say on the matter. Loader is unable to comprehend how Hebrews can place purgative weight to Jesus' heavenly offering, yet also remain doctrinally aligned with other NT writings that appear to locate purgation with Jesus' death. Jamieson sums this up when he asks, 'if Hebrews ascribes no particular atoning significance to Jesus' death per se, how might we explain such a conspicuous departure from the early Christian kerygma?'[46]

Maybe this is the wrong question to ask when exploring Hebrews. Alternatively, one might ask, 'how does Hebrews hope to *advance* Christian kerygma in order to address its own hermeneutical and pastoral concerns?' For instance, it was argued previously that the early Christian kerygma inherited by the recipients could not deal with the problem of συνείδησις (§1.2, §2.2). Restricting Hebrews to what other NT writings say prevents Hebrews from speaking independently. After all, no other text in the NT depicts Jesus as a high priest, yet Hebrews does. This is not a departure from Christian kerygma but an advancement. Scholars should not begin by deciding whether Hebrews is compatible with other NT writers; instead, they should explore the unique innovations whilst asking what it is that the author is trying to say.

The unfortunate consequence of Moffitt's work is that some scholars approach it with their own preconditions rather than engaging with Moffitt's own conclusions.[47] Perhaps this is a weakness on Moffitt's part, since Jesus' death cannot be limited to a preparatory act within a Yom Kippur framework. A solution to this is to observe Hebrews' selective use of Yom Kippur, as argued below.

---

[42] Ribbens, 'Ascension', 23 n. 119.
[43] Ribbens, 'Ascension', 20.
[44] So Kibbe, 'Finished', 25–61.
[45] Jamieson, 'When and Where', 338–68, esp. 338–9.
[46] Jamieson, 'When and Where', 359.
[47] So Loader, 'Revisiting', 263.

3.3 Yom Kippur and Hebrews

Yom Kippur remains the foremost *tertium comparationis* for Hebrews' cultic discussions concerning Christ,[48] but is this justified? This second section will argue that 'elements' of Yom Kippur certainly play a significant role in Hebrews, yet an exact Yom Kippur hermeneutical narrative is not evident. Instead, Hebrews' sacrificial and salvific picture is multifaceted and complex, with Hebrews blending Yom Kippur with other sacrifices and OT narratives. 'Atonement' is also a problematic term and requires close examination; it should be differentiated and not assimilated from other terms like 'redemption', 'forgiveness' and 'purification'. This section establishes an important premise for the next section; it frees both Jesus' earthly life of obedience (culminating in death) and his heavenly offering from the umbrella of a Yom Kippur hermeneutic, allowing both to be viewed as possessing significant and distinctive achievements.

3.3.1 Yom Kippur

Yom Kippur[49] (יום הכפרים/ἡμέρα ἐξιλασμοῦ) is a central ritual at the heart of Jewish and early Christian *imaginaire*, including Hebrews. Regulations for the festival are found in a few places (Lev. 23.26-32; Num. 29.7-11) with Lev. 16 containing a thorough description – a chapter many regard as the heart of the book and the climax of Torah itself.[50] Leviticus 16 notes that the ritual was conducted by the high priest on behalf of the whole community, requiring no pilgrimage to the tabernacle, making Yom Kippur unique in this regard. After bathing himself and putting on a linen tunic and turban (Lev. 16.3-4), the high priest receives two male goats (for a sin-purification offering) and a ram (for a burnt offering). Once the priest has made atonement for himself, lots are cast for the two goats, resulting in one for Azazel (עזאזל) being sent into the

---

[48] As Gelardini notes, it is of 'fundamental importance for the interpretation of Hebrews', 'The Inauguration of Yom Kippur According to the LXX and its Cessation of Perpetuation According to the Book of Hebrews: A Systematic Comparison', *Atonement*, 227. Also A. N. Chester, 'Hebrews: The Final Sacrifice', in *Sacrifice and Redemption: Durham Essays in Theology*, ed. S. W. Sykes (Cambridge: Cambridge University Press, 1991), 57–72; Rissi, *Theologie*, 72–8; Harold W. Attridge, 'The Uses of Antithesis in Hebrews 8–10', *HR* 79 (1986): 1–9. For a critical analysis see Hermann, *Hermeneutische*, 293–328; Fuhrmann, *Vergeben*, 175–83; Gäbel, *Kulttheologie*, 254–79, esp. 276–9; Susan Haber, 'From Priestly Torah to Christ Cultus: The Re-Vision of Covenant and Cult in Hebrews', *JSNT* 28.1 (2005): 105–24.

[49] The HB and later Jewish sources (Tannaim/Amoriam) refer to the festival as the 'Day of Atonements' (יום הכפרים) but the 'Day of Atonement' (יום כפר) is common by the Middle Ages. 'Fasting' and 'affliction' are other descriptors used in referring to this ritual, with Philo often labelling the day simply as ἱλασμός (*Congr.* 89.107; *Her.* 179; *Poster. C.* 48). For useful overviews see Hans M. Moscicke, *The New Day of Atonement: A Matthean Typology*, WUNT 2.517 (Tübingen: Mohr Siebeck, 2020), 55–98, esp. 62–5; Christian A. Eberhart, 'To Atone or Not to Atone: Remarks on the Day of Atonement Rituals According to Leviticus 16 and the Meaning of Atonement', in *Sacrifice, Cult, and Atonement in Early Judaism and Christianity: Constituents and Critique*, ed. Henrietta L. Wiley and Christian A. Eberhart, RBS 85 (Atlanta: SBL, 2017), 197–231; Daniel Stökl ben Ezra, *The Impact of Yom Kippur on Early Christianity: The Day of Atonement from Second Temple Judaism to the Fifth Century*, WUNT 163 (Tübingen: Mohr Siebeck, 2003), 78–141.

[50] Hundley, *Heaven*, 2–3; Nihan, *Priestly*, 371–5. Contra Graeme Auld, 'Leviticus at the Heart of the Pentateuch?', in *Reading Leviticus: A Conversation with Mary Douglas*, ed. John F. A. Sawyer, JSOTSup 227 (Sheffield: JSOT Press, 1996), esp. 49–51.

wilderness (16.8) and the other being presented to the Lord. From this point the priest enters the Holy of Holies and sprinkles blood from the bull and goat onto the mercy seat (16.11-14). After washing his attire, the priest offers a final sacrifice for the people, and then for himself (16.23-8). Yom Kippur is a decisive 'day of purgation'[51] which cleanses the people from 'all their sins' (16.30).

Yom Kippur has caused scholars to not only examine this ritual closer, but to reflect on the very nature of sacrifice.[52] Historically, the violent slaughter of the sacrificial victim has dominated discussions.[53] This approach, as Kathryn McClymond argues, 'ignores or minimizes the other activities that are applied to the sacrificial offering, and in so doing they exaggerate the importance of killing, characterizing it as the essential feature of sacrificial activity.'[54] McClymond, and Christian Eberhart too, point to a variety of elements which constitute sacrifice, not simply slaughter.[55] They note that sacrifice is not synonymous with slaughter/death, but is a holistic narrative often devoid of slaughter.[56] Thus, the role and application of blood within the sacrificial ritual is understood by some scholars to be the essential moment and not the death of the victim.[57] This presents a challenge to contemporary notions for what the term 'sacrifice' often denotes.

3.3.2 Yom Kippur in Hebrews

Various instances in Hebrews allude to Yom Kippur. In particular, 9.1-10 outlines the requirements of worship for the earthly cult. The Holy Place is distinguished from the Holy of Holies and the various paraphernalia and priestly duties are observed briefly (9.2-3; §2.4.3). It is not that Hebrews is unable to provide more information about this 'παραβολή' (9.9) – like other Hellenistic allegorical midrash[58] – but due to his present purposes he cannot speak in detail (9.5). Hebrews confirms that Yom Kippur occurs annually (9.7, 25; 10.1-4) with particular animals (9.13; 10.1, 4) and is performed by

---

[51] For Milgrom it is the 'Day of Purgation', *Leviticus 1-16*, 1009-84.
[52] See my relevant discussion in §5.4.3.3.
[53] René Girard, *Violence and the Sacred*, trans. Patrick Gregory (London: Athlone, 1995), 1-38; *Things Hidden Since the Foundation of the World*, trans. Stephen Bann and Michael Mann (Stanford: Stanford University Press, 1987), 167-8, 205-7, 213-14; Walter Burkert, *Greek Religion: Archaic and Classical*, trans. John Raffan (Oxford: Blackwell, 1985), 54-9; H. Hubert and M. Mauss, *Sacrifice: Its Nature and Function*, trans. W.D. Halls (1898; repr., Chicago: University of Chicago Press, 1964), 1-49.
[54] Kathryn McClymond, *Beyond Sacred Violence: A Comparative Study of Sacrifice* (Baltimore: Johns Hopkins University Press, 2008), 17, esp. 1-24 for an overview of scholarship. So too Eberhart, 'Introduction: Constituents and Critique of Sacrifice, Cult, and Atonement in Early Judaism and Christianity', *Sacrifice*, 1-29.
[55] McClymond, *Beyond*, 29-33, 44-64; Christian A. Eberhart, *Studien zur Bedeutung der Opfer im Alten Testament: Die Signifikanz von Blut- und Verbrennungsriten im kultischen Rahmen*, WMANT 94 (Neukirchen-Vluyn: Neukirchener Verlag, 2002), 187-221.
[56] As McClymond notes, the vegetal sacrifices are often ignored, *Beyond*, 65. Thus, sacrifice (θυσία) can be devoid of death altogether (Lev. 2.1-15) with atonement not limited to slaughter either (Num. 16.46-50).
[57] Nelson, 'Offered', 251-65; Milgrom, *Leviticus 1-16*, 1031-5.
[58] Extensive commentaries and symbolic interpretations of the tabernacle furnishings are given by Josephus (*Ant.* 3.123, 181-3; *War* 5.213-18) and Philo (*Vit. Mos.* 2.74-160, 2.81-2). See n. 8 in §2.2.

priests who offer sacrifices for themselves and for the people (5.3; 7.25; 9.7). Christ is described as a 'ministering' (8.2) 'high priest' (2.17; 3.1; 4.14-15; 5.5, 10; 6.20; 7.20-8; 8.1-3; 9.11) who enters into a heavenly tabernacle (9.12, 24-5) separated by a 'curtain' (6.19; 9.3; 10.20) in order to bring an 'offering' (7.27; 8.3; 9.7-15, 25-6; 10.12-14) through blood manipulation (9.7;[59] 13.11) resulting in purgation (1.3; 9.14, 23; 10.22) ending with the disposal of animal corpses (13.11).[60]

Hebrews draws on Yom Kippur to display the superiority of Christ as high priest. The Levitical priests entered annually into an earthly tabernacle, but Jesus entered once-for-all into the heavenly one (9.12, 24-5). Jesus did not enter with another's blood (9.7, 25); he entered heaven with his own blood (9.12, 24-5). Earthly sacrifices encountered problems (9.9; 10.1-3), but Jesus' heavenly offering achieved a decisive purgation (9.13-14, 23; 10.22). Yom Kippur is undoubtedly an essential motif which runs throughout Hebrews, but scholars have criticized both Hebrews' 'inaccurate' employment of this ritual, as well as the extent to which Yom Kippur should govern Hebrews' overall argumentation.

3.3.3 An overarching Yom Kippur hermeneutic

To what extent should Hebrews' sacrificial argumentation be governed by an overarching Yom Kippur hermeneutic which is initiated by the slaughtered victim and culminates with blood manipulation? For Moffitt, Yom Kippur is one of *the* prime frameworks for understanding the process of Jesus' sacrifice. Jesus' death equates with the sacrificial animal and its blood equates to Jesus' heavenly offering. Moffitt further suggests that the Yom Kippur ritual is currently in motion and will only end when Jesus leaves the tabernacle to return to earth (cf. Heb. 9.28), since this is what indicated the end of the Yom Kippur rite initially.[61] Such a dominant narrative would only be possible if Hebrews cited Leviticus directly, which the author never does.[62] There are a few problems with this hermeneutic. First, Hebrews never explicitly says that 'Jesus' death mirrors the death of sacrificial animals on Yom Kippur' or even that 'Jesus' blood was brought into the heavenly Holy of Holies and sprinkled on the mercy seat'. As will become evident, Hebrews is quieter on the former as opposed to the latter. As Loader points out:

---

[59] Hebrews uniquely describes the act of blood manipulation in the Holy of Holies as an 'offering' (προσφέρω, 9.7). Davies shows that 'entering' heaven with blood is the same as 'offering' himself in heaven, 'Heavenly', *Studia*, 384-7; Brooks, 'Perpetuity', 209; Gäbel, *Kulttheologie*, 276-8; Jamieson, *Death*, 39-40. Contra Wilfred Stott, 'The Conception of "Offering" in the Epistle to the Hebrews', *NTS* 9.1 (1962): 62-7; Church, *Temple*, 416 n. 212. Some LXX references do use προσφέρω in reference to blood (Lev. 1.5; 7.33; Ezek. 44.7, 15). Contra Christian A. Eberhart, *Kultmetaphorik und Christologie: Opfer- und Sühneterminologie im Neuen Testament*, WUNT 306 (Tübingen: Mohr Siebeck, 2013), 144.

[60] The disposal of animal corpses is contrasted with Jesus' earthly suffering; but the bringing of blood is the main comparison, Davies, 'Heavenly', *Studia*, 387.

[61] See Moffitt, 'Interceding', 545. Moffitt is not limited to a Yom Kippur reading, see 'Modelled on Moses: Jesus' Death, Passover, and the Defeat of the Devil in the Epistle to the Hebrews', in *Mosebilder: Gedanken zur Rezeption einer literarischen Figur im Frühjudentum, frühen Christentum und der römisch-hellenistischen Literatur*, ed. Michael Sommer et al., WUNT 390 (Tübingen: Mohr Siebeck, 2017), 279-97; 'Wilderness', *Muted Voices*, 153-72. However, the Yom Kippur narrative (slaughter and blood presentation) is the overriding typology for Moffitt.

[62] Loader, 'Revisiting', 244; Fuhrmann, *Vergeben*, 175-6. Although Philip argues this is deliberate, *Leviticus*, 78. See Heb. 13.11 as a possible parallel with Greek Leviticus.

Employing Atonement Day typology in order to expound the significance of Jesus was therefore far from a simple matter of matching up details ... It simply will not do to read Hebrews in the light of the Old Testament and Jewish tradition and ignore what had already taken place within the traditions of believers in Jesus ... This means we must proceed with caution in interpreting the author's employment of Atonement Day typology. It cannot, for instance, be automatically assumed that because the weight of significance in the antitype lies with the sprinkling of the blood not the slaughter of the animal whence it came, the same must apply to how the author saw Jesus' death. It may be so, but cannot be assumed simplistically.[63]

Loader does not deny that Hebrews employs Yom Kippur typology,[64] but he questions whether it has been correctly employed by Hebrews' interpreters.

A weakness in Moffitt's argument is that it notes rightly the climactic value of blood manipulation, but then deduces that Jesus' death must equate to the slaughtered victim. This is an *argumentum ex silentio*; Hebrews never explicitly makes this connection.[65] This is the setback with applying an overarching Yom Kippur narrative to Hebrews' sacrificial argumentation. By equating Jesus' death with the slaughter of the victim, the weight of soteriological worth shifts to the moment of blood manipulation. As a result, scholarship becomes polarized. But does Yom Kippur typology *have* to be applied to Jesus' death? Is Hebrews expected to draw a correlation between the burning of fat on the altar (Lev. 16.25) and the sacrifice of Jesus as well?

A second problem with this hermeneutic is threefold: the absence of key elements relating to Yom Kippur, the blending of other rituals into Yom Kippur, and the inclusion of other OT narratives associated with Jesus' death. In terms of the inaccuracies, the odd location of the incense within the Holy of Holies (Heb. 9.4),[66] the absence of Azazel and the inclusion of the red heifer ritual[67] are but a few criticisms of Hebrews' employment of Yom Kippur.[68] Some equate these omissions with Hebrews' disinterest in Yom Kippur typology.[69] It is worth noting that 'inaccuracies' may be a misleading

---

[63] Loader, 'Revisiting', 248–9. See also Fuhrmann, *Vergeben*, 175–9.
[64] Loader, 'Revisiting', 264.
[65] Hebrews 13.11-12 provided the author with a perfect opportunity to make this connection, instead, he chooses to associate Jesus' *suffering* and not exclusively his death, with the burnt carcasses outside the camp at the end of Yom Kippur.
[66] This could potentially be a scribal error corrected in the Codex Vaticanus (B) and the Sahidic MSS. See Bruce M. Metzger, *A Textual Commentary on the Greek New Testament: A Companion Volume to the United Bible Societies' Greek New Testament*, 2nd edn (Stuttgart: Deutsche Bibelgesellschaft, 1994), 264. Gelardini interprets the misplacing as deliberate, 'Inauguration', *Atonement*, 252. Alternatively see 2 Bar. 6.7 which locates the incense in the Holy of Holies.
[67] For a defence of the red heifer and its association with Yom Kippur, see Gäbel, *Kulttheologie*, 322–75; esp. 374–5, where Gäbel notes that in Philo and later Jewish writings the ritual was understood as restoring people to participate in the cult. Also Haber, 'Priestly', 105–24; W. Horbury, 'The Aaronic Priesthood in the Epistle to the Hebrews', *JSNT* 19 (1983): 43–71; Delitzsch, *Hebrews*, 2:92–4. Contra Loader, 'Revisiting', 250.
[68] Loader, 'Revisiting', 243–8; Hermann, *Hermeneutische*, 314–15; Fuhrmann, *Vergeben*, 175–83; 'Failures Forgotten: The Soteriology in Hebrews revisited in the light of its quotation of Jeremiah 38:31-4 [LXX]', *Neot* 41.2 (2007): 296–316; Felix H. Cortez, 'From the Holy to the Most Holy Place', *JBL* 125.3 (2006): 527–47; Ezra, *Kippur*, 180–97; Knöppler, *Sühne*, 188–219.
[69] Rascher, *Schriftauslegung*, 151–3; Cortez, 'Holy', 529.

term here. These inaccuracies or omissions can be viewed as deviations and may point to the diverse interpretation and application of Yom Kippur across various literature.[70] Additionally, Hebrews does not limit itself to Yom Kippur. The red heifer ritual (9.13-14; 10.22; Num. 19), the ordination of priests (Lev. 8; Heb. 9.21) and the covenant inauguration (9.18-21; Exod. 24) are all significant texts which the author draws upon. Additionally, Hebrews blends Yom Kippur with the daily sacrifices in Leviticus.[71] Most importantly, other OT narratives and themes are drawn upon, such as 'redemption' and the paschal lamb (§3.4.2, §3.4.3). The burden of proof lies with those who uphold an overarching Yom Kippur hermeneutic. If Hebrews does employ an overarching Yom Kippur hermeneutic, what tradition of Yom Kippur is being followed exactly and how are the deviations or omissions to be accounted for?

A fair conclusion might be that Hebrews is not concerned with the 'mathematical precision'[72] of ritual, but close attention should be given to what *is* included. Just as the description of the tabernacle furnishings are not in detail (Heb. 9.5b), the implementation of Yom Kippur is deliberately selective and at the same time innovative. Rather than focusing on matching exact details, Hebrews invites the recipients to focus on the 'ritual signs' it provides, such as 'blood' or entrance into the 'Holy of Holies', since these host diverse and crucial meanings.[73] This selective approach allows Hebrews to draw upon and blend an array of important early Christian depictions of Christ and his salvific work (§3.4.2, §3.4.3). The remainder of this study will show that Yom Kippur *is* utilized by Hebrews, but the prime focus is blood sprinkling and Jesus' heavenly offering.

3.3.4 The problem with 'atonement'

The next chapter will explore in more detail what exactly is happening in the heavenly tabernacle with respect to blood and 'atonement'. For now, it is worth briefly highlighting a problem with how 'atonement' has been understood and applied in Hebrews, since this adds to the overarching Yom Kippur hermeneutic. First, 'atonement' is an unhelpful and slippery term and the act is arguably absent from Hebrews all together (§4.2.2). As Moffitt rightly concludes, '[a]tonement is a theological term, not a biblical one'.[74] Thus, Hebrews scholarship has explored the highly disputed *piel* verb כִּפֶּר, typically rendered 'atone'.[75] The root for כִּפֶּר occurs 149 times in the MT, with ἐξιλάσκομαι being the most

---

[70] Rightly Hermann, *Hermeneutische*, 313.
[71] The linking of 'unintentional sin' with Yom Kippur (9.7) and references to 'daily' offerings (7.27; 10.11) all point to the daily sacrifices in Leviticus. See the discussion towards the end of §4.3.5 and n. 119 in §4.4.2.
[72] Hundley, *Heaven*, 21.
[73] Hundley, *Heaven*, 23; Fuhrmann, *Vergeben*, 175; Davies, 'Heavenly', *Studia*, 387.
[74] Moffitt, 'Finished', *So Great*, 166.
[75] For an overview see Greenberg, *Atonement*, 3–6, 165–88; M. A. Bennett, *Narratives in Conflict: Atonement in Hebrews and the Qur'an* (Eugene, OR: Wipf & Stock Publishers, 2019), 46–62; Eberhart, 'Atone', *Sacrifice*, 197–231; 'Atonement', *EBR* 3:24–32; *Kultmetaphorik*, 157–77; Hundley, *Heaven*, 159–72, 186–9; Sklar, *Sin*, 1–10, 121–4; Gane, *Cult*, 133–6, 144–62, 217–41, 267–84; Gilders, *Blood*, 28–9, 135–9; Bernd Janowski, *Sühne als Heilsgeschehen: Traditions- und religionsgeschichtliche Studien zur priesterschriftlichen Sühnetheologie*, 2nd edn, WMANT 55 (Neukirchen-Vluyn: Neukirchener Verlag, 2000), 1–26; Milgrom, *Leviticus 1–16*, 253–78, 1010, 1033, 1079–84; 'Sanctuary', 390–9; Frank H. Gorman, *The Ideology of Ritual: Space, Time and Status in the Priestly Theology*, JSOTSup 91 (Sheffield: JSOT Press, 1990), 51–2, 55, 61–102.

frequent LXX rendering (eighty-three times).[76] Milgrom notes that while 'atone' or 'expiate' is the 'customary rendering of kipper ... this is, at best, imprecise'.[77] Some have sought to connect כִּפֶּר with the Akkadian *kapāru/kuppuru*,[78] evoking meanings such as 'rub off' and 'wipe', or with the Arabian *kaffara*,[79] meaning 'to cover'. Over time these cognates have lost credibility.[80] More recently Sklar[81] has encouraged a reading of כִּפֶּר which incorporates the related verb כֹּפֶר 'ransom', thus defining כִּפֶּר as a 'ransom-purgation'.[82] The difficulty here is that כֹּפֶר is a broadly nuanced term and is absent from Leviticus,[83] leading Schwartz to disparage a connection between the two terms as 'false ... unrelated homographs'.[84] Those who read כֹּפֶר as 'ransom' – a payment for wrong – struggle to show how legal contexts apply to sacrifice.[85] Further renderings for כִּפֶּר have been suggested, such as to 'effect removal',[86] or a 'protective connection'.[87]

The problem arises when Hebrews scholarship applies Sklar's definition of כִּפֶּר ('ransom-purgation')[88] to Jesus' heavenly offering. It is worth quoting Moffitt in full here:

> [I]t is remarkable to note that the author of Hebrews seems to work with a notion of atonement very similar to the one Sklar deduces in his synchronic study of the Pentateuch. Hebrews, that is, uses both the language of redemption (λύτρωσις, 9:12; ἀπολύτρωσις, 9:15) and of purification (καθαρίζω and cognates, 1:3; 9:13–14, 22–23; 10:2). Correlated with these terms are the words for or related to forgiveness (ἄφεσις, 9:22; 10:18; ἀθέτησις, 9:26 ἀφαιρέω, 10:4; περιαιρέω, 10:11) and forms of the verb 'to sanctify' (ἁγιάζω, 2:11; 9:13; 10:10, 14, 29; 13:12). As Sklar's hypothesis in particular would suggest, all four terms – redemption, forgiveness, purification, and sanctification – are closely collocated in Hebrews with the function and effect of sacrificial blood ... The act of bringing the blood into God's presence is, in keeping with one of the central emphases in Leviticus, the central act that effects both ransom (λύτρωσις) and purification (καθαρσιμός).[89]

---

[76] Ἐξιλάσκομαι does not occur in the NT, with the other LXX rendering, ἱλάσκομαι, occurring just six times. For a discussion on these LXX terms see *GELS* 251–2; Dirk Büchner 'Ἐξιλάσασθαι: Appeasing God in the Septuagint Pentateuch', *JBL* 129.2 (2010): 237–60; Lyonnet and Sabourin, *Sin*, 137–46.

[77] Milgrom, 'Kipper', *EncJud* 10:180; *Leviticus 1–16*, 1079, 1079–84.

[78] For a summary see Sklar, *Sin*, 44 n. 2; Janowski, *Sühne*, 20–2; Levine, *Leviticus*, 23–4.

[79] Michel Cuypers, *The Banquet: A Reading of the Fifth Sura of the Qur'an* (Miami: Convivium, 2009).

[80] For criticisms see Greenberg, *Atonement*, 3–6; Isabel Cranz, *Atonement and Purification: Priestly and Assyro-Babylonian Perspectives on Sin and its Consequences*, FAT 2.92 (Tübingen: Mohr Siebeck, 2017), 119–21; Yitzhaq Feder, 'On *kuppuru*, *kipper* and Etymological Sins that cannot be Wiped Away', *VT* 60 (2010): 535–45, esp. 540–1; Gilders, *Blood Ritual*, 28–9.

[81] For a summary of Sklar's argument, see 'Sin and Impurity', *Perspectives*, 18–31; *Sin*, 67–79.

[82] Sklar, *Sin*, 187.

[83] Cranz, *Atonement*, 120. Gorman claims כִּפֶּר can have a dual meaning, *Ritual*, 59.

[84] Baruch J. Schwartz, 'The Prohibitions Concerning the "Eating" of Blood in Leviticus 17', in *Priesthood and Cult in Ancient Israel*, ed. Gary A. Anderson and Saul M. Olyan, JSOTSup 125 (Sheffield: JSOT Press, 1991), 54. Viewing כִּפֶּר as 'ransom' is entirely alien to the חטאת offering, rightly Greenberg, *Atonement*, 26.

[85] Rightly Greenberg, *Atonement*, 8; Yitzhaq Feder, *Blood Expiation in Hittite and Biblical Ritual: Origins, Context, and Meaning*, WAWSup 2 (Atlanta: SBL, 2011), 169–70.

[86] Gilders, *Blood*, 135.

[87] Greenberg, *Atonement*, 51.

[88] Sklar, *Sin*, 187.

[89] Moffitt, *Atonement*, 269, 256–76, esp. 263–5.

The issue with this conclusion is that it takes Sklar's highly contested definition of כִּפֶּר and applies it to a plethora of terms in Hebrews. The result is that 'atonement' becomes an umbrella concept for every term in Hebrews associated with the work of Christ (forgiveness, redemption, purification and sanctification). Additionally, since 'atonement' occurs in heaven (within an overarching Yom Kippur hermeneutic), then so does forgiveness, redemption, purification and sanctification. The irony here is that Yom Kippur is focused solely around purgation and says nothing about forgiveness or ransoming. Instead, the renderings 'purge', 'purify' or 'effect purgation'[90] unmistakably capture the essence of כִּפֶּר, at least in relation to Yom Kippur and the 'sin-purification' (חטאת) offering.[91] Other *piel* verbs that accompany כִּפֶּר, such as 'remove sin, purify' (חטא) and the dominant 'purify' (טהר), further complement the meaning of כִּפֶּר as to 'purge'.[92] Furthermore, as argued shortly, 'redemption' is located with Jesus' earthly life and death, not with his heavenly blood offering, with the latter obtaining purification.

3.4 A death that redeems (Heb. 9.11-17)

This is the first of three sections which seek to locate soteriological worth to both Jesus' earthly offering and his heavenly blood offering. Here both purgative (Heb. 9.12-14) and redemptive language (9.12, 15-19) are used to display the earthly and heavenly soteriological achievements of Christ. Jesus is both the paschal lamb who redeems God's people from slavery, as well as the high priest who purges the heavenly Holy of Holies with his own blood.

3.4.1 Having obtained an eternal redemption (Heb. 9.11-14)

Hebrews 9.11-12 presents readers with a flurry of διά prepositions. Christ came (1) διά the greater and perfect tabernacle, not (2) διά the blood of goats and calves, but (3) διά his own blood.[93] 'He entered' (εἰσῆλθεν) 'once-for-all' (ἐφάπαξ) into the 'Holy of Holies' (τὰ ἅγια)[94] 'having obtained an eternal redemption' (αἰωνίαν λύτρωσιν εὑράμενος, 9.11-12).[95] These three διά prepositions have been read in a local ('through') and instrumental sense ('with', 'by means of').[96] It is likely that the first διά is local, 'through' (9.11), since the Yom Kippur imagery is suggestive of movement. The second and third occurrences of διά, with the

---

[90] See Joshua M. Vis 'The Purgation of Peoples Through the Purification Offering', *Sacrifice*, 47; Milgrom, *Leviticus 1-16*, 1040, 1080-2; Levine, *Presence*, 56-61.
[91] Milgrom, *Leviticus 1-16*, 255.
[92] Eberhart, 'Atonement', *EBR* 3:27.
[93] Rendering διά as 'with' has caused hesitancy as to the extent with which to push a literal meaning, see Schreiner, *Hebrews*, 268; Attridge, *Hebrews*, 248. See my later discussion §4.2.1.
[94] See my justifications in the previous chapter for rendering τὰ ἅγια as 'Holy of Holies' and not the entirety of the tabernacle (§2.4.3).
[95] Redemption is 'eternal', not in a temporal sense, but in its quality, rightly Grässer, *Hebräer*, 2:153.
[96] Cockerill, *Hebrews*, 393. Moffitt sees διά (9.11) as locative, and the other two occurrences of διά (9.12) as instrumental, *Atonement*, 222 n. 12. Also, Jamieson, *Death*, 60-1; Mackie, *Eschatology*, 92; Telscher, *Opfer*, 257; Koester, *Hebrews*, 408-9; Cody, *Heavenly*, 164-5. Hebrews 9.6 points to the continual nature of διά (BDAG 224). Contra Church who distinguishes between 'with' and 'by means of', *Temple*, 417-19.

genitive, refer to agency (9.12), that is, *by the means of* blood entrance into the sanctuary is possible.[97] At the same time Jesus' life of obedience, his *own* offering, might be viewed as the reason why he was able to enter, not necessarily because he entered 'with' blood (§3.6.1, §3.6.2). He did not require blood for himself, since he was blameless (7.26; 9.14). Rendering the second and third occurrences of διά as 'through', as opposed to 'with', does not imply the agency/instrumental sense any less,[98] since Jesus entering 'through' the heavenly sanctuary implies that he did this *by* means of his own blood. Agency is further supported by the general context too. The Levitical high priest entered the Holy of Holies, 'not without blood, which he offers for himself' (οὐ χωρὶς αἵματος ὃ προσφέρει ὑπὲρ ἑαυτοῦ, 9.7) but he enters annually 'with another's blood' (αἵματι ἀλλοτρίῳ, 9.25).

Moreover, there remains dispute as to *when* 'eternal redemption'[99] (9.12) occurred. This depends mostly on how the phrase 'εἰσῆλθεν . . . εὑράμενος' is understood. The action of an aorist verb (perfective tense-forms) is typically understood as *preceding* the action of the main verb in a sentence. Yet, recent linguistic discourse challenges this view by exploring examples where the action of an aorist verb occurs *after* the action of a main verb,[100] with the same principle being applied to aorist participles.[101] Thus, this has led some to understand the phrase 'εἰσῆλθεν . . . εὑράμενος' (9.12) to mean that Jesus 'obtained' (εὑράμενος) redemption *after* 'he entered' (εἰσῆλθεν) heaven.[102] Conversely, this reading is not common in the NT,[103] and in Hebrews aorist participles refer to a prior action in relation to the main verb (cf. 1.3). This remains the most common temporal construction for an aorist participle in the NT.[104] Nicholas Moore argues that Heb. 9.12 refers to a subsequent action ('obtaining redemption in heaven') but reads the same construction in 1.3 as denoting a prior action.[105] Moore reads 9.12 in this manner since 'we have' to interpret Hebrews within the Yom Kippur rite 'wherever possible'.[106]

But as argued before, it is not possible, or right, to force Hebrews into an overarching Yom Kippur hermeneutic (§3.3.3). After all, since the issue in 9.12 is 'redemption', why

---

[97] Heinrich von Siebenthal, *Ancient Greek Grammar for the Study of the New Testament* (New York: Peter Lang, 2019), 257; Jamieson, *Death*, 163–4; Gäbel, *Kulttheologie*, 285–6 ('*mit seinem Blut*').

[98] See Wallace, *Grammar*, 368–9; Stanley E. Porter, *Idioms of the Greek New Testament*, 2nd edn (Sheffield: JSOT Press, 1994), 148–50.

[99] Hebrews chooses an uncommon term (λύτρωσις) found elsewhere (Lk. 1.68; 2.38). Its use in the LXX denotes redeeming people and possessions (Lev. 25.29, 48; Num. 18.16; Ps. 110.9).

[100] The extent to which Greek verbal forms grammaticalize time is an ongoing discussion, see Siebenthal, *Greek*, 304–17; Steven E. Runge and Christopher J. Fresh, eds, *The Greek Verb Revisited: A Fresh Approach for Biblical Exegesis* (Bellingham: Lexham Press, 2016); Constantine R. Campbell, *Basics of Verbal Aspect in Biblical Greek* (Grand Rapids: Zondervan, 2008), 11–52. A significant parting of opinion is represented by Porter and Fanning. See Stanley E. Porter, *Verbal Aspect in the Greek of the New Testament, with Reference to Tense and Mood*, SBG 1 (New York: Peter Lang, 1989); Buist M. Fanning, *Verbal Aspect in New Testament Greek*, OTM (Oxford: Oxford University Press, 1990). I am thankful for the years of dialogue with James Sedlacek on this topic, see his published thesis, *The Verbal Aspect Integral to the Perfect and Pluperfect Tense-Forms in the Pauline Corpus: A Semantic and Pragmatic Analysis*, SBG 22 (New York: Peter Lang, 2022).

[101] See Porter, *Verbal*, 385–7.

[102] Ribbens, *Levitical*, 218–20; Moffitt, 'Blood', *Atonement*, 212; *Atonement*, 222–3 n. 13; Gäbel, *Kulttheologie*, 287–89; Porter, *Idioms*, 190.

[103] Siebenthal, *Greek*, 384–5; Campbell, *Basics*, 94; Kibbe, 'Finished', 8–9.

[104] Harris, *Hebrews*, 224.

[105] Moore, 'Session', 527–8; 'Vaine', *Son*, 130–2.

[106] Moore, 'Session', 527.

should 9.12 be collapsed into a Yom Kippur framework when Yom Kippur is concerned primarily with purgation and not redemption? Thus, the language of 'redemption' in 9.12 should lead us to other OT narratives (§3.4.2, §3.4.3), not to Yom Kippur. Additionally, if the grammar in 9.12 is read consistently with other examples within Hebrews (1.3), then 'redemption' occurred *on earth* – presumably in relation to Jesus' death (cf. 9.15-17) – not in heaven.[107] As a result, 'εὑράμενος' denotes a prior action preceding the aorist verb 'εἰσῆλθεν'.[108] Hebrews 9.12 may not explicitly link 'redemption' with Jesus' death, but as explored below (§3.4.2), 9.15-17 does.[109]

It is of further importance to note that the death of Jesus in 9.12-17 possesses its own unique purpose (securing eternal redemption). This is an *objective* and eternal ransoming from sin. Yet it is limited, or restricted, in terms of its purgative nature. Alongside 'redemption' in this passage is the more dominant imagery of the sacrificial cult (9.11-14). The statement regarding Jesus entering the heavenly tabernacle with his own blood (9.12) is the beginning of Jesus' heavenly cultic work and relates specifically to the *subjective* purging of the consciousness. Jesus' heavenly achievements are connected to his earthly ones in that together they form an overall ongoing salvific reality, but their purpose is different: one relates to *objective* redemption, the other to *subjective* purification. From 9.14 Hebrews begins to form one of its prime *a fortiori* arguments (πόσῳ μᾶλλον, cf. 2.1-4; 10.28-9; 12.25); *how much more* will Jesus' blood purify the consciousness from 'dead works' to worship the living God? (9.14). This verse will be examined in greater detail later (§4.4.2). For now, it is important to witness Hebrews ascribing distinctive soteriological accomplishments to both Jesus' earthly life and his heavenly activity. What scholars often fail to notice is that Hebrews is inadvertently asserting that Jesus' earthly accomplishments do not relate to the purging of the συνείδησις.

3.4.2 Death and redemption (Heb. 9.15-17)

If 9.12 stated *when* redemption occurred, then 9.15 explains *how* it occurred. The contrast between the earthly and heavenly tabernacles obliquely leads to a contrast between the 'new covenant' (διαθήκης καινῆς) and the 'first covenant' (πρώτη διαθήκη, 9.15). Hebrews shifts its focus from cult to covenant to explain *how* the Jeremiah prophecy was enacted (8.8-12). It states that Jesus is 'a meditator of a new covenant' (διαθήκης καινῆς μεσίτης) and those who are called into this covenant are promised an 'eternal inheritance', because 'a death has occurred that redeems them' (θανάτου γενομένου εἰς ἀπολύτρωσιν)[110] from the transgressions under the first covenant (9.15).

---

[107] Stolz outlines the supporters of this view, *Höhepunkt*, 227–30.
[108] A different viewpoint is to understand 'αἰωνίαν λύτρωσιν εὑράμενος' (9.12) as an exclusive reference to Jesus, while the subsequent reference to redemption (ἀπολύτρωσιν) in 9.15 refers to the recipients. Jesus 'finds redemption for himself' (εὑράμενος) since he is 'saved from death' (c.f. 5.7), see Fuhrmann, *Vergeben*, 196–98. Contra, Grässer, *Hebräer*, 2:154.
[109] Rightly Loader, 'Revisiting', 258; Cockerill, *Hebrews*, 394–5; Backhaus, *Hebräerbrief*, 320, 328–9.
[110] While λύτρωσις was used in 9.12 (see n. 99), in 9.15 the more common ἀπολύτρωσις is used (Lk. 21.28; Rom. 3.24; 8.23; 1 Cor. 1.30; Eph. 1.7, 14; 4.30; Col. 1.14; Heb. 11.35). Both these terms and others which derive from λύω have a general sense of emancipation/liberation, see Spicq, 'λύτρωσις, ἀπολύτρωσις', *TLNT* 2:423. Montefiore understands redemption here as 'costly liberation', *Hebrews*, 154. Koester links it to forgiveness, *Hebrews*, 417.

Hebrews commences to explain this further by comparing a covenant with a 'testament' or a 'will' (διαθήκη) in a *double entendre*,[111] noting how the latter is established through the death of the one who made it (9.16-17). Every 'covenant' necessitates a death, because no 'testament/will' is legal until the testator dies.[112] Hebrews' creative use of διαθήκη helps to explain the role of Christ's death in establishing a new covenant. Yet his death is the 'presupposition rather than the conclusion of the argument'.[113] The Sinaitic covenant's failure to perfect God's people (7.11) – or to remain blameless by itself (8.7) – is compounded by human transgression (8.8; 9.15). While angels were the initial meditators of the law on Mount Sinai (2.2),[114] Jesus has become the final 'mediator' (μεσίτης) of the new covenant (8.6; 9.15; §5.4.2).

3.4.3 The paschal lamb who redeems (Heb. 2.14-15)

A final question at this point is what exactly is 'redemption' and how does Hebrews connect this with Jesus' death? It will be argued that 'redemption' language (Heb. 9.12-15) should not be conflated with the surrounding Yom Kippur imagery,[115] but serves as a reference to the Passover and the general Pentateuchal narrative of deliverance from Egypt.[116] The majority of scholarship affirms that Hebrews does not link Passover with Jesus' death.[117] This will be argued against below.

The Passover was initially a pre-deuteronomic apotropaic localized family ritual, as observed in Exod. 12. It later developed into a national holiday to be remembered (Deut. 7.8; 9.26; 13.5; 15.15) and became associated with the Festival of Unleavened Bread (Deut. 16.1-8; 2 Kgs 23.21-3; 2 Chron. 30.1-27; Ezra 6.19-22).[118] In the Exodus narrative Moses commands each household to obtain a sheep (or goat), slaughter it and apply its blood to the doorposts (Exod. 12.1-7, 21-2). By doing this, 'the Destroyer' (τὸν

---

[111] The temptation to find a singular meaning for διαθήκη in Hebrews is unconvincing, contra Scott W. Hahn, 'A Broken Covenant and the Curse of Death: A Study of Hebrews 9:15–22', *CBQ* 66.3 (2004): 416–36. As a Hellenistic Jew, Hebrews likely applied both understandings of διαθήκη as ברית/testament, see Filtvedt, *Identity*, 118–20; Moffitt, *Atonement*, 290–1; Lindars, *Hebrews*, 95–6. Hence, they 'inherit' salvation (1.14; 6.12), see Koester, *Hebrews*, 364, 417–18, 425–6.

[112] Based on Attridge's reasoning, *Hebrews*, 254. Contra K. S. Kim who argues for a singular meaning, 'The Concept of διαθήκη in Hebrews 9.16–17', *JSNT* 43.2 (2020): 248–65.

[113] Koester, *Hebrews*, 425.

[114] Angels as 'mediators' of Torah is common in the 2TP (*Jub.* 1.27, 29; 2.1; Josephus, *Ant.* 15.136), with the reference to Mount Sinai a likelihood here, see Attridge, *Hebrews*, 64–5. Jesus as Torah is not explicit.

[115] Contra Moffitt, *Atonement*, 224, 257, 269, 289, 290, 292; Eberhart, 'Characteristics', *Hebrews: Contemporary Methods*, 58–9. Johnsson notes the strange inclusion of redemption, 'Defilement', 297–8.

[116] Hebrews uses the term ἀπολύτρωσις later for those released from prison (11.35) further strengthening the idea of slavery/imprisonment and subsequent redemption. My conviction at this point is similar to Moffitt, 'Modelled', *Mosebilder*, 279–97; Hughes, *Hebrews*, 500, 577.

[117] Koester, *Hebrews*, 504; Bruce, *Hebrews*, 314–15.

[118] Passover was celebrated throughout the 2TP (Josephus, *War* 2.280; b. *Pesaḥ*. 64b). See Daniel K. Falk, 'Festivals and Holy Days', *EDEJ* 636–8; Louis Jacobs, 'Passover', *EncJud* 15:678–80. See Bernard M. Levinson's arguments for a pre-deuteronomic apotropaic rite, *Deuteronomy and the Hermeneutics of Legal Innovation* (Oxford: Oxford University Press, 1997), 57–62. Some attest that it later returned as a family celebration (Lk. 2.41; Josephus, *Ant.* 11.109; Philo, *Spec. Leg.* 2.148, 245; *Vit. Mos.* 2.224; m. *Pesaḥ.* 8.1).

ὀλεθρεύοντα) will pass by and will not enter the houses of the people of Israel to kill their firstborns (Exod. 12.23 LXX). Passover is the ultimate depiction of redemption in the biblical narrative and celebrates the liberation of God's people from slavery in Egypt. Hebrews connects Passover with Jesus' death in a few ways.

First, like the Passover, Jesus' death possesses apotropaic ability. In Exod. 12 the Destroyer is unable to enter the homes of God's people due to the slaughtered lamb and the sprinkled blood on the doorposts. We read that the people are 'protected' from the Destroyer and his striking down of all the firstborns (Exod. 12.1-30).[119] Some argue that the Passover functioned as a powerful apotropaic rite, warding off evil and protecting people from demonic forces.[120] Turning to Hebrews, it is intriguing how the author describes the effects of Jesus' death, noting that through Jesus' death, the Devil, who has the power of death, has been rendered powerless (καταργέω, Heb. 2.14). Because of the 'fear of death' (φόβῳ θανάτου) God's people, all their lives, were in a state of slavery (δουλεία). Through Jesus' death they have been set free (2.15). Jesus is pictured in a Herculean-like manner[121] as the one who comes to bring redemption.

Poignantly, the *power* of Jesus' death is said to have defeated the one who possessed the *power* of death.[122] Jesus' death was not a ransom or a substitution, but a triumph over death (*Christus Victor*).[123] Christ did not face death as a victim, but as an assailant who 'intruded into death's domain in order to overcome it'.[124] Being freed from the 'fear of death' does not denote immortality, nor is it a reference to outside pressures.[125] It may mean that death as an inevitability (9.27) is no longer something to be feared; nevertheless, freeing the recipients from the 'fear of death' should not be limited to confidence in dying. It is important to not overlook the connection the author makes between 'death' and the 'devil'. Outside of Hebrews the close relationship between these two concepts was well established in Jewish apocalyptic writings, where people were anticipating the arrival of a Messiah who would put an end to all demonic oppression.[126] In associating 'death' with the devil (διάβολος), one might read this not as a reference to mortality, but to active demonic oppression. This is aided by the act of freedom (ἀπαλλάσσω). While previously fearful of death – and subsequently the διάβολος – this present fear has been removed. The recipients no longer have to live in fear. Just as the Passover possessed apotropaic ability and prevented death from striking down the firstborns, so too Jesus' death has rendered the devil powerless, meaning that believers are confident of the overall diminishment of his power in their lives.[127]

---

[119] Thus, Passover (פסח) meant 'protection' not 'pass over', Levinson, *Deuteronomy*, 57–8.
[120] T. B. Dozeman, *Exodus*, ECC (Grand Rapids: Eerdmans, 2008), 268–9, 272, 282; Levinson, *Deuteronomy*, 57–8. By repeating the practice of Passover people are continually protected from evil (*Jub.* 49.13-15).
[121] See Jason A. Whitlark's discussion, *Resisting Empire: Rethinking the Purpose of the Letter to the 'Hebrews'*, LNTS 484 (London: Bloomsbury T&T Clark, 2014), 143–52.
[122] Dyer, *Suffering*, 87.
[123] Rightly Allen, *Hebrews*, 219–21. Pace Jamieson, *Death*, 123–4, 170. See later discussions §3.5.3, §5.4.3.3.
[124] Koester, *Hebrews*, 240.
[125] Whitlark's analysis is intriguing, *Resisting*, 124–32.
[126] *1 En.* 10.13; *4 Ezra* 13.1; *Ass. Mos.* 10.1; 1QM I, 1-17. See also Dyer, *Suffering*, 86–8; Schreiner, *Hebrews*, 269; Cockerill, *Hebrews*, 395 n. 39.
[127] If Hebrews was referring to the Passover in 2.14-15, moving to the wilderness motif in the preceding chapters would be a logical progression.

Second, there is a possibility that Hebrews understands the Passover 'Destroyer' (ὁ ὀλοθρεύων, Heb. 11.28) to be the same figure Jesus defeats in 2.14.[128] In terms of the identity of the 'Destroyer' in the Exodus story, there are numerous viewpoints. Some Jewish commentators point back to Exod. 12.12, which affirms that the Lord himself was the subject of the final plague. However, other 2TP texts and later Rabbinic texts read the Exod. 12.23 reference to the Destroyer as a reference to 'Mastemah', a significant figure and chief tactician of demonic oppression in a number of texts.[129] In its retelling of the Passover, *Jubilees* notes that all the powers of 'Mastemah' were let loose to slay all the firstborns in Egypt (*Jub.* 49.2-3).[130] Essentially, Mastemah is *Jubilees*' term for Satan and thus is understood to be the Destroyer (*Jub.* 10.11).

Interestingly, Hebrews' only explicit reference to the Passover mentions the 'Destroyer'. By faith Moses kept 'the Passover and the sprinkling of blood, so that the destroyer of the firstborn would not touch the firstborn of Israel' (τὸ πάσχα καὶ τὴν πρόσχυσιν τοῦ αἵματος, ἵνα μὴ ὁ ὀλοθρεύων τὰ πρωτότοκα θίγῃ αὐτῶν, Heb. 11.28). As with *Jubilees*, the question is whether Hebrews understands the Destroyer here to be the Devil mentioned earlier (2.14). *Jubilees* identifies the Destroyer as Mastemah, and so Mastemah with Satan, but it is not clear, or vital, as to whether Hebrews does the same.[131] Whether Mastemah, διάβολος/σατανᾶς, or Belial refer to the same figure or not, they each fall under the umbrella of figures/descriptors which aim to derail and oppress the people of God. If Hebrews had said that Jesus' death 'destroyed the Destroyer', then this would have been an unmistakable connection.

Regardless, Heb. 2.14-15 and Exod. 12 share corresponding conceptual themes that link Jesus' death with Passover. Both events lead to God's people being set free from slavery (δουλεία, Heb. 2.15). The term δουλεία is found ten times in Exodus and Deuteronomy, and on each occasion it refers to being enslaved in Egypt. In both Hebrews and Exodus, God's people are 'redeemed' by an oppressor. For the Exodus narrative, whether under the influence of Mastemah or not, the oppressor is Pharaoh. In Hebrews, the oppressor is the Devil. The means of this redemption in Exodus and Hebrews is also similar. In the former, the slaughtering of the paschal lamb and the sprinkling of its blood on the doorposts protects the people from the Destroyer. For Hebrews, the death of Christ is the medium for obtaining redemption and destroying the power the Devil has over God's people (2.14-15). Further, in Heb. 9.12 the term

---

[128] Recently Moffitt has sought to make this connection, 'Modelled', *Mosebilder*, esp. 283–95; 'Wilderness', *Muted Voices*, 164–6.

[129] Mastemah means 'hostility' (Hos. 9.7-8) and at Qumran the term is closely connected with 'Belial', another important term potentially synonymous with Mastemah, see L. T. Stuckenbruck, *The Myth of Rebellious Angels: Studies in Second Temple Judaism and New Testament Texts* (Grand Rapids: Eerdmans, 2017), 95–102; J. W. van Henten, 'Mastemah', *DDD* 553–4; *Jub.* 1.19-20; 10.5-6. See Moffitt for references, 'Modelled', *Mosebilder*, 286–7.

[130] In seeking to associate feasts with certain patriarchs later texts associated the Passover with the 'Binding of Isaac' (Akedah). In the same way that Mastemah's plot to kill Isaac failed, so too the blood of the paschal lamb protects the people from Mastemah (*Jub.* 18.18-19). Isaacs' self-offering was later imitated by the Maccabean martyrs, see Geza Vermes, *Scripture and Tradition in Judaism: Haggadic Studies* (Leiden: Brill, 1961), 194–227; James Swetnam, *Jesus and Isaac: A Study of the Epistle to the Hebrews in the Light of the Aqedah* (Rome: Biblical Institute Press, 1981); Barry D. Smith, *The Meaning of Jesus' Death: Reviewing the New Testament's Interpretations* (London: Bloomsbury T&T Clark, 2017), 62–71, 105–13.

[131] Pace Moffitt, 'Modelled', *Mosebilder*, 289.

λύτρωσις (redemption) is employed. Interestingly, the verbal form (λυτρόω) is used frequently in the LXX as a reference to the Lord delivering Israel from slavery in Egypt (Exod. 6.6; 13.15; 15.13; Deut. 7.8; 9.26; 13.15; 15.15; 24.18). This connection further strengthens the idea that Heb. 2.14-15 and 9.12-15 denotes 'redemption' and the Exodus narrative of liberation from slavery.

Finally, Heb. 2.14-15 – when coupled with Jesus' redemptive accomplishment (9.12, 15) – contains a strong connection to Passover in Exod. 12. From this, Hebrews aligns itself with other early Christian writings that depict Jesus as the paschal lamb.[132] When all of this is brought together, the notion that Jesus' death in Hebrews is limited to a preparatory slaughter within an overarching Yom Kippur framework is significantly weakened. Instead, his death is aligned with Passover, unassociated with the purification of the sacrificial cult.[133] Jesus' earthly suffering and death achieved the destruction of demonic oppression and the redemption of God's people from slavery.

3.5 Not to offer himself again and again (Heb. 9.24-8)

The following segment will continue to locate the earthly and heavenly achievements of Christ, with the latter primarily in focus. Jesus actively 'offers himself' in heaven (Heb. 9.25-6) yet is also described passively as being 'offered up' on earth (9.28). Nevertheless, he is offered up *in order to* (εἰς τὸ) 'bear away the sins of many'. Isaiah 53.12 may be evident here (Heb. 9.28), but a substitutionary view of sacrifice is foreign to Hebrews' emphasis on blood purgation.

3.5.1 He offered himself (Heb. 9.24-6)

As before (Heb. 9.11-12), the narrative of Yom Kippur continues to play a key role once Jesus enters the heavenly tabernacle, contrasted here with the earthly hand-made tabernacle (9.24). The primary and initial starting point is Jesus' entrance into the heavenly tabernacle to bring his own blood (9.24-5).[134] This is where his heavenly blood offering is located, not on earth.[135] This is bolstered by the preceding verses which point towards heavenly blood purification (9.22-3; cf. §4.2.2). The purpose of Christ entering the heavenly tabernacle was not to 'offer himself again and again' (πολλάκις προσφέρῃ ἑαυτόν) like the Levitical priests who enter 'with another's blood' (αἵματι ἀλλοτρίῳ, 9.25). Rather, as the subsequent hypothetical argument notes, the reason Jesus was not meant to offer himself in heaven repeatedly was because he would have had to suffer repeatedly since the foundation of the world (9.26). Rather, 'he has

---

[132] See Jn 1.29, 36; 1 Cor. 5.7; Rev. 5.6. Also 1 Pet. 1.18-19; 2.24; 1 Jn 3.5. For Luke, Jesus' death is an ἔξοδος (Lk. 9.31) and subsequently the Eucharist (Mat. 26.17-29; Mk 14.12-25; Lk. 22.15-20).

[133] Janowski argues Passover became a sacrifice post-exile, *Sühne*, 248–9. See also Dany Christopher, *The Appropriation of Passover in Luke-Acts*, WUNT 2.476 (Tübingen: Mohr Siebeck, 2018), 24–5; Telscher, *Opfer*, 124–5.

[134] This is implicitly stated through both the contrast with 9.11-12 and with what has already been said regarding Jesus' blood (9.12-14).

[135] Contra Lane, *Hebrews*, 2:249.

appeared once' (ἅπαξ ... πεφανέρωται) in order to remove (ἀθέτησις) sin by 'his sacrifice' (θυσίας αὐτοῦ, 9.26). This antithetical argument is supported by the contrasting terms 'ἅπαξ ... πολλάκις'. As Delitzsch notes, this 'sets the Lord's own great historical self-oblation for the putting away of the world's sin in contrast with the frequently repeated παθεῖν of the sacrificial victims for atonement'.[136] The Levitical priests' sacrificial responsibilities required repetitive sacrificial acts, whereas Christ's heavenly offering was once-for-all (ἅπαξ), intended to remove sin completely (9.26). Thus, 9.26 is key in maintaining the illustration of Yom Kippur, which relies on blood manipulation inside a sanctuary.[137]

3.5.2 He was offered up (Heb. 9.27-8)

Following the past (Heb. 9.11) and present (9.24) appearances of Jesus, his future appearance is now spoken of (9.28).[138] Just as 'humans die once and after that judgement' (9.27), in the same way Christ, 'having been offered up in order to bear the sins of many' (προσενεχθεὶς εἰς τὸ πολλῶν ἀνενεγκεῖν ἁμαρτίας)[139] 'will appear a second time, not in reference to sin, but to bring salvation to those who are waiting for him' (9.28).[140] With these verses (9.27-8), scholars either argue for coherence with 9.24-6 (continuing the heavenly offering motif), or as a reference to an earthly offering. Hebrews 9.27-8 is the closest the author comes to assimilating 'offering' language with 'death' (cf. 5.7), so it poses difficulties for those who exclusively locate Jesus' offering in heaven.

3.5.3 Offered up on earth in order to bear away the sins of many in heaven (Heb. 9.24-8)

It is possible to view the entirety of this section (Heb. 9.24-8) as a comparison between the earthly and the heavenly. This can be viewed from Table 3. The first column (1) sees a contrast between Christ 'not' (οὐ) entering a hand-made tabernacle (1a), 'but' (ἀλλ᾿) into heaven (the heavenly tabernacle, 1b). This contrast is implied by the progressive negatives (οὐ/ἀλλά). The second column (2) is a contrast between Christ 'not' (οὐδ᾿) having to offer himself 'again and again' (πολλάκις, 2a) on earth, 'but now' (νυνὶ δὲ) he has appeared at the end of the ages to remove sin by his self-sacrifice in heaven (2b). It is a contrast between plurality and singularity, strengthened by the 'οὐδέ'/'νυνί δέ' construction.

The final contrast (3) is one of distinctiveness. 'Just as' (καθ᾿ ὅσον) humans are appointed to die ἅπαξ (3a) on earth, 'thus' (οὕτως) Christ was offered ἅπαξ (9.28) in heaven. The emphasis here is not death but distinctiveness (ἅπαξ). This comparison is

---

[136] Delitzsch, *Hebrews*, 2:131.
[137] Moffitt, *Atonement*, 293–4. Contra Loader, 'Revisiting', 260.
[138] Guthrie points to an *inclusio* here with 9.11-12, *Structure*, 86–7. Contra Cockerill, *Hebrews*, 424 n. 27.
[139] Neither is this a 'divine passive', *Pace* Jamieson, *Death*, 64; Bénétreau, *Hébreux*, 2:95; Westcott, *Hebrews*, 279. Jesus chooses (through obedience) to be an offering in accordance with God's θέλημα.
[140] Ribbens, *Levitical*, 221–2; Cockerill, *Hebrews*, 421–7.

Table 3 Earthly-heavenly contrast (Heb. 9.24-8)

Earthly	9.24a (1a) <u>οὐ</u> γὰρ εἰς χειροποίητα εἰσῆλθεν ἅγια Χριστός	9.25-6a (2a) <u>οὐδ᾽</u> ἵνα πολλάκις προσφέρῃ ἑαυτόν	9.27 (3a) καὶ <u>καθ᾽ ὅσον</u> ἀπόκειται τοῖς ἀνθρώποις ἅπαξ ἀποθανεῖν
Heavenly	9.24b (1b) <u>ἀλλ᾽</u> εἰς αὐτὸν τὸν οὐρανόν	9.26b (2b) <u>νυνὶ δὲ</u> ἅπαξ ἐπὶ συντελείᾳ τῶν αἰώνων εἰς ἀθέτησιν ἁμαρτίας διὰ τῆς θυσίας αὐτοῦ πεφανέρωται	9.28 (3b) <u>οὕτως</u> καὶ ὁ Χριστὸς ἅπαξ προσενεχθείς

strengthened again with the 'κατὰ ὅσος'/'οὕτως' construction.[141] By viewing 9.24-8 in this way, there is no reason to assume that by mentioning death (9.27), Hebrews was invoking Christ's death. This reading allows Jesus' heavenly offering to remain the focus throughout 9.24-8.

For some Heb. 9.28 provides an almost certain allusion to the suffering Isaianic servant motif (Isa. 52.13–53.12),[142] potentially echoing other NT traditions (cf. 1 Pet. 2.24). The following comparison reveals close textual links between these two passages:

Isa. 53.12 (LXX)	Heb. 9.28a
αὐτὸς <u>ἁμαρτίας πολλῶν ἀνήνεγκεν</u> καὶ διὰ τὰς ἁμαρτίας αὐτῶν παρεδόθη	ὁ Χριστὸς ἅπαξ προσενεχθεὶς <u>εἰς τὸ πολλῶν ἀνενεγκεῖν ἁμαρτίας</u>

The prime parallel is the phrase 'πολλῶν ἀνενεγκεῖν ἁμαρτίας'. Hebrews 9.28 may well be a reference to Jesus' death and possibly to Isa. 53.12. Nonetheless, the extent to which Hebrews imports a substitutionary understanding of sacrifice into 9.28 via Isa. 53.12 needs to be addressed.

According to Jamieson, 'Hebrews' allusion to this passage [Isa. 53.12] affirms that, in his death, Christ bore the judicial burden of others' sins . . . As the substitute for "many", Christ bears the retributive consequences of their sins so that those consequences do not accrue to them.'[143] Thus, '[p]recisely by being offered as a sacrificial victim on his people's behalf, Christ bears the penal consequences of their sins',[144] leading to Jamieson's main conclusion that '[w]hat he achieved when he was offered as victim is what he offered when, as both high priest and victim, he presented himself to God in heaven'.[145] The issue here is that a reference to Isa. 53.12 in Hebrews is not unequivocal and neither is a substitutionary reading of Isa. 53. Imposing a substitutionary understanding of sacrifice into Hebrews – Jesus as the 'substitute for many' – is an unwarranted leap.

---

[141] See Gäbel, *Kulttheologie*, 297, for similar reasoning.
[142] Jamieson, *Death*, 169–76; Ribbens, *Levitical*, 222–3; C. Joslin, 'Christ Bore the Sins of Many: Substitution and the Atonement in Hebrews', *SBJT* 11.2 (2007): 88–91; Otfried Hofius, 'The Fourth Servant Song in the New Testament Letters', in *The Suffering Servant: Isaiah 53 in Jewish and Christian Sources*, ed. Bernd Janowski and Peter Stuhlmacher, trans. Daniel P. Bailey (Grand Rapids: Eerdmans, 2004), 163–88, esp. 184–5; Grässer, *Hebräer*, 2:198. F. Hägglund argues for a non-cultic reading of אשם (Isa. 53.10), *Isaiah 53 in the Light of Homecoming After Exile*, FAT 2.31 (Tübingen: Mohr Siebeck, 2008), 68–73.
[143] Jamieson, *Death*, 170. So too Ribbens, *Levitical*, 223.
[144] Jamieson, *Death*, 174.
[145] Jamieson, *Death*, 175.

Hofius likewise sees a reference to Isa. 53.12, but warns against reading a substitutionary motif into Hebrews' argument.[146] Writing against Hofius' convictions, Jamieson says that '[w]hen Heb 9:28 says that Christ "bore the sins of many" in his death as sacrificial victim, the idea of "substitutionarily" bearing the penal consequences of others' sin is not foreign to the overarching cultic framework but instead derives from it and depends on it'.[147] Yet a substitutionary reading is not only foreign to Hebrews' sacrificial thought, but is, as Richard Nelson states, foreign to Israelite cultic logic as well, being found only in later Western traditions.[148] This substitutionary motif, and the function of 'blood', will be explored more closely later (§5.4.3.3); for now it is important to briefly address some of Jamieson's assertions before offering an interpretation of 9.28.

The previous chapter argued that defilement is a severe problem in Hebrews. Since sin acts *like* defilement, then purification must be its remedy. It is apparent that Hebrews sees the prime purpose of blood as purgative (9.7, 12, 13, 14, 21, 22, 25; 10.19, 22; 12.24; 13.11-12). Sin and defilement are not treated as needing to be ransomed or forgiven but done away with (περιαιρέω, 10.11),[149] taken away (ἀφαιρέω, 10.4),[150] removed (ἀθέτησις, 9.26), sprinkled clean (ῥαντίζω, 9.13; 10.22) and purged (καθαρίζω/ καθαρισμός, 1.3; 9.14, 22, 23; 10.2; §4.4.3).[151] Therefore, blood has a unique function apart from death. One does not approach the heavenly tabernacle via the death of Jesus, but via his blood (10.19); it is here that his blood is presently speaking independently, not his death (12.24; §5.4.4). 'Dead works' are not purged with death, but with blood (9.14). Even when Hebrews seems to focus on the importance of death in relation to a covenant (9.15-17) he does not conclude by saying that covenants cannot be created 'without death' but 'without blood'.[152] As Moffitt writes, it is 'highly unlikely that the author of Hebrews thinks that Jesus effected purification by bringing his death into God's presence'.[153] Blood as a 'metonym' for death contradicts Hebrews' insistence on blood as the medium of purgation.[154]

Consequently, in arriving at 9.28, it should be second nature at this point to read ἀναφέρω in line with the terms mentioned above. Elsewhere in Hebrews ἀναφέρω refers to earthly priests who bring an 'offering' as well as Jesus who 'offered' himself (7.27) and finally to 'offering' a sacrifice of praise (13.15). To read ἀναφέρω as 'to bear' in relation to sin in 9.28 seems anomalous. Similarities between 9.26 and 9.28 suggest synonymity[155] between ἀθέτησις and ἀναφέρω:

---

[146] Hofius, 'Servant', *Suffering*, 184–5. So too Johnsson, 'Defilement', 316–17.
[147] Jamieson, *Death*, 174.
[148] Nelson, *Raising*, 79.
[149] BDAG 798.
[150] BDAG 154.
[151] BDAG 24.
[152] Rightly, Johnsson, 'Defilement', 316.
[153] Moffitt, *Atonement*, 275.
[154] Karrer makes this conclusion too, *Hebräer*, 2:156. I am not claiming that blood is not associated with death in Hebrews, it is in places (cf. 9.18; 13.20), but the overwhelming concentration is on blood as *purgative*, with Hebrews deliberately silent about death in this regard (§4.4.3, §5.4.3, §5.4.4). Additionally, while Hebrews connects blood with suffering (9.26; 12.4; 13.12), suffering should not be treated as synonymous with death. Suffering equally describes Jesus' life of temptation and being perfected vocationally (2.10, 14, 17; 9.26; 12.4; 13.12; §4.4.1). Death in this regard is not the focus, but Jesus' ability to suffer and *experience* death; τὸ πάθημα τοῦ θανάτου (2.9).
[155] See Ribbens, *Levitical*, 222–3; Gäbel, *Kulttheologie*, 306–7. Contra Ellingworth, *Hebrews*, 482.

9.26 (A) ἅπαξ . . . (B) εἰς ἀθέτησιν [τῆς] ἁμαρτίας . . . (C) διὰ τῆς θυσίας αὐτοῦ
9.28 (A) ἅπαξ . . . (B) εἰς τὸ πολλῶν ἀνενεγκεῖν ἁμαρτίας . . . (C) προσενεχθείς

Thus, reading too much into 'bearing sin' in 9.28 should be cautioned against. After all, as Bruce notes, the 'bearing of sin implies the removing of sin from others'.[156] Johnsson's rendering of ἀναφέρω as to 'bear away' or to 'take away' sin is compelling, since this is the general tone of Hebrews in relation to sin.[157]

Having said this, it is possible to locate an earthly and heavenly offering in 9.28. This is because the language in 9.25-6 is solely active. Christ 'offers himself' (προσφέρῃ ἑαυτόν, 9.25); it is 'his sacrifice' (θυσίας αὐτοῦ, 9.26) and he is the active subject of sacrifice.[158] With 9.28 however, ἀναφέρω is placed alongside the passive 'having been offered' (προσενεχθείς, 9.28). This active–passive distinction may well point to an earthly and heavenly offering.[159] Nonetheless, the 'εἰς τὸ' infinitive clause would still suggest that ἀναφέρω is the purpose of 'προσενεχθείς' (9.28),[160] that is, Jesus was offered up on earth 'in order to bear away the sins of many' (εἰς τὸ πολλῶν ἀνενεγκεῖν ἁμαρτίας, cf. 2.17) in heaven. This fits with the following discussion which views Jesus' earthly life, culminating in death, as an initial offering (§3.6). Even if Jesus' earthly death is being described in 9.28 as 'bearing sin', it still does not solve the present problem of consciousness of sin, hence Hebrews' emphasis elsewhere on a heavenly blood offering.

3.6 An offering of obedience and a heavenly offering (Heb. 10.5-14)

The following text exists within a larger structure (Heb. 10.1-18).[161] After addressing the inability of the law to bring perfection through sacrifices (10.1-4), a purposeful contrast is invited between the Levitical cult and Jesus' sacrifice (10.5-14). Typically, 10.5-14 is understood by the majority of secondary literature as an exclusive reference to Jesus' earthly death.[162] Even though Jesus' death is not mentioned in these verses, 'offering' terminology (10.8, 10, 12, 14) dovetailed with a reference to Jesus' 'body' (σῶμα, 10.10) are treated as synonymous with death/slaughter.[163] More recently a

---

[156] Bruce, *Hebrews*, 232.
[157] Johnsson, 'Defilement', 251, 452.
[158] In Hebrews προσφέρω is flexible. It denotes a blood offering (Heb. 9.7; §4.2.2) but it also has a metaphorical nuance (5.7; 10.10; cf. §3.6.2). Likewise, θυσία focuses on the act of sacrifice; Jesus offers his blood as a sacrifice. See n. 1.
[159] Rightly Jamieson, *Death*, 48–51, 63–5.
[160] See Wallace, *Grammar*, 590–4.
[161] Cynthia Long Westfall, *A Discourse Analysis of the Letter to the Hebrews: The Relationship between Form and Meaning*, LNTS 297 (London: T&T Clark, 2005), 219–30.
[162] See n. 5. Additionally, Harris, *Hebrews*, 255–66; Jean-René Moret, *Christ, la Loi et les Alliances: Les lettres aux Hébreux et de Paul: regards croisés*, TB 3 (Berlin: LIT Verlag, 2017), 68; Moore, *Repetition*, 175; Compton, *Psalm 110*, 149; Hermann, *Hermeneutische*, 324–6; Backhaus, *Hebräerbrief*, 347, 350–1; Fuhrmann, *Vergeben*, 223–7; Ellingworth, *Hebrews*, 511; Weiss, *Hebräer*, 510–11; Bruce, *Hebrews*, 243; Braun, *Hebräer*, 299.
[163] Jesus' σῶμα is his sacrifice *and* obedience to God's will. See Filtvedt, *Identity*, 158–9; Schreiner, *Hebrews*, 300–1; Lane, *Hebrews*, 2:266; Koester, *Hebrews*, 439.

handful of scholars have taken a different approach, understanding the reference to σῶμα not as a reference to Jesus' earthly body, but rather as a reference to his heavenly *resurrected* body. The result of this reading means that Jesus' 'offering' takes place in heaven (10.10-14), not on earth.[164] Gäbel innovatively attempts to locate both the death and heavenly offering of Jesus in this passage (10.5-14), with both offerings forming one offering in 10.14.[165] In what follows, Hebrews' use of Ps. 40 (Ps. 39.7-9 LXX) in this passage (Heb. 10.5b-7) will be viewed from two perspectives. The first purpose for employing Ps. 40 is to display that Jesus' earthly *sacrificial life* of obedience to the will of God in the midst of suffering (10.5-10) constitutes Jesus' own earthly offering. The second function of Ps. 40 is to show that Jesus' *literal* cultic heavenly offering fulfils Ps. 40 (Heb. 10.11-14) on behalf of his followers. Essentially, Hebrews argues that Jesus fulfils Ps. 40, both in his own sacrificial life of obedience and in a literal sense for his followers.[166] I will follow Gäbel in arguing for an earthly and heavenly offering.[167] Unlike Gäbel, however, I will read Heb. 10.14 as denoting Jesus' heavenly offering only.[168]

3.6.1 The sacrificial life of Jesus (Heb. 10.5-10)

Psalm 40 (39.7-9 LXX)[169] is one of Hebrews' longest cited Psalms, being only the second time where Jesus speaks in Hebrews.[170] Psalm 40 touches on important themes concerning thanksgiving, deliverance, hope, prayer and obedience. The portion of Ps. 40 that Hebrews utilizes concerns God's desire for obedience as opposed to sacrifice. The words are placed on Jesus' lips upon his entrance into the world: 'sacrifices and

---

[164] Moffitt, *Atonement*, 231. Similarly, Ribbens, 'The Sacrifice God Desired', 284-304; *Levitical*, 134, 146-8; Jamieson, *Death*, 81, esp. 71-82.

[165] Gäbel, *Kulttheologie*, 193-201.

[166] It is not a choice between 'Christ's obedience' or a 'literal cultic offering' – it is both. See Hermann, *Hermeneutische*, 326. Pace Ribbens, 'The Sacrifice God Desired', 289-93; Moffitt, *Atonement*, 241.

[167] Moffitt explores the nature of Jesus' offering in Hebrews in the patristic writers. He observes a dual offering in Origen's *Homilies*. Except Origen maintains that it is not the heavenly blood but Jesus *himself* which is the offering in heaven, 'Heavenly Sacrifice', 63. Jesus is not the offering in heaven, but his blood (§5.4.3, §5.4.4).

[168] I adopt Gäbel's language in relation to 10.5-14. Although he ultimately labels both offerings as a single offering, *Kulttheologie*, 201, 473-4. Unlike Gäbel I do not see the forgiveness of sins as linked to Jesus' intercession or heavenly offering, *Kulttheologie*, 418-22, 480, 483, 486. Jesus' heavenly blood and Jesus himself have distinct functions (§5.4).

[169] For a detailed analysis see Madison N. Pierce, *Divine Discourse in the Epistle to the Hebrews: The Recontextualization of Spoken Quotations of Scripture*, SNTSMS 178 (Cambridge: Cambridge University Press, 2020), 113-34; Wolfgang Kraus, 'Psalm 40(39):7-9 in the Hebrew Bible and in the Septuagint, with its Reception in the New Testament (Heb 10:5-10)', in *XVI Congress of the International Organization for Septuagint and Cognate Studies: Stellenbosch, 2016*, ed. Gideon R. Kotzé, Wolfgang Kraus and Michaël N. Van Der Meer (Atlanta: SBL, 2019), 119-31; Karen H. Jobes, 'Putting Words in His Mouth: The Son Speaks in Hebrews', *So Great*, 40-50; 'Rhetorical Achievement in the Hebrews 10 "Misquote" of Psalm 40', *Bib* 72.3 (1991): 387-96; Martin Karrer, 'LXX Psalm 39:7-10 in Hebrews 10:5-7', in *Psalms and Hebrews*, 137-43; Walser, *Old Testament*, 90-102; Steyn, *Vorlage*, 282-97.

[170] See Heb. 1.12-13, also Steyn, *Vorlage*, 282-97; Johnson, *Hebrews*, 250.

offerings you have not desired, but a body[171] you have prepared for me; in burnt offerings and sin offerings[172] you have taken no pleasure. Then I said, "See, God, I have come to do your will, O God"' (10.5b-7). Immediately the Psalm is applied to the establishment of a second (δεύτερος) covenant (10.9), inferring that Jesus has come to enact the Jeremiah prophecy (Jer. 31.31-4) and establish a new covenant (Heb. 8.8-12; 10.16-17)[173] through his death (9.15-17). A key point Hebrews takes from Ps. 40 is that no sacrifice can ever match what God truly desires, since his desire is an obedient servant whose heart has internalized the law (תורה, Ps. 40.8, cf. 1.2).[174] A life so conformed to God's commands and teachings results in obedience and a life that God delights in.

Hebrews follows this discussion around Ps. 40 by stating that, 'we have been made holy by the offering of the body of Jesus Christ once-for-all' (ἡγιασμένοι ἐσμὲν διὰ τῆς προσφορᾶς τοῦ σώματος Ἰησοῦ Χριστοῦ ἐφάπαξ, Heb. 10.10). As mentioned already (§3.6), the reference to σῶμα (10.10) has been interpreted as both a direct reference to Jesus' earthly death, as well as a reference to Jesus' heavenly resurrected body. The former may be possible, but is it fair to limit σῶμα as a reference only to death? How does this interpretation account for the presence of Ps. 40 and its focus on a *life* of obedience? Alternatively, the 'offering of Jesus' body' might be viewed as a reference to Jesus' earthly life of obedience culminating in death, as outlined below.

Contextually, the offering of Jesus' σῶμα likely takes place on earth, since Hebrews places the Psalm on Jesus' lips, not when he enters heaven, but when he 'enters the world' (10.5). It is earth where Jesus has come to do the will of God (10.7). Although a minor point, the compound name 'Ἰησοῦ Χριστοῦ' occurs only here in Hebrews, with Ἰησοῦς potentially reinforcing an earthly setting. Consequently, an earthly setting seems possible for the offering of Jesus' σῶμα. But how should σῶμα and its designation as an 'offering' (προσφορά) be understood? Most interpreters read σῶμα as a 'body' being offered (on earth or in heaven), yet σῶμα could also symbolize Jesus' earthly life of obedience, for several reasons.

First, σῶμα, as well as θέλημα and προσφορά, are unusual terms for Hebrews in reference to purgative and sacrificial language and are only imported here via Ps. 40. Generally, when Hebrews speaks of an offering (προσφέρω) in a *literal* cultic sense it refers to either 'sacrifice/gifts' (5.1, 3; 7.27, ἀναφέρω; 8.3, 4; 9.9; 10.1, 2, 8, 11, 12, 18, προσφορά; 11.4, 17), 'blood' (9.7, cf. 9.25), or Jesus (9.14, 25, 28). But 'offering' is also

---

[171] The inclusion of 'body' instead of 'ears' is the most notable deviation from the LXX tradition. Rahlfs LXX maintains 'ears' with Brenton assuming 'body'. It is probable that ΗΘΕΛΗΣΑΣΩΤΙΑ was misread as ΗΘΕΛΗΣΑΣ(Σ)ΩΜΑ in LXX traditions, see Ellingworth, *Hebrews*, 500. I agree with Bruce who states that 'if our author had preferred the Hebrew wording, it would have served his purpose almost as well', *Hebrews*, 240. Whether 'ear' or 'body' as Isaacs notes, 'it is the human person', *Sacred*, 202. See too Gäbel, *Kulttheologie*, 190.

[172] Psalm 39.7 and 𝔓⁴⁶ D and Vulgate MSS support the singular phrase 'ὁλοκαύτωμα'. Hebrews pluralizes them 'ὁλοκαυτώματα καὶ περὶ ἁμαρτίας' (Heb. 10.6), this is supported by א A C K L P Ψ 𝔐 and other uncial and miniscule MSS.

[173] Gäbel, *Kulttheologie*, 196. The omission of the end clause in Ps. 40.8 (39.9 LXX) does not dampen the link with the Jeremiah prophecy, since the establishment of a δεύτερος covenant is mentioned (Heb. 10.9), contra Johnson, *Hebrews*, 251.

[174] L. Michael Morales' argument that the reference to a 'burnt offering' (Heb. 10.6) is symbolic for Jesus' earthly life of obedience, with his death being the 'capstone', is helpful, 'Atonement in Ancient Israel: The Whole Burnt Offering as Central to Israel's Cult', *So Great*, 37.

used to denote obedience (5.7) and praise (13.15, ἀναφέρω, cf. 12.7). Reading the 'offering' of Jesus' σῶμα in a literal cultic sense would seem odd, given that elsewhere Hebrews puts so much emphasis on the offering of blood (§4.2, §4.4, §5.4.3, §5.4.4).[175]

Elsewhere in Hebrews σῶμα is used in contexts that describe suffering, obedience and faithfulness. In 10.22, the washed 'body' is essentially a 'vehicle of obedience'.[176] In 13.3 σῶμα refers to imprisonment and those who were tortured. Finally, σῶμα is used in reference to the disposal of sacrificial bodies, which Hebrews juxtaposes with Jesus' suffering outside the gate, that is, on earth (13.11-12). Following this analogy, Hebrews exhorts the recipients to offer (ἀναφέρω) a sacrifice of praise, the fruit of their lips, as they, like Jesus, continue to suffer outside the camp (παρεμβολή, 13.13-15). Outside of Hebrews, Paul uses similar cultic language metaphorically to describe a life of obedience with the exhortation 'to present your bodies as a living sacrifice' (παραστῆσαι τὰ σώματα ὑμῶν θυσίαν ζῶσαν, Rom. 12.1). As Richard Longenecker writes, Paul is not referring to a 'killed, bloody, or dead sacrifice, as were the animal sacrifices at the Jewish tabernacle and temple, but as the sacrifice of one's entire person in all its created vibrancy and aliveness'.[177]

By drawing on Ps. 40, Hebrews contrasts the many 'sacrifices and offerings and burnt offerings and sin offerings' (10.8) with the greater sacrifice of a life lived in obedience to God and his will – the offering of Jesus' σῶμα (10.10).[178] Reading σῶμα as a reference to Jesus' earthly life of obedience fits the logic of Ps. 40: obedience trumps sacrificial offerings. There is not necessarily anything abhorrent with rendering σῶμα as 'body', but it is what 'body' *signifies* that matters. Jesus has come to live a life of obedience and he has come to do this within the σῶμα *prepared* for him (10.5). The 'offering' of Jesus' σῶμα should not be limited to his death, but it is broader and concerns his 'his entire somatic existence'.[179]

Accordingly, rather than juxtaposing the obedience spoken of in Ps. 40 with a literal cultic offering, Hebrews, at least initially, uses sacrificial language to describe Jesus' obedience to God's will.[180] Some of Eberhart's conclusions can be critiqued, but he is right in stating that when Hebrews uses sacrificial language, it is not exclusively cultic, but also 'points to Christ's whole life as an example of Christian love'.[181]

3.6.2 Jesus' personal offering? (Heb. 5.1-10; 7.26-8)[182]

A question rarely addressed in scholarship is whether Jesus' life constituted an offering for himself, as well as for others, but certain passages in Hebrews make this assertion

---

[175] *Pace* Ribbens, 'The Sacrifice God Desired', 292–3.
[176] Cockerill, *Hebrews*, 474. I will say more on 10.22 in the next chapter (§4.4.4).
[177] Richard N. Longenecker, *The Epistle to the Romans: A Commentary on the Greek Text*, NIGTC (Grand Rapids: Eerdmans, 2016), 920.
[178] Further Pauline examples exhibit a broader understanding to what it means to offer oneself as a sacrifice to God (Phil. 4.18; Eph. 5.1-2).
[179] Johnson, *Hebrews*, 253; Bruce, *Hebrews*, 240–3.
[180] *Pace* Ribbens, *Levitical*, 147.
[181] Eberhart, 'Characteristics', *Hebrews: Contemporary Methods*, 63. Contra Easter, *Faith*, 109, who equates solidarity with being able to make atonement.
[182] See Justin H. Duff's unpublished thesis which engages with this question in greater detail, 'With Loud Cries and Tears': Sin and the Consecration of the Incarnate Son in the Epistle to the Hebrews (Ph.D. diss., University of St Andrews, 2019).

possible. In two passages (Heb. 5.1-10; 7.26-8) the dual offering of the earthly high priests (for themselves and for the people) is mentioned, but immediately following, Jesus is described as 'offering' something. In Heb. 5.1-10 the requirements of the high priests are set out. They are chosen and appointed to act on behalf of people in relation to God 'to offer gifts and sacrifices for sins' (5.1). These priests are able 'to deal gently' (μετριοπαθεῖν) or 'to restrain one's anger'[183] towards the people, since they themselves are subject to weakness (5.2). The author then adds a clause which is echoed elsewhere in the epistle (cf. 7.27; 9.7), stating that he is obligated to offer a sacrifice 'for his own sins as well as for those of the people' (5.3). At this point one might wonder why the author repeats the need for earthly priests to offer something for themselves, as well as for the people. Was Jesus also required to offer something? This primer regarding the earthly priests (5.1-4) leads to a contrast with Christ (5.5-10). It states that in the days of Jesus' flesh (σάρξ) he offered up (προσφέρω) 'prayers and supplications, with loud cries and tears, to the one who was able to save him from death, and he was heard because of his reverent submission' (5.7). This verse is explored in detail later, with a reference to Gethsemane argued for (§5.3.2). But a discussion around προσφέρω is warranted at present.

Some see προσφέρω as indicating an earthly sacrifice,[184] yet the following verses (5.8-9) suggest that προσφέρω is a generic reference to Jesus' earthly obedience.[185] Hebrews states that 'although being Son' (καίπερ ὢν υἱός)[186] Jesus 'learned obedience through what he suffered, and having been made perfect, he became the source of eternal salvation for all who obey him' (5.8-9). This is his own 'vocational' perfection (§4.4.1). This passage suggests that Jesus' earthly life of obedience, through suffering and temptation, constituted an 'offering' (προσφέρω). Significantly, this verse and 10.10 both link Jesus' perfection and earthly obedience with salvific accomplishments for his followers. It may be suggested, therefore, that Jesus' earthly life was his own offering to God and his own vindication as a high priest who offers his blood on behalf of the people. Within a few short verses a contrast is formed between what the earthly priests need to offer (προσφέρω) for themselves and the people (5.3) and Jesus' own offering (προσφέρω) of obedience (5.7).

A similar passage comes from 7.26-8. Hebrews once more highlights Jesus' moral superiority (7.26) in the context of the earthly high priests who needed to offer a double daily offering, for themselves and for the sins of the people.[187] Hebrews then concludes with an intriguing clause: 'for this he [Jesus] did when he offered himself once' (τοῦτο γὰρ ἐποίησεν ἐφάπαξ ἑαυτὸν ἀνενέγκας, 7.27). The question for commentators here is what exactly does the demonstrative pronoun 'τοῦτο' refer to? It

---

[183] This term (μετριοπαθέω) may include the Stoic notion of 'moderating one's feelings', see Mitchell, *Hebrews*, 108; BDAG 643. It is not to be confused with συμπαθέω in Heb. 4.15 (§5.3.4).
[184] Cockerill, *Hebrews*, 241–2; Lane, *Hebrews*, 1:119.
[185] Rightly, Jamieson, *Death*, 29–30, 30 n. 20.
[186] The NIV, NRSV and NASB render this as 'although he was Son', but the present εἰμί in the verse suggests Jesus 'being' Son was concurrent with his suffering.
[187] See Exod. 29.28-42; Num. 23.3-8.

is favourable to conclude that 'τοῦτο' cannot refer to Jesus needing to offer something for his sins, but only for the sins of others, since Jesus was sinless (4.15).[188] But equally 'τοῦτο' may refer to the whole prior clause (πρότερον ὑπὲρ τῶν ἰδίων ἁμαρτιῶν θυσίας ἀναφέρειν ἔπειτα τῶν τοῦ λαοῦ) or simply to Jesus' own offering (for himself). This reading would not mean that Jesus had to offer something to compensate for his own sin; Hebrews is clear on Jesus' sinlessness (4.15; 7.26). But this verse (7.27) could mean that Jesus, like other priests, needed to bring an offering for himself in order to bring one for the people. Westcott is helpful in stating that '[w]hatever the Aaronic Highpriest did in symbol, as a sinful man, that Christ did perfectly as sinless in His humanity for men'.[189] The earthly priests had to offer blood for themselves and for the people (9.7), yet Jesus was found to already be blameless (9.14), with his own blood becoming the means of purgation for his followers. When Hebrews states that Jesus was 'without sin' (4.15), 'holy', 'blameless' and 'undefiled' (7.26), it does not denote Jesus' inability to sin, but describes Jesus' life of obedience to the will of God – Jesus' own vindication and earthly offering.

3.6.3 Made holy by Jesus' earthly offering (Heb. 2.5-11; 10.5-10)

If Jesus' σῶμα refers to his sacrificial life of obedience, what does it mean that 'we have been made holy' (ἡγιασμένοι ἐσμὲν) by the offering of Jesus' σῶμα (Heb. 10.10)? Hebrews' previous discussion (2.5-18) parallels this passage (10.5-10) and offers additional material which aids this question. Among the possible parallels, two important threads stand out.

First, Jesus' incarnation, obedience and solidarity with humankind (10.5, 6-10) are anticipated earlier (2.5-18). Prior to Jesus' glorification and enthronement (1.3-14) he underwent temptation (2.17-18), being made temporarily 'a little lower than the angels' (2.7a, 9) and in full solidarity with humankind (cf. 2.14; §5.2.2). This description of Jesus' incarnational earthly life (2.5-18) parallels with the σῶμα prepared for Jesus when he entered the world to do the will of God (10.5-10).

Second, the soteriological impact of Jesus' earthly obedient life ('being made holy') from incarnation to death (10.9-10) is also anticipated (2.10-11). We read that God is able to 'bring many children to glory' *because* Jesus was made 'perfect through sufferings' (διὰ παθημάτων τελειῶσαι, 2.10). The following 'τε γὰρ' in 2.11 tightens the connection with 2.10,[190] which states, using the same verb as in 10.10, that the one[191] who 'sanctifies' (ἁγιάζων) and 'the ones who are being sanctified' (οἱ ἁγιαζόμενοι) all have one Father (2.11).[192] From 2.10-11, as in 10.5-10, Hebrews makes a direct link between Jesus'

---

[188] Harris, *Hebrews*, 186; Cockerill, *Hebrews*, 343; Johnson, *Hebrews*, 195; Ellingworth, *Hebrews*, 394; Attridge, *Hebrews*, 214.
[189] Westcott, *Hebrews*, 199.
[190] Ellingworth, *Hebrews*, 163.
[191] See Attridge's conclusion, *Hebrews*, 88–9.
[192] Soteriological significance is attributed to Jesus' death (Heb. 2.14) but must be considered in the context of his whole life.

earthly obedience, including suffering, with God's people being made holy. Jesus' life, culminating in death – that is, his perfection – sanctifies the children of God (2.10-11; 10.5-10).

Thus, when 2.5-11 is read alongside 10.5-10, a connection can be observed. The idea of being sanctified through the perfecting of Christ shares similarities with Johannine thought (cf. Jn 17.17, 19).[193] This is not to say that Jesus did not offer his body on earth, in terms of a historical crucifixion, but rather that the offering of his body was an 'unkultische Darbringung'[194] and was part of a broader act of obedience to the will of God throughout Jesus' life – the main point of Ps. 40. The language of purgation is not used in either of these passages (2.10-11; 10.10), but the earthly offering of Jesus' obedient life brings the people of God into his family by making them holy (2.10-11).[195] 'Being made holy' (10.10) changes the status of God's people from a 'profane' state to a 'holy' state, in order that they might approach the heavenly realm.[196] It is an *objective* transformation. Nevertheless, being able to approach is not the same as *feeling* able to approach. Burdened by their consciousness of sin, the recipients require *subjective* assurance concerning purification. This is solved via Jesus' heavenly blood offering.

3.6.4 The sacrificial offering of Jesus (Heb. 10.11-14)

Having offered his life in obedience to the will of God (10.5-10), Jesus as high priest now offers himself as a cultic heavenly sacrifice (10.11-14). The 'καὶ' (10.11) signals a shift in conversation as the priestly comparison is reintroduced. The Levitical priests stand 'daily' (καθ' ἡμέραν, cf. 7.27; κατ' ἐνιαυτὸν, 9.25; 10.1) offering the same sacrifices which can never 'take away sins' (περιελεῖν ἁμαρτίας, 10.11), but Jesus' 'one sacrifice' (μίαν . . . θυσίαν) is offered 'perpetually' (εἰς τὸ διηνεκές, 10.12).[197] 'For' (γὰρ) with a 'single offering' Jesus 'has perfected perpetually those who are being made holy' (τετελείωκεν εἰς τὸ διηνεκὲς τοὺς ἁγιαζομένους, 10.14; cf. 1.3).

While Gäbel views 10.10 and 10.14 as a reference to an earthly offering,[198] most scholars read 10.5-14 as a reference to a single offering (§3.6). As Jamieson points out, all three references to Jesus' offering in 10.10-14 point to the 'singularity' of Christ's offering (ἐφάπαξ, 10.10; μίαν . . . θυσίαν, 10.12; μιᾷ . . . προσφορᾷ, 10.14), meaning this 'emphatic singularity signals that the author is spinning a single thread'.[199] However, plurality can exist within singularity. Additionally, ἐφάπαξ in 10.10 equally compliments ἁγιάζω rather than προσφορά. Nonetheless, differences exist between 10.5-10 and 10.11-14 which further point to two offerings.

---

[193] Gäbel, *Kulttheologie*, 199–200. Also, Ribbens, *Levitical*, 213–15; Attridge, *Hebrews*, 88 n. 107.
[194] 'Uncultic offering', Gäbel, *Kulttheologie*, 193.
[195] Sanctification is not synonymous with purification (§4.4.1), contra Mitchell, *Hebrews*, 203.
[196] It enables them to partake in the heavenly cult and leave behind the earthly cult, Gäbel, *Kulttheologie*, 197–8.
[197] See my later discussion regarding this temporal phrase (§5.4.3.1).
[198] Unlike Gäbel, I read 10.14 as a reference *only* to Jesus' heavenly blood offering, with Jesus' earthly offering being for himself *and* his followers. Gäbel views both offerings as a single offering, *Kulttheologie*, 201.
[199] Jamieson, *Death*, 76.

Unlike 10.5-10, 10.11-14 is focused around 'removing sins', with its focus being purgative. The focus of 10.5-10 is around Christ coming into the world (10.5), while the focus in 10.11-14 is heavenly, with Christ positioned in heaven 'sat down at the right hand of God' (10.12). A few further additions of cultic terminology are notable in 10.11-14. Jesus, now as heavenly high priest, offers a single sacrifice 'for sins' (ὑπὲρ ἁμαρτιῶν, 10.12). Thus, Jesus' heavenly purposes are purgative (cf. 9.14-15, 23-6; 10.22). The addition of θυσία (10.12) clarifies that a *literal* sacrificial offering is now being discussed.[200]

In 10.10 the effects of Jesus' earthly offering were described using a perfect participle: 'we have been made holy' (ἡγιασμένοι). This perfective nature is strengthened through the use of ἐφάπαξ. Yet in 10.14, when referring to Jesus' heavenly offering, a present passive participle for the same verb is employed (τοὺς ἁγιαζομένους). This perfect–passive semantic contrast can be considered as deliberate in order to display the unique purposes of Jesus' earthly offering and his heavenly offering.[201] Christ's earthly offering obtains an objective static/positional holiness (ἐφάπαξ), whereas in 10.14 his heavenly offering is dynamic and durative, concerned with the ongoing sanctification of being made holy. This is obtained through Jesus' heavenly activity[202] – a subjective aid for practical Christian holiness. This notion of 'divine help' will be introduced later (§5.3).

Moreover, a key term in 10.14 which is missing in the preceding verses is τελειόω. The perfecting of God's people in Hebrews is associated with the consciousness of sin and access (cf. 9.9; 10.1-2). Perfection, while distinct from purification, is in this sense the totality of purgation (§4.4.1). This is highlighted by the contrast between 10.1 and 10.14. In the former, the perpetual nature (εἰς τὸ διηνεκὲς) of Levitical sacrifice is weak since they need to be offered annually. They are unable to perfect those who approach (10.1) and cause a reminder of sin (10.3). Yet the perpetual nature (εἰς τὸ διηνεκὲς) of Christ's heavenly offering has 'perfected' (τετελείωκεν) God's people, leading to a more permanent and dynamic priestly ministry of purgation and the impartation of holiness (10.14).

3.7 Conclusion

This chapter argued that Hebrews purposefully distinguishes between what Jesus achieves on earth and what he achieves in heaven. Hebrews is not pitting Jesus' death against a heavenly offering, or blurring them into one 'singular, sacrificial act'.[203] Rather, Jesus' incarnational life of obedience, culminating in death, is a multifaceted salvific image obtaining certain objective soteriological realities (§3.4, §3.4.1, §3.4.2, §3.4.3,

---

[200] Gäbel, *Kulttheologie*, 201.
[201] Allen, *Hebrews*, 503; Lane, *Hebrews*, 2:266; Attridge, *Hebrews*, 280–1. There is also the option to take 'ἁγιαζομένους' as middle, which places the responsibility for being made holy on the believers.
[202] One might say that 'the enduring effects of Christ's act is an ongoing present reality', Attridge, *Hebrews*, 281. Also Gordon J. Thomas, 'The Perfecting of Christ and the Perfecting of Believers in Hebrews', in *Holiness and Ecclesiology in The New Testament*, ed. Kent E. Brower and Andy Johnson (Grand Rapids: Eerdmans, 2007), 303–4.
[203] *Pace* Ribbens, *Levitical*, 133. See also Moore, *Repetition*, 12–13; Cody, *Heavenly*, 170–9.

§3.6.3). Yet, only Jesus' heavenly offering is purgative and only this purges the subjective consciousness of sin (§3.4.1, §3.5.1, §3.6.4). Thus, at points, it may be conceivable to speak of two offerings[204] (§3.6.3, §3.6.4). However, it is not simply that Jesus' earthly offering is 'nicht opferkultisch',[205] but that it lacks the purgative power of his heavenly blood offering, in relation to the consciousness of sin.

Yom Kippur is an important ritual for Hebrews, but the author only seems to draw out its significance once Jesus enters the heavenly tabernacle. Therefore, an overarching Yom Kippur hermeneutic, beginning with the slaughtered victim comparison, is elusive in Hebrews. This hermeneutic causes significant terms ('redemption'/'sanctification') to lose their own distinctiveness, as they are absorbed into the 'atonement' and the 'logic' of Hebrews' apparent overarching Yom Kippur narrative. Additionally, it hinders the richness and diversity of Hebrews' argumentation. On earth, Jesus obtained eternal redemption (§3.4, §3.4.1, §3.4.2). He is the paschal lamb whose earthly offering defeated the Devil and obtained apotropaic assurance (§3.4.3). Jesus' earthly life from beginning to end displayed unmatchable obedience, so much so that his earthly life can be said to sanctify believers (§3.6.3). Hebrews' use of Ps. 40 emphasizes that Jesus' life and heavenly activity constitutes two offerings. Jesus' very life was an offering for himself and for others (§3.6.2). Jesus was 'offered up' on earth (§3.5.3), but 'self-offered' in heaven (§3.5.1, §3.6.4). While Jesus' earthly achievements are vast, the purification of the consciousness is not one of them. It is only through Jesus' heavenly blood offering that the purgation of the consciousness can be located.

---

[204] Rightly Gäbel, *Kulttheologie*, 201, 473–4.
[205] 'Non sacrificial', Gäbel, *Kulttheologie*, 9. Hebrews shows that Jesus' death lacks the purgative power of the heavenly offering. Contra Ribbens, *Levitical*, 134 n. 230. While Christ's earthly life and enthronement are tied together, they are not to be associated with purgative language. Hebrews' employment of Ps. 110 acts as a motivation for the recipients and a celebration of the Son (§5.2.2).

4

How much more the blood of Christ? Ritual, perfection and the finality of purgation

4.1 Introduction

The previous chapter located the earthly and heavenly achievements of Christ and concluded that the heavenly offering was restricted to the purgation of the consciousness. The purpose of this chapter is to take a detailed look at the role of συνείδησις within Hebrews' cultic argumentation. Therefore, the role of blood and the purification of the heavenly tabernacle will be a necessary starting point. Most scholars understand purification in Hebrews as a συνείδησις–σάρξ/internal–external juxtaposition, whereby Levitical sacrifice purged externally (σάρξ) rather than internally (συνείδησις). This embellished contrast will be critiqued with the relationship between συνείδησις and σάρξ being examined. It will be argued that Levitical sacrifice *is* concerned with the συνείδησις, as seen through the concept of אָשֵׁם. This term is typically rendered as 'to be guilty', yet 'being conscious of sin' will be my suggestive rendering. By linking συνείδησις and אָשֵׁם the psychological significance of sacrificial ritual is unearthed and the supposed negative internal–external juxtaposition can be disregarded. It was not that the earthly cult could not purify the consciousness but that it required repetitive sacrifices to do so. This conclusion raises the question of 'distinctiveness' and so the 'how much more' of Christ's heavenly blood offering will be regarded as a qualitative type of purification. It is 'perfection' – the finality of purgation.

4.2 Purifying the heavenly tabernacle

Sin and defilement impact – and subsequently connect – both people and the heavenly tabernacle in Hebrews (§2.3.1, §2.3.3, §2.5.6). Jesus' heavenly blood offering provides a solution to this defilement (§3.4.1, §3.5.1, §3.6.4). The purpose of the following section is to bring these ideas together and look closer at the implications of Jesus' heavenly blood offering and the purgation of the heavenly tabernacle.

4.2.1 Entering with blood

According to Hebrews, the solution to a defiled heavenly tabernacle is purification and the medium of this purgation is blood. Hebrews never says 'Jesus offered his blood in heaven', but it is strongly implied. For instance, in describing the work of an earthly priest, Hebrews states that he goes into the Holy of Holies 'not without blood which he offers' (οὐ χωρὶς αἵματος ὃ προσφέρει) for himself and for the unintentional sins of the people (Heb. 9.7). This statement confirms that blood is brought into a tabernacle in order to purge sins. This verse is also important because it describes blood as an 'offering'. Consequently, when Hebrews speaks of Jesus entering into the heavenly tabernacle with 'his own blood' (ἰδίου αἵματος) a few verses later (9.11-12), it is instinctively assumed (via 9.7) that Jesus offered his blood in heaven.

Hebrews 9.24-6 reiterates this same pattern but with further additions. As before, Jesus is described as entering a heavenly sanctuary (9.24), it states that Jesus did this not to 'offer himself' (προσφέρῃ ἑαυτόν) again and again, as the high priest enters the Holy of Holies year after year with blood that is not his own (9.25). Here 'offering himself' is paralleled with blood, showing that Jesus' blood offering in heaven somehow is linked to offering his very self to God. Offering himself could be linked to his earthly life and death, which inevitably leads to offering his blood in heaven. Or, offering himself could be viewed as shorthand for offering his own blood in heaven. This same construction is evident earlier (7.26-7; 9.14). Furthermore, 9.26 describes this blood self-offering as 'his sacrifice' (θυσίας αὐτοῦ).[1] Further examples enforce the notion that what Jesus brought into the heavenly tabernacle was blood (12.24; 13.11-12).

4.2.2 Purifying the heavenly tabernacle (Heb. 1.3; 2.17; 9.23)

Yom Kippur provides the context for Jesus' heavenly blood purgation (§3.3.2) and there are a couple of key passages which point to this. Before his enthronement Jesus made 'purification for sins' (1.3). Of course, this can be read as occurring at any given time prior to the act of sitting down, but Hebrews consistently locates purgative language in the heavenly realm and so this leads one to believe that 'purification for sins' is a heavenly event. Hebrews 2.17 also provides a reference to Jesus' heavenly blood purgation. It states that Jesus' solidarity with humanity enabled him to be a faithful high priest 'to make a sacrifice of atonement for the sins of the people' (εἰς τὸ ἱλάσκεσθαι τὰς ἁμαρτίας τοῦ λαοῦ, NRSV). The term ἱλάσκομαι divides scholars and ties into the earlier discussion concerning 'atonement' (§3.3.4). Typically, ἱλάσκομαι is understood as either 'to propitiate'[2] or 'to expiate'.[3] Some argue for a blend of the two,[4] as Ribbens writes, '[i]t is only by means of Christ's expiatory sacrifice that God's wrath toward sin is appeased'.[5]

---

[1] This can be read as a possessive ('his sacrifice') or verbal genitive ('sacrifice of himself') see Harris, *Hebrews*, 247.
[2] Lane, *Hebrews*, 1:65–6.
[3] Knöppler, *Sühne*, 36–56, 118–216.
[4] Ribbens, *Levitical*, 206–11; Joslin, 'Bore', 74–103; Mitchell, *Hebrews*, 77; Koester, *Hebrews*, 241; Spicq, *Hébreux*, 2:257.
[5] Ribbens, *Levitical*, 208, 211.

Yet, since 'propitiate' denotes opposing the wrath of a specific person, 'expiate' seems more favourable,[6] since its direct object is sin and not God.[7] God's wrath is clearly displayed in Hebrews,[8] but sin requires purgation, not propitiation (cf. 1.3). Kistemaker claims that those who choose 'expiate' over 'propitiate' do so because they do not want to represent an angry God over a God of love.[9] Although, propitiation can depict God positively, since he removes the condemnation brought by sin. Others have suggested a non-cultic rendering for ἱλάσκομαι, since the phrase 'ἱλάσκεσθαι τὰς ἁμαρτίας' has no LXX equivalent. It is understood in the light of Christ's high priestly intercession, either as 'to have mercy'[10] or as a generic reference for helping believers overcome temptation to sin (as opposed to help after they have sinned).[11]

It may be possible to define ἱλάσκομαι as 'atonement', but this depends on how atonement is defined. In the context of Yom Kippur, כִּפֶּר, via the sin-purification offering (חַטָּאת) means to 'purge' (§3.3.4). In Heb. 2.17, the context is the heavenly tabernacle implied by Jesus' priestly function. Since the direct object of ἱλάσκομαι is the 'sins of the people' in 2.17 (cf. Lev. 16.16, 30, 34) then it makes sense to render ἱλάσκομαι similarly as to 'purge'. The sins are being purged and removed from the heavenly tabernacle (cf. Heb. 1.3; 9.14; 22-3; 10.2). In this sense, it may be right to conclude that Hebrews never once refers to 'atonement'.[12]

Hebrews' most explicit reference to purging the heavenly tabernacle is found in 9.23. This verse was introduced earlier with relation to defilement (§2.5.6), but its connection with purification has been unexamined. Sandwiched between blood purgation (9.21-2) and Jesus' heavenly offering (9.24-6; §3.5.1), 9.23 states, 'thus, on the one hand, it is necessary for the sketches of the heavenly things to be purified with these, but, on the other hand, the heavenly things themselves [require] better sacrifices than these' (Ἀνάγκη οὖν τὰ μὲν ὑποδείγματα τῶν ἐν τοῖς οὐρανοῖς τούτοις καθαρίζεσθαι, αὐτὰ δὲ τὰ ἐπουράνια κρείττοσιν θυσίαις παρὰ ταύτας, 9.23).[13] The suggestion that the heavenly things required purification stuns some readers. Scholars

---

[6] See Ribbens, *Levitical*, 209–12; Attridge, *Hebrews*, 96 n. 192; David Hill, *Greek Words and Hebrew Meanings: Studies in the Semantics of Soteriological Terms*, SNTSMS 5 (Cambridge: Cambridge University Press, 1967), 25–36; Michel, *Hebräer*, 168–96; Spicq, *Hébreux*, 2:48; Delitzsch, *Hebrews*, 1:145–50; C. H. Dodd, 'ΙΛΑΣΚΕΚΘΑΙ, its Cognates, Derivatives, and Synonyms, in the Septuagint', *JTS* 32.128 (1931): 352–60.
[7] See Richardson, *Pioneer*, 33; Fuhrmann, 'Failures', 310.
[8] Yet it is saved for those who reject him (Heb. 2.2, 3; 3.11, 18; 4.5; 6.8; 9.22; 10.27, 30–1, 39; 12.25, 29).
[9] Simon J. Kistemaker, 'Atonement in Hebrews: "A Merciful and Faithful High Priest"', in *The Glory of the Atonement: Biblical, Historical & Practical Perspectives: Essays in Honour of Roger Nicole*, ed. Charles E. Hill and Frank A. James III (Downers Grove, IL: InterVarsity Press, 2004), 164.
[10] Gäbel, *Kulttheologie*, 213–27; Fuhrmann, 'Failures', 309–12; *Vergeben*, 24–30 (cf. Lk. 18.13). Contra Knöppler who sees the plurality of sins (τὰς ἁμαρτίας) as a reference to Yom Kippur, *Sühne*, 215–17; Richardson, *Pioneer*, 34–5. See my later discussion (§5.3.3).
[11] Loader, 'Revisiting', 268–9.
[12] Elsewhere the *place* of atonement is mentioned (ἱλαστήριον, 9.5; possibly ἵλεως, 8.12), see Knöppler, *Sühne*, 192–5). Yet 'atonement', lexically in reference to the act is absent in Hebrews. Rightly George H. Guthrie, 'Time and Atonement in Hebrews', *So Great*, 212.
[13] I understand 'these' (τούτοις) as a reference to the blood manipulation discussed earlier, see n. 171 in §2.5.6.

are hesitant to accept this interpretation,[14] describing it as 'preposterous'.[15] The result of this apparent absurdity has conjured up multiple interpretations.[16]

This verse is treated as an apocalyptic reference to Satan being cast from heaven.[17] This motif does occur in the NT (Lk. 10.18; Jn 12.31; Rev. 2.9) and evil beings are present in the heavens (Eph. 6.12; Col. 1.20), but Hebrews scholarship shows little enthusiasm for this theme. Others understand Heb. 9.23 as a metaphorical reference to an ecclesiological purification of the church, as the temple,[18] or the συνείδησις.[19] Rather than seeing *both* the συνείδησις and the heavenly tabernacle as being purged (as argued below), this viewpoint interprets heavenly purification as a symbolic reference for the purification of the church. It is also unlikely that the purification of the heavens/συνείδησις refers to degrees of pollution,[20] since this assumes a Platonic dualistic reading, whereby the earthly cult relates to external purity and the heavenly cult deals with internal purity (συνείδησις). A contrast is undoubtedly made between the earthly cult and the heavenly cult, except it is not metaphysical. The heavens and earth are created realms (Gen. 1.1), so the potential for either of these realms to become defiled is not unfounded, but a defiled heaven in a Platonic worldview is inconceivable.

Alternatively, the language of purification (καθαρίζω) is read as inauguration (ἐγκαινίζω)[21] or both.[22] This is due to the previous verses which connect inauguration and blood manipulation (Heb. 9.18-22), discussed in more detail below (§4.4.3). Nevertheless, supplementing inauguration language within 9.23 betrays and distorts Hebrews' insistence elsewhere concerning purification (9.14, 22; 10.2; cf. 1.3). Even if consecration or inauguration language was employed, it would not solve the difficulty of 9.23, since consecration still requires sacrificial blood and subsequent cleansing.[23] Covenant inauguration is the context for 9.23, yet the *immediate* context, the verse prior, is concerned with removing sin through the purification of blood (9.22).

---

[14] Harris, *Hebrews*, 242; Loader, 'Revisiting', 259-60; Schenck, 'Archaeology', *Hebrews in Contexts*, 253; Moore, *Repetition*, 169 n. 90; Schreiner, *Hebrews*, 283; Montefiore, *Hebrews*, 160; Spicq, *Hébreux*, 2:266-7; Moffatt, *Hebrews*, 132.

[15] Schenck, *Cosmology*, 168.

[16] For a thorough summary see Jamieson, *Death*, 16-17, 40-2, 49-51; '9.23', 569-87; Ribbens, *Levitical*, 119-23; Gäbel, *Kulttheologie*, 419-24. D. J. MacLeod proposes at least nine perspectives on 9.23, 'The Cleansing of the True Tabernacle', *BSac* 152.605 (1995): 60-71, but is hesitant towards a literal reading, 70.

[17] Michel, *Hebräer*, 323-4. Hebrews does not employ Satan (σατανᾶς) like other NT writers; however, the Devil (διάβολος) is mentioned (Heb. 2.14) but not to the extent with which to warrant Michel's conclusions. See *1 En*. 6-7.

[18] Fuhrmann, *Vergeben*, 217-19; Bruce, *Hebrews*, 228-9; Cody, *Heavenly*, 192-6.

[19] Schenck, 'Archaeology', *Hebrews in Contexts*, 253; *Cosmology*, 168; Thompson, *Hebrews*, 192; Isaacs, *Sacred*, 212 n. 2; Attridge, *Hebrews*, 261-62; Montefiore, *Hebrews*, 160; Schierse, *Verheissung*, 48.

[20] Pace Gäbel, who argues for an internal-external dualism. He aligns the purification of the συνείδησις with the severity of sins and the degrees of pollution; the συνείδησις is a 'deeper' purification, *Kulttheologie*, 422-4. Instead, purifying the συνείδησις relates to one's general awareness of sin and need for ritual assurance.

[21] Spicq, *Hébreux*, 2:267; Westcott, *Hebrews*, 272-3. Since the second clause in 9.23 does not contain an overt verb, καθαρίζω is implied. Examples where καθαρίζω and ἐγκαινίζω are used interchangeably (Exod. 29.36; Lev. 8.15) does not mean they are equivalent in Hebrews.

[22] Gäbel, *Kulttheologie*, 420-4; Compton, *Psalm 110*, 138-41; Ribbens, *Levitical*, 122-3; McKelvey, *Pioneer*, 96; Richardson, *Pioneer*, 42; Cockerill, *Hebrews*, 417; Moffitt, *Atonement*, 225 n. 20.

[23] Delitzsch, *Hebrews*, 2:124.

Furthermore, the 'therefore' (οὖν) beginning 9.23a does not automatically presuppose covenant inauguration in 9.23b.[24] Rather, the occurrence and meaning of καθαρίζω in 9.22 supplies the same meaning in 9.23. To understand καθαρίζω as inauguration in 9.23 leads to a 'watering-down'[25] of the text. Throughout Hebrews blood as the medium of purgation is the central concern, not whether ἐγκαινίζω and καθαρίζω are synonymous. After all, *blood* is what inaugurates (9.20; 10.29), provides access (9.7, 12, 25; 10.19), holiness (9.13), purgation (9.14, 22) and perfection (9.9, 14; 10.14).

Others accept Heb. 9.23 as a reference to purifying the heavens,[26] with some scholars pointing to Jewish apocalyptic texts which affirm the importance of maintaining purity for ministering angels (4Q400 1 I, 15-20) and sinful angels (*1 En.* 7.1-6; 12.3-4; 15.1-7). Thus, Hebrews' assertion that the heavenly tabernacle had to be purified might have been acceptable within Jewish apocalyptic thought.[27] Nonetheless, these texts do not speak of heavenly *things* becoming defiled, only angels. While it is true that a defiled individual is a threat to his or her environment,[28] references to the heavens becoming defiled are absent in these texts and likewise defiled angels are absent in Hebrews. The *Songs of the Sabbath Sacrifice* and Hebrews are both aware of the threat of heavenly defilement, yet angels in the Qumran *Songs* are only protecting from possible impurity (4Q400 1 I, 14-20; 4Q402 4, 3-10).[29] It is only Jesus in Hebrews who actually purges the heavens.

Parallels with Second Temple texts are not required; after all, Yom Kippur already affirms that a holy sanctuary can become defiled and purged. Employing Yom Kippur typology in relation to the heavenly realm allows Hebrews to affirm defilement and purgation within the heavenly tabernacle. This is possible since the following verses (Heb. 9.24-6) locate 9.23 within a Yom Kippur framework (§3.5.1).[30] The importance of Jacob Milgrom has already been raised (§2.3.1). By viewing the tabernacle as collecting and, through sacrifice, removing defilement, Milgrom showed that it is the sanctuary that requires purging, not the people.[31] Therefore, the question might be asked, in speaking of bringing blood into a heavenly sanctuary and purging it, might Hebrews also share a similar understanding of the cult which Milgrom expresses? Might Hebrews interpret sin like a 'miasma', attaching itself to the heavenly tabernacle? As shown earlier, Hebrews understands the status of God's people to be intrinsically linked to the status of the heavenly tabernacle (§2.3.1, §2.3.3, §2.5.6). If Hebrews includes the recipients as worshippers within a heavenly cult, then the same reasoning applies with regards to defilement and purgation. If Israelite sin defiled the sancta (Lev. 16.16, 19; 20.3; 21.23; Num. 19.20) and Yom Kippur purified both the community and the

---

[24] Ribbens, *Levitical*, 120.
[25] Johnsson, 'Defilement', 44.
[26] Jamieson, '9.23', 582; Calaway, *Sabbath*, 157-8; Cockerill, *Hebrews*, 415-17; Mackie, *Eschatology*, 177; Koester, *Hebrews*, 421, 427; Grässer, *Hebräer*, 2:188; Weiss, *Hebräer*, 484; Lane, *Hebrews*, 2:247; Johnsson, 'Defilement', 330-3.
[27] Jamieson, '9.23', 582. See Church, *Temple*, 153; Ezra, *Kippur*, 184 n. 180, 184. Furthermore, Job 15.15 is often drawn upon in support of this, with similar comparisons made later (*1 Clem.* 39.5).
[28] Moffitt, *Atonement*, 225-6 n. 20.
[29] See Calaway, *Sabbath*, 158; Alexander, *Mystical Texts*, 13-73, esp. 22-3.
[30] Loader misses the link between Heb. 9.11-12 and 9.24-5, with 9.11-12 informing and implying a blood offering in 9.23-6, 'Revisiting', 259-60 (cf. §3.5).
[31] Milgrom, *Leviticus 1-16*, 254-8.

tabernacle (Lev. 16.16, 30),[32] then the same rationale can be applied to the recipients of Hebrews and the heavenly cult.[33] Furthermore, a connection between the defilement of the heavenly tabernacle and the recipients' συνείδησις is evident here. If purging the heavenly tabernacle results in the purification of the συνείδησις (Heb. 9.14; 10.2, 22) it can be argued that the recipients were concerned with the status of the heavenly tabernacle just as much as the author. Perhaps the recipients' own consciousness of sin may have been triggered by an awareness of the defilement of the heavenly tabernacle? Purging the heavenly tabernacle appears to create a sense of assurance for the recipients whereby they are purified from guilt and the awareness of sin (§5.4).

4.3 The drama of sacrifice: Purifying the consciousness

The majority of scholarship affirms that the purification of the συνείδησις is unique to Hebrews because Levitical sacrifices were supposedly 'limited' to external purification. The juxtaposing of συνείδησις and σάρξ (Heb. 9.13-14) apparently confirms this assertion. This section will instead argue that σάρξ and συνείδησις represent an earthly–heavenly contrast, not an internal–external contrast. Additionally, Levitical אשם provides a connection with συνείδησις and further endorses the belief that both Hebrews and Levitical sacrifices had an internal impact.

4.3.1 An internal–external/συνείδησις–σάρξ purification contrast?

The most popular understanding of purification in Hebrews scholarship is the internal–external model. This concludes that Levitical sacrifices were concerned primarily with 'external' purgation, while Jesus' offering resulted in 'internal' purgation.[34] Hebrews 9.13-14 is an example of this (cf. 9.9-10; 10.22):

9.13 εἰ γὰρ τὸ αἷμα τράγων καὶ ταύρων καὶ σποδὸς δαμάλεως ῥαντίζουσα τοὺς κεκοινωμένους ἁγιάζει πρὸς τὴν τῆς <u>σαρκὸς καθαρότητα</u>
9.14 πόσῳ μᾶλλον τὸ αἷμα τοῦ Χριστοῦ, ὃς διὰ πνεύματος αἰωνίου ἑαυτὸν προσήνεγκεν ἄμωμον τῷ θεῷ, <u>καθαριεῖ τὴν συνείδησιν ἡμῶν</u> ἀπὸ νεκρῶν ἔργων εἰς τὸ λατρεύειν θεῷ ζῶντι

---

[32] The extent to which Yom Kippur purged people (as well as the sancta) remains an ongoing debate. For a summary of this discussion see C. Nihan, *From Priestly Torah to Pentateuch: A Study in the Composition of the Book of Leviticus*, FAT 2.25 (Tübingen: Mohr Siebeck, 2007), 371–5; N. Kiuchi, *Leviticus*, AOTC 3 (Nottingham, UK: Apollos, 2007), 310; *Purification*, 26; Gäbel, *Kulttheologie*, 411–12 n. 349; Gane, *Cult*, 230–3, 273–5, 298–300; Sklar, *Sin*, 188–93; John Dennis, 'The Function of the חטאת Sacrifice: An Evaluation of the View of Jacob Milgrom', *ETL* 78.1 (2002): 124–6; Milgrom, *Leviticus 1–16*, 1033, 1056. Inadvertent sins have the power to pollute as far as the incense altar and accidental sins can pollute the outer, but cannot enter the sanctuary, see Greenberg, *Atonement*, 153–88; Vis, 'Purification', *Sacrifice*, 33–57.
[33] As Koester notes 'one need not envision heavenly beings committing sins to think that purification of heaven would be appropriate', *Hebrews*, 421.
[34] See the scholarship mentioned in n. 139 in §1.4.2.

Since συνείδησις and σάρξ appear in close proximity with regards to purification, it is assumed that Hebrews not only deliberately contrasts these two terms but understands their purification as belonging to two separate covenants.[35] For instance, as Ribbens writes, '[t]he old covenant sacrifices are performed in the earthly realm as symbols connecting to a greater sacrifice that is actually efficacious. Thus, the old covenant sacrifices are external signs, which do not attain any internal effect by their own merit but only because God established them as a means of accessing the efficacy of Christ's sacrifice.'[36] The result of this reading is that OC offerings are viewed as inferior – or at least limited in purpose – since they only purified the σάρξ; Christ's offering, however, purifies the συνείδησις.

This apparently is because the 'gifts and sacrifices' (Heb. 8.3; 9.9) offered under the OC were 'devoid of divine power and thus unable to change the heart or transform the person'[37] since 'the whole sacrificial system was restricted to outward purification.'[38] Levitical sacrifices seemingly had 'nothing explicitly to do with the soul or conscience. The cleansing of that inner sphere is the sort of sanctification that Christ's sacrifice affords.'[39] In short, this prevailing stance proposes a contrast between one type of purification which cleanses the σάρξ, and another type of purification which cleanses the συνείδησις.[40] This hermeneutic has a further impact on how σάρξ is understood in Hebrews, with decisive phrases such as 'δικαιώματα σαρκὸς' (9.10) and 'σαρκὸς καθαρότητα' (9.13) being rendered as 'fleshly' or 'outward' purification/regulations. This internal–external perspective will be challenged by first exploring σάρξ and then through studying the nature of Levitical sacrificial ritual.

4.3.2 Σάρξ

While σάρξ might conjure up negative associations for some,[41] it is not a negative term in Hebrews,[42] but a reference to the earthly realm. Of the six times σάρξ is mentioned (Heb. 2.14; 5.7; 9.10, 13; 10.20; 12.9) three are in reference to Jesus. The most tentative example is 10.20, a verse 'bristling as it is with both syntactical and hermeneutical difficulties.'[43] It states that we have confidence to enter the Holy of Holies by the blood of Jesus by the 'new and living way which he opened for us through the curtain, by means of his flesh' (ἣν ἐνεκαίνισεν ἡμῖν ὁδὸν πρόσφατον καὶ ζῶσαν διὰ τοῦ καταπετάσματος, τοῦτ' ἔστιν τῆς σαρκὸς αὐτοῦ). The core of interpretation here

---

[35] Thompson aligns it with Platonic thought, *Hebrews*, 185.
[36] Ribbens, *Levitical*, 190.
[37] Cockerill, *Hebrews*, 385. See also Allen, *Hebrews*, 494.
[38] Cockerill, *Hebrews*, 397.
[39] Attridge, *Hebrews*, 250. Attridge points to Jewish exegetical practices evidenced here, since the heifer is mentioned alongside the high priest. Ribbens too notes, '[o]ther efficacies, such as the purification of the conscience, are simply not in the realm of possibility for the levitical sacrifices', *Levitical*, 192.
[40] Ribbens helpfully maps some of the scholarship here, *Levitical*, 6. For Thompson, this is additional proof of Platonic dualism; emphasising a metaphysical superiority of the heavenly (συνείδησις) over the earthly (σάρξ), 'Middle Platonism', *Reading*, 42.
[41] Schenck, *Cosmology*, 133.
[42] Rightly Johnsson, 'Defilement', 287. Contra Thompson, *Beginnings*, 44–52.
[43] Church, *Temple*, 384.

depends on syntax, namely what the phrase 'τοῦτ' ἔστιν τῆς σαρκὸς αὐτοῦ' is in reference to. Typically, three options have surfaced, as outlined by Table 4.[44]

In Table 4 the first interpretation shows that the 'flesh of Jesus' (τῆς σαρκὸς αὐτοῦ) depends grammatically on 'the new and living way' (ὁδὸν πρόσφατον καὶ ζῶσαν),[45] meaning that the new and living way is Jesus' σάρξ. This becomes unlikely, since 'τοῦτ' ἔστιν' typically stands in apposition with terms in the same case (Heb. 2.14; 7.5; 9.11; 11.16; 13.15).[46] The second reading in Table 4 views 'his flesh' acting appositionally with 'the curtain' (τοῦ καταπετάσματος) with the preposition 'through' (διὰ) being extended, not only to govern the preceding genitive (τοῦ καταπετάσματος) but also 'his flesh' (τῆς σαρκὸς αὐτοῦ).[47] Thus, the curtain is described as Jesus' σάρξ. The third reading in Table 4 sees the entire clause beginning 10.20 as the referent of 'his flesh', yet this interpretation supplies a second instrumental διά preposition to avoid associating 'his flesh' with the 'veil'.[48] So Jesus, by means of his flesh, has opened the new and living way, through the curtain.

Table 4 By means of his flesh (Heb. 10.20)

	The referent of τοῦτ' ἔστιν τῆς σαρκὸς αὐτοῦ (10.20b)	Possible rendering	Meaning
1	The new and living way (ὁδὸν πρόσφατον καὶ ζῶσαν).	The new and living way, the way of his flesh, which he opened for us through the curtain.	The new and living way is the flesh of Christ.
2	The curtain (διὰ τοῦ καταπετάσματος).	Through the curtain, that is, [through] his flesh.	The curtain is further defined as the flesh of Christ.
3	The whole clause (ἐνεκαίνισεν ἡμῖν ὁδὸν πρόσφατον καὶ ζῶσαν διὰ τοῦ καταπετάσματος).	He has opened a new and living way through the curtain, that is, [by means of] his flesh.	Christ has opened the new and living way, through the curtain, by means of his flesh.

---

[44] Harris, *Hebrews*, 273–4; Church, *Temple*, 383–6. Cf. Jamieson, *Death*, 86–91, who outworks further nuances.

[45] Notably Gäbel, *Kulttheologie*, 203–7; Grässer, *Hebräer*, 3:14–19, esp. 18–19; Montefiore, *Hebrews*, 173–4; Cody, *Heavenly*, 161–2; Nairne, *Hebrews*, 161, 381–2; Spicq, *Hébreux*, 2:316; Westcott, *Hebrews*, 321–3.

[46] Attridge, *Hebrews*, 286. Although Heb. 7.5 and 13.15 show that there can be some distance between 'τοῦτ' ἔστιν' and its substantive.

[47] Harris, *Hebrews*, 274; Church, *Temple*, 385–6; Calaway, *Sabbath*, 114; Mitchell, *Hebrews*, 211; Bénétreau, *Hébreux*, 2:110–11; Johnsson, 'Heavenly Sanctuary', *Issues*, 48–9; N. H. Young, 'ΤΟΥΤ' ΕΣΤΙΝ ΤΗΣ ΣΑΡΚΟΣ ΑΥΤΟΥ (Heb. x. 20): Apposition, Dependent, or Explicative?', *NTS* 20.1 (1973): 103–4; N. A. Dahl, 'New and Living Way: The Approach to God According to Hebrews 10:19-25', *Int* 5.4 (1951): 404–5.

[48] Rose, *Hebräerbrief*, 161; Jamieson, *Death*, 90–1; Cockerill, *Hebrews*, 467–71; David M. Moffitt, 'Unveiling Jesus' Flesh: A Fresh Assessment of the Relationship Between the Veil and Jesus' Flesh in Hebrews 10:20', *PRSt* 37.1 (2010): 72; Svendsen, *Allegory*, 197; Koester, *Hebrews*, 443–4; Lane, *Hebrews*, 2:275–6; Wiley, *Hebrews*, 298–9; Hofius, *Vorhang*, 81–3; J. Jeremias, 'Hebr. 10:20: τοῦτ' ἔστιν τῆς σαρκὸς αὐτοῦ', *ZNW* 62 (1971): 131; Moffatt, *Hebrews*, 143; Delitzsch, *Hebrews*, 2:172–3.

Of the literature surveyed, it is the third view which is the most compelling, for a few reasons. First, as outlined previously (§2.4.3, §2.4.5), Hebrews does not allegorize the heavenly tabernacle but describes it and reveals it to be a very real structure with the curtain included (cf. 9.3). Also, the curtain has already been referred to in Hebrews as something Jesus passed through (6.19-20). These reasons cast doubt on aligning the curtain with Jesus' flesh, or as a symbol of negative separation.[49] Second, it is proposed that a parallel between 10.19 and 10.20 should be recognized,[50] allowing the 'blood' of Jesus (10.19) to be aligned with the 'curtain' (10.20). Yet a parallel between 10.19 and 10.21-2 is more persuasive.

For instance, 10.19 highlights three things: (a) it exhorts believers to approach the heavenly tabernacle (b) with 'boldness' (παρρησία) (c) because of the blood of Jesus. These three motifs are picked up and altered slightly in 10.21-2. Beginning with the hortatory subjunctive (προσερχώμεθα), 'we' are (a) exhorted to approach (the Holy of Holies) (b) with the fullness of faith (c) due to the blood which has purged the consciousness. Therefore, the purpose of 10.20 is not to parallel 10.19, but to describe the heavenly tabernacle which 'has been opened' (ἐνεκαίνισεν) by Jesus.[51]

Finally, something which scholars seem to ignore is the connection between the ὁδός (the way) in 10.20 and the ὁδός mentioned earlier (9.8). Access into the heavenly tabernacle and the establishment of a new heavenly cult is not possible while the current earthly one has legal standing (§2.2). However, Jesus' suffering, obedience and death establishes a NC, ushers in the time of correction (9.10) and opens the ὁδός into the heavenly tabernacle (9.8). Turning to 10.20, the opening of the ὁδός can be interpreted as occurring through Jesus' σάρξ, as shown in 9.8. Yet, as the crux of this study has sought to argue, the problem is not whether the heavenly ὁδός is open, or even whether one has been sanctified and so made objectively holy in order to enter the heavenly sanctuary (2.11; 10.10). The problem is whether one *feels* subjectively able to approach. It is a subjective concern put right when Jesus offers his blood in heaven. This again confirms the objective achievements of Jesus' earthly life of obedience (culminating in death) and his subjective heavenly achievements (purging the consciousness) (§3.7). This is why Jesus acts as a forerunner into the heavenly tabernacle (6.20) in order to purge it (9.14, 23) thereby removing the consciousness of sin (9.14; 10.22) and allowing for boldness to approach (10.19).

One question remains, however: what is Jesus' σάρξ? Jesus' incarnation,[52] death[53] and heavenly offering[54] have all been suggested; nevertheless, Jesus' σάρξ is best understood as a reference to his earthly life. When Jesus' σάρξ is mentioned elsewhere, his earthly

---

[49] The curtain, Christ's flesh, as a barrier separating heaven and earth is unwarranted, contra Käsemann, *Wandering*, 225–7. So is the Synoptic tradition of the 'torn veil', rightly Attridge, *Hebrews*, 286–7. Contra Moffatt, *Hebrews*, 143. The body/flesh of Jesus is not viewed as a barrier in Hebrews but a gift, rightly Backhaus, *Hebräerbrief*, 358.
[50] Church, *Temple*, 386; Anderson, *Hebrews*, 274; Barnard, *Mysticism*, 195; Cockerill, *Hebrews*, 470–1; Mitchell, *Hebrews*, 211; Ellingworth, *Hebrews*, 520–1.
[51] As a result, in 10.20 the recipients pass through the veil, not Jesus.
[52] Backhaus, *Hebräerbrief*, 358–9.
[53] Rose, *Hebräerbrief*, 161; Attridge, *Hebrews*, 287.
[54] Moffitt, *Atonement*, 281–3; 'Unveiling', 71–84.

life is always in view. In Heb. 5.7 Jesus is described as offering up prayers 'in the days of his flesh' (ἐν ταῖς ἡμέραις τῆς σαρκὸς αὐτοῦ). In 2.14, a passage devoted to the incarnation (2.5-18), Jesus is said to have shared 'flesh and blood' (αἵματος καὶ σαρκός) with the children of God. Σάρξ is used later to describe earthly familial relations (12.9). In short, Jesus' σάρξ includes his earthly life of obedience, from incarnation to his suffering and ultimate death.[55] On this reading, Hebrews connects Jesus' life of obedience (σάρξ) with the heavenly sanctuary in 10.20;[56] Jesus' obedient life ushers in a NC and grants access via a new and living ὁδός.[57] Nonetheless, the purging of the sanctuary is a separate action that relates to the consciousness.

4.3.3 Earthly regulations/purifications

Now that all other occurrences of σάρξ have been addressed, a good foundation exists for interpreting both 'δικαιώματα σαρκὸς' (Heb. 9.10) and 'σαρκὸς καθαρότητα' (9.13). Table 5 shows a range of contemporary English translations which display the distinctive interpretative decisions.

Phrases vary from defining σάρξ as 'external', 'bodily', 'fleshly', 'outwardly' and 'ceremonial impurity'. The analysis so far suggests that σάρξ refers to that which is earthly, not inferior or sinful. Hebrews does not understand anthropological terminology competing in an internal–external manner, or in an earthly–heavenly manner, but holistically (§1.4.2, §2.4.1).[58] Therefore, the problem with 'external'/'fleshly', as displayed in the internal–external purification perspective, is that these regulations/purifications are viewed as either inferior or distinct from what Christ achieves.

Beginning with 'δικαιώματα σαρκὸς' (9.10), the surrounding discussion (9.1-15) suggests a comparison between the earthly cult and the heavenly cult, not a negative

Table 5 Renderings for 'δικαιώματα σαρκὸς' (9.10) and 'σαρκὸς καθαρότητα' (9.13)

	NIV	ESV; NRSV	NET	NASB	NLT	NKJV
δικαιώματα σαρκός (9.10)	external regulation	regulations for the body	external regulations	regulations for the body	physical regulations	fleshly ordinances
σαρκὸς καθαρότητα (9.13)	outwardly clean	purification of the flesh/flesh is purified	provided ritual purity	regulations for the body	cleanse people's bodies from ceremonial impurity	purifying of the flesh

---

[55] Similarly Grässer, *Hebräer*, 3:18–19.
[56] Luck, 'Himmlisches', 208–11. Although I would not agree that Hebrews makes this connection with the curtain, as Luck goes on to state, 'Das Leiden und Sterben Jesu ist der Vorhang', 209.
[57] There may be more significance to the ὁδός which has not been fully explored in Hebrews (cf. Jn 14.6).
[58] Contra Schenck, *Cosmology*, 133. Ethical dualism is to be discredited, rightly Williamson, *Philo*, 268–76.

internal–external contrast. Elsewhere the author places value on making the 'body' (σῶμα) holy (10.22; cf. 10.10; §4.4.4). Thus, reading 'δικαιώματα σαρκὸς' as 'earthly' or 'human' 'regulations' complements Hebrews' cultic argumentation.[59] These 'earthly regulations' are for the 'earthly tabernacle' (τό ἅγιον κοσμικόν, 9.1). This is further supported by the conclusions made earlier regarding the contrast between cults (§2.2). If Hebrews is writing from a pre-70 CE setting, the recipients exist within a cultic interim period. According to the author there is 'the present time' (τὸν καιρὸν τὸν ἐνεστηκότα, 9.9) of earthly sacrifices – which is wearing away and will soon disappear (8.13) – and the 'time of correction' (καιροῦ διορθώσεως, 9.10), that is, Christ's heavenly cultic ministry (9.11-14). In a sense, the 'present time' and the 'time of correction' refer to the same thing, since the exaltation of Christ in these last days (1.1-3) places the recipients in an overlap of the ages. This 'present time' deals only with 'food and drink and various baptisms' since these are 'earthly regulations' until the 'time of correction' (9.10; cf. §2.5.2).

A key once more is 9.9, which indirectly argues that sacrifices were offered in an attempt to deal with the consciousness of sin, yet it was not that they were unable to, but that they were unable to 'once-for-all'. This is shown through Hebrews' preference for perfection terminology (τελειόω) in 9.9 and 10.1, as opposed to purification language (καθαρίζω, cf. 9.14; 10.22), demonstrating that perfection (total purgation) was the limitation for Levitical sacrifice, not internal cleansing. If sacrifices could perfect the worshipper, then they would have no consciousness of sin, 'having been purged once-for-all' (ἅπαξ κεκαθαρισμένους, 10.1-2; §2.5.3, §4.4.2). The contrast therefore is not internal–external, but a contrast between earthly purification and heavenly purification. It is also possible to read 9.9-10 as a positive affirmation regarding the role of 'food and drink and various baptisms' in helping to ease one's consciousness of sin (9.9-10). Hebrews states that offerings cannot perfect (totally purge) the consciousness, but deal 'only' (μόνον) with 'food and drink and various baptisms'. Read in this manner, Hebrews appears once more to be hinting towards the positive impact Levitical sacrifice played in dealing with the consciousness of sin.[60]

The renderings in Table 5 for 'σαρκὸς καθαρότητα' greatly misrepresent Hebrews' argumentation. The phrase 'σαρκὸς καθαρότητα' (9.13) should be read as another subjective genitive, 'earthly' or 'human' 'purification'. This is more than apparent given that 9.13-14 is a comparison between earthly purification, through animal blood (9.13), and heavenly purification, via Jesus' heavenly blood (9.14). Additionally, the contrast between σάρξ and συνείδησις (9.13-14) should be viewed as a contrast between two blood types – the blood of 'goats and bulls' and the 'blood of Christ'. There is something more powerful and effective about human blood, especially the 'spotless' (ἄμωμον) blood of Christ (9.14). In turning to the impact of Levitical sacrificial ritual now, it will become even more apparent that this internal–external purification contrast is unfounded in Hebrews.

---

[59] Ribbens, *Levitical*, 189–92; Cody, *Heavenly*, 190–1.
[60] Karrer, *Hebräer*, 2:156.

4.3.4 The drama of ritual

In the introductory parts of this study it was argued that Hebrews' sacrificial argumentation cannot be emptied of its ritual impact (§1.5). In other words, cultic language – in relation to the consciousness of sin and Jesus' heavenly blood offering – are not just symbolic but represent very real matters for the community. In Hebrews, the consciousness of sin, when purged, enables access to God (cf. Heb. 9.14; 10.22), suggesting that the consciousness of sin acts as *the* problem in approaching him. But what ritual impact did Levitical sacrifices possess in this regard?

The assertion that OT sacrificial ritual possessed only an 'external' purification can be challenged. Levitical sacrifice provided a holistic cleansing and possessed powerful psychological benefits for those involved. *How* this happened, however, is not so easily understood. As James Greenberg notes, 'with some confidence, scholars conclude that sacrifice fixes a problem between the offeror and YHWH. However, determining how and why sacrifice fixes this problem is elusive.'[61] In recent times scholars have begun to explore the role of ritual in order to explain how sacrifice 'works'.[62] Viewing sacrifice as a 'drama' is a helpful motif for this. The 'drama of sacrifice',[63] as Nelson defines it, enables social cohesion and restores the equilibrium for a given community. The readers 'must step into relatively fixed roles ... [since] the very actions themselves are believed to actually do something that affects reality'.[64] Like a drama, the participants play certain roles (victim, priest, giver, audience) and are drawn into a story intended to impact those involved; suspense builds as the impure people of God are made pure. Sacrifice is hence a 'dramatic "performance" both in the sense of *acting out* a communication event and in the sense of *bringing into being* the reality being communicated'.[65]

Sacrifice is not merely an outward act but possesses powerful internal consequences for those involved. Ritual impacts the psychology of its participants, appearing to be of more benefit to the people involved, rather than to the one whom sacrifices are offered. As Lindars notes, in reference to Yom Kippur, '[m]odern readers are liable to underestimate the psychological importance of what is involved here. The mental pain of a sense of guilt is too great to be dealt with internally, and needs to be objectified in practical action and to be shared with others who can help to bear the burden'.[66] At times the lucidity of sacrificial ritual defies empirical reasoning – 'a bloody mess does not empirically clean anything'[67] – but it nonetheless works.[68] Sacrifice in this sense represents a 'spontaneous expression of felt needs, and the outward act and the inward meaning were completely at one'.[69] An important question to turn to now is, what role does Levitical sacrifice play in reference to the consciousness of sin?

---

[61] Greenberg, *Atonement*, 1.
[62] Greenberg, *Atonement*, 1–11; Hundley, *Heaven*, 20–37; Feder, *Blood*, 147–65; Gane, *Cult*, 3–24.
[63] I borrow this phrase from Nelson, *Raising*, 71–3.
[64] Hundley, *Heaven*, 22.
[65] Nelson, *Raising*, 72 (emphasis his own).
[66] Lindars, *Hebrews*, 85.
[67] Hundley, *Heaven*, 24.
[68] Hundley, *Heaven*, 25.
[69] Lindars, *Hebrews*, 89.

4.3.5 Levitical אָשָׁם and the consciousness of sin

Hebrews is clear that perfection cannot be attained under the earthly cult (Heb. 7.11, 19; 9.9-10; 10.1) yet it never claims that one's consciousness of sin (συνείδησις) could not be purified.[70] To claim that sacrifices under the earthly cult were unable to impact the consciousness of the worshipper, or deal with internal realities, shows a lack of appreciation for sacrifice as ritual.

The five Levitical offerings (Lev. 1–7), specifically both the 'sin-purification'[71] (חטאת/περὶ ἁμαρτίας) and the 'guilt-reparation' (אשם/πλημμέλεια) offerings (Lev. 4.1–6.7)[72] are essential for understanding purification in relation to sin. Moreover, these offerings are an important albeit neglected aspect for understanding purification in relation to the consciousness of sin. The establishment of the law and the covenant (Exod. 19–24), as well as the creation of a tabernacle and its priestly maintenance (Exod. 15–40),[73] provides the necessary backdrop for these Levitical offerings (Lev. 1–7). Exodus shows *where* the Lord is to be worshipped, Leviticus says *how*, by beginning the book with instructions on how to bring an 'offering' (קרבן, Lev. 1.2), that is, how to 'draw near' to the Lord. In Chapter 2 two the impact of sin and defilement within the sacrificial cult was outlined. Sin's defiling effects impacted the individual, those associated with the culprit and also the sanctity of the Lord's sanctuary (§2.3.1). The remedies for sin and its defiling effects included punishment – even death – but also consisted of rituals that rectified physical impurity (such as isolation, oil and water).[74] The sin-purification/guilt-reparation offerings (Lev. 4.1–6.7) dealt with intentional/unintentional sins[75] and were integral for maintaining the covenant relationship with the Lord by removing both physical and moral defilement.[76] Leviticus 4 contains five purification rites for various groups of people[77] – anticipating the חטאת offerings on the annual Yom Kippur (Lev. 16)[78] – with Lev. 5 detailing what specific sins

---

[70] See my comments earlier (§1.3.4, §1.4.1).

[71] Milgrom's point that the חטאת should be translated as 'purification' and not 'sin' offering is based on other texts (Lev. 12.6-7; 14.10-31; 15.14-15, 29-30) where sin is not mentioned but defilement, meaning a 'purification' offering is meant, *Leviticus 1–16*, 253; *Studies in Cultic Theology and Terminology*, SJLA 36 (Leiden: Brill, 1983), 67–69; 'Sin-Offering or Purification-Offering?', *VT* 21.2 (1971): 237–9. This has been generally accepted by most scholars, although some have critiqued Milgrom and maintain 'sin offering', see Feder, *Purity and Pollution*, 99–106; Lam, *Sin*, 59–61, 220; Eberhart, *Studien*, 113–14, 267. See also Kiuchi's rendering as 'to hide oneself', *Leviticus*, 90–2; *A Study of Hata and Hatta't in Leviticus 4-5*, FAT 2.2 (Tübingen: Mohr Siebeck, 2003), 84. The likelihood in Lev. 4–5 is that it is both: sin-purification offering, Nihan, *Priestly*, 186–90.

[72] Understanding these two offerings as complementary is suggested by Jay Sklar, *Leviticus: An Introduction and Commentary*, TOTC 3 (Downers Grove, IL: InterVarsity Press, 2013), 107–8.

[73] See Mark J. Boda, *A Severe Mercy: Sin and Its Remedy in the Old Testament* (Winona Lake, IN: Eisenbrauns, 2009), 35–48, 49–85.

[74] Boda, *Severe*, 55–8.

[75] See my prior discussion (§2.5.5).

[76] Cf. Lev. 6.1-6 (5.20-5 MT) with 14.12-28 and 4.1-35 with 5.2-3.

[77] These range from responsibilities held, from high priests (Lev. 4.3-12) to the community as a whole (4.13-21) and to specific leaders (4.22-6) or individuals (4.27-35).

[78] The חטאת offering was also performed on Yom Kippur and required the same sacrificial animals (Lev. 4.3, 23; 16.3, 5). Rather than observing variances between the חטאת offering in Lev. 4 and the חטאת offering in Lev. 16, it is possible to see a continues process, reaching its completion in Lev. 16 when the entire sanctuary is purged, rightly Cranz, *Atonement*, 36–37; Nihan, *Priestly*, 188–9, 193–4, 197–8. Leviticus 16 represents a greater purgation than was offered in Lev. 4–5, Kiuchi, *Purification*, 157. Greenberg chooses to focus on the dissimilarities between Lev. 16 and Lev. 4–5, *Atonement*, 181–2.

required purification (5.1-13). The אשם offering (Lev. 5.14–6.7) focuses on 'reparation', as opposed to purification. What is significant to consider at this point is that the trigger for initiating these sacrificial offerings is once guilt (אָשֵׁם) has been recognized (Lev. 4.13, 22, 27; 5.2-5, 17, 19, 6.4).[79]

The verb אָשֵׁם has received much scholarly attention.[80] Traditionally it is rendered as 'to be guilty' (*qal*) which emphasizes the objective status of the sinner.[81] This is further emphasized through the LXX with the passivity of the phrase 'the sin be made known to him' (γνωσθῇ αὐτῷ ἡ ἁμαρτία, Lev. 4.22).[82] The sinner, after breaking the law, becomes guilty. However, the traditional rendering of אָשֵׁם only states that someone has 'become guilty', it does not explain how or why guilt has arisen, or when a person is supposed to bring an offering. Because of this anomaly there have been various suggestions of how to best define אָשֵׁם.[83] An important addition has been to acknowledge the subjective aspect of אָשֵׁם as 'being conscious' of one's own sin, that is 'he [or she] feels his [or her] guilt'.[84] This rendering is possible for a few reasons. In one example it states the following:

> If anyone of the ordinary people among you 'sins unintentionally' (תחטא בשגגה) in doing any one of the things that by the Lord's commandments ought not to be done and 'feels guilty' (אָשֵׁם), 'or the sin that you have committed is made known to you' (או הודע אליו חטאתו אשר חטא), you shall bring a female goat without blemish as your offering, for the sin that you have committed.
>
> Lev. 4.27-8, cf. 22-3

The particle 'or' (או) is significant here as it shows that אָשֵׁם cannot mean 'becomes guilty' since it also states that the sin is 'made known' to the one who has sinned. Instead, אָשֵׁם as 'feels guilt' adds a subjective element to אָשֵׁם.[85]

A further example from the אשם offering highlights this issue again. This particular example regards a person who has sinned against a neighbour, for instance, through robbery:

> When you have sinned and realize your guilt (אָשֵׁם) and would restore what you took by robbery or by fraud ... You shall pay it to its owner when you realize your

---

[79] Lev. 4.1–5.26 (MT) is labelled 4.1–6.18.
[80] See Joshua M. Vis, 'The Purification Offering of Leviticus and the Sacrificial Offering of Jesus' (Ph.D. diss., Duke University, 2012), 164–77; Sklar, *Sin*, 25–43.
[81] Levine, *Leviticus*, 19–22; *HALOT* 95–6.
[82] Mark Awabdy, *Leviticus: A Commentary on Leueitikon in Codex Vaticanus* (Septuagint Commentary Series; Leiden: Brill, 2019), 206–7.
[83] As Milgrom notes, 'it is absurd in a legal text to state that after a deliberate crime, one incurs guilt (NEB) becomes guilty (RSV) or realizes guilt (NJPS) ... The sinner is stricken with conscience: he feels his guilt', *Cult and Conscience: The ASHAM and the Priestly Doctrine of Repentance*, SJLA 18 (Leiden: Brill, 1976), 10 (emphasis his own). Contra Janowski, *Sühne*, 256–9. Kiuchi sees it as to 'realize guilt', *Leviticus*, 95–6; *Purification*, 34. Levine prefers 'incurs guilt', *Leviticus*, 22–3. Sklar renders the phrase as 'to suffer guilt's consequences', *Sin*, 24–41. Although his conclusions can be challenged, see Boda, *Severe*, 63–4. Boda prefers the phrasing to 'recognize' guilt, 62–4. Greenberg prefers 'compelled by guilt', *Atonement*, 25, 26 n. 56.
[84] Milgrom, *Cult*, 10.
[85] Kiuchi, *Leviticus*, 97.

guilt (אשמה). And you shall bring to the priest, as your guilt offering (אשם) to the Lord, a ram without blemish ... The priest shall make atonement (כִּפֶּר) on your behalf before the Lord, and you shall be forgiven for any of the things that one may do and incur guilt (אשמה) thereby.

Lev. 6.4-7 [5.23-6 MT]

If the traditional phrasing for אָשֵׁם ('becomes guilty') is applied to this passage, then it makes no sense as to why the one who committed the offence should seek to rectify it. Rather, if it is rendered to 'feel guilt' or 'realize guilt' then it explains why an offering was brought initially.[86]

It is important to recognize that both the objective and subjective aspects of אָשֵׁם are evident in these passages. As Boda notes, אָשֵׁם is 'a phase distinct from yet intermediate between the sinful/impure act and the sacrificial act'.[87] Either the sin is pointed out by the community, or it is realized by one's own consciousness. It is also interesting to note the phraseology used by scholars when interpreting these offerings. Milgrom describes אָשֵׁם as 'psychological guilt',[88] with Kiuchi understanding אָשֵׁם as 'consciousness of sin'.[89] Kiuchi's rendering has important implications for Hebrews and creates close conceptual links with Hebrews' conception of the consciousness of sin. Similarly, while Hebrews and Philo have their differences with respect to συνείδησις (§1.3.4, §1.4.1), Philo does make use of the 'convicting conscience' in his retelling of the אשם offering in Lev. 6.4-7 (5.23-6 MT). Philo uniquely shows the important role that one's own consciousness plays within the sacrificial cult. You can escape the judgement of others, but according to Philo, you can never escape 'being convicted inwardly by conscience' (ἔνδον ὑπὸ τοῦ συνειδότος ἐλεγχθείς, *Spec. Leg.* 1.235; cf. *Spec. Leg.* 4.6). Unintentional sin is evident through the absence of an accusing conscience (τὸ συνειδός) whereas intentional sin provokes the inner judgement of τὸ συνειδός (*Deus Imm.* 128-9).

What is significant to highlight from this discussion is that sacrificial ritual – as displayed in both the חטאת/אשם offerings – is prompted by the worshipper's own 'consciousness of sin' (אָשֵׁם), to use Kiuchi's rendering. In order to relieve their burden participants enter the sacrificial drama to bring an offering.[90] Their consciousness of sin and the sacrificial ritual are bound together. Therefore, the claim that Levitical sacrifices had nothing to do with the consciousnesses of sin is not entirely true. It would be wrong, as Bruce notes, to state 'that faithful men and women in Old Testament times did not enjoy peace of conscience and a sense of nearness to God'.[91] Christ's heavenly offering is not understood as being offered by the recipients themselves, but it no

---

[86] Greenberg claims that these definitions still do not explain the motivation behind bringing an offering, but one has to assume that 'feeling guilt' denotes an awareness that an accepted law or custom has been violated, *Atonement*, 25–6.
[87] Boda, *Severe*, 64.
[88] Milgrom, *Cult*, 11. Although see Sklar, *Leviticus*, 110–14; *Sin*, 38–9.
[89] Kiuchi, *Hata*, 11; *Purification*, 32–4. So too Boda, *Severe*, 64.
[90] The motive behind bringing an offering is not entirely certain. Greenberg suggests that it is a conscious act to avoid divine punishment, *Atonement*, 25. However, a general feeling of guilt or uncleanliness is also an assumed motivation behind bringing an offering. Rightly Nelson, 'Offered', 260–1; Lindars, *Hebrews*, 88–9.
[91] Bruce, *Hebrews*, 169.

doubt connects with their own experience and impacts them psychologically. Given its first century context, Hebrews is to be read and treated as a sacrificial ritual text, with the recipients/participants playing their own role within Jesus' heavenly offering. As Wesley Bergen notes, the hearers of ritual texts, although potentially far removed from the practice of sacrifice, are nonetheless called to identify themselves as active participants, provoking them to be 'deeply concerned with sin and its effects'.[92]

If the notion of אָשָׁם is anchored within the 'present problem' of συνείδησις (§1.2, §2.2), then it would be sufficient to argue that Hebrews is writing in order to address the psychological void which exists within their own Christian community. A further aspect to consider is the consciousness of unconscious sin, that is, 'unintentional' sin. It is easy to conceive from the examples above how one becomes conscious of sin following a deliberate sin, but what about the role of אָשָׁם in relation to unconscious sin (cf. Lev. 5.17-19)? Unintentional sin can be pointed out by others (Lev. 4.27-8) with this leading logically to the consciousness of a sinful act. Also, since 'unintentional sin' (שגגה) has its root in שגה ('going astray'), Milgrom has argued that unintentional sin involves a certain degree of consciousness from the offender.[93]

Alternatively, Milgrom argues that the presence of psychical and physical suffering causes individuals to assume they have committed an unintentional sin; their present suffering causes them to assume the worst.[94] Kiuchi disagrees and rightly points out that someone is able to possess the consciousness of an act without incurring guilt.[95] What is apparent in these discussions is that 'guilt exists whether or not the offender is aware of it at the time ... Guilt may "begin" even before the offender realizes what he has done.'[96] The possibility that someone may have sinned unintentionally seems to create a sense of suspicion and fear. This confronts one's consciousness and leads individuals to bring an offering by simply assuming the worst.

Traditionally, unintentional sin is not directly associated with Yom Kippur. However, in Heb. 9.7 the author innovatively claims that on Yom Kippur the high priest offers blood for 'unintentional sin' (9.7; §2.5.5). Elsewhere the daily offerings (7.27; 10.11) are clearly within Hebrews' argumentation,[97] yet describing a blood offering on Yom Kippur for unintentional sin is entirely original. This innovation has implications. By associating Yom Kippur with unintentional sin (9.7) Hebrews alludes once more to the notion of אָשָׁם and its relationship with unintentional sin. What does Hebrews intend through this assimilation? It is possible that Hebrews is wanting to provide further reassurance for the recipients; even their unintentional sin, which they may or may not be fully conscious of, is dealt with through Christ's heavenly blood offering. The lingering doubt and fear concerning sin's defiling effects is vanquished through the assurance which Christ's heavenly blood brings (§5.4.4).

In summary, the common assumption that συνείδησις and σάρξ represent two opposing forms of purification, namely, an internal–external dichotomy, greatly

---

[92] Wesley Bergen, *Reading Ritual: Leviticus in Postmodern Culture*, JSOTSup 417 (London: T&T Clark, 2005), 40.
[93] Milgrom, *Cultic Terminology*, 122–4.
[94] Milgrom, *Leviticus 1–16*, 332–3.
[95] Kiuchi, *Purification*, 26–7. Leviticus 5.17 likely parallels Lev. 4.2, 13, 22, 27, Milgrom, *Leviticus 1–16*, 331.
[96] Levine, *Leviticus*, 22.
[97] See n. 120.

distorts Hebrews' argumentation. Rather, the internal connectedness of ritual and sacrifice reveals the holistic nature of the cult. Levitical אשם corresponds conceptually to and informs Hebrews' notion of συνείδησις. The earthly offerings foreshadow the 'good things that have come' (9.11), that is, Christ's heavenly entrance and subsequent offering. The real issue then is not internal–external purification, but as shall be argued shortly, perfection and the finality of purgation.

4.4 How much more? Perfection and the finality of purgation

If Levitical sacrificial ritual solves the problem of אשם, or συνείδησις (albeit temporarily), then how does Jesus' sacrifice deal with the present problem of συνείδησις? If the internal–external purification model is to be rejected, then what difference does Christ's heavenly offering make with regards to the purging of the consciousness? In other words, what is the 'how much more' (Heb. 9.14)? This final section argues that Jesus' heavenly blood offering provides a 'qualitative purgation', with respect to the problem of συνείδησις. This is expressed in various places (9.13-14, 22; 10.1-4, 22).

4.4.1 Perfection and purification

It is not possible to understand purification in Hebrews without understanding its relationship with *and* differentiation from perfection and vice versa. Hebrews is clear that perfection was unattainable under the first covenant (Heb. 7.11, 19; 9.9-10; 10.1) yet the author never claims the same for purification (cf. 9.13). What does it mean that the OC was unable to 'perfect' the worshipper with regards to συνείδησις (9.9; 10.2) and how does this relate to the purification of the συνείδησις (9.14; 10.22)? Before turning to these and other related passages, it is necessary to introduce perfection language, since this has only been touched upon briefly.

Τελειόω has the basic lexical value of 'bringing to completion' or 'bringing to an end'.[98] Hebrews employs the concept fourteen times through lexical variations,[99] displaying both the author's creativity and concern for the concept.[100] Perfection shapes how Hebrews understands Christ (2.10; 5.9; 7.28; 12.2), the limitations of OC sacrifices (7.11, 19; 9.9; 10.1) and the perfection of NC believers (5.14; 6.1; 10.14; 11.40; 12.23). Scholars interpret perfection language in Hebrews in diverse ways.[101] First, some

---

[98] BDAG 996.
[99] As well as τελειόω (2.10; 5.9; 7.19, 28; 9.9; 10.1, 14; 11.40; 12.23) Hebrews employs τέλειος (5.14; 9.11), τελειότης (6.1), τελείωσις (7.11) and τελειωτής (12.2). It is worth noting other nouns/verbs of completion, such as τέλος (3.14; 6.8, 11; 7.3), παντελής (7.25), ἐπιτελέω (8.5; 9.6), συντελέω (8.8), συντέλεια (9.26) and τελευτάω (11.22).
[100] Moisés Silva, 'Perfection and Eschatology in Hebrews', *WTJ* 39.1 (1976): 60.
[101] Four categories are generally recognized, see Ribbens, *Levitical*, 171-6; Kevin B. McCruden, *Solidarity Perfected: Beneficent Christology in the Epistle to the Hebrews*, BZNW 159 (Berlin: de Gruyter, 2008), 6-24; 'Christ's Perfection in Hebrews: Divine Beneficence as an Exegetical Key to Hebrews 2:1', *BR* 47 (2002): 40-62. Seth M. Simisi gives five, *Pursuit of Perfection: Significance of the Perfection Motif in the Epistle to the Hebrews* (Eugene, OR: Wipf & Stock, 2016), 38-42, 128-210, 211-16. Both McCruden's 'attestation' approach and Simisi's 'eschatological' understanding of perfection might constitute two additional categories.

understand perfection as moral progress, or human development.[102] The call to perfection is certainly evident in Hebrews (5.14; 6.1), but when this understanding of perfection is applied to Jesus it can create Christological issues. Jesus' moral development might not seem to require any further progress (1.3; 4.15; 7.26; 9.14). Second, perfection as 'cultic consecration' is a favourable nuance for some, understanding Jesus' perfection as priestly consecration in line with the LXX.[103] Third, perfection as 'vocational', or to borrow Otto Michel's phrase, 'berufliche Vollendung',[104] was promoted by David Peterson.[105] Vocational perfection signifies an educational process of development through human solidarity and suffering, yet it is not strictly ethical, but enables and qualifies Jesus to become a high priest. As high priest, Jesus helps humanity, who likewise are called to live a life of endurance through suffering, leading to perfection.[106] While this viewpoint might carry shades of the first and second perspective, it is Jesus' own solidarity and *experience* that stands out here. By identifying himself with humankind, Jesus was 'personally experiencing what obedience entailed'.[107] Finally, perfection as 'eschatological' provides a helpful addition. Through the exaltation of Christ, believers are provided with soteriological benefits via their high priest in these last days.[108] In the light of Christ and his perfect priestly ministry, the imperfections of the OC sacrificial system are laid bare. Hebrews employs perfection terminology 'to describe a significant messianic and soteriological reality'.[109]

It is possible to categorize scholars into various camps of interpretation, but it is unlikely that 'perfection' holds one meaning; 'perfection' might have multiple meanings depending on the context. For instance, the importance of Jesus' earthly educational and vocational perfecting (2.10; 5.9; 7.28) must be acknowledged as necessary for him to function as a sympathetic high priest (4.15). Perfection for Jesus means solidarity, enduring sufferings and preparation for his priestly ministry. The vocational perfection of Jesus overlaps with God's eschatological purposes.[110] Yet, 'perfection' in relation to the participants is less vocational and more experiential or declarative; they are perfected in order to draw near to God (10.14; 11.40; 12.23). Perfection is certainly a state to

---

[102] Oscar Cullmann, *The Christology of the New Testament*, 2nd edn (London: SCM Press, 1963), 92–7; Allen Paul Wikgren, 'Patterns of Perdition in the Epistle to the Hebrews', NTS 6 (1960): 160–1. This notion of perfection can be paralleled with 'Wesleyan' discussions concerning Christian Perfection.

[103] Much of this relies on the phrase 'to perfect the hand' (τελειώσεις τὰς χεῖρας). For helpful overviews see Pierce, *Divine Discourse*, 128–33; Ribbens, *Levitical*, 172–4, 242–5. The association of 'perfection' and 'priestly ordination' in the Greek form of Exodus and Leviticus maybe facilitated in Hebrews, Cockerill, *Hebrews*, 139 n. 67.

[104] 'Vocational perfection', Otto Michel, 'Die Lehre von der christlichen Vollkommenheit nach der Anschauung des Hebräerbriefes', TSK 106 (1934–5), 139.

[105] David G. Peterson, 'Perfection: Achieved and Experienced', in *The Perfect Savior: Key Themes in Hebrews*, ed. J. Griffiths (Nottingham: InterVarsity, 2012), 125–45; *Perfection*, 74–103. See also A. Vanhoye, 'La "Teleiôsis" du Christ: Point capital de la Christologie sacerdotale d'Hébreux', NTS 42.3 (1996): 321–38; G. B. Caird, 'Just Men Made Perfect', LQHR 191 (1966): 89–98.

[106] It is not moral or ethical, but experiential.

[107] McCruden, *Solidarity*, 22.

[108] Simisi, *Perfection*, 211–16; Ribbens, *Levitical*, 177–8; Gordon, *Hebrews*, 113; Lane, *Hebrews*, 1:195–6. Perfection as resurrection might also be included here, see Easter, *Faith*, 94–9; Moffitt, *Atonement*, 38, 181, 198–200.

[109] Ribbens, *Levitical*, 170.

[110] Harris, *Hebrews*, 55.

be maintained (5.14-6.1) but it might be better to understand perfection in Hebrews as the 'flow of perfection'; as the Father perfects the Son, so too the Son perfects the people of God.

Additionally, perfection must be distinguished from purification[111] yet simultaneously viewed as interconnected. If perfection is the totality of God's eschatological accomplishments, then purification is included within this scope. As Peterson notes:

> Perfection is not synonymous with cleansing from sin, though it involves the latter as a most significant element. Perfection is also not synonymous with sanctification, though the two concepts are closely related. The terminology of perfection is used to proclaim the fulfilment or *consummation* of men and women in a permanent, direct and personal relationship with God.[112]

Whilst distinct from purification, perfection includes the totality of purgation.[113] Perfection in relation to NC believers might therefore be described as containing a 'qualitative purgation'.

4.4.2 Qualitative purgation (Heb. 9.13-14; 10.1-4)

The purification of the consciousness through Christ's heavenly offering can be viewed as a type of 'qualitative purgation', as opposed to a συνείδησις–σάρξ/internal–external contrast. For instance, in 9.13-14 the 'how much more' (πόσῳ μᾶλλον) is a contrast between the blood of animals and the blood of Christ, not between σάρξ and συνείδησις (§4.3.3). These verses constitute a fundamental claim for the author of Hebrews. If the blood of goats and bulls with the sprinkling of the 'ashes of a heifer' (σποδὸς δαμάλεως) 'make holy the ones who have been defiled' (τοὺς κεκοινωμένους ἁγιάζει) for 'earthly purification' (σαρκὸς καθαρότητα); how much more will the blood of Christ, who through the eternal Spirit 'offered himself' (ἑαυτὸν προσήνεγκεν) without blemish to God 'purify our consciousness from dead works' (καθαριεῖ τὴν συνείδησιν ἡμῶν ἀπὸ νεκρῶν ἔργων) to worship the living God (9.13-14). These verses display once more the importance of defilement and purgation. The author continues the contrast between the earthly cult and the heavenly cult, being strict to maintain the importance of being made holy (ἁγιάζω) and being purged (καθαρότης) from defilement (κοινόω) in order to approach the presence of God.[114] Yom Kippur typology is maintained ('goats and bulls'), yet an intriguing addition of the 'ashes of a heifer' introduces the sole NT occurrence of the red cow ritual (Num. 19.1-21).[115] With Heb. 9.13 both purification and sanctification are granted key roles within the Levitical cult.

---

[111] Perfection is not synonymous with purification, contra Isaacs, *Sacred*, 101-2.

[112] David G. Peterson, *Possessed by God: A New Testament Theology of Sanctification and Holiness*, NSBT (Grand Rapids: Eerdmans, 1995), 36 (emphasis his own). Pace Moffitt, 'Weak', in *Lawlessness*, 100.

[113] Koester, *Hebrews*, 399; Peterson, *Perfection*, 136. Although, a distinction should be made between the perfection of Jesus and of believers. Perfection may involve purgation for believers, but this connotation does not apply to the Son (Heb. 4.15).

[114] Backhaus, *Hebräerbrief*, 320.

[115] Some understand the red heifer as just another 'external' purification rite, Koester, *Hebrews*, 415; Peterson, *Perfection*, 260 n. 78. See n. 67 in §3.3.3.

Hebrews draws on these rituals to demonstrate the superiority of Christ's *sprinkled* blood in the heavenly tabernacle, since central to both the red heifer and Yom Kippur rituals is the act of sprinkling. The author uses this comparative technique (πόσῳ μᾶλλον) to display the purgative power blood has in purifying the consciousness from 'dead works', enabling a participation in the heavenly cult. The reason Hebrews focuses on συνείδησις in relation to Christ's blood is because the author is responding to a need in the community (§1.2, §2.2). There might be a probable juxtaposing between σάρξ and συνείδησις here, but it should be understood as a contrast in cults (earthly–heavenly), not in anthropology.

Additionally, Heb. 10.1-4 is paramount for understanding the relationship between the earthly and heavenly cults in relation to the purification of the consciousness (§2.5.3). This passage reintroduces the notion of 'foreshadowing' with regards to the earthly and heavenly cult (§2.4.5; cf. 8.5). The law foreshadows (σκιά) the good things to come (10.1) which are being experienced now. The nature of the earthly cult and its perpetual sacrifices 'are never able to perfect the ones that approach' (οὐδέποτε δύναται[116] τοὺς προσερχομένους τελειῶσαι, 10.1).[117] The following conditional clause states that if they were able to, offerings would cease, because the worshippers would have no 'consciousness of sin' (συνείδησιν ἁμαρτιῶν) 'having been purged once-for-all' (ἅπαξ κεκαθαρισμένους, 10.2), yet 'in these [sacrifices there is] a reminder of sin annually' (10.3). The conclusion to this segment states 'for it is impossible for the blood of bulls and goats to take away[118] sins' (ἀδύνατον γὰρ αἷμα ταύρων καὶ τράγων ἀφαιρεῖν ἁμαρτίας, 10.4).[119] This passage (10.1-4) was introduced earlier (§2.5.3), but there are a few more additional points to raise here.

First, Hebrews displays an intrinsic connection between sacrifice and memory (of sin), both in a negative and positive manner.[120] On the one hand, Hebrews affirms that the repetitive nature of Levitical sacrifice only leads to a 'reminder of sin' (ἀνάμνησις ἁμαρτιῶν, 10.3). While 'memory/memorial' plays an important part in Jewish thought,[121] Hebrews focuses on the negative reminder of sin at this point.[122] But on the other hand, Hebrews also acknowledges a positive connection between sacrifice and memory (of sin) by stating that if perfection was attainable under the earthly cult (10.1) then the worshippers' consciousness of sin would have been cleansed once-for-all (10.2). Perfection here is defined indirectly as 'having been purged once-for-all' (ἅπαξ κεκαθαρισμένους) showing perfection to contain a qualitative type of

---

[116] Textual support for the plural form 'δύνανται' is notable (ℵ A C D¹ and other uncial and miniscule MSS), see Metzger, *Textual*, 600.
[117] The distinction here between priests (προσφέρω) and worshippers – the ones who bring the offerings (προσέρχομαι) – is evident, Delitzsch, *Hebrews*, 2:144.
[118] BDAG 154 has the sense of 'remove' too (cf. Heb. 10.11, περιαιρέω).
[119] References to the 'annual' (κατ' ἐνιαυτόν) reminder of sin points to Yom Kippur. While Heb. 10.4 may point to Yom Kippur, 10.11 – which parallels closely – points to daily sacrifices (every priest 'stands daily'). Contra Delitzsch who misses this distinction, *Hebrews*, 2:144–5. See Ellingworth for a helpful discussion concerning Heb. 10.4, *Hebrews*, 497–8.
[120] The plural 'ταῖς . . . θυσίαις' is umbrellaed with reference to the law (Heb. 10.1), further suggesting a generic reference to sacrifice, not only Yom Kippur.
[121] G. Boccaccini, *Middle Judaism: Jewish Thought, 300 B.C.E.-200 C.E.* (Minneapolis: Fortress, 1991), 230–40.
[122] Rightly Moore, *Repetition*, 174.

definite purgation, as opposed to an inferior form of purification.[123] Hebrews does not disparage the link between offerings and the removal of the consciousness of sin. Instead, this perpetual sacrificial routine is weak and not as effective as total purgation, simply because it requires repetition, not because it was ineffective or unable to purify the consciousness. If it were ineffective, one could deduce that the worshippers themselves would have refrained from this practice, but, on the contrary, they *believed* in this perpetual routine (§1.2, §2.2).[124] The repetitive nature of ritual may be weak, but it is not ineffective (§4.3.4).[125]

Hebrews does not deny that sacrifice and the removal of the memory of sin (consciousness of sin) was possible for the earthly cult, but that the earthly cult lacked a superior form of purification. This is highlighted when Hebrews chooses perfection terminology (τελειόω) in 9.9 instead of purification (καθαρίζω), suggesting that the old cultus could not bring about a totality of purgation (§4.3.3).[126] Hebrews is not joining in with contemporary debates concerning the internal connectedness of worship. Rather, Hebrews is arguing that Christ's heavenly offering has a distinctive qualitative superiority. Hence, when Hebrews says that 'it is impossible for the blood of bulls and goats to take away sins' (10.4), he means this in an absolute sense; their blood can take away sins, just not unequivocally (cf. 9.13-14). Lane is right therefore in stating that '[t]he issue is not whether the blood of bulls and goats sacrificed during the annual observances of the Day of Atonement ... has any power to effect cleansings, but whether it has the potency to effect a *decisive* cleansing'.[127] Conversely, it is not simply that it is a *better* form of purification, but that, as argued shortly, it only requires one single offering, as opposed to repetitive offerings (§5.4.3, §5.4.4).

The additional nuances regarding συνείδησις in 10.2 were introduced earlier (§2.5.3), with the term further defined as 'consciousness of sin' (συνείδησιν ἁμαρτιῶν, 10.2), a 'reminder of sin' (ἀνάμνησις ἁμαρτιῶν, 10.3) and simply, 'sins' (ἁμαρτίας, 10.4). Hence, by connecting these descriptors with συνείδησις it is reasonable to state that Hebrews is acknowledging the role of the consciousness/awareness of sin within sacrificial ritual. The earthly cult acts as a perpetual cycle reminding people of the problem they are attempting to solve – their consciousness of sin. Of course, sacrificial ritual and specifically Yom Kippur in this context (10.4) purifies God's dwelling place, but in Hebrews it also has a negative psychological impact for those involved.

4.4.3 Without αἱματεκχυσία there is no ἄφεσις (Heb. 9.22)

If the purification of the heavenly tabernacle coincides with the purification of the consciousness, then how might Heb. 9.22 be interpreted? In this verse two important

---

[123] Lane renders this as 'decisively to purge', *Hebrews*, 2:255.
[124] T. G. Stylianopoulos notes that sin was removed in the earthly cult (Heb. 9.18-23) but Christ's heavenly offering is plural (9.23), 'Shadow and Reality: Reflections on Hebrews 10:1–18', *GOTR* 17.2 (1972): 223–4.
[125] Moore, *Repetition*, 8, 166. Contra Westcott, *Hebrews*, 307–9.
[126] See Johnsson, 'Defilement', 282.
[127] Lane, *Hebrews*, 2:261–2 (emphasis his own).

terms require investigation: αἱματεκχυσία and ἄφεσις. First, the potentially coined[128] *hapax legomenon* αἱματεκχυσία[129] is traditionally rendered as the 'shedding of blood', and denotes ritual slaughter.[130] Others understand the term based on its compounds αἷμα and ἐκχύσις/ἐκχέω and their combined use in the LXX, meaning to 'pour out' at the end of cultic rituals (Exod. 29.12; Lev. 4.7, 18, 25, 30, 34; 8.15; 9.9).[131] Thornton in particular drives much of this viewpoint.[132] While these viewpoints have scholarly proponents, they both rely on input from outside of Hebrews in order to understand αἱματεκχυσία. Alternatively, the meaning behind αἱματεκχυσία can be grasped based on the preceding and subsequent verses in Hebrews, with the term being understood roughly as denoting the idea of 'blood manipulation'.[133]

The surrounding context (Heb. 9.18-23) includes the themes of covenant inauguration and heavenly purgation. The death of Jesus is likened to the inauguration of a covenant (9.18). Hebrews then references Exod. 24 and the inauguration of the Sinai covenant (Heb. 9.19-20). However, from 9.21 the καί represents a shift in topic, since it states that the tabernacle and all its objects were sprinkled, evoking Levitical language. The problem here is that the tabernacle was not yet built in Exod. 24. Yet in shifting topic and echoing Levitical language (concerning the tabernacle sprinkled with blood), Hebrews provides the necessary context for discussing heavenly tabernacle purgation from 9.22 onwards. Thus, 9.22a shows that almost everything is purged with blood under the law, but the καί is adversative; everything is purged with blood under the law, *but*, without blood manipulation (αἱματεκχυσία) there is no purgation (ἄφεσις). In this way, 9.22 as a whole relates to the OC and the NC. The difference between the two is in what follows, with 9.23 speaking of a 'better' heavenly sacrifice.

Central throughout 9.18-23 (and Hebrews typically) is the power of blood; it is *the* overarching theme. Johnsson is helpful here:

> Throughout, he has stressed the idea of blood as a religious force of surpassing potency: blood provides access, blood perfects the συνείδησις, blood inaugurates, blood cleanses ritual objects as well as the people, blood purges almost everything

---

[128] Bruce, *Hebrews*, 227 n. 143; T. C. G. Thornton, 'The Meaning of αἱματεκχυσία in Heb. IX.22', *JTS* 15.1 (1964): 63–5. Contra Allen, *Hebrews*, 483 n. 1042; N. H. Young, 'αἱματεκχυσία: A Comment', *ExT* 90.6 (1979): 180.

[129] A search of the TLG corpus reveals sixty-three other later occurrences of the term (although some of these are citations of Heb. 9.22). For summaries see Jamieson, *Death*, 141–56; Ribbens, *Levitical*, 155–6.

[130] Brondos, *Death*, 2:1021–2; Schreiner, *Hebrews*, 279–80; Cockerill, *Hebrews*, 410; Backhaus, *Hebräerbrief*, 332; Young, 'αἱματεκχυσία', 180; Michel, *Hebräer*, 321; Moffatt, *Hebrews*, 130; Delitzsch, *Hebrews*, 2:121–2. Ellingworth alludes to a Markan eucharistic setting, *Hebrews*, 474. See Mk 14.24; BDAG 27. Jamieson interprets this through the blood canon (Lev. 17.11), *Death*, 150–1.

[131] Church, *Temple*, 422; Ribbens, *Levitical*, 156; Moffitt, *Atonement*, 291–2 n. 157; Gäbel, *Kulttheologie*, 418; Koester, *Hebrews*, 420; Lane, *Hebrews*, 2:232, 246; Weiss, *Hebräer*, 482, n. 32; Attridge, *Hebrews*, 259; Braun, *Hebräer*, 279–80; Thornton, 'αἱματεκχυσία', 63–5; Spicq, *Hébreux*, 2:265.

[132] His strengths lie in outlining the process of sacrifice in his septuagintal analysis of the compounds in αἱματεκχυσία, Thornton, 'αἱματεκχυσία', 64. Yet, the pouring out of blood is not atoning, rightly Jamieson, *Death*, 143, see 142–50 for a detailed engagement and critique of Thornton's arguments.

[133] See also Heb. 11.28 and the Passover reference to the *hapax legomenon* πρόσχυσις (sprinkling [of blood]). It is not clear to what extent this informs Hebrews' prior discussion concerning sprinkling.

under the old law. He does not say: the high priest, after taking the life of the sacrificial animal, was able to enter the Most Holy; nor: Christ by his death perfected the συνείδησις; nor: the death of the covenant animals inaugurated the first covenant; nor: purgation under the old law required the killing of animals. This is the way we are prone to put the argument! If we are willing to let him present the argument in his own way, then by αἱματεκχυσία he must signify the *application* of blood.[134]

Blood is both powerful and versatile in that it provides access to and purgation of the heavenly tabernacle and the συνείδησις (9.7-14, 23) whilst also relating to death and covenant inauguration (9.15-20; §3.4). Therefore, in arriving at αἱματεκχυσία in 9.22, it would make sense to view the term as denoting the force or application of blood, not simply a reference to slaughter.

Hebrews seems to highlight the flexibility of blood when stating that just as blood sprinkling inaugurates a covenant, *likewise* (ὁμοίως) blood sprinkling is used to purge the tabernacle and its vessels (9.21). Thus, blood manipulation provides access, it purges the tabernacle, yet it also inaugurates; blood is essential for many things. By 9.22, Hebrews expresses this very idea when it states that 'almost everything is purified with blood' (σχεδὸν ἐν αἵματι πάντα καθαρίζεται). One might expect this to be the end of the clause, what much is there left to say? Yet Hebrews has not just been speaking about blood as an entity, or as a symbol, but as something which requires the active force of sprinkling (ῥαντίζω, 9.19, 21), with 9.23 a further reference to blood sprinkling in relation to the purging of the heavenly tabernacle (§4.2.2). Hebrews never speaks of spilling or pouring out blood, but references blood sprinkling instead (9.13, 19; 10.22; 12.24). Since both the preceding and subsequent verses (9.21, 23) discuss the importance of blood sprinkling, as well as 9.22 being sandwiched between the concept of καθαρίζω (9.22, 23), then one would expect αἱματεκχυσία in 9.22 to be rendered conceptually as 'blood manipulation' or 'blood use', with the 'shedding of blood' making little sense alongside the language of purgation.[135] It might also refer to sprinkling, yet ῥαντίζω would have been expected.

The second issue is how the term ἄφεσις is understood, here in 9.22 and subsequently in 10.18. Like αἱματεκχυσία, ἄφεσις has a few renderings. The most popular is 'forgiveness',[136] with translators reinforcing this idea by supplying the

---

[134] Johnsson, 'Defilement', 322–3 (emphasis his own).
[135] Rightly Harris, *Hebrews*, 238.
[136] Jamieson, *Death*, 133–4; Laansma, *The Letter to the Hebrews: A Commentary for Preaching, Teaching, and Bible Study* (Eugene, OR: Cascade, 2017), 213; Filtvedt, *Identity*, 105, 159–60; Moore, *Repetition*, 177; Schreiner, *Hebrews*, 279, 310–11; Easter, *Faith*, 69, 109; Amy L. B. Peeler, *You Are My Son: The Family of God in the Epistle to the Hebrews*, LNTS 486 (London: T&T Clark, 2014), 17, 136; Thompson, *Hebrews*, 197; Mackie, *Eschatology*, 188; Mitchell, *Hebrews*, 190, 204; Schenck, *Cosmology*, 84, 101–2; Johnson, *Hebrews*, 242, 254; Grässer, *Hebräer*, 2:185; Löhr, *Umkehr*, 253; Weiss, *Hebräer*, 482, 516; Bruce, *Hebrews*, 226–7; Attridge, *Hebrews*, 259; Riggenbach, *Hebräer*, 279; Hughes, *Hebrews*, 378, 408, 436; Moffatt, *Hebrews*, 130. Others understand the term as 'forgiveness' but see it within the larger scope of purification, Ribbens, 'Positive Functions', Son, 104–8; *Levitical*, 157; Moffitt, *Atonement*, 269, 291; Allen, *Hebrews*, 483; Gäbel, *Kulttheologie*, 410–12; Koester, *Hebrews*, 420.

absent genitive qualifier 'of sins' (ἁμαρτιῶν) in translations of 9.22 and 10.18 (ESV; NRSV).[137] This is often argued by drawing on the more common LXX verbal form, ἀφίημι, which frequently denotes the idea of forgiveness.[138] Nevertheless, Hebrews already employs ἀφίημι twice, with neither occurrence denoting 'forgiveness' (2.8; 6.1). Nowhere in the LXX does ἄφεσις denote 'forgiveness', but 'sending away'.[139] Others have suggested ἄφεσις as 'release' in Hebrews, with this including the appeasement of God's wrath. Except this requires αἱματεκχυσία to mean 'shedding', that is, Jesus' death absorbs humanity's penalty.[140] The most compelling rendering of ἄφεσις is 'decisive purgation'.[141] This can be put forward for a few reasons.

Some understand ἄφεσις to denote forgiveness because, apparently, 'forgiveness is an explicit goal of blood sacrifice',[142] yet this is not exclusively true. While the חטאת sacrifice on occasions does include 'forgiveness' (סלח, Lev. 4.20, 26), elsewhere, especially on Yom Kippur, forgiveness is never mentioned, rather, the purification of sins is prevalent (Lev. 16.19, 30). To quote Milgrom, כִּפֶּר in relation to the חטאת on Yom Kippur always means to '"purge" and nothing else',[143] since, for Milgrom, the sanctuary is being cleansed. Likewise, Hebrews understands sins as needing purification (Heb. 1.3), not forgiveness. Even when forgiveness (סלח) is mentioned in relation to the חטאת (Lev. 4.20, 26) Milgrom questions the notion of forgiveness. He writes, 'the offender who brings the ḥaṭṭā't does so because he knows that his wrong, though committed inadvertently, has polluted the altar and, hence, has alienated him from God. By his sacrifice he hopes to repair the broken relationship. He therefore seeks *more* than forgiveness.'[144] In returning to αἱματεκχυσία, the surrounding context suggests ἄφεσις should be associated with purgation, since it is juxtaposed alongside the notion of blood sprinkling and καθαρίζω (9.22, 23). Hebrews connects these ideas of purgation with the purification of the heavenly tabernacle (οὖν, 9.23a), thus, it does not make sense to render ἄφεσις as 'forgiveness', since the heavenly tabernacle requires purging, not forgiving.

Similarly with 10.18, ἄφεσις denotes a removal of sin. The context here is the Jer. 31.33-4 citation (Heb. 10.16-17). Interestingly, this second occurrence of Jer. 31 in Hebrews differs from the first citation (Heb. 8.8-13). The first citation is evidently longer than the second. The reference to putting laws in their minds and writing it on their hearts (8.10) –which denotes greater knowledge and enabled obedience – is

---

[137] The genitive ἁμαρτιῶν alongside ἄφεσις is the standard in most places (Mat. 26.28; Mk 1.4; Lk. 1.77; 3.3; 4.18; 24.47; Acts 2.38; 5.31; 10.43; 13.38; 26.18; Col. 1.14).

[138] Ribbens, *Levitical*, 154–60; Gäbel, *Kulttheologie*, 410–12. The verbal form occurs 125 times in the LXX, twelve of these occurring in Lev. 4–5 (Lev 4.20, 26, 31, 35; 5.6, 10, 13, 16, 18, 26; 16.10; 19.22). In Lev. 16.10, 26, ἄφεσις and ἀφίημι both refer to the 'sending away' of the scapegoat.

[139] Ellingworth, *Hebrews*, 474. While it is true that the NT often does employ ἄφεσις in reference to forgiveness, there are exceptions (cf. Lk. 4.18). Also, unlike Hebrews, most of the occurrences of ἄφεσις are accompanied alongside ἁμαρτία, see n. 137. The semantic range of ἄφεσις/ἀφίημι warrants a definition faithful to the context of Hebrews.

[140] Cockerill, *Hebrews*, 410–11; Spicq, *Hébreux*, 2:265; Westcott, *Hebrews*, 271.

[141] Anderson, *Hebrews*, 266; Ellingworth, *Hebrews*, 474, 515; Lane, *Hebrews*, 2:232–4, 247, 257, 269; Johnsson, 'Defilement', 328, 351–2. See also Braun, *Hebräer*, 280.

[142] Jamieson, *Death*, 134.

[143] Milgrom, *Leviticus 1-16*, 255.

[144] Milgrom, *Leviticus 1-16*, 245 (emphasis my own).

exchanged in the second citation, where laws are now written on minds and put into hearts (10.16). The first citation includes a reference to the Lord being 'merciful' (ἵλεως) towards iniquities (8.12), but this is omitted in the second citation, where the focus appears fixed on the Lord 'forgetting sins' (10.17).

It might be argued that the second citation of Jer. 31 (Heb. 10.16-17) describes both the earthly (objective) and heavenly (subjective) achievements of Christ (§3.7). The establishment of a new covenant through Jesus' death (§3.4.2) enables true obedience (the law written on minds and put into hearts, 10.16), this is Jesus' earthly objective achievement (cf. §3.6.3). However, the second aspect of this citation (10.17) connects more with Jesus' heavenly achievement. The Lord is spoken of emphatically as remembering their sins no more (οὐ μή). This is followed by a resumptive δέ[145] and the phrase 'where [there is] a decisive purgation of these, [there is] no longer [any] offering for sin' (ὅπου ... ἄφεσις τούτων, οὐκέτι προσφορὰ περὶ ἁμαρτίας, 10.18). The antecedent of the demonstrative pronoun (τούτων) points back to the sins and lawlessness (10.17). Importantly, Hebrews connects the Lord forgetting sins with the purgation (ἄφεσις) of sin (10.17-18). This juxtaposition implies that the Lord 'no longer remembering their sins' is another way of Hebrews referring to Jesus' heavenly blood offering. As argued previously, if not dealt with, sin threatens the departure of the Lord's presence in the tabernacle (§2.3.1, §4.2.2). However, Jesus' heavenly blood offering removes, not only the recipients' consciousness of sin, but the Lord's consciousness of *their* sins. Just as the Lord no longer remembers sin, so too, believers, through Christ's heavenly blood offering, are no longer to remember theirs (cf. 10.3).

Finally, when the needs of the recipients and the language of purgation throughout Hebrews is considered, it must be questioned as to whether a sermon on forgiveness was required. It has been argued throughout this study that Hebrews' prime concern is purging defilement and the present consciousness of sin. The theme of forgiveness, in the sense of a debt owed, is unwarranted in Hebrews. Johnsson is right when he states that, '[humankind's] problem here is not that he [or she] lacks righteousness, so that he [or she] cries out for 'right-wishing' nor is it a debt that he [or she] owes, so that he [or she] seeks forgiveness ... [humankind] faces the difficultly of the stain, the blot, the corruption of his [or her] person – that is, defilement'.[146] Forgiveness represents an unsatisfactory doctrine for the recipients (§1.2, §2.2). They do not require a sermon on forgiveness, but a promise of purgation for their consciousness of sin. Hebrews might understand the death of Jesus as obtaining forgiveness, but this is not the author's present concern. As Milgrom notes above, participants in sacrificial ritual often require *more* than forgiveness. Defilement and the consciousness of sin require 'purging' (1.3; 9.14, 22, 23; 10.2), 'doing away with' (10.11), 'taking away' (10.4) and 'removing' (9.26). This is because sin behaves like defilement and so within this semantic domain sin requires purging, as opposed to a debt that needs forgiving (§2.3, §2.5.3, §3.5.3).

---

[145] Rightly Ellingworth, *Hebrews*, 515. Contra Harris, *Hebrews*, 269.
[146] Johnsson, 'Defilement', 252.

4.4.4 Washing and sprinkling (Heb. 10.22)

Hebrews 10.22 supplies an additional layer to the purging of the consciousness.[147] After laying out the means of access into the heavenly sanctuary, the author includes himself in the hortatory subjunctive (προσερχώμεθα), to approach with true hearts in full assurance of faith '[and our] hearts sprinkled from a consciousness of evil and [our] body washed with pure water' (ῥεραντισμένοι τὰς καρδίας ἀπὸ συνειδήσεως πονηρᾶς καὶ λελουσμένοι τὸ σῶμα ὕδατι καθαρῷ, 10.22).[148] The meanings of both participles, 'sprinkling' (ῥεραντισμένοι) and 'washing' (λελουσμένοι), have attracted the attention of scholars.[149]

First, 'sprinkling' and 'washing' are understood as a reference to the recipients' prior baptism (cf. Heb. 6.1-2). There is no internal–external contrast between καρδία and σῶμα here, but both participles refer to the same reality, that is, interior sprinkling is a result of external washing.[150] Gäbel encourages a parallel reading with 1 Pet. 3.20-2, stating '[d]ie Taufe reinigt den Leib und das Herz'.[151] Others understand the 'sprinkling' as a reference to the blood of Christ's sacrifice on earth[152] and the 'washing' of bodies as Christian baptism.[153] The difficulty here is that sprinkling elsewhere refers to blood, not water (9.13, 19, 21; 12.24), which reverts the attention back to blood purgation and not baptism. Although it is true that water and blood are combined features in places (9.13, 19, 21), this view fails to account for the presence of blood.

A different approach points towards priestly consecration and argues that the first participle ('ῥεραντισμένοι') is the sprinkling of the blood of priestly consecration (cf. Exod. 29.20-1; Lev. 8.23-30), understood as Christ's earthly sacrifice. The second participle ('λελουσμένοι') refers to the washing of priests (cf. Exod. 29.4, 21; Lev. 8.6, 30), fulfilled in Christian baptism.[154] The implication is that the recipients form a

---

[147] Note the *inclusio* with Heb. 4.14-16.
[148] The choice to render the phrase 'συνειδήσεως πονηρᾶς' as 'consciousness of evil' is based on the conclusions in the introduction (§1.4.1).
[149] A eucharistic reading is proposed by Eberhart, *Kultmetaphorik*, 146-8; Weiss, *Hebräer*, 2:165-6; Wilhelm Thüsing, *Studien zur neutestamentlichen Theologie* (Tübingen: Mohr Siebeck, 1995), 184-200, esp. 186; 'Lasst uns hinzutreten (Hebr 10:22): zur Frage nach dem Sinn der Kulttheologie im Hebräerbrief', *BZ* 9.1 (1965): 1-17. Sacraments are not a domineering theme in Hebrews, rightly Pfitzner, *Hebrews*, 42.
[150] Greenlee, *Hebrews*, 376-7; Koester, *Hebrews*, 449; Bruce, *Hebrews*, 254-6; Hughes, *Hebrews*, 412; Montefiore, *Hebrews*, 174-5; Spicq, *Hébreux*, 2:317; Dahl, 'Living', 401-12, esp. 406-9. Similarly, Samuel Byrskog, 'Baptism in the Letter to the Hebrews', in *Ablution, Initiation, and Baptism: Late Antiquity, Early Judaism, and Early Christianity*, ed. David Hellholm et al., BZNW 176 (Berlin: de Gruyter, 2011), 595-7; Ellingworth, *Hebrews*, 523-4; Weiss, *Hebräer*, 530. Barnard argues for continuous washings, *Mysticism*, 196-208.
[151] 'Baptism purifies the body and the heart', Gäbel, *Kulttheologie*, 400. He reads this passage through the lens of the red heifer (as he does with 9.13-14; 12.24), 320-424, for 10.22 esp. 385-92, 424.
[152] Backhaus, *Hebräerbrief*, 359; Lane, *Hebrews*, 2:287.
[153] Harris, *Hebrews*, 275; Stolz, *Höhepunkt*, 217-20; Moore, *Repetition*, 189-91; Anderson, *Hebrews*, 276-7; Thompson, *Hebrews*, 204; Mitchell, *Hebrews*, 211-12; Bénétreau, *Hébreux*, 2:114; Johnsson, 'Defilement', 404-5.
[154] Westcott, *Hebrews*, 324-5; Delitzsch, *Hebrews*, 2:174-9. Other references to washings can be made (Exod. 40.12; Lev. 11.40; 14.8-9; 15.5-6; 16.4, 24, 26; 17.15; 22.6; Num. 19.7-8). See also Löhr, *Umkehr*, 263-5.

priesthood.¹⁵⁵ The priesthood of Christ is a clear motif in Hebrews, but the inauguration of a 'priesthood of believers' is not so apparent.¹⁵⁶

The fourth proposal is equally uncommon and views both participles as describing the purification which Christ's sacrifice achieves (obtained on earth, not in heaven)¹⁵⁷ with a possible further reference to Ezek. 36.25-6.¹⁵⁸ Schreiner concludes, '[s]aying that the body is "washed in pure water" is another way of describing the cleansing that comes through Jesus' offering of himself'.¹⁵⁹ The strengths of this viewpoint is that it focuses on the effects of Christ's offering and follows the narrative of Hebrews so far, without imposing less dominant themes like 'baptism' and the 'priesthood of believers'. The weaknesses are that it locates the referent of 10.22 to the earthly sphere and fails to consult what Jesus achieves in heaven.

Alternatively, it is possible to view the 'washing' and 'sprinkling' in this verse as occurring separately on earth and in heaven, in accordance with the conclusions of the previous chapter. Both perfect participles display the continuous effects of 'washing' and 'sprinkling' via Jesus' earthly and heavenly offerings.¹⁶⁰ Similar to the fourth view above, baptism does not seem to be in view. The washing of bodies may well be metaphorical, given that the heart was just described as being 'sprinkled' clean. It is likely that 'sprinkling' is a reference to Christ's heavenly blood offering (which purges the consciousnesses)¹⁶¹ and the 'washing' is a reference to the sanctification of believers, obtained by Christ on earth. The 'washing' of bodies 'represents the life of obedience'¹⁶² and is the objective sanctification of believes, being brought into the NC (cf. §3.6.3).

Furthermore, the reference to σῶμα here must be linked with the previous discussion concerning the obedience of Jesus' σῶμα (§3.6.1). The washed σῶμα in 10.22 is the vehicle of obedience – people made holy by Jesus' own obedience and earthly offering.¹⁶³ The 'sprinkling' of hearts from a consciousness of evil is the subjective effect of the purged heavenly tabernacle. It grants assurance (πληροφορία, 10.22) and it is by this heavenly blood that access and confidence (παρρησία) is granted (10.19). The 'heart' is a reference to the Jeremiah prophecy mentioned a few verses before (Heb. 10.16) – the NC enacted by Christ's earthly offering (§3.6.1). Commentators are tempted to connect the writing/putting of the law on minds/hearts (8.10; 10.16) as a reference to the cleansing of the συνείδησις.¹⁶⁴ Yet the purification of the consciousness and its removal from the heart are spoken of as two separate entities. The need to sprinkle this

---

¹⁵⁵ Peter J. Liethart, 'Womb of the World: Baptism and the Priesthood of the New Covenant in Hebrews 10.9-22', *JSNT* 22.78 (2000): 51-5; Moffatt, *Hebrews*, 144-5. Similarly, John M. Scholer, *Proleptic Priests: Priesthood in the Epistle to the Hebrews*, JSNTSup 49 (Sheffield: JSOT Press, 1991), 130-1.
¹⁵⁶ Cockerill, *Hebrews*, 474 and n. 39; Attridge, *Hebrews*, 288.
¹⁵⁷ Church, *Temple*, 387; Schreiner, *Hebrews*, 318-19; Cockerill, *Hebrews*, 474; Rissi, *Theologie*, 99-100.
¹⁵⁸ Cockerill, *Hebrews*, 474. See Thompson too, *Hebrews*, 204.
¹⁵⁹ Schreiner, *Hebrews*, 318.
¹⁶⁰ Rightly Moore, *Repetition*, 190. Not permissive middles, contra Cockerill, *Hebrews*, 475.
¹⁶¹ Cf. Heb. 9.13, 19, 21; 12.24. Rightly Gäbel, who sees the blood as analogous with the function of the water in Num. 19, *Kulttheologie*, 384.
¹⁶² Cockerill, *Hebrews*, 474.
¹⁶³ I agree mostly here with Cockerill's conclusions, *Hebrews*, 474-5. I differ though in seeing the blood as a reference to Jesus' heavenly offering.
¹⁶⁴ See my '*democratization* of συνείδησις' discussion in §1.4.2.

heart from an evil consciousness reveals that the consciousness of sin may well have been a hindrance to true obedience within the community. As argued previously, the enacting of a NC is to be associated with Jesus' earthly achievements and the purging of the consciousness with his heavenly achievements (§4.4.3).

With regards to sprinkling, outside of 10.22 the act of 'sprinkling' occurs four other times in Hebrews: three times in the verbal form (ῥαντίζω, 9.13, 19, 21) and once in the substantive (ῥαντισμός, 12.24). Hebrews might associate sprinkling with Christ, but as is the author's custom, he never spells out *explicitly* where or even how this sprinkling takes place in relation to Christ. As Davies states, sprinkling in Hebrews 'is present only by implication if at all'.[165] This is purposeful for Loader, who argues that Hebrews deliberately avoids 'anything that matches the high priest's taking blood with him into the Holiest place and sprinkling it on the mercy seat'.[166] As argued already, the cultic imagery of 'blood' refers to something more tangible and to Christ bringing his blood into the heavenly Holy of Holies. Although not a popular perspective, the sprinkling in 10.22 should be viewed as a reference to blood and its location being the heavenly tabernacle. This fits the narrative of Jesus *bringing* his blood into the heavenly tabernacle (§3.4.1, §4.2.1) as well as the connection between purging both the heavenly tabernacle and the consciousness of sin with blood (§4.2.2).[167]

4.5 Conclusion

This chapter began by re-establishing the connection between the status of people and the tabernacle within the cult. The solution to heavenly defilement is Christ's heavenly blood, which in turn coincides with the purification of the consciousness (§4.2.2). In turning to the impact of Jesus' heavenly offering, Hebrews' understanding of cultic purification was explored. Scholarship frequently interprets purification as a συνείδησις–σάρξ/internal–external negative juxtaposition (§4.3.1), however this was shown to be a misguided hermeneutic for two reasons. First, σάρξ is not a reference to external or inferior purification, but to earthly realities. Hebrews, therefore, is contrasting the present earthly cult with the present heavenly cult, maintained by Jesus' heavenly offering. The earthly cult possessed 'earthly regulations' and an 'earthly purification', not external ones (§4.3.3). The contrast between σάρξ and συνείδησις is an earthly–heavenly cultic blood contrast, not an internal–external one.

Second, Levitical sacrificial ritual was not merely an external exercise but contained a very real internal element. One's consciousness of sin, one's אָשָׁם, triggered the need to bring an offering in order to lessen the burden of guilt. The study of אָשָׁם further

---

[165] Davies, 'Heavenly', *Studia*, 388.
[166] Loader, 'Revisiting', 264. Also, Stolz, *Höhepunkt*, 238.
[167] So too Jamieson, *Death*, 164–5; Ribbens, *Levitical*, 133; Brooks, 'Perpetuality', 209. Contra, Loader, 'Revisiting', 243; Moffitt, 'Serving', *Hebrews in Contexts*, 276; Schenck, 'Archaeology', *Hebrews in Contexts*, 244; Schreiner, *Hebrews*, 268 n. 430; Cortez, 'Holy', 528; Mackie, *Eschatology*, 159, 167, 181–2; Ezra, *Kippur*, 188; Nelson, 'Offered', 256; Cody, *Heavenly*, 181. If Hebrews' sacrificial language is 'homeomorphic' then sprinkling must be affirmed, *pace* Moffitt, 'Serving', *Hebrews in Contexts*, 276.

complemented Hebrews' notion of the 'consciousness of sin', showing that Hebrews is writing in order to address a psychological void (§4.3.5). After differentiating perfection and purification (§4.4.1) it was argued that Hebrews understands the heavenly cult to possess a 'qualitative' type of purification (§4.4.2). The 'how much more' of Christ's blood refers to sin needing to be 'done away with' (10.11), 'taken away' (10.4), 'removed' (9.26), 'purged' (1.3; 9.14, 22, 23; 10.2) and 'sprinkled clean' (10.22; §4.4.3, §4.4.4). The Lord will never remember their sins because Jesus' heavenly offering has obtained a decisive purgation (ἄφεσις, 10.17-18).

The conclusions of this chapter provoke further questions which will be dealt with in the following chapter, such as, what does a purified consciousness look like? How exactly does Jesus' heavenly blood purify the consciousness? Is this blood offering once-for-all or perpetual? How does Jesus, as heavenly high priest, relate to and help his followers and how does this connect or differentiate from the theme of purification?

Part Three

Assurance and the purified consciousness

5

Divine help, assurance and perpetual blood

5.1 Introduction

This study has addressed the problem facing the recipients (consciousness of sin) and the sacrificial solution (heavenly purgation), but how does Hebrews understand Jesus and his heavenly blood offering relating to his followers *presently* with specific reference to their consciousness of sin? What constitutes Jesus' heavenly offering and what is the 'nature' and 'substance' of this offering? What relationship does Jesus' enthronement share with his heavenly offering? Does Jesus' seated posture indicate the finalization or beginning of his work? Is this offering once-for-all or perpetual? These questions also provoke further discussion of terms such as 'intercession' and 'meditation'.

To address these questions, this chapter is structured in the following manner. First, Jesus becoming high priest and his session is the starting point. It will argue that the enthronement of Christ is the culmination and celebration of his earthly life of obedience and while linked, it is not connected to the status of Jesus' heavenly offering. Instead, sitting down will not be equated with a finished work. Second, Jesus' role as high priest towards his followers will be looked at. Jesus as 'praying' or 'atoning' for his followers will be cautioned against. 'Divine help' is what Jesus primarily offers as high priest, with this 'divine help' aligned with access into the heavenly tabernacle, or, entering the 'rest'. In the third section the tensions around a once-for-all/perpetual offering will be resolved by viewing Jesus and his heavenly blood functioning as two independent agents – both convey 'perpetual assurance'. Jesus' role as 'guarantor' and 'mediator' are key aspects of 'assurance', but his heavenly blood offers ongoing perpetual assurance concerning purgation in relation to the consciousness of sin. Jesus' heavenly blood is his heavenly offering which 'speaks' purgation and assurance. It enables confidence, boldness and sacrificial amnesia.

5.2 Becoming the enthroned high priest

One of Hebrews' unique contributions to NT thought is the explicit designation of Jesus as high priest.[1] His function as heavenly high priest cannot be detached from his

---

[1] Although see Cullmann, *Christology*, 83–107.

earthly life of obedience; Jesus' enthronement is the reward and manifestation of his earthly obedience. Furthermore, Jesus' priestly work is tied to and informed by his earthly experiences; his ability to emphasize and offer help is because of Jesus' incarnational solidarity with humankind. Jesus' enthronement is often aligned with a finished sacrificial work. This section will conclude that Jesus' enthronement is the culmination of his suffering and life offering (§3.6.1). Jesus' heavenly session – while linked to his heavenly offering – marks the culmination and celebration of the enthroned obedient Son. The heavenly enthronement of Christ acts as both a messianic marker and a motivational narrative for the recipients' own perseverance.

5.2.1 The eternal Son (Heb. 1.1-14)

The exordium and catena establish both the eternal unchanging identity of the Son (Heb. 1.1-4)[2] and his superiority above all (1.5-14). 'What the Son has been from all eternity comes to fruition and full expression in his exaltation and session.'[3] Some have likened the description of Jesus in the exordium to personified Wisdom or the divine *Logos*,[4] leading scholars to deny a personal pre-existence of Jesus in Hebrews; 'Christ only exists as a function of God'.[5] Hebrews no doubt joins in with contemporary terminology, yet as Peeler notes, '[this] does not prove that it [Hebrews] uses that language in the same way'.[6] The language may be that of Wisdom or Philo, but as Bruce puts it, '[for Hebrews] the language is descriptive of a man who had lived and died in Palestine . . . but who nonetheless was the eternal Son and supreme revelation of God'.[7] Hence, the exalted Son *is* the eternal Son. The same Son who was instrumental in creation (1.2b; cf. Jn 1.3; Col. 1.16) has arrived in these final days to bring about a heavenly purgation before sitting at the right hand of the majesty on high (Heb. 1.3c; cf. 1.13; 8.1; 10.12-13; 12.2).

Since the purification of sins is in close proximity with Jesus' enthronement (1.3), this is typically viewed as denoting a finished sacrificial work.[8] Enthronement and heavenly purgation share a locational connection (1.3), but both of these acts are

---

[2] The exordium is a 'favour winning' mechanism, see M. W. Martin and J. A. Whitlark, eds, *Inventing Hebrews: Design and Purpose in Ancient Rhetoric*, SNTSMS 171 (Cambridge: Cambridge University Press, 2018), 193–201.
[3] Cockerill, *Hebrews*, 96.
[4] Wisdom 'rules' the world and 'sits' by the heavenly throne (Wis. 9.1-4) is active in creation (7.22; 9.2; Prov. 8) and resembles God in likeness (Wis. 7.25-6). Compare Hebrews' description of Jesus as a 'reflection' (ἀπαύγασμα) of God's glory (Heb. 1.3) with Wisdom's description of Sophia as a 'reflection of eternal light' (ἀπαύγασμα . . . φωτὸς ἀϊδίου, Wis. 7.26). Similarities with Philo's *Logos* are also likened to Jesus, see Thompson, *Hebrews*, 34–6.
[5] Kenneth L. Schenck, 'Keeping His Appointment: Creation and Enthronement in Hebrews', *JSNT* 19.66 (1997): 115, 119. Also 'A Celebration of the Enthroned Son: The Catena of Hebrews 1', *JBL* 120.3 (2001): 469–85. See James D. G. Dunn, *Christology in the Making: A New Testament Inquiry into the Origins of the Doctrine of the Incarnation* (London: SCM, 1980), 163–212, 213–49.
[6] Peeler, *Son*, 26, esp. 26–9. Also, Barnard, *Mysticism*, 153–4; Cockerill, *Hebrews*, 99–100.
[7] Bruce, *Hebrews*, 48.
[8] Moore, 'Session', 531; Harris, *Hebrews*, 16; Mason, 'Sit', *Teacher*, 907–12; Mackie, *Eschatology*, 169; David M. Hay, *Glory at the Right Hand: Psalm 110 in Early Christianity*, SBLMS 18 (Nashville: Abingdon, 1973), 87.

independent with unique purposes. Enthronement acts as the 'celebration of the enthroned son';[9] it is the culmination of Jesus' life and obedient earthly offering (§3.6.1). Enthronement is related to sonship; it is confirmation of the divine Son's unmatchable glory. Enthronement confirms the Son but it is not directly for the benefit of others. Likewise, Jesus' heavenly offering benefits others, but it is not for the benefit of the Son. Therefore, Jesus 'sitting down' showcases the Son's glory but it does not indicate the nature of Jesus' heavenly offering. While seated, Jesus functions as high priest through his heavenly ministry.

Hebrews continues its praise of the Son by contrasting him with the angels in a flurry of citations (1.5-14). The Son is not only superior to all, but all things are now subject to him (1.13). Enthronement is not divorced from incarnation and so the first two chapters of Hebrews should be read harmoniously. Hebrews' implementation of Ps. 8 (Heb. 2.6-8) is especially intended to be informed by Hebrews' first chapter.[10]

5.2.2 The narrative of the enthroned son (Heb. 2.5-9)

After introducing the first of his warnings (Heb. 2.1-4) Hebrews continues the theme of 'subjection' (1.13). The author asks, if the coming world was not subjected to angels, who was it subjected to (2.5)? We know it was subjected to the Son (1.13), but Hebrews now shows *how* it became subject to him, through the implementation of Ps. 8 (Heb. 2.6-8).[11] In Ps. 8 both the creative nature of the Lord is displayed and humankind's inability to understand creation. The 'heavens' and the 'moon and stars' leave the psalmist in awe, asking 'what are human beings that you are mindful of them?'[12] As a result the psalmist 'becomes intensely aware of his existence within the cosmos'.[13] In reflecting on the work of God's hands the psalmist considers humanity, who, as part of God's creation not only possesses worth (Ps. 8.5) but status (8.6) and responsibility too (8.6-8). The psalmist declares that the Lord has 'put all things under their feet' (8.6b). In short, Ps. 8 describes humankind with the utmost dignity and appraisal, of which, 'no humanist ever dreamed'.[14] But who does Hebrews understand the referent in the Psalm to be? Whose 'feet' are all things under (Heb. 2.8)?

---

[9] Taken from Schenck, 'Celebration'.

[10] Caird, 'Exegetical', 47–9.

[11] For a thorough examination of Hebrews' use of Ps. 8 see Angela Costley, *Creation and Christ: An Exploration of the Topic of Creation in the Epistle to the Hebrews*, WUNT 2.527 (Tübingen: Mohr Siebeck, 2020), 202–35.

[12] My choice to render ἄνθρωπος here as 'human beings' is based on the NRSV and partly on Craig L. Blomberg's conclusions, '"But We See Jesus": The Relationship Between the Son of Man in Hebrews 2.6 and 2.9 and the Implications for English Translations', in *A Cloud of Witnesses: The Theology of Hebrews in its Ancient Contexts*, ed. Richard Bauckham et al., LNTS 387 (London: T&T Clark, 2008), 88–99.

[13] Gerda de Villiers, 'Reflections on Creation and Humankind in Psalm 8, the Septuagint and Hebrews', *Psalms and Hebrews*, 69–82. The Hebrew Psalm uses two terms to refer to humans, אנוש (8.4a) and the more common, אדם (8.4b). The term אנוש suggests human frailty and weakness, with the LXX employing ἄνθρωπος for both terms, reducing the 'beauty of the poem', 78.

[14] Donald G. Miller, 'Why God Became Man: From Text to Sermon on Hebrews 2.5-18', *Int* 23.4 (1969): 413.

Scholars typically interpret Hebrews' use of Ps. 8 in three ways: 'Christological',[15] 'anthropological',[16] or a blend of both.[17] Understanding Ps. 8 as telling 'the story of Jesus'[18] is the most convincing reading.[19] The anthropological reading claims that Ps. 8 was originally addressed to humanity, yet the Psalm has an eclectic interpretative history, where it is understood as describing certain individuals, either Moses, Adam, Abraham, or a future Messiah.[20] Additionally, it is important that Ps. 8 is not isolated but viewed within a family of Psalms with a common messianic tradition, which Hebrews cites.[21] Even if Ps. 8 was initially addressed to humanity, in the light of Jesus' incarnation and exaltation in Hebrews, the Psalm takes on supplementary meaning. God has now spoken through his Son (Heb. 1.2) and so, Hebrews interprets Scripture in the light of this revelation whilst being keen to listen to what the Holy Spirit is saying now (3.7; 10.15). Early Jewish texts applied Ps. 8 to humanity's dominion over creation,[22] but for Hebrews' NT contemporaries Ps. 8 was messianic.[23] The creation mandate is possibly in the author's view (Gen. 1.26-30) although Adamic typology and notions of

---

[15] Jason Maston, '"What is Man?" An Argument for the Christological Reading of Psalm 8 in Hebrews 2', ZNW 112.1 (2021): 89–104; Harris, Hebrews, 45–50; Amy L. B. Peeler, 'The Eschatological Son: Christological Anthropology in Hebrews', in Anthropology and New Testament Theology, ed. Jason Maston and Benjamin E. Reynolds, LNTS 529 (London: T&T Clark, 2018), 161–76; Cockerill, Hebrews, 126–35; G. H. Guthrie and R. D. Quinn, 'A Discourse Analysis of the Use of Psalm 8:4-6 in Hebrews 2:5–9', JETS 49.2 (2006): 235–46; Aquila H. I. Lee, From Messiah to Preexistent Son: Jesus' Self-Consciousness and Early Christian Exegesis of Messianic Psalms, WUNT 2.192 (Tübingen: Mohr Siebeck, 2005), 221–3; Robert L. Brawley, 'Discursive Structure and the Unseen in Hebrews 2:8 and 11:1: A Neglected Aspect of the Context', CBQ 55.1 (1993): 81–98; Lane, Hebrews, 1:48; Bruce, Hebrews, 72–4; Attridge, Hebrews, 72.

[16] Jamieson, Death, 101–7; Church, Hebrews, 293–303, esp. 301–3; Compton, Psalm 110, 38–51; Easter, Faithfulness, 35–45; Blomberg, 'Jesus', Cloud, 88–99; Gäbel, Kulttheologie, 134–48; Ellingworth, Hebrews, 150; Bénétreau, Hébreux, 1:109–10; L. D. Hurst, 'The Christology of Hebrews 1 and 2', in The Glory of Christ in the New Testament: Studies in Christology in Memory of George Bradford Caird, ed. L. D. Hurst and N. T. Wright (Oxford: Oxford University Press, 1987), 153–4; Moffatt, Hebrews, 21–3; Westcott, Hebrews, 41–5. English translators add to this viewpoint by referring to 'human beings' in the Psalm citation (CEV; NLT; NRSV; TNIV).

[17] Moore, Repetition, 109–11; Moffitt, Atonement, 120–9; Chris L. De Wet, 'The Messianic Interpretation of Psalm 8:4-6 Part II', Psalms and Hebrews, 123–5; Schenck, Cosmology, 53–60; Koester, Hebrews, 364; deSilva, Perseverance, 108–11; Dale F. Leschert, Hermeneutical Foundations of Hebrews (Lewiston: Edwin Mellen, 1994), 98–115. Whether Hebrews implies a 'ruling with Christ' (cf. 1 Cor. 6.2-4; 2 Tim. 2.12; Rev. 20.6) is not certain.

[18] Peeler, 'Eschatological', Anthropology, 163; Cockerill, Hebrews, 131.

[19] Peeler notes, '[t]he Son's story, as described in Psalm 8, is not just his own, however, but becomes the template and doorway for all others', 'Eschatological', Anthropology, 161.

[20] For a survey, see M .S. Kinzer, '"All Things Under His Feet": Psalm 8 in the New Testament and in Other Jewish Literature of Late Antiquity' (PhD diss., University of Michigan, 1995). For messianic readings of Ps. 8, see C. W. Retief, 'A Messianic Reading of Psalm 8', OTE 27.3 (2014): 992–1008.

[21] Ps. 2.7 (Heb. 1.5); Ps. 45.6-7 (Heb. 1.8-9); Ps. 8 (Heb. 2.6-8); Ps. 110.1 (Heb. 1.13); 4QFlor 1, 1-19; Pss. Sol. 17.23-8; Midr. Ps. 2.9 are often included in this discussion. See Leschert, Hermeneutical, 14–15, 77, 95–7, 121; F. J. Maloney, 'The Reinterpretation of Psalm VIII and the Son of Man Debate', NTS 27.5 (1981): 656–72. For messianism in Ps. 2 see Midr. Gen. Rab. 44.8; b. Sukkah 52a.

[22] Other early Jewish readings of Ps. 8 link it to dominion granted to humankind at creation. Creation being subject to humanity (2 En. 31.1-5; 58.2-3) and human beings having dominion over creation (Wis. 9.2; Sir. 17.4; 4 Ezra 6.45-6, 54; Jub. 2.14; 4Q504 8 I, 4-5 (אדם)); Philo, Op. Mund. 52; 84; b. Sanh. 38b). See Georg Gäbel, 'Rivals in Heaven: Angels in the Epistle to the Hebrews', in Angels: The Concept of Celestial Beings: Origins, Development and Reception, ed. Friedrich V. Reiterer, Tobias Nicklas and Karin Schöpflin, DCLY 2007 (Berlin: de Gruyter, 2007), 357–76.

[23] Mat. 21.16; 1 Cor. 15.27-8; Eph. 1.20-2. Cf. Phil. 3.21; 1 Pet. 3.22.

the 'fall' are unwarranted.[24] Hebrews' use of Ps. 8 does not provide 'a ready vehicle for Adam Christology'.[25]

Second, when Hebrews refers to the Greek Psalm, it is noteworthy that the author omits part of the citation, 'the works of your hands' (τὰ ἔργα τῶν χειρῶν σου, Ps. 8.7) and the one who has dominion over the animals (Ps. 8.8-9). This inclusion would have enhanced an anthropological reading; its omission may imply that Hebrews sought to make the Psalm more about Jesus and less about humanity.[26] Third, the practice of blending Ps. 110.1 with Ps. 8 elsewhere (cf. 1 Cor. 15.25-8; Eph. 1.20-2) indicates further that Ps. 8 refers to Jesus. This example of 'gezera shawa' is important since Ps. 110 and Ps. 8 both speak of submission and the putting of 'enemies' (Ps. 110.1), or 'all things'[27] (Ps. 8.6) under feet (Pss. 8.6; 110.1). Together, both Psalms provide a now/not yet eschatological tension, since Ps. 8 refers to that which has already been subjected and Ps. 110 refers to that which is yet to be subjected. Hebrews 'responds to the question, "Which is it: have all things been submitted to the Son, or does his universal reign lie in the future?" His answer: "Yes to both!"'[28] By attaching Ps. 110.1 to Jesus previously (Heb. 1.3, 13), it makes sense that Ps. 8 would refer to Jesus later (Heb. 2.6-8). The blending of both Psalms further strengthens the unity of thought in the first two chapters of Hebrews. Jesus naturally fits the personage of Ps. 8 if the first two chapters of Hebrews are read harmoniously and not in isolation. Jesus' divinity and superiority over angels does not end in Heb. 1.14 but continues into Ps. 8 (Heb. 2.6-8). Hook words unite the first two chapters, with μέλλω (1.14, 2.5) and ἄγγελος (1.13, 2.5) creating a natural transition. These hook words are important because they infer that the previous comparison between Jesus and the angels (1.13-14) is supposed to be held onto as Ps. 8 is introduced (2.5-6).[29]

Fourth, Jesus is the 'Son of Man' in Ps. 8. An anthropological reading of Ps. 8 is encouraged by the fact that Jesus (Ἰησοῦς) is not explicitly mentioned until Heb. 2.9.[30] The 'ambiguous' personal pronouns in the cited Psalm (Heb. 2.6b-8) could refer to anyone.[31] This is a weak argument, since Ἰησοῦς is not mentioned in the exordium or catena either. The contentious personal pronouns (2.6b-8) *do* refer to Jesus, the 'Son of Man' (υἱὸς ἀνθρώπου, Heb. 2.6). Each personal pronoun (2.6b-8) finds its grammatical antecedent with either 'υἱὸς ἀνθρώπου' or 'ἄνθρωπος' (2.6), or both,[32] meaning that it is possible Hebrews understood the reference to 'υἱὸς ἀνθρώπου' as a Christological nuance. It is true that 'υἱὸς ἀνθρώπου' could mean 'human being',[33] but a first century early Christian reading was likely messianic.[34] It is 'hard to imagine' as France argues, 'that any Christian,

---

[24] Pace Jamieson, *Death*, 102; Compton, *Psalm 110*, 51; Gäbel, 'Rivals', *Angels*, 361–71.
[25] Dunn, *Christology*, 109.
[26] MS evidence for omitting Ps. 8.7a include 𝔓⁴⁶ B D² K L and other witnesses. The longer reading (ℵ A C D* Ψ) may exhibit a scribal enlargement of the text, Metzger, *Textual*, 593–4.
[27] 'All things' as Peeler rightly notes, 'encompasses much more than the earth alone', *Son*, 68.
[28] Guthrie and Quinn, 'Discourse', 242.
[29] Guthrie and Quinn, 'Discourse', 239–40; Westfall, *Discourse*, 100.
[30] Jamieson, *Death*, 100–1; Compton, *Logic*, 43.
[31] NA²⁸ brackets the first mention of 'αὐτῷ' in Heb. 2.8, with 𝔓⁴⁶ B d v and Vulgate MSS excluding it. The decision to include it is supported favourably by ℵ A C D K L P Ψ 𝔐 and other uncial and miniscule MSS. See Church's discussion, *Temple*, 300–1 n. 121. Although 'δὲ' can function as a conjunction, Wallace, *Grammar*, 671. The interpretive decision must be made concerning 'αὐτῷ' (2.8).
[32] See Ellingworth, *Hebrews*, 149–53.
[33] De Wet, 'Messianic', *Psalms and Hebrews*, 122.
[34] Moffitt points out various 2TP texts which support this reading, *Atonement*, 125.

particularly a Greek-speaking Christian, after the middle of the first century could have heard the phrase υἱὸς ἀνθρώπου without thinking of Jesus'.[35] Jesus as the 'υἱὸς ἀνθρώπου' may also have been foreshadowed by other occurrences of υἱός (1.2, 5, 8; 3.6; 4.14; 5.5, 8; 6.6; 7.3; 10.29) with the occurrence in the exordium providing a further link with 2.6-8.[36] In arriving at 2.9 it becomes evident that the 'Son under discussion is finally identified as a particular human being – Jesus'.[37] This is further supported since each personal pronoun in the Psalm citation (Heb. 2.6b-8) is singular. Finally, the claim that Ps. 8 is abstruse in its referent is difficult to maintain. As Barrett noted, the 'figure who stands over against the angels is, as ch[apter] 1 makes unmistakably clear, not man in general but the Son of God; it is to him that the world to come is made subject'.[38]

In sum, by understanding Ps. 8 as describing the 'narrative of the enthroned Son', it is possible to view Jesus' enthronement as the culmination of Jesus' obedient journey and not simply as indicating the nature of his heavenly purgation. Psalm 8 describes the Son's status as well as his incarnation and solidarity with humankind. In this way it shares similarities with other early Christian hymns (Phil. 2.5-11) that describe the lowering and elevating of Jesus. Through Ps. 8, Hebrews notes that Jesus (ἄνθρωπος) was made temporarily 'a little while' (βραχύ τι) lower than the angels (Heb. 2.7a; 2.9) before being enthroned with all things under his feet (2.7-8). That 'βραχύ τι' refers to 'time' over 'degree' is likely.[39] Some argue that the participle 'being made lower' (ἠλαττωμένον) should override the meaning of 'βραχύ τι' (2.9), resulting in Jesus' continued state as a human.[40] It is more likely that 'βραχύ τι' is modifying the participle 'ἠλαττωμένον', meaning that 'being made lower' ends 'after a little while'. This is further highlighted later when Jesus is described as 'having shared' (μετέσχεν) 'flesh and blood' (2.14).

Sitting down indicates the Son's status, power and accomplishment. It is the culmination of Jesus' obedience and suffering, not necessarily an announcement regarding a finished cultic work. Jesus certainly sat down after making purification for sins, but the act of sitting down is to be understood alongside the narrative of the enthroned Son, as displayed in Heb. 1-2.

5.2.3 A high priest, like Melchizedek (Heb. 5.1-10; 7.1-28)

The Son might have sat down, but Jesus' priestly role has just begun.[41] According to Hebrews every high priest is chosen from among humans to 'offer gifts and sacrifices for sins' (Heb. 5.1) for themselves and for the people (5.3). Jesus' earthly life of obedience,

---

[35] R. T. France, 'The Writer of Hebrews as Biblical Expositor', *TynBul* 47.2 (1996): 262. This relies on the Greek speaker being aware of the Hebrew background to the term, Guthrie and Quinn, 'Discourse', 243–4.

[36] It is true that the phrase lacks the typical definite article that accompanies it in the Gospels, with Jesus referring to himself 80 times as 'the Son of Man', although see Dan. 7.13.

[37] Moffitt, *Atonement*, 125.

[38] C. K. Barrett, *On Paul: Aspects of His Life, Work and Influence in the Early Church* (London: T&T Clark, 2003), 202.

[39] See *GELS* 122; Isa. 57.17; Jn 6.7.

[40] Cockerill, *Hebrews*, 133.

[41] Much has been written concerning 'when' Jesus becomes a high priest. For a recent overview see Jamieson, *Death*, 25–35. Many point to Heb. 8.4 as proof of Jesus becoming a priest in heaven, yet this verse might be read as referring to him being able to *function* as a high priest. Like becoming a 'Son' (1.4-5; 5.5) Jesus was always high priest, but only functioned in this role in heaven.

through suffering and death, bypasses any need for Jesus to perform a literal sacrifice for himself (§3.6.2). He fulfils the true desire/will of the Lord, as outlined in Ps. 40 (§3.6.1). This is what Hebrews displays in the following verses (Heb. 5.7-10) – a persevering description of the Son's obedience. Jesus' earthly 'vocational' perfection (§4.4.1) is bound up in his sonship and leads to his priestly ministry. Thus, Hebrews can state 'although being Son' (καίπερ ὢν υἱός) Jesus 'learned obedience through what he suffered' (5.8).

To illustrate the nature of Jesus' high priesthood the enigmatic figure of Melchizedek is drawn upon, cited briefly through Ps. 110.4 (Heb. 5.6, 10; 6.20) but expounded upon later (7.1-28). Hebrews draws on the Gen. 14 narrative to introduce Melchizedek and his priesthood (Heb. 7.1-2, 4-10) whilst adding three alpha privatives further defining him as 'without father, without mother, without genealogy' (ἀπάτωρ ἀμήτωρ ἀγενεαλόγητος).[42] The Melchizedekean priesthood is superior to the Levitical priesthood because it remains forever (7.23-4); Melchizedek is 'likened' (ἀφωμοιωμένος) to Jesus, since his priesthood 'remains forever' (7.3). Melchizedek's 'eternity' and superior priesthood have caused scholars to speculate as to how this fits alongside Jesus' eternal priesthood. Some place Melchizedek alongside the ministering angels in the opening chapter (1.5-14).[43] Others have gone further, arguing that Hebrews sought to pit Jesus against the rise of the Qumran Archangel Warrior-Redeemer, Melchizedek.[44]

Despite these claims, there are no clear indications within Hebrews of a 'Melchizedek speculation'. Melchizedek is never described as an angel in Hebrews, nor is he disparaged or pitted against Jesus.[45] Melchizedek is merely 'likened' to Jesus, with 7.3 pointing to Melchizedek's elusiveness in Scripture, not his ontology. His eternity anticipates, not rivals, Jesus' eternal priesthood.[46] Hebrews might be said to be 'harvesting exegetical fruit from the typological trees [in the OT]'.[47] 'It is inconceivable', as Cockerill notes, 'that the author would insist on the Son's eternity in contrast to the angels' temporality in Heb. 1.5-14 and then use an angel to affirm the Son's eternity'.[48] Instead, Hebrews relies on the only two OT texts which describe Melchizedek (Gen. 14.17-24; Ps. 110.4), leaving the recipients with no supplemented data other than the fact that this mysterious figure acts as a signpost towards Jesus' heavenly priestly ministry.[49]

---

[42] Lane translates this phrase as '[h]is father, mother and line of descent are unknown', *Hebrews*, 1:157.
[43] Barnard, *Mysticism*, 121-30, esp. 128-30; Moffitt, *Atonement*, 203-8; Mason, *Priest*, 138-90; Rissi, *Theologie*, 89.
[44] Richard N. Longenecker, 'The Melchizedek Argument of Hebrews: A Study in the Development and Circumstantial Expression of New Testament Thought', in *Unity and Diversity in New Testament Theology: Essays in Honor of George E. Ladd*, ed. Robert A. Guelich (Grand Rapids: Eerdmans, 1978), 161-85.
[45] Other 2TP texts are relatively transparent about the identity of Melchizedek, whether an 'angelic being' (11Q13) a 'priest' (4Q401) or a 'human' (Philo, *Abr.* 253; *Congr.* 99; *Leg. All.* 3.79-82; Josephus, *Ant.* 1.179-81; *War* 6.438) but Hebrews appears evasive.
[46] Cockerill, *Hebrews*, 302.
[47] C. Bird, 'Typological Interpretation Within the Old Testament: Melchizedekian Typology', *CJ* 26 (2000): 48.
[48] Gareth L. Cockerill, 'Melchizedek Without Speculation: Hebrews 7.1-25 and Genesis 14.17-24', *Cloud*, 132.
[49] See Regev, *Temple*, 260-1; Cockerill, *Hebrews*, 298-98 n. 14, 300-6; 'Melchizedek or "King of Righteousness"', *EvQ* 63.4 (1991): 305-12; Richard Bauckham, 'The Divinity of Jesus in the Epistle to the Hebrews', *Hebrews*, 28-31; Leschert, *Hermeneutical*, 232-3; Hay, *Glory*, 153.

The inability of the Levitical priesthood to bring 'perfection' explains the need for a different priest to arise (Heb. 7.11), one from the tribe of Judah, anticipated in Ps. 110.4 (Heb. 7.13-14). This priest resembles Melchizedek, arising not through genealogy, but through the power of an 'indestructible life' (7.15-16). The reference to an indestructible (ἀκατάλυτος) life is regarded as a type of qualitative eternal life, obtained when Jesus rose from the dead.[50] Conversely, attributing indestructible life to Jesus' resurrection body and not to his earthly incarnate body might be said to undermine Hebrews' previous emphasis regarding the eternal nature of Jesus (1.1-4; cf. 13.8). 'Indestructible life' can equally be applied to Jesus' divinity, innate to him throughout his earthly and heavenly functioning.[51] Any claim that Jesus did not possess indestructible life before his resurrection is unfounded in Hebrews; if anything, rising from the dead *proves* his indestructible life.

5.3 Divine help

According to Hebrews, its main point (κεφάλαιον)[52] is that the recipients presently have a ministering high priest in the heavenly tabernacle (Heb. 8.1-2),[53] yet how does Jesus function as a heavenly ministering high priest and what are the implications for the recipients? The term 'intercession' is often used by scholars to describe this priestly work, although 'intercession' means different things to different scholars. Moore understands intercession as involving prayer,[54] but claims that it is not associated with atonement since Jesus' seated position denotes the end of his cultic work. Sitting, however, might denote ongoing work, since he must sit down *until* all enemies are under his feet (Ps. 110.1). In contrast, Moffitt describes intercession as 'the ongoing work of making his people holy and perfect'.[55] Intercession is 'sanctifying', 'atoning' and enables 'complete salvation',[56] ensuring that the 'new covenant is being maintained',[57] and also involves prayer.[58] The recipients require ongoing atonement and sanctification for sin via Jesus' intercessory role, according to Moffitt.[59] Instead, Moore follows others in viewing

---

[50] The language of another priest arising (ἀνίστημι, Heb. 7.11, 15) has been understood as a reference to the resurrection, see Regev, *Temple*, 262; Jamieson, *Death*, 30–3; Alan Kan-Yau Chan, *Melchizedek Passages in the Bible: A Case Study for Inner-Biblical and Inter-Biblical Interpretation* (Berlin: de Gruyter, 2016), 192; Moore, *Repetition*, 165–6; Moffit, *Atonement*, 148, 203, 208, 218; Karrer, *Hebräer*, 2:84. Alternatively, the messianic apocalyptic notion of someone 'arising' makes good sense, see Cockerill, *Hebrews*, 316 n. 13, 320 n. 36.
[51] Cockerill, *Hebrews*, 323–4.
[52] I take κεφάλαιον to refer to Heb. 8.1 and beyond, see Lane, *Hebrews*, 1:204; BDAG 541.
[53] Key here is the *place* of his exaltation, rightly Moffitt, 'Interceding', 545; McKelvey, *Pioneer*, 101.
[54] Moore connects this to the תמיד (Exod. 28.29-30; cf. Heb. 9.6; 13.15).
[55] Moffitt, 'Finished', *So Great*, 158–9, 174. Also 'Interceding', 547.
[56] Moffitt, 'Finished', *So Great*, 168. In relation to Heb. 7.25 he writes that, 'were it the case that Jesus were not actively interceding for his people, their complete salvation would not be possible. Yet this implication suggests another: Jesus' followers are in need of ongoing atonement', 168.
[57] Moffitt, 'Interceding', 547.
[58] Moffitt, 'Interceding', 548–51.
[59] Like Moffitt I have sought to draw out similarities between Hebrews and the Levitical cult rather than pitting them against one another (§4.3.3, §4.3.4, §4.3.5). Yet while the NC and OC offered ongoing atonement – including purging the consciousness of sin – the prime difference is that Jesus' heavenly blood is offered once perpetually, offering assurance for their consciousness of sin, as will be argued in the final section (§5.4).

intercession as helping the recipients to *not* sin, as opposed to further forgiveness when they do.[60] Both Moore and Moffitt use 'intercession' broadly, although the term only occurs once in Hebrews (7.25). In light of this, 'intercession' will not be used in such a broad manner in what follows. This section will argue that Jesus' prime function as a heavenly priest is to offer 'divine help' for his followers, not atonement or forgiveness.

5.3.1 Holiness, fighting temptation and post-baptismal sin

One of the primary threats facing the recipients is the temptation to leave their community (§1.2, §2.6.3). The author's solution is to centre his rhetoric around the cosmic purgation of Christ. The recipients have been made holy by Jesus' life culminating in death (§3.6.3) and their consciousness of sin has been purified by his heavenly blood. Holiness is a state they share in (Heb. 2.11; 3.1; 10.10, 29; 13.12, 24); nevertheless it still requires pursuit (10.14; 12.10, 14). A heavenly crowd of witnesses[61] might surround them, but so does sin[62] (εὐπερίστατος, 12.1).[63] Sin is a weight (ὄγκος) to be thrown off, so that they might better compete.[64] Just as Jesus suffered, the recipients are expected to suffer. The author's coupling of the terms 'to struggle against' (ἀνταγωνίζομαι)[65] and 'to resist' (ἀντικαθίστημι) depicts their fight against sin as a bloody boxing match.[66] Temptation is the 'challenger in the corner' if you will, but they are barely putting up a fight. Like Cain in Gen. 4.7 the recipients are to rule over sin, being weary of its besetting nature.

The language of 'fighting' sin raises a question over how this relates to the author's insistence on purging the consciousness of sin. In other words, what is the relationship between post-baptismal sin and the consciousness of sin? It was argued earlier that post-baptismal sin has a threefold distinction in Hebrews (§2.5.5): unintentional (ἀγνόημα), intentional/explicable (πλανάω) and high-handed/inexplicable (ἑκουσίως). Regarding the latter (ἑκουσίως), the recipients must resist the temptation to leave the community in search of a ceremonial solution to their consciousness of sin, failure to do so is interpreted by the author as apostasy (§1.2, §2.2, §2.6.3). In terms of explicable (πλανάω) and unintentional (ἀγνόημα) post-baptismal sin, this is dealt with by Jesus' earthly objective achievements (§3.7); they are made positionally holy (§3.6.3) and they are eternally redeemed (§3.4.1, §3.4.2, §3.4.3). However, in terms of the recipients' own subjective

---

[60] Some of Moffitt's and Moore's exegetical points are engaged with indirectly in my earlier analysis. My interpretation of Heb. 10.5-14 (§3.6) differs with Moore's interpretation, 'Session', 530-1, with my understanding of 9.27-8 (§3.5.3) differing from Moffitt's understanding, 'Interceding', 546-8.
[61] 'Cloud' equates to 'crowd', see BDAG 670.
[62] The singular ἁμαρτία does not refer to specific sins, nor to a generalized sense of sin, but to one sin only, apostasy and the recipients' temptation to leave their faith behind. Contra Mitchell, *Hebrews*, 265.
[63] The term εὐπερίστατος was perhaps coined by the author, meaning to 'surround', see BDAG 410; LSJ 726, as well as 'seeking to be in control', L&N 472-3.
[64] Athletic imagery is likely in view again here (cf. Heb. 10.32). See Scott D. Mackie, 'Visually Oriented Rhetoric and Visionary Experience in Hebrews 12:1-4', *CBQ* 79.3 (2017): 476-97. See Zoe Hollinger for a critique, 'Rethinking the translation of τρέχωμεν τὸν . . . ἀγῶνα in Heb. 12.1 in light of ancient Graeco-Roman literature', *BT* 70.1 (2019): 94-111.
[65] The present middle participle 'ἀνταγωνιζόμενοι' displays the very real and current 'fight' against sin, Porter, *Idioms*, 67-70.
[66] Bénétreau, *Hébreux*, 2:177; L&N 496.

consciousness of present and past sin, it is only Jesus' perpetual heavenly blood which offers them ongoing assurance (§5.4) by removing their consciousness of sin (§3.4.1, §3.5.1, §3.6.4, §4.2.2, §4.4.2, §4.4.3, §4.4.4). Similarly, the dual occurrence of 'dead works' discussed earlier (§2.5.4) revealed that sin can be repented from – as a foundation to faith (6.1) – but sin still requires purging by the heavenly blood of Christ (9.14).

Yet, we might ask, what about 'forgiveness' for ongoing sin? However, this would mean raising a question which Hebrews is not addressing at present. As argued already, 'forgiveness' may be understood as being obtained via Jesus' earthly life, culminating in death (§4.4.3), but purification for their consciousness of sin is a *present problem* (§1.2, §2.2) which Jesus' death is unable to solve. This can only be dealt with via Jesus' heavenly blood. Thankfully, in their fight against temptation, they have a high priest who offers divine help.

5.3.2 The father helps the son (Heb. 5.7-8)

Jesus models what it looks like to receive divine help. Interestingly, whenever Hebrews mentions Jesus' priestly help towards the recipients, the author links it back to Jesus' own life of temptation (Heb. 2.18; 4.15; cf. 12.3-4). Hebrews could have simply stated that 'Jesus is able to help in times of temptation', without any reference to the temptations Jesus faced himself. Yet the author chooses to include Jesus' solidarity with them, not only to highlight his sympathy as a high priest but to display Jesus' life as an example to follow.

Hebrews 5.7 displays what has already been defined as an example of Jesus' earthly obedience (§3.6.2). On earth Jesus offered up (προσφέρω) prayers and supplications, with loud cries and tears, to the one who was able to save him 'from death' (ἐκ θανάτου) and he was heard 'because of [his] reverent submission' (ἀπὸ τῆς εὐλαβείας, 5.7). Previously the term προσφέρω was examined (§3.6.2), now the 'praying' element of this verse will be explored. Scholars are divided over what Jesus prayed for and where he prayed in 5.7.[67] Viewing this passage as Jesus receiving 'divine help' through temptation is possible. First, if the context is Gethsemane and not Golgotha, as some propose,[68] then readers are naturally led to see Jesus as wrestling with the temptation of whether to escape the suffering that awaits him, or to submit to the will of God. Gethsemane is certainly not a given reference in Hebrews, offering no synoptic verbal parallels (Mat. 26.36-46; Mk 14.32-42; Lk. 22.40-6),[69] but Jesus 'praying' with 'loud cries and tears' to be delivered from death might have struck the recipients as a possible reference.

---

[67] For a useful summary of the debates see Dyer, *Suffering*, 90–3; Richardson, *Pioneer*, 74–89. Also, Claire Cliva, *L'ange et la sueur de sang (Lc 22, 43-44) ou comment on pourrait bien écrire l'histoire*, BTS 7 (Leuven: Peeters, 2010); 'The Angel and the Sweat like "Drops of Blood" (Lk 22:43-4): $\mathfrak{P}^{69}$ and f^{13}', *HTR* 98.4 (2005): 419–40.

[68] Weiss, *Hebräer*, 312; Bénétreau, *Hébreux*, 1:211–12; Peterson, *Perfection*, 86–92; William R. G. Loader, *Sohn und Hoherpriester: Eine traditionsgeschichtliche Untersuchung zur Christologie des Hebräerbriefes*, WMANT 53 (Neukirchen-Vluyn: Neukirchener Verlag, 1981), 87; Spicq, *Hébreux*, 2:113. For locating this at the cross see Richardson, *Pioneer*, 75–80; Laub, *Bekenntnis*, 127.

[68] Contra Richardson, *Pioneer*, 74–89.

[69] Although some argue for a different Gethsemane tradition, Loader, *Sohn*, 87.

If this is the case, the exegetical problem surrounds the final clause: 'εἰσακουσθεὶς ἀπὸ τῆς εὐλαβείας'. The verb εἰσακούω means 'to hear' but implies 'answered', causing some to note that Jesus could not have prayed to be delivered from death, since Hebrews says his prayer was heard/answered.[70] Except, it is not clear what Jesus prayed for, whether this prayer was answered immediately, or even if it was answered in the manner Jesus requested. Attridge's solution is to read the phrase 'ἐκ θανάτου' as Jesus praying to be saved 'out of the realm of death' as opposed to 'impending death'.[71] But the verse suggests impending suffering (σῴζειν αὐτὸν), with the next verse further indicating that his earthly obedience in the face of death is in view (5.8). Furthermore, the phrase 'ἀπὸ τῆς εὐλαβείας' has vexed interpreters. Was Jesus heard *because of* his 'godly fear'/'reverence' or was he heard/delivered 'from [his] fear [of death]' (cf. 2.14-15; 12.28).[72] Even if εὐλάβεια is rendered 'godly fear', 5.7 still depicts Jesus as being afraid, hence, he prays loudly with tears to be delivered from death. Additionally, Jesus being heard because of his godly fear/reverent submission might also imply submission to God's will,[73] further suggesting a Gethsemane reference. This clause can be interpreted as Jesus praying for deliverance from impending suffering on the one hand, but on the other, having reverence for God and wanting to submit to his will. To quote Clark Pinnock, '[a]s human, Jesus cried out for the cup to pass from him, but as Spirit-filled he prayed for God's will to be done'.[74]

What is evident from 5.7 is that Jesus appeals to God for *help* in a testing situation and God in turn hears/answers Jesus, implying some form of 'divine help'. Gethsemane might supply the context here, since it portrays a key moment in Jesus' earthly obedience, as well as depicting a conflict of wills.[75] Thus, Jesus praying to be delivered from death might be a reference to this conflict. Clearly God did not deliver Jesus from death, but it might be implied that God offered divine help and supplied Jesus with help to face and endure death, when he was otherwise tempted to not do so. By receiving divine help, Hebrews states that Jesus learned obedience through his sufferings (5.8). Therefore, if 5.7 is read as an example of God helping Jesus, then Jesus' role as high priest can be understood in a similar manner and explains why Hebrews refers to Jesus' own temptations alongside the recipients' need for help (2.18; 4.15). Jesus' deliverance (σῴζω) through divine help (5.7) might also be paralleled later when it is said that Jesus delivers (σῴζω) the recipients through his own priestly ministry (7.25; §5.3.5).

5.3.3 Helping the descendants of Abraham (Heb. 2.16-18)

The first reference to Jesus offering divine help as high priest is anchored in the narrative of the enthroned Son. From Heb. 2.14 the author attaches Jesus' life and

---

[70] Allen, *Hebrews*, 320.
[71] Attridge, *Hebrews*, 150.
[72] For a summary see Harris, *Hebrews*, 121–2.
[73] The NIV and NRSV render it as 'reverent submission' further suggesting a Gethsemane setting (cf. ESV; NLT).
[74] Clark H. Pinnock, *Flame of Love: A Theology of the Holy Spirit* (Downers Grove, IL: InterVarsity Press, 1996), 90.
[75] Rissi, *Theologie*, 67–8.

exaltation with temptation and divine help. Jesus 'shared' of the same things (2.14) and he was 'made like' the recipients for the sole purpose that 'he might be a merciful and faithful high priest' in the service of God 'to purge the sins of the people' (εἰς τὸ ἱλάσκεσθαι τὰς ἁμαρτίας τοῦ λαοῦ, 2.17). Jesus has not come to help (ἐπιλαμβάνομαι)[76] angels but the seed of Abraham (2.16). Because Jesus was tempted by what he suffered[77] he is able to help those who are being tempted (2.18). When commenting on these verses the attention of scholars is fixed on the phrase 'εἰς τὸ ἱλάσκεσθαι τὰς ἁμαρτίας τοῦ λαοῦ' (2.17). This is because, while it seems clear that one of Jesus' priestly roles is to offer divine help (ἐπιλαμβάνομαι (x2), 2.16; βοηθέω, 2.18), it is not clear how this coincides with purging the sins of the people (εἰς τὸ ἱλάσκεσθαι τὰς ἁμαρτίας τοῦ λαοῦ). Is Jesus' priestly role one of 'helping' *and* 'purging/atoning'? Or has the meaning of ἱλάσκομαι been misunderstood?

Previously the various renderings for ἱλάσκομαι were introduced (§4.2.2). Typically, the term is read cultically with the two main renderings being 'propitiation' or 'sacrifice of atonement' (cf. NIV; NRSV). However, some have opted to read ἱλάσκομαι as 'to have mercy', a reference to Jesus' intercessory role which includes both 'help' and 'forgiveness' for sins.[78] This is because 'help' and intercession not only dominate these verses but are conceived of as an ongoing reality (2.14-18), thus, the clause 'εἰς τὸ ἱλάσκεσθαι' is also treated as a reference to ongoing intercession.[79]

Rather than opting for a cultic or non-cultic understanding for ἱλάσκομαι and 2.14-18, this passage can be read as a reference to both Jesus' heavenly offering and his ongoing offer of divine help. Jesus' priestly help is evident in these verses, but Jesus' heavenly offering can be located in the phrase 'ἱλάσκεσθαι τὰς ἁμαρτίας τοῦ λαοῦ', a topic which will be developed in detail in the later portions of the epistle. In the previous chapter ἱλάσκομαι was read as 'purgation' (§4.2.2) and it parallels with 5.1 nicely:

2.17 ἵνα . . . τὰ πρὸς τὸν θεὸν εἰς τὸ ἱλάσκεσθαι τὰς ἁμαρτίας τοῦ λαοῦ
5.1 τὰ πρὸς τὸν θεόν ἵνα προσφέρῃ δῶρά τε καὶ θυσίας ὑπὲρ ἁμαρτιῶν

With 5.1, as in 2.17, Hebrews describes the purpose of the high priest 'in the service of God' to offer gifts and sacrifices for sins, described as ἱλάσκομαι in 2.17. In both examples the topic of sacrifice and its direct impact (purgation) is not intended to be discussed in detail, only mentioned in passing. The prime focus in 2.17 and 5.1 is the

---

[76] The verb ἐπιλαμβάνομαι (Heb. 2.16) has a vast interpretative history, see Allen, *Hebrews*, 221-3 for a useful summary. Fuhrmann renders ἐπιλαμβάνομαι as 'angreifen' (to attack) with the Devil the subject, not Jesus (cf. 2.14-15), *Vergeben*, 61-4. Although, it is typically rendered 'help' with Jesus as the subject of the main verb (ESV; NASB; NIV; NRSV). BDAG 374 has the sense of to 'take hold of'/'grasp' (cf. Heb. 8.9).

[77] The perfect 'πέπονθεν' should be read as intensive (Wallace, *Grammar*, 574-6) with the participle 'πειρασθείς' as temporal not causal: 'Jesus suffered *when* he was tempted'.

[78] Jesus' offering, not forgiveness, is the focus here. Rightly Loader, 'Revisiting', 268-9.

[79] Gäbel, *Kulttheologie*, 213-27, esp. 226-7. Gäbel differentiates between a once-for-all offering (1.3) and the ongoing intercession/forgiveness of Jesus (2.17), although he does acknowledge a connection between the two, 131.

role of the priest, in relation to God, with the people the indirect object. The purpose of 2.17, as revealed by the author (ἵνα . . . γένηται), is Jesus becoming a priest. By moving from incarnation and solidarity (becoming like his brothers and sisters) to Jesus' cultic heavenly offering (purgation for the sins of the people) in the space of one verse (2.17), the author wants to highlight the narrative of Jesus' earthly obedience and his heavenly conclusion/celebration once more. Similarly, with 1.3, enthronement is the foreground and heavenly purgation the background which will be discussed later in the epistle.

If ἱλάσκομαι is a minor reference to Jesus' heavenly offering, then the rest of the passage is centred around ongoing divine help from Jesus, as outlined above. Thus, 2.17-18 can be read in this manner: Jesus offers divine help and the people can receive this divine help, *because* their sins have been purged. Jesus 'helps' those who are *being* tempted. The present passive (τοῖς πειραζομένοις) is significant because it affirms that Jesus' priestly aid comes *during* temptation, not after they have sinned, indicating once more that forgiveness or atonement are not what Jesus offers, but divine help.

5.3.4 Mercy and grace to help in time of need (Heb. 4.14-16)

Hebrews 4.14-16 sheds further light on Jesus' priestly offer of divine help and is intended to be read and interpreted alongside 2.17-18. This is displayed by hook words such as ἀρχιερεύς (2.17; 4.14, 15), ἐλεήμων/ἔλεος (2.17; 4.16), πειράζω (2.18; 4.15), βοηθέω/βοήθεια (2.18; 4.16) and ἁμαρτία (2.17; 4.15), displaying lexical cohesion and purposeful transitioning. Yet 4.14-16 adds a couple of additional key elements: (1) the sympathetic (συμπαθέω) nature of Christ towards their weaknesses (ἀσθένεια), (2) Jesus' sinlessness under temptation (χωρὶς ἁμαρτίας),[80] as well as (3) the exhortation to approach the throne.

First, what does it mean for Christ to be able to 'sympathize with our weaknesses' (4.15)? Weakness (ἀσθένεια) has been read as either 'physical' (weariness),[81] 'social' weakness (abuse/imprisonment), or as 'vulnerability' to sin (cf. 5.2; 7.28).[82] Weakness and sin are linked[83] but they are not synonymous.[84] This is evident by Jesus' compassion (συμπαθέω) towards it. Michaelis describes συμπαθέω not as sympathy, but as a 'fellow-feeling',[85] further denoting one's 'helplessness'[86] and need for help. Jesus' earthly solidarity enabled him to feel and know ἀσθένεια. The difference is that Jesus remained without sin (4.15). The exhortation to approach the throne (4.16) is aligned with

---

[80] See Williamson for a useful discussion, 'Hebrews 4:15 and the Sinlessness of Jesus', *ExpTim* 86 (1974): 4–8. Contra Rascher, *Schriftauslegung*, 112–13.
[81] Westcott, *Hebrews*, 108.
[82] Cockerill, *Hebrews*, 225; Koester, *Hebrews*, 283. Ellingworth links ἀσθένεια to intellectual/moral weakness, *Hebrews*, 208.
[83] As Löhr states 'Schwachheit und Sünde sind nicht dasselbe, aber es besteht ein Sachzusammenhang zwischen beiden', *Umkehr*, 134. The threefold Wesleyan distinction of sin might be helpful here, see 'Christian Perfection', *John Wesley's Sermons: An Anthology*, ed. Albert C. Outler and Richard P. Heitzenrater (Nashville: Abingdon Press, 1991), 73.
[84] Grässer conflates ἀσθένεια with temptation and ultimately apostasy, *Hebräer*, 1:253–4. Cf. Jamieson, *Death*, 30–1.
[85] W. Michaelis, 'συμπαθής, συμπαθέω', *TDNT* 5:936. Cf. Heb. 10.34; 4 *Macc.* 5.25.
[86] BDAG 142 (cf. Rom. 8.26).

receiving mercy and empowering grace (cf. 13.9), adding a significant element to intercession, as explored below. Yet, the throne does not give grace, as Mackie rightly asserts, but the one who sits on it.[87]

5.3.5 He makes intercession for them (Heb. 7.25)

After describing the eternal priesthood of Christ, Hebrews concludes (ὅθεν) stating that Jesus is able 'to save completely'[88] (σῴζειν εἰς τὸ παντελὲς) those that approach God through him, because he 'always lives to make intercession for them' (πάντοτε ζῶν εἰς τὸ ἐντυγχάνειν ὑπὲρ αὐτῶν, Heb. 7.25).[89] The common verb σῴζω is typically understood here under the guise of 'salvation'.[90] Yet 'to save' is a broad rendering. Like the other occurrence of σῴζω in Hebrews (5.7), the term depicts deliverance from a specific situation. Rendering the term as 'to deliver' or 'to rescue' is more appropriate as it complements the need for 'help' in temptation (2.18; 4.14-16).

Due to the broad semantic range given to the term ἐντυγχάνω (to intercede) noted above (§5.3), a closer examination is required. The term is one of Hebrews' many *hapax legomena* (7.25). Generally, intercession is interpreted as Jesus representing his followers before God in heaven.[91] This is further evident in 9.24.[92] The language of appearing 'before the face of God for us' (τῷ προσώπῳ τοῦ θεοῦ ὑπὲρ ἡμῶν, 9.24) echoes back to 7.25, which refers to Jesus being able to save 'those who approach God through him'. As a representative, Jesus' intercessory role means he is an advocate who 'petitions' on behalf of his followers, leading some to marry intercession with mediation.[93] Jesus as an advocate is viewed as twofold, including a 'plea for assistance' and a 'plea for forgiveness',[94] and for some it involves Jesus actively praying for believers.[95] Jesus praying for his people is understood as comparable to priests praying on Yom Kippur.[96] In Philo's account of Agrippa's letter to Gaius, the high priest is referred to as praying in the Most Holy Place (*Leg. Gai.* 306). This is the only tenable link to a priest praying for people on Yom Kippur, with the HB silent on the matter.[97] Some include intercession alongside atonement/expiation and under the umbrella of Yom Kippur,[98] others detach it.[99]

---

[87] Scott D. Mackie, '"Let us draw near... but not too near": A Critique of the Attempted Distinction between 'Drawing Near' and 'Entering' in Hebrews' Entry Exhortations', in *Listen, Understand, Obey: Essays in Honor of Gareth Lee Cockerill*, ed. Caleb T. Friedeman (Eugene, OR: Wipf & Stock, 2017), 22.

[88] See Harris for the various options, *Hebrews*, 183.

[89] The NIV takes the participle 'ζῶν' as causal.

[90] Cockerill's idea of 'complete salvation' is unwarranted, *Hebrews*, 334–5.

[91] Cockerill, *Hebrews*, 336; Johnson, *Hebrews*, 194; Lane, *Hebrews*, 1:190; Bruce, *Hebrews*, 173.

[92] Telscher, *Opfer*, 270; Grässer, *Hebräer*, 2:191–2.

[93] Johnson, *Hebrews*, 193–4; Koester, *Hebrews*, 365; Lane, *Hebrews*, 1:190; Bruce, *Hebrews*, 173–5.

[94] Koester, *Hebrews*, 366. Cockerill too notes, 'Christ's intercession results in his providing cleansing for sin, access to God and grace to overcome all temptation and opposition', *Hebrews*, 336. Cf. Gäbel, *Kulttheologie*, 202, 478.

[95] Schreiner, *Hebrews*, 234; Bruce, *Hebrews*, 174.

[96] Moffitt, 'Intercession', 548–51.

[97] See Moore for a critique of this, 'Intercession', 531–4.

[98] Moffitt, 'Intercession', 548–51. Similarly, Cody, *Heavenly*, 198–202.

[99] Moore, 'Intercession', 534–7; *Repetition*, 178–84.

This notion of Jesus perpetually petitioning on behalf of believers has been criticized. David Hay famously described this notion of intercession as a 'foreign body'[100] in Hebrews, taken possibly from another Christian tradition (cf. Rom. 8.34).[101] There is no need for Jesus to petition, since his sacrifice has been accepted. Typically, ἐντυγχάνω is understood as 'to petition',[102] but others have challenged this. Ellingworth and Thompson contend that ἐντυγχάνω must be read as denoting 'help' given, since Jesus' priestly ministry elsewhere refers to this divine aid (2.16-18; 4.14-16).[103] While others have argued similarly,[104] the synergistic element is often lost regarding intercession; intercession is not received passively but sought after by the recipients. What is significant, as with 4.16, is that the author aligns the exhortation to approach (προσερχώμεθα) with deliverance, or as in 4.16, with receiving mercy and empowering grace (cf. 13.9). This suggests that divine help is not one-sided but synergistic, requiring human obedience and initiative. The cultic hortatory subjunctive 'let us approach' (προσερχώμεθα, 4.16; 7.25; 10.1, 22; 11.6; 12.18, 22) can be further understood when read in the light of the 'rest' motif.

5.3.6 Divine help, approach and entering the rest

Divine help has a synergistic element to it; divine help is made available when one approaches (Heb. 4.16; 7.25) because the blood of Christ has removed the consciousness of sin and replaced it with boldness to approach (4.16; 10.19). 'Approach' and 'entrance' terminology (εἰσέρχομαι/προσέρχομαι) is a contested topic. Who is 'entering' or 'approaching' and when, where and what does this look like?[105] It is possible to read the 'drawing near' (to receive divine help) exhortations in 4.16 and 7.25 within the framework of the wilderness and rest motifs. Drawing near to receive divine help looks like entering the rest to receive divine help. The failure of the wilderness generation to enter the promised rest (κατάπαυσις) is a depiction of apostasy, sin and faithlessness. The wilderness motif is not employed to depict the Christian life as a desert wandering experience (until they enter a post-mortem κατάπαυσις) but as a very present example (ὑπόδειγμα, 4.11) to be avoided, not imitated (§2.6.3). The κατάπαυσις is a depiction of faithfulness and obedience. Heuristically, the author places a choice before the recipients: apostasy and sin, or faithfulness and obedience.

Entering the κατάπαυσις (3.11, 18; 4.1, 3 (x2), 4, 5, 11) is often viewed as an eschatological heavenly homeland, as reflected in apocalyptic traditions.[106] It is, as Laansma notes, a *'spatially conceived* goal of the Christian journey'.[107] It motivates

---

[100] Hay, *Glory*, 132. Also, Cockerill, *Hebrews*, 336.
[101] Hay, *Glory*, 132-3; Cody, *Heavenly*, 49.
[102] BDAG 241.
[103] Thompson, *Hebrews*, 161; Ellingworth, *Hebrews*, 392.
[104] Loader, 'Revisiting', 271-3; Attridge, *Hebrews*, 212.
[105] For a helpful summary see Nicholas J. Moore, 'Heaven's Revolving Door? Cosmology, Entrance and Approach in Hebrews', *BBR* 29.2 (2019): 187-207; '"In" or "Near"? Heavenly Access and Christian Identity in Hebrews', *Muted Voices*, 185-98; Mackie, 'Let us draw near', *Listen*, 17-36.
[106] See *2 Bar.* 73.1; 85.9-11; *1 En* 39; 45; *4 Ezra* 7.36-8; 8.52; *T. Dan* 5.10-13; *Josh. Asen.* 8.9. Also Barnard, *Mysticism*, 180-1.
[107] Laansma, *Rest*, 10 (emphasis his own). See esp. 252-335.

believers to persevere; it is the homeland (11.13-16) and the heavenly city (11.9-10; 12.22). The wilderness generation and the promised κατάπαυσις (3.7-4.11) stand in parallel with the faithful generation (11.1-40) and their invitation into this heavenly city (12.22) – the final rest.[108] This view no doubt reflects the fact that 3.7–4.11[109] is frequently treated as a non-cultic tangent, detached from Hebrews' priestly discussion.[110] Others read 3.7–4.11 as cultic, conflating κατάπαυσις with the heavenly Holy of Holies;[111] supported by OT texts which bring rest and the sanctuary together[112] and the nearby *inclusio* (4.14-16; 10.19-22). In viewing κατάπαυσις in this manner, Hebrews might be reflecting the increasing post-exilic propensity to shift the focus from the land to the cult place.[113] For the majority there is 'nothing in 3:1–4:13 that suggests present entrance';[114] it is simply 'an eschatological event'.[115] Some stretch to a 'process of entering into rest'[116] or an iterative present.[117]

Lincoln proposes that commentators have been misled and encourages the eschatological tensions to be acknowledged. For instance, the future heavenly city is yet to come (11.10; 13.14) yet the audience have already arrived at Mount Zion, the heavenly city of the living God (12.22). This explains why Hebrews affirms that a Sabbath rest (σαββατισμός)[118] remains for the people of God to be entered (4.8). Thus, for Hebrews, 'spatial concepts do not stand for the eternal in the sense of that which is ideal and timeless but rather signify that the future is already present in heaven and therefore available now'.[119] Present entry into the rest, God's presence, is made more evident with the appropriation of the term 'today' (σήμερον, 3.7, 13, 15; 4.7 (x2)) via Ps. 95 (Heb. 3.7). The term σήμερον acts as an anchor which exhorts the recipients to enter the rest *today*.[120] The repetition of σήμερον emphasizes a present choice placed before the recipients to not be like the wilderness generation who sinned and fell away. By

---

[108] Cockerill, *Hebrews*, 198 n. 11.
[109] Kim's suggestion of extending the traditional discourse from Heb. 3.7-4.11/3.7-4.13 to 3.1-4.16 would be welcomed, 'Jewish', *Hebrews in Contexts*, 35–6.
[110] Docherty, 'Recent', 385. See Nicholas Moore's discussion, 'Jesus as "The One Who Entered his Rest": The Christological Reading of Hebrews 4.10', *JSNT* 36.4 (2014): 384–6.
[111] Calaway, *Sabbath*, 62–3; Koester, *Hebrews*, 258; Andrew T. Lincoln, 'Sabbath, Rest and Eschatology in the New Testament', in *From Sabbath to Lord's Day: A Biblical, Historical and Theological Investigation*, ed. D. A. Carson (Eugene, OR: Wipf & Stock, 1982), 209; Hofius, *Katapausis*, 53–5, 91–101, 106–10, 115, 144–51.
[112] Deut. 12.11; 1 Chron. 6.31; Ps. 131.8; Isa. 66.1.
[113] Isaacs, *Sacred*, 83–4.
[114] Cockerill, *Hebrews*, 200. Also, Koester, *Hebrews*, 271; Laansma, *Rest*, 307; Ellingworth, *Hebrews*, 26, 224, 246; Weiss, *Hebräer*, 1:279; Hofius, *Katapausis*, 180 n. 352; Rissi, *Theologie*, 18 n. 43.
[115] Laansma, *Rest*, 307.
[116] David A. deSilva, 'Entering God's Rest: Eschatology and the Socio-Rhetorical Strategy of Hebrews', *TJ* 21.1 (2000): 25–43; Attridge, *Hebrews*, 126.
[117] Neva F. Miller, *The Epistle to the Hebrews: An Analytical and Exegetical Handbook* (Dallas: Summer Institute of Linguistics, 1988), 106.
[118] As Barnard notes 'κατάπαυσις is σαββατισμός – it is the Sabbath into which God himself entered at creation and is therefore the state that believers may experience in the immediate presence of God', *Mysticism*, 181.
[119] Lincoln, 'Sabbath', *Sabbath*, 211. See also Gäbel's discussion, *Kulttheologie*, 426–34.
[120] Dominique Angers, *L'Aujourd'hui' en Luc-Actes, chez Paul et en Hébreux: Itinéraires et associations d'un motif deutéronomique*, BZNW 251 (Berlin: de Gruyter, 2018), 361–409; Allen, 'Numbers', 140; Frevel, 'σήμερον', *Psalms and Hebrews*, 190.

speaking of entering the κατάπαυσις, Hebrews is exhorting the recipients to draw near to receive divine help, *today* and avoid the example of disobedience.

5.4 The perpetual assurance of Jesus and his heavenly blood offering

This final section will explore the 'nature' of Jesus' heavenly offering. Rather than viewing it as once-for-all (à la Moore), or perpetually through Jesus' presence (à la Moffitt and Gäbel), is there a middle way? Most discussions concern Jesus' role in heaven, but little is said concerning the role of Jesus' blood. This section will argue that both Jesus and his blood are independent agents in the heavenly tabernacle. The motif of 'assurance' is a helpful aid in understanding this. As discussed above, Jesus' primary role is offering divine help for his followers as they approach him. Yet, Jesus is given two other key titles: guarantor and meditator.[121] Jesus offers assurance for his followers, he guarantees and meditates the NC and its benefits. Jesus' blood likewise offers perpetual assurance, but in relation to purgation. Jesus' blood is alive in the heavenly tabernacle and speaks (12.24) on behalf of the recipients.

5.4.1 Jesus as guarantor

Jesus as the guarantor (ἔγγυος) of a 'better covenant' (Heb. 7.22; cf. 6.17) is a key descriptor for added assurance. The term ἔγγυος is another of Hebrews' *hapax legomena*, carrying legal connotations in Hellenistic literature denoting somebody who absorbs the obligations of a debt, as well as offering their life for another.[122] With Hebrews, Jesus is described as a ἔγγυος to reassure the recipients that he guarantees the promises of this 'better covenant', this 'better hope' (7.19). In this sense ἔγγυος encapsulates much of the argumentation of Hebrews' seventh chapter. The recipients are assured that they do not have to worry about the expiration of Jesus' priesthood. This divine high priest is not hindered by death (7.16, 23-4), human weakness (7.26-7) or nepotism (7.20), instead, he is called to become a high priest through a divine unchanging oath (5.5-6; 6.17; 7.17, 21). Jesus *is* the guarantor for the 'better covenant' and therefore guarantees its benefits.[123]

---

[121] I view guarantor (ἔγγυος) and mediator (μεσίτης) as having two separate meanings, rightly Harris, *Hebrews*, 196–7; Michael Kibbe, *Godly Fear or Ungodly Failure? Hebrews 12 and the Sinai Theophanies*, BZNW 216 (Berlin: de Gruyter, 2016), 169–72; Cockerill, *Hebrews*, 330 n. 79; Koester, *Hebrews*, 378–9; Lane, *Hebrews*, 1:188–9; Nairne, *Hebrews*, 351. Others maintain a synonymous link between the two terms, see Stolz, *Höhepunkt*, 196–7; Wolfgang Kraus, 'Jesus als "Mittler" im Hebräerbrief', in *Vermittelte Gegenwart: Konzeptionen der Gottespräsenz von der Zeit des Zweiten Tempels bis Anfang des 2. Jahrhunderts n. Chr*, ed. Andrea Taschl-Erber and Irmtraud Fischer, WUNT 367 (Tübingen: Mohr Siebeck, 2016), 308, 314; Allen, *Hebrews*, 427–8, 444; Backhaus, *Hebräerbrief*, 280; Johnson, *Hebrews*, 171; Ellingworth, *Hebrews*, 388–9, 410; Attridge, *Hebrews*, 208–9; R. H. Nash, 'The Notion of Mediator in Alexandrian Judaism and The Epistle to The Hebrews', *WTJ* 40.1 (1977): 89–115, esp. 114–15.

[122] Prov. 17.18; 22.26; Sir. 29.14-19. For Spicq, since Ἰησοῦς follows ἔγγυος (Heb. 7.22) the legal meaning of ἔγγυος is meant, 'ἔγγυος', *TLNT* 1:390–5. See Philo (*Cher.* 45) and Josephus (*Ant.* 6.2).

[123] Contra Grässer who sees the guarantee as not yet obtained, *Hebräer*, 2:57. L&N renders it as 'one who guarantees the reality of something', 668.

Christ 'absolutely guarantees that God's people can be cleansed of sin and come into God's presence'.[124] Delitzsch is helpful:

> [Christ as guarantor enables a] personal security for continuance and completion. As truly as He is Priest and King, so assuredly will the promises of the covenant be fulfilled in us ... And all He has obtained was obtained for us. He exists and lives for us eternally. His indissoluble life as Priest and King is the indissoluble bond which unites us with God and assures us of the endurance of this blissful fellowship.[125]

Furthermore, as priestly ἔγγυος, Jesus guarantees and reassures the recipients concerning the consciousness of sin. The purgation of the heavenly tabernacle guarantees unclouded communion, since they now have a priest over the house of God, they can approach (10.21-2) – it is guaranteed.

5.4.2 Jesus as meditator

Hebrews also describes Jesus as a mediator (μεσίτης, Heb. 8.6; 9.15; 12.24) of a 'better' or 'new' covenant. First, in reflecting on Moses as the initial mediator, Hebrews stresses the superiority of Jesus as the present ministering heavenly mediator of this 'better covenant' (8.1-6) foretold in Scripture (8.8-12; 10.16-17). Second, as addressed earlier (§3.4.2), Jesus' death enacts a new covenant of which Jesus is described as a mediator (9.15-17). Third, rather than describing the covenant as new (καινός, cf. 8.8, 8.13; 9.15), Hebrews opts for a different but similar term in νέος (12.24).[126] Interestingly, Jesus as meditator is placed alongside his sprinkled blood which speaks, a motif explored below. Christ as the 'mediator' of a NC adds further assurance for the recipients.

As a theological term 'mediation' carries baggage. For some, Jesus as μεσίτης[127] means that he stands in the gap and prevents or appeases a wrathful God from destroying his sinful creation.[128] Nevertheless, it seems counter-intuitive that a divinely initiated and divinely gifted covenant requires retrospective mediation, at least in this sense.[129] It is true that a 'mediator' stands between two parties,[130] but it must be remembered that Jesus is not a '*neutraler* Vermittler'.[131] His solidarity with humankind and divine status enables him to not only be on both sides,[132] as it were, but to maintain perfect harmony. Any ontological or moral distance between humanity and God is meditated through Christ's priesthood because of God's desire to commune with his

---

[124] Cockerill, *Hebrews*, 330. Similarly, Schreiner, *Hebrews*, 230; Brian C. Small, *The Characterization of Jesus in the Book of Hebrews*, BibInt 128 (Leiden: Brill, 2014), 193; Koester, *Hebrews*, 370.
[125] Delitzsch, *Hebrews*, 1:368–9. See Fuhrmann's helpful discussion, *Vergeben*, 79–84.
[126] Only here does νέος modify διαθήκη in all biblical Greek, Harris, *Hebrews*, 389.
[127] Cf. Gal. 3.19-20; 1 Tim. 2.5.
[128] See Reinhard Feldmeier and Hermann Spieckermann, *God of the Living: A Biblical Theology*, trans. Mark E. Biddle (Waco, TX: Baylor University Press, 2011), 335.
[129] Stolz, *Höhepunkt*, 194–202; Ellingworth, *Hebrews*, 410.
[130] Vanhoye, *Different*, 245–6.
[131] 'Neutral mediator', Stolz, *Höhepunkt*, 200 (emphasis his own).
[132] J. Schlosser, 'La médiation du Christ d'après l'Épître aux Hébreux', *RevScRel* 63 (1989): 181.

people.[133] Additionally, Hebrews speaks of Christ meditating the NC, not two separate parties.[134]

5.4.3 Perpetual heavenly blood

If Jesus' very presence in heaven offers assurance through his ministry as guarantor and meditator, what about his blood offering? In terms of the 'nature' of Jesus' heavenly offering scholars fall into two camps. For instance, Moffitt does not view the 'once-for-all' statements in Hebrews as the finalization of Jesus' work; 'the sacrificial work of Jesus is not finished'.[135] His work is incomplete because he is yet to leave the heavenly tabernacle and bring salvation to his people (Heb. 9.28).[136] Jesus as a 'ministering' (8.2) and 'interceding' (7.25) high priest is interpreted as Jesus continuing his salvific work.[137] This can be obtained since Jesus' sacrificial work is not limited to past events but continues through the person of Jesus, *the* perpetual offering, continually offering himself to the Father;[138] 'it is a sacrifice that is timeless'.[139] Moffitt interprets Jesus leaving the heavenly tabernacle as concluding the Yom Kippur event. Moore sees the act of Jesus sitting down as indicating a finished sacrificial work;[140] Jesus is the embodiment of Ps. 110.1, he has sat down at the right hand of the Father and so his sacrificial work is finished. For Moore, purification precedes session (Heb. 1.3) and the only present heavenly activity is intercession through Jesus the high priest. Thus, Jesus' 'session is not simply a close but rather a hinge; it brings his sacrifice to a definitive end and at the same time inaugurates his royal rule and priestly intercession'.[141] By bringing 'atonement' and 'intercession' together, Moore argues that Moffitt 'runs the risk of espousing an insufficiently realized account of Hebrews' eschatology'.[142] Moffitt's response to this is that maybe he is.[143]

These two viewpoints are not innovative,[144] but Moore and Moffitt, with their own unique nuances, represent them effectively. Nonetheless, neither discusses the

---

[133] Rodriques' review of the different theological models of priesthood is helpful, *Priestly*, 23–54.
[134] Kraus argues that Jesus cannot be a mediator between parties because he reflects God, 'Mittler', *Vermittelte*, 314.
[135] Moffitt, 'Finished', *So Great*, 175.
[136] Moffitt, 'Interceding', 545. Yom Kippur has not finished, because '*Jesus has not yet left the space where the high priest ministers on the Day of Atonement*', 546 (emphasis his own). Thus, the act of sitting down does not disregard, 'Jesus remaining who and where he is until he returns to his people', 549.
[137] Moffitt, 'Interceding', 545.
[138] Moffitt, 'Interceding', 551–2.
[139] Moffitt, 'Interceding', 545.
[140] Moore, 'Intercession', 537.
[141] Moore, 'Session', 531. 'Hebrews deploys the enthronement motif in two different ways in close proximity, first to delineate a finished cultic work and secondly to introduce a continuing work which is both cultic and royal', 528.
[142] Moore, 'Session', 537.
[143] Moffitt, 'Interceding', 548. Rather than viewing these tensions as realized/over-realized eschatologies, an imputed/imparted righteousness tension might be more helpful. Moore would fit imputation, while Moffitt fits impartation.
[144] Bengel suggested a few centuries ago that Jesus' blood was poured out throughout his life, beginning in Gethsemane and ending in heaven, Johann Albrecht Bengel, *Gnomon of the New Testament*, 5 vols, ed. Ernest Bengel, A. R. Fausset and J. C. F. Steudel, 2nd edn (Edinburgh: T&T Clark, [1759] 1858–59), 4:474–90. See also Brooks, 'Perpetuity', 212–14; Cody, *Heavenly*, 78–82; George Milligan, *The Theology of the Epistle to the Hebrews* (Edinburgh: T&T Clark, 1899), 141–61; Delitzsch, *Hebrews*, 2:29, 85–9.

possibility that Jesus' heavenly blood could, as an independent agent, continue to have some form of purgative power. Jesus' heavenly blood offering, for those who locate it in that realm (cf. §3.2) was argued in the previous chapter as being *the* qualitative difference against the earthly sacrifices (§4.4.2). But the question of the temporal nature of this heavenly blood offering has been left until now. In what remains, it will be argued that Jesus' heavenly blood is an independent agent that was offered once in the heavenly Holy of Holies and provides ongoing purgation and assurance. Jesus' heavenly blood offering was offered once (never to be repeated) but it has a perpetual element to it, in that the heavenly blood, as an independent agent, offers perpetual assurance for the recipients with regards to their permanent and ongoing purgation. Two related questions need to be addressed: the nature and the substance of Jesus' heavenly offering.

5.4.3.1 *The nature of Jesus' heavenly offering*

Rather than arguing for a once-for-all or a perpetual offering, both are apparent. Hebrews does assert a once-for-all offering through adopting a qualitative distinction between the one offering of Jesus (ἐφάπαξ/ἅπαξ, esp. Heb. 7.27; 9.12, 28; 10.10) and the many of the earthly priests (κατὰ ἐνιαυτός/κατὰ ἡμέρα/πολλάκις, esp. 7.27; 9.24-6; 10.1). This is a clear distinction and a fundamental part of Hebrews' sacrificial argumentation.[145] Equally, however, the eternal effects of this offering are apparent. Just as Jesus is the eternal Son and high priest (1.8; 5.6; 6.20; 7.17, 21, 24, 28; 13.8) his heavenly offering is described as 'εἰς τὸ διηνεκὲς' (10.12, 14, cf. 7.3 10.1), with translators rendering this phrase in many ways 'forever'/'continually'/'for all time'/'perpetual'.[146] The role of 'εἰς τὸ διηνεκὲς' is key, especially in 10.12-14 (§3.6.4). Scholars are divided over whether this temporal phrase modifies Jesus' offering ('προσενέγκας', 10.12) or his session ('ἐκάθισεν', 10.12). Evidence points to Jesus' offering being 'perpetual' as opposed to Jesus sitting 'perpetually',[147] for the following reasons.

First, the argument of the previous verse (10.11) suggests that 'εἰς τὸ διηνεκὲς' refers to Jesus' offering:

10.11 Καὶ πᾶς μὲν ἱερεὺς ἕστηκεν καθ᾽ ἡμέραν λειτουργῶν καὶ τὰς αὐτὰς <u>πολλάκις προσφέρων θυσίας</u> αἵτινες οὐδέποτε δύνανται περιελεῖν ἁμαρτίας
10.12 οὗτος δὲ μίαν ὑπὲρ ἁμαρτιῶν <u>προσενέγκας θυσίαν εἰς τὸ διηνεκὲς</u> ἐκάθισεν ἐν δεξιᾷ τοῦ θεοῦ

A contrast between earthly priests standing and Jesus sitting is evident, but there is an additional contrast between offering repeated sacrifices ('πολλάκις προσφέρων θυσίας', 10.11) and Jesus' offering which has perpetual effects ('προσενέγκας θυσίαν εἰς τὸ

---

[145] James W. Thompson, *Strangers on the Earth: Philosophy and Rhetoric in Hebrews* (Eugene, OR: Wipf & Stock, 2020), 92–107; 'EPHAPAX: The One and the Many in Hebrews', *NTS* 53.4 (2007): 566–81; Grässer, *Hebräer*, 2:58.
[146] BDAG 245, has the sense of 'without interruption' or 'being continuous'.
[147] *Pace* Moore, 'Session', 530–1; Ellingworth, *Hebrews*, 510.

διηνεκές, 10.12). This is an important and neglected contrast. Jesus' offering is offered once with perpetual effects. It does not need to be offered continually since it continually has an impact in heaven. Repeated earthly offerings could not take away sin, but Jesus' offering is perpetual and so is able to remove all sins, past, present and future.

Second, not only do most English translators read 'εἰς τὸ διηνεκὲς' as modifying Jesus' offering in 10.12 (ESV; NASB; NET; NIV; NLT; NRSV) but to read 'εἰς τὸ διηνεκὲς' as modifying 'ἐκάθισεν' is contrary to the usage in Hebrews.[148] Elsewhere, as in 10.12, 'εἰς τὸ διηνεκὲς' follows what it modifies (7.3; 10.1, 14). Hebrews' point by invoking Ps. 110.1 (Heb. 10.12-13) and elsewhere (1.3, 13; 8.1; 12.2) is not that Jesus is seated 'perpetually' (εἰς τὸ διηνεκὲς), but about *who* is now seated and *where* – Jesus, our heavenly ministering high priest. Also, nowhere else does Hebrews link the phrase 'εἰς τὸ διηνεκὲς' with Ps. 110.1. Logically, Heb. 9.28 indicates that Jesus does not plan on being seated for too long. His heavenly blood offering on the other hand continues to have an eternal impact.

5.4.3.2 The substance of Jesus' heavenly offering

For most scholars, Jesus does not perform any blood manipulation in heaven. The previous discussion argued that by entering 'with blood' and 'sprinkling' it, blood manipulation is implied (§4.2.1, §4.4.4). Jamieson, Moore and Moffitt all interpret heavenly blood imagery as another way of referring to Jesus himself, so the question about *what* Jesus' heavenly blood offering constitutes becomes redundant. In speaking of a 'perpetual' heavenly offering, Moffitt states that Jesus' presence is his perpetual offering:

> Jesus' sacrifice does not consist simply in the events or work that he performs. He is the sacrifice that he offers. That the resurrected Jesus is himself the offering he presents to the Father helps explain why his atoning work can be understood to be ongoing. By his very presence in the heavenly holy of holies, the sacrifice, Jesus himself, is perpetually in the Father's presence.[149]

For Moffitt, a 'perpetual' heavenly offering – understood as ongoing atonement – looks like Jesus' very presence in heaven. Moffitt does not claim that Jesus is repeatedly performing a sacrifice, or endlessly sprinkling his blood, but that the *presence* of Jesus himself 'is the sacrifice that he offers'.[150] In this way Moffitt does affirm a once-for-all offering, but like Gäbel, sees Jesus' priestly presence as bringing his prior atonement to the fore.[151]

Jamieson too notes that 'the act that constitutes Jesus' self-offering in heaven simply is his entrance there and appearance before God'.[152] Heavenly blood imagery is redundant. Jamieson states:

---

[148] Westcott, *Hebrews*, 316. Also Rose, *Hebräerbrief*, 154; Lane, *Hebrews*, 2:256; Peterson, *Perfection*, 148–9.
[149] Moffitt, 'Interceding', 551–2.
[150] Moffitt, 'Interceding', 552.
[151] Gäbel, *Kulttheologie*, 131.
[152] *Pace* Jamieson, *Death*, 164. Jamieson says Jesus must enter heaven and offer his blood, but also that Jesus does not offer his blood in heaven, 164.

In depicting Christ's heavenly offering Hebrews invokes the cultic category of blood as material offered but does not posit a distinct, corresponding act. Blood's role as sacrificial material is conceptual, not physical. 'Blood' names something about the significance and effect of Christ's sacrifice without entailing a distinct act in heaven.[153]

Jamieson's argument appears confusing. Jesus' heavenly blood is described as a 'metonym' for Jesus' death, but Jesus' blood does not constitute his heavenly offering but his entrance into heaven. Based on this reasoning, it seems odd that Hebrews would place such a high value on blood throughout the epistle, that it would be robbed of all significance as it reaches the heavenly realm.

5.4.3.3 What does Jesus' heavenly blood represent?

When this question is asked, often times the so-called 'blood canon' of Lev. 17.11 is drawn upon. This states that the 'life (נֶפֶשׁ) of the flesh is in the blood; and I have given it to you for making atonement (כִּפֶּר) for your lives on the altar; for, as life, it is the blood that makes atonement'.[154] In this verse, blood represents the very life of the sacrificial animal. Turning to Hebrews, Moffitt concludes, based on this verse that 'Jesus' blood represents Jesus' life/living presence appearing in the presence of God'.[155] Jesus' blood contains his life and his blood atones, not his death.

There is a very different reading of Lev. 17.11, which reads the dubious *piel* verb כִּפֶּר, as a 'ransom'[156] for the life of the offeror – that is, the life of the blood is a life-for-life exchange for the offeror.[157] From this vantage point, scholars have read a substitutionary view of sacrifice into Hebrews. More recently, Jamieson has argued this extensively (§3.5.3). He writes that '[w]hat Jesus' blood conveys to God is the value of the life he gave when he died',[158] and 'by presenting his blood to God in heaven Jesus offers what his sacrificial death achieved'.[159] Thus, '[t]he achievement of the cross is what he offers in heaven',[160] 'what Jesus offered to God in heaven was his death'.[161] For Jamieson, '"blood" is shorthand for Jesus' sacrificial slaughter'.[162] Blood is a 'currency'; a medium of exchange.[163] He states, '[i]t is only [Jesus'] death that renders blood a currency for life'.[164] In short, Jamieson argues that the imagery of Jesus' heavenly blood represents

---

[153] Jamieson, *Death*, 165.
[154] For a discussion concerning the בּ preposition as instrumental (by means of), see Milgrom, *Leviticus 1–16*, 706–7.
[155] Moffitt, *Atonement*, 273. For his discussion around blood and death, see 289–95.
[156] This is often triggered by Sklar's analysis. For further discussions around this and כִּפֶּר see §3.3.4. For criticisms of this reading of Lev. 17.11, see Greenberg, *Atonement*, 8; Feder, *Blood*, 169–70.
[157] See my earlier section for a critique of 'ransoming' as opposed to 'purging' (§3.3.4, §3.5.3).
[158] Jamieson, *Death*, 167.
[159] Jamieson, *Death*, 166.
[160] Jamieson, *Death*, 165.
[161] Jamieson, *Death*, 168.
[162] Jamieson, *Death*, 166.
[163] Jamieson, *Death*, 167.
[164] Jamieson, *Death*, 159.

and is a metonym for Jesus' death, since the life of the flesh is in the blood and blood is only attained through death.

It is entirely possible that Hebrews incorporates Lev. 17.11 and it is also possible that Lev. 17.11 possesses a substitutionary view of atonement. But why does this mean that every other blood sacrifice in Leviticus must also involve substitutionary ransoming? Ribbens states that '[t]his maxim [Lev. 17.11] is central to Leviticus's sacrifice theology'.[165] Yet, the extent to which Lev. 17.11 – and the often accompanying 'ransom' motif – should dictate the rationality of blood sacrifice throughout Lev. 1–16 is rejected by many scholars.[166] Milgrom questions the rationale behind needing to ransom someone who has either committed wrong inadvertently,[167] or someone who has given birth (Lev. 12.7-8).[168] For Milgrom, the ransoming of Lev. 17.11 relates only to removing the guilt that occurs after killing an animal, since it is classed as murder to kill an animal without first offering its life-blood back to God. This occurs via the 'well-being' (שלם) offering (Lev. 3; 7.11-34; 17.1-10).[169] By offering the blood of animals on the altar, according to Milgrom, Israel is spared from the guilt of slaughter during the consumption of meat.[170]

Whether one agrees with Milgrom's reading of Lev. 17.11 or not, there is no cause for applying a substitutionary theory of sacrifice to all sacrifices based on a substitutionary reading of Lev. 17.11.[171] Previous OT scholarship viewed sacrifice as substitutionary,[172] that is, sacrifice was a substitute for the punishment due to the offeror, but since the nineteenth-century this interpretation of sacrifice has been widely rejected.[173] Julia Rhyder goes as far as to conclude that there 'is no notion, neither in P nor elsewhere in the Hebrew Bible, that blood might substitute for human life'.[174] Substitution and vicarious suffering may be evident in other NT writers (cf. Mk 10.45; Rom. 3.25; 2 Cor. 5.21) but it is alien to Hebrews' sacrificial argumentation.[175] Alternatively, Joshua Vis's recent interaction with Lev. 17.11 opens up the possibility that כִּפֶּר should maintain the meaning 'purge', since this is the same nuance a few verses earlier (Lev. 16.30) by the same author (H) in relation to Yom Kippur.[176] In this sense,

---

[165] Ribbens, *Levitical*, 155.
[166] See Julia Rhyder for a summary, *Centralizing the Cult: The Holiness Legislation in Leviticus 17-26*, FAT 134 (Tübingen: Mohr Siebeck, 2019), 218–23.
[167] Dealt with via the 'sin-purification' (חטאת/περὶ ἁμαρτίας) and the 'guilt-reparation' (אשם/πλημμέλεια) offerings (Lev. 4.1–6.7).
[168] Milgrom, *Leviticus 17–22*, 1475.
[169] Milgrom, *Leviticus 17–22*, 1474–8. Contra, R. Rendtorff, 'Another Prolegomenon to Leviticus 17:11', *Pomegranates*, 26–8.
[170] This could represent a 'case of inner-biblical exegesis, almost midrashic in nature', Schwartz, 'Prohibitions', *Priesthood*, 59–60.
[171] While the function of Lev. 17.11 may inform our understanding of certain sacrifices, it should not impinge on the sin-purification offering, since 17.11 says nothing about blood sprinkling/smearing, see Feder, *Blood*, 147–8. Relating to 17.11 see, 196–206, 266–8.
[172] See Greenberg, *Atonement*, 2–3.
[173] Thus, כִּפֶּר as 'to cover' means that the sacrificial animal is viewed as the means by which the effects of sin and defilement are removed and the relationship with YHWH is restored.
[174] Rhyder, *Cult*, 220.
[175] Rightly the NRSV ('by means of the life it contains'), contra the NIV ('the blood atones for a life'). See Janowski, *Sühne*, 242–7.
[176] Vis, 'Purification', 209–30, esp. 224–5.

Lev. 17.11 is making a general comment concerning the nature of sacrificial blood. While P emphasizes the purgation of the tabernacle (Lev. 16.1-28), H emphasizes the purgation of the people (Lev. 16.29-34), via Yom Kippur.[177]

Hebrews' keen interest in Yom Kippur and the high priest bringing a blood offering into the inner sanctum (Heb. 9.7) should lead scholars towards *this* ritual, where 'atonement' simply means 'purge' and not 'ransom'.[178] It is not the 'day of ransoming', but as Milgrom states, 'the day of Purgation'.[179] Blood is the medium of purgation (§4.4.3), its purpose is to purge defilement, not to ransom it (§3.5.3, §4.2.2, §4.4.3). Hebrews' prime concern is not what blood represents, but what blood *does*.

5.4.4 Blood that is speaking (Heb. 11.4; 12.24)

The nature of Jesus' heavenly offering is perpetual (rightly Moffitt), but nowhere in Hebrews does this offering denote Jesus' presence or heavenly entrance. Rather, Jesus' blood fulfils this role. Hebrews states that Jesus brought his blood into heaven (Heb. 9.12) to purge the consciousness of sin (9.14, 22, 26, 28; 10.12-14, 22) via the purging of the heavenly Holy of Holies (9.23) enabling ongoing access into God's presence (10.19). The very presence of this blood grants unhindered access. This blood '*will* purify' (καθαριεῖ) the consciousness from 'dead works' (9.14). The curious use of the future tense here is virtually ignored in commentaries, yet it suggests an ongoing effect attributed to Jesus' blood. This heavenly blood will continue to purify. Attached to this once more is the motif of 'assurance'. The present problem of consciousness of sin lacks assurance (§1.2, §2.2). By being assured that Jesus' heavenly blood offering has an ongoing purgative reality, the recipients' consciousness of sin is eased. Their sin and subsequent consciousness of sin has been purged and will continue to be purged. A motif which further supports this notion is that this heavenly blood is speaking (12.24).

The motif of Jesus' heavenly blood as 'speaking' further suggests an ongoing independent role related to Jesus' blood. In describing Jesus' sprinkled blood as 'speaking' better than Abel's, Hebrews adds further continued assurance for the recipients. But what does Hebrews intend by comparing the blood of Abel with Jesus' sprinkled blood and how is it better and what does the author mean when he describes Jesus' blood as 'speaking' (λαλοῦντι)?[180] It is common to view a reference to Abel's blood as representing the victims of sin 'crying out' for punishment.[181] Abel's blood cries out for judgement

---

[177] Vis, 'Purification', 224–5.
[178] Milgrom, *Leviticus 1–16*, 255.
[179] Milgrom, *Leviticus 1–16*, 1009–84.
[180] Abel's 'blood' is admittedly implied/supplied in translation, leading some to question any association with Abel's blood in Hebrews, see especially Harris, *Hebrews*, 390; Kyu Kim, 'Better Than the Blood of Abel? Some Remarks on Abel in Hebrews 12:24', *TybBul* 67.1 (2016): 129–32; Gene Smillie, '"The One who is Speaking" in Hebrews 12:25', *TybBul* 55.2 (2004): 280. Kevin McCruden focuses more on the fidelity of Abel/Jesus as the prime contrast, 'The Eloquent Blood of Jesus: The Neglected Theme of the Fidelity of Jesus in Hebrews', *CBQ* 75.3 (2013): 504–20. Nonetheless, παρά plus an accusative ('τὸν Ἄβελ', Heb. 12.24) often infers a comparison with something in Hebrews (cf. 1.4; 3.3; 9.23; 11.4), see Wallace, *Grammar*, 297 n. 10. Also, 𝔓⁴⁶ and other MSS trade 'τὸν Ἄβελ' for 'τὸ Ἄβελ' in order that 'τὸ' links with 'αἵματι' and makes the comparison with Abel's blood clearer (12.24).
[181] Stolz, *Höhepunkt*, 226–7; John Byron, 'Abel's Blood and the Ongoing Cry for Vengeance', *CBQ* 73.4 (2011): 743–56, esp. 752; Cockerill, *Hebrews*, 659; Ellingworth, *Hebrews*, 573; Bruce, *Hebrews*, 361.

(Gen. 4.10) but Jesus' blood cries out for grace and forgiveness.[182] This is probable, although it requires reading further details from Genesis that are absent in Hebrews, namely, the murder of Abel. Instead, the contrast in Heb. 12.24 might be made between Jesus' heavenly sprinkled blood and the blood of Abel's *sacrifice*, not Abel's blood. This is possible through a close reading of Hebrews' only other mention of Abel in 11.4.

In this first occurrence Hebrews states that Abel offered (προσφέρω) a more acceptable sacrifice (θυσία) to God than Cain, because of this, Abel was declared 'righteous', but more significantly, 'through it, although dead, it speaks' (δι' αὐτῆς ἀποθανὼν ἔτι λαλεῖ, 11.4). But what is it that 'still speaks'? Is it Abel's unjust death crying out for justice or his example of faith?[183] A nuanced version of the latter is possible. Although 11.4 is included within this 'faith chapter', 'faith' is not necessarily the reason Abel was commended as righteous, nor is 'faith' the thing that 'still speaks'. Both prepositional phrases and relative pronouns ('δι' ἧς'/'δι' αὐτῆς', 11.4) are often read as pointing to the rhetorical device of anaphora, 'by faith' (πίστει, 11.4; cf. NIV).[184] Yet 'sacrifice' (θυσίαν) also agrees with the antecedent in the first relative phrase, being nearer to the first relative ('δι' ἧς') too.[185] With this reading, Abel was attested as righteous because of his *sacrifice* (cf. NLT). The following clause also complements this reading, stating that God 'approved his gifts'.[186] Accordingly, if the first relative phrase refers to Abel's sacrifice, it makes sense to render the final relative phrase ('δι' αὐτῆς') as a reference to Abel's sacrifice as still speaking and not his faith or his death. Abel's sacrifice was better because it derived from an obedient, faithful and devoted heart.

If 11.4 is read in this way (as Abel's sacrifice still speaking) then 12.24 can be read, not as reference to the blood of Abel speaking, but to the sprinkled blood of Abel's sacrifice speaking. The blood of Abel's sacrifice is still speaking because it was offered by Abel, a righteous faithful servant. There is no clear evidence as to whether Abel's offering contained the act of blood sprinkling, however it remains significant that Hebrews does not merely compare 'blood' but 'sprinkled blood', implying a cultic context. The contrast in 12.24 therefore, might be read as a contrast between two offerings by two righteous offerors. If this is the case, how is Jesus' sprinkled blood 'better' than Abel's? The sprinkled blood that speaks is better for many reasons. It is better because, as Hebrews says frequently, it belongs to a better covenant, with a better mediator, in a better heavenly cult.[187] More significantly, Jesus' heavenly sprinkled blood purges the consciousness (§4.4.4). Abel's blood speaks from earth, possibly a reference to the earthly cult, but Jesus' blood is speaking from heaven (12.24-5). Jesus' sprinkled blood is better because

---

[182] I would caveat this by saying that Jesus' blood cries out, or speaks, purgation and enabled communion with God. While Abel's blood accuses, Jesus' blood cleanses, contra Stolz, *Höhepunkt*, 220.
[183] Bruce, *Hebrews*, 283.
[184] See Greenlee, *Hebrews*, 419. I agree mostly with Kim, 'Blood', 132–6, but I understand the emphasis of Heb. 11.4 and 12.24 to be on the superior blood offering of Christ, over Abel's blood offering.
[185] The ESV, NASB and the NRSV leave it down to interpretation by translating the relative phrase simply as 'by which'.
[186] Rightly Bruce, *Hebrews*, 280. See also Ellingworth, *Hebrews*, 572; Attridge, *Hebrews*, 317 n. 139. Lane is right when he says '[w]hat fixed the attention of the writer on Abel was that he and his sacrifice were pleasing to God', *Hebrews*, 2:335.
[187] Similarly Kim, 'Blood', 131–6.

it speaks assurance from heaven. This can be argued if the speaking blood of Jesus is read within the overarching Sinai–Zion contrast (12.18-24).

This contrast is viewed by some as a heavenly–earthly contrast,[188] an old–new covenant contrast,[189] or simply as two possible paths for the recipients.[190] The Sinai–Zion comparison is much more than a covenantal contrast; it is a multifaceted contrast which brings together numerous themes from Hebrews. Sinai conceals God, Zion reveals him fully. Sinai is a fearful place one readily departs ('οὐκ ἔφερον', 12.20), Zion is a joyful gathering (πανήγυρις, 12.22). More importantly, Sinai–Zion is a contrast of 'access'. This, after all, is another of the author's cultic exhortations to approach (προσέρχομαι) the heavenly cult (12.18, 22; cf. 4.16; 7.25; 10.1, 22; 11.6). Sinai is untouchable, dark and terrifying and the Lord's voice piercing; even Moses, their mediator, was afraid (12.18-21). But Zion is a vibrant joyful heavenly city (12.22-3). This covenant still requires cooperation (12.25-9) but it is the sprinkled blood of the eternal meditator (12.24) which maintains its availability.

This 'sprinkled blood' which 'speaks better than [the blood of] Abel's [sacrifice]' (12.24) provides ongoing assurance of access. This speaking blood announces unrestricted access (10.19-22) and it assures the recipients of their ongoing purification and holiness (9.14). Thus, Jesus' heavenly blood offering is not static, but dynamic, it is an unfolding reality across space and time – it is still speaking.[191]

5.4.5 Purifying the consciousness: Confidence, assurance and amnesia

One of the key background assumptions of this study is the present problem of the 'consciousness of sin' (§1.2, §2.2). Outside of Hebrews the concept of συνείδησις was often accompanied with feelings of timidity and fear (§1.3.4, §1.3.5). A defiled consciousness in Hebrews culminates in restricted access, dread, timidity and the general stain of defilement (§2.6.1, §2.6.2), as well as temptation to abandon the community (§2.6.3). Hebrews' solution to these problems is Jesus' heavenly blood, which purges the συνείδησις and grants the recipients confidence and boldness to approach the presence of God. As Hebrews states, the recipients now have 'boldness to approach the Holy of Holies by the blood of Jesus' (παρρησίαν εἰς τὴν εἴσοδον τῶν ἁγίων ἐν τῷ αἵματι Ἰησοῦ, 10.19). They can approach (προσέρχομαι) accompanied with full assurance (πληροφορία) since their συνείδησις has been sprinkled clean (10.22). The temptation to return to former Jewish practices relates potentially to the issue of assurance, regarding συνείδησις. After all, sacrificial ritual, as stated previously, gives participants assurance that their consciousness of sin is being dealt with (§4.3.4, §4.3.5). If rituals are removed or no longer practised, then a lack of assurance arises

---

[188] See Stolz's analysis, *Höhepunkt*, 373–90.
[189] Christopher T. Holmes, *The Function of Sublime Rhetoric in Hebrews: A Study in Hebrews 12:18-29*, WUNT 2.465 (Tübingen: Mohr Siebeck, 2018), 143.
[190] Cockerill, *Hebrews*, 643–5.
[191] Hebrews' concept of time in relation to sacrifice warrants further research. See Guthrie, 'Time and Atonement', *So Great*, 227; P. Steensgaard, 'Time in Judaism', in *Religion and Time*, ed. N. Balslev and J. N. Mohanty (Leiden: Brill, 1993), 63–108; Augustine, *Conf.* 11.

regarding guilt and the consciousness of sin, culminating in a general awareness of sin and defilement.

With this in mind, one of the problems in dismissing a once-for-all offering (à la Moffitt) is that it leaves the recipients with further doubts as to whether their sins are purged. If ongoing atonement is required, then this only seems to fuel the issue of συνείδησις. The recipients need perpetual assurance, not perpetual doubt. On the other hand, affirming a once-for-all offering (à la Moore) raises questions about how practically ongoing issues of sin and guilt are dealt with ritually. This is where the motif of perpetual heavenly assurance may be helpful, as it affirms that Jesus' heavenly blood is alive and speaking and so offers the assurance of ongoing purgation. Knowing that Jesus' heavenly blood offering is offering perpetual purgation eases the burden of the consciousness of sin. One no longer *feels* defiled or guilty, since they are part of a perpetual ritual which assures ongoing purgation.

Moreover, might a more literal interpretation be intended too? Consciousness of sin possibly includes the consciousness of unconscious sin (§2.5.5, §4.3.5) but it no doubt includes the awareness of present sin, or by extension, the present awareness of the memory of sin. The memory of past sin lingers, conjuring up feelings of shame, timidity and guilt. In this manner, Hebrews may be arguing for a type of sacrificial amnesia. The heavenly blood of Christ purifies the consciousness and so removes the memory of sin. This was implied earlier (§2.5.3, §4.4.2) with the logic of 10.1-4 being of central importance. It states, rather provocatively, that if Levitical sacrifices could make perfect those who approached, then the cult participants would have no consciousness of sin (10.1-2). These rituals cause a 'remembrance' of sin (10.3). But as argued previously, Jesus' heavenly blood offering *does* obtain perfection, that is, the finality of purgation (§4.4.1, §4.4.2). By Hebrews' logic, the perfection of Christ's heavenly blood offering, unlike Levitical offerings (10.3), does not cause a 'remembrance' of sin, but an 'amnesia' of sin! Thus, 'purifying the consciousness' might be interpreted as preventing bringing the awareness of sin to the consciousness, or, it might additionally denote removing the memory of sin.

5.5 Conclusion

This chapter has sought to argue that Jesus' activity as a high priest should be distinguished from his heavenly blood. Jesus' session is the culmination and celebration of his earthly life of obedience. This is linked to his role as high priest, since he is now able to offer 'divine help' for his followers (§5.3.3, §5.3.4, §5.3.5, §5.3.6) just as he received 'divine help' during his earthly trials (§5.3.2). The final section focused on the role of Jesus' heavenly blood offering and the motif of assurance. Jesus' presence in heaven as guarantor and mediator offers assurance; his priestly presence *guarantees* and *mediates* the benefits of the NC (§5.4.1, §5.4.2). Yet it is Jesus' perpetual heavenly blood that offers assurance for ongoing purgation. Within Hebrews scholarship the idea of Jesus' blood as a substance possessing a distinctive role from his priestly work is often frowned upon. Focus is placed on what Jesus' blood represents, but this chapter suggests that Hebrews is more concerned with what Jesus' blood *does* and is *doing*.

Jesus' blood is the medium of purgation and continues to speak and offer assurance to the people of God regarding their own pure status, as they continue to walk faithfully with him. They approach the presence of God with boldness and full assurance, since their consciousness has been purged. They no longer live with dread and timidity, since their memory of sin has been removed (§5.4.5).

6

Conclusion

This study has argued that the consciousness of sin and its subsequent purification is a vital motif for understanding Hebrews' sacrificial argumentation and vice-versa. The *present* problem of consciousness of sin is *why* Jesus' heavenly blood offering is so significant for the audience. In this final chapter, the key points of this study will be brought together and the different contributions will be outlined. The limitations and opportunities for further research will be suggested. Finally, the implications of this study for the wider church will be stated.

6.1 Summary

This study began by arguing that recent Hebrews scholarship has failed to consider the role of the recipients within Hebrews' sacrificial argumentation, especially with respect to the motif of συνείδησις – their consciousness of sin. The introductory chapter found that this motif was not only underappreciated but greatly misunderstood and warranted further research. A brief diachronic exploration into the background of συνείδησις and the related σύνοιδα word group helped to unearth the rich development of the concept (§1.3). Philo's use of συνείδησις and Josephus' too (§1.3.5) denoted 'consciousness' or 'awareness', typically of sin and this seemed to be the general sense within Hebrews (§1.4.1). Philo, unlike Hebrews, treats the convicting nature of τὸ συνειδός almost as a divine concept (§1.3.4). In turning to Hebrews scholarship, two issues revealed confusion: what συνείδησις denotes and what purification language means in relation to συνείδησις. A plethora of explanations and ideas were discovered (§1.4.2). For some, συνείδησις evoked a Platonic worldview denoting an unseen world, for others it was just another term for the 'heart', 'soul' or 'mind'. Some rightly saw συνείδησις as denoting consciousness/awareness of sin, but their understanding of purification was divided. Purging the consciousness was interpreted as another way of speaking about 'forgiveness', 'redemption' or even 'justification'. Again, many rightly interpret συνείδησις as needing to be purged, but this is typically defined as a 'deeper' purification obtained by Christ. Christ offers internal purification – a supposed impossible feat for Levitical sacrifices which were 'limited' to external purification.

A helpful starting point for establishing some clarity came with the assumptions of Lindars concerning the background of Hebrews and what he describes as the 'crucial issue'[1] of consciousness of sin (§1.2). The analysis of Lindars positions Hebrews within its own unique setting and allows readers to see the consciousness of sin as a unique problem for the recipients. Yet tensions were highlighted in the work of Lindars. He observes the importance of ritual in solving the problem of consciousness but he does not offer a convincing solution for how the recipients are supposed to deal with this problem with respect to Christ's sacrifice. Rather than focusing on the death of Christ, as Lindars does, the question was asked: how might the inclusion of Jesus' heavenly offering speak into the problem of συνείδησις? Additionally, how might Levitical sacrifices speak into the issue of συνείδησις?

To answer these questions, the main body of the study was structured into three parts. Part One ('The Defiled Consciousness') and Chapter 2 centred around the problem of συνείδησις and the centrality of defilement within Hebrews' cultic argumentation. It began by anchoring Hebrews within the 'present problem' of consciousness of sin (§2.2). The problem of συνείδησις exists within an interim period, characterized by the wearing away of the earthly cult (Heb. 1.10-11; 8.13) and the inauguration of the NC (9.11-14). Hebrews describes these two states as the 'present time' and the 'time of correction' (9.9-10). The problem with this present time is that the earthly cult is unable to perfect the worshipper with respect to their consciousness of sin (9.9). Examining the OT background of cultic defilement helped in understanding the heavenly tabernacle in Hebrews. The ὑπόδειγμα and σκιά which Moses constructed pointed to this heavenly tabernacle (§2.4.5).[2] It was concluded that in the cultic sphere sin *behaves* like defilement and, in agreement with Milgrom's 'aerial miasma' (§2.2.1), attaches itself to the tabernacle. Defilement was argued as having communal and cosmic effects in Hebrews. Sin is *conscious* defilement (§2.5.3, §2.5.4), hence Hebrews' insistence on *purging* the συνείδησις (9.14; 10.2, 22). It is a 'stain' which culminates in 'dread' and 'timidity' (§2.6.2). Those with a consciousness of sin suffered from restricted access and the inability to approach God's divine presence, leaving apostasy as a possible solution to this problem (§2.6.1, §2.6.3). Sin also polluted the heavenly tabernacle (§2.5.6), further suggesting a link between the status of the people and God's dwelling place (§2.3.3).

Part Two ('Purifying the Consciousness: Cosmic Purgation') and Chapters 3 and 4 explored Hebrews' cultic argumentation and the solution to a defiled συνείδησις, outlined in Part One. Chapter 3 argued that Hebrews purposefully distinguishes between Jesus' earthly and heavenly achievements. Yom Kippur dictates much of Hebrews' heavenly cultic dialogue but should be cautioned against dictating Hebrews' overall soteriological pronouncements. As paschal lamb (§3.4.3) Jesus' earthly life and death obtained eternal redemption (§3.4, §3.4.1, §3.4.2) and sanctification (§3.6.3). Jesus' very life was an offering for himself and for others (§3.6.2). Jesus was 'offered up' on earth (§3.5.2), but 'self-offered' in heaven (§3.5.1, §3.6.4). This reading allows important early Christian narratives to exist together in harmony.

Chapter 4 looked closer at the purification of the συνείδησις and Jesus' heavenly blood offering, beginning by arguing that the purification of the heavenly tabernacle

---

[1] Lindars, *Hebrews*, 88.
[2] Gäbel, *Kulttheologie*, 244.

coincides with the purification of the consciousness (§4.2.2). The dominant συνείδησις–σάρξ/internal–external purification contrast (§4.3.1) was argued against; the contrast between σάρξ and συνείδησις is an earthly–heavenly cultic blood contrast, not an internal–external negative contrast (§4.3.2, §4.3.3). Levitical sacrificial ritual was not an external exercise but contained a very real internal element. One's consciousness of sin, their אָשָׁם, triggered the need to bring an offering in order to lessen the burden of guilt. The exploration of Levitical אָשָׁם complements Hebrews' notion of the 'consciousness of sin'. Thus, the earthly cult *was* able to purge the consciousness, but repetitive sacrifices created problems (Heb. 10.1-4). They lacked a qualitative type of purgation, that is 'perfection' (§4.4.2). Furthermore, the supposed notion of 'forgiveness' disrupts Hebrews' cultic argumentation, since the focus is on purging sins, not forgiving them. The consciousness of sin needs 'removing' (9.26), 'doing away with' (10.11), 'taking away' (10.4) and 'purging' (1.3; 9.14, 22, 23; 10.2). The recipients require what Milgrom describes as *more* than forgiveness (§4.4.3). By purging the heavenly tabernacle, the Lord is unable to remember their sins (10.17-18) and the recipients are encouraged to do the same.

Part Three ('Assurance and the Purified Consciousness') and Chapter 5 addressed the tensions concerning Jesus' session, present heavenly activity and blood offering. What is the link between these issues and the consciousness of sin? It was argued that Jesus' session was the culmination and celebration of his earthly life of obedience. Ps. 110.1 celebrates the Son, not his heavenly blood offering. Jesus sits and offers 'divine help', but his priestly work is not atoning. Jesus' presence in heaven *guarantees* and *mediates* the benefits of the new covenant (§5.4.1, §5.4.2), but Jesus' perpetual heavenly blood is a separate entity, offering assurance for ongoing purgation. Like the blood of Abel's sacrifice, Jesus' blood speaks apart from himself (§5.4.4). Jesus' blood is a substance and solution for the consciousness of sin. Hebrews is not concerned with what Jesus' blood represents but what his blood *does* and is *doing*. His blood purges and speaks assurance to the people of God regarding their own pure status. They are free to approach the presence of God with boldness and full assurance, since their consciousness and their memory of sin has been done away with (§5.4.5).

6.2 Contributions

The 'summary' section above outlines the argumentation of this study, as well as how it contributes to and pushes Hebrews scholarship forward. Yet, there are a few particular contributions which are worth highlighting in this section. Defining συνείδησις as 'consciousness' of sin opens up a new way of reading Hebrews. Rather than diluting συνείδησις into a general 'interiority' or viewing it as a synonym for the 'heart' or 'soul', the language of 'consciousness' points to 'present awareness' and the 'memory' of sin (cf. Heb. 10.1-4). At least in Hebrews, συνείδησις is not 'conscience', since this term is often suggestive of an active moral agent that either helps individuals decide moral decisions, or affirms and condemns moral choices (§1.3.1). As shown throughout this study, συνείδησις is representative of both memory and the present awareness of sin. Because sin behaves like defilement, the consciousness of sin is spoken of as needing to be 'purged' and 'washed' (9.14; 10.22). In this sense, συνείδησις is more passive than active. It does not actively decide moral choices but brings sin to the consciousness, requiring purification. When purged, Hebrews may speak of the συνείδησις as good (καλός, 13.18), that is, the lack of an awareness of sin. When one has no consciousness of sin, the συνείδησις may be said to be dormant. This, once more, is fundamentally different from other writers, like Philo, who views τὸ συνειδός as divine, functioning as God's reproof; it does not require purgation (§1.3.4). The purification of the συνείδησις, therefore, is entirely unique to Hebrews.

The 'consciousness of sin' is the leitmotif throughout Hebrews. It is not limited to only the occurrences of συνείδησις (9.9, 14; 10.2, 22; 13.18) but was shown to be expressed in a variety of ways: as 'dead works' (6.1; 9.14), a 'reminder' or 'remembrance' of sin (10.3) and simply as 'sins' (10.4; §2.5.3, §2.5.4). Furthermore, heavenly purgation denotes further reference to this motif (1.3; 9.22, 23, 26; 10.4, 11): a defiled heavenly tabernacle culminates in one's consciousness of sin (§4.2.2); a purged heavenly tabernacle purifies the consciousness. The solution to the consciousness of sin should not be understood as 'justification' or 'forgiveness' but purgation – removing the present awareness of sin. So often commentators have read the consciousness of sin as a 'debt' that needs to be paid rather than a stain that needs to be purged. After all, the recipients have already repented from their sin (§2.5.4); what they require now is the removal of their consciousness of sin and defilement. The issue is a deeply personal and subjective one; it is, as Bouquet puts it, a 'numinous uneasiness'.[3]

Reading Hebrews in this manner provokes the possibility that 'consciousness of sin' was an unexpected and new problem facing the recipients. The consciousness of unconscious sin is a possible motif in Hebrews too (§2.5.5, §4.3.5), with ongoing perpetual purification assuring the recipients of their past, present and future pure status (§5.4.3, §5.4.3.3). This study offers a contemporary overview of the debates concerning the location of Jesus' sacrificial offering (§3.2, §3.2.1, §3.2.2, §3.2.3) as well as debates concerning 'atonement' (§3.3.4, §4.2.2). In addition, an overarching Yom Kippur hermeneutic was critiqued (§3.3.3) and a different perspective was argued for in viewing the earthly and heavenly achievements of Jesus. Here it was shown that while Jesus' earthly achievements have their own soteriological purpose – dealing especially with the objective issues of sin (§3.7) – only Jesus' heavenly blood offering can purge the συνείδησις and deal with the ongoing subjective consciousness of sin.

By drawing on the conceptual links between Levitical אָשָׁם and συνείδησις (§4.3.5) and by dismissing the internal–external purification model, Levitical sacrifices are shown to foreshadow Jesus' sacrifice, rather than pitting them against one another. Gäbel is right, 'Hebrews is concerned with two priesthoods, two sanctuaries and the cults performed therein, but not with two religions'.[4] Levitical sacrifices were argued to have been able to purge the consciousness. The main difference with Jesus' offering, however, is that this possesses a qualitative type of purification; it only needs to be offered once, since it is perpetually purifying (§4.4.2, §5.4.3). Most scholars frown upon the notion of Jesus' blood being a heavenly substance, yet this study argues that Jesus'

---

[3] Bouquet, 'Numinous Uneasiness', 203–9.
[4] Gäbel, 'Permission', *Son*, 173.

session and priestly ministry can co-exist yet be distinguished from his perpetual heavenly blood (§5.2, §5.3, §5.4). The motif of perpetual 'assurance' further complements an understanding of a purified consciousness, which may further be understood as sacrificial amnesia (§5.4, §5.4.5).

6.3 Limitations and further research

This study is limited by the methodology it employs. Second Temple texts and other later writings were incorporated throughout, but the brevity of this study meant that a thorough historical examination into motif of 'consciousness of sin' was not possible. This raises the question as to whether the motif was present in other communities and writings. Further research into the consciousness of sin and its relationship with ritual outside of Hebrews would complement a reading of Hebrews. A modern heuristic approach into 'consciousness' might also provide further insights. 'Consciousness' and its associations with 'guilt' and 'shame' are prominent topics for clinical psychologists and other subdisciplines of psychology. How might these discussions inform our current mental health crisis? If the consciousness of sin is the process of bringing sin and the feelings of defilement to our attention and if this cognitive process is purged, this provides further implications for treatments like cognitive behavioural therapy (CBT), where negative mental habits are replaced with positive ones. Applying this field of research within biblical studies would provide intriguing points of discussion for Hebrews.

6.4 Pastoral implications for the contemporary church

Certain aspects of Hebrews may seem alien to contemporary ears. Sin as a defiling force which stretches to the heavens is not likely to be spoken or thought about too often. Nevertheless, this study does raise a few important pastoral implications for the church today. The consciousness of sin and related aspects of guilt continue to be a challenge for many, even if someone believes that they are forgiven. Like the recipients in Hebrews, an isolated message of Christ dying for past sins does not seem to be satisfactory for addressing the present consciousness of sin (§1.2, §2.2). Thomas Long recalls the difficulties of walking with and reassuring church members who, although they know they are forgiven, struggle to fight the sense of guilt and awareness of sin.[5] Long draws on Joseph, a character in Franz Kafka's novel, *The Trial*.[6] Joseph, with no memory of having done anything wrong, is arrested for an unknown crime. He is brought before a court and although he is unaware of any fault, he begins to *feel* like he has done something wrong. As Long notes, 'the congregation of Hebrews would readily understand the plight of Joseph ... the debilitating possibility of being on trial indefinitely, of being obsessed by guilt over a crime one cannot remember or name'.[7]

---

[5] Thomas G. Long, 'Bold in the Presence of God: Atonement in Hebrews', *Int* 52.1 (1998): 53–5.
[6] Franz Kafka, *The Trial*, trans. Mike Mitchell (Oxford: Oxford University Press, 2009): 5–29.
[7] Long, 'Bold', 60.

The conclusion of this study is that Jesus' heavenly blood offering grants perpetual assurance for the recipients concerning their consciousness of sin. A perpetually purged heavenly tabernacle equates to the absence of the consciousness of sin; there is no need to be conscious of sin, since the heavenly tabernacle has been ridden of the effects of sin – defilement. A further implication is that one's memory of sin might also be purged (§5.4.5). Additionally, Gordon Thomas raises an interesting question: what about the victims of sin? Thomas notes that many people in the church struggle not with a 'tormented conscience but a traumatised consciousness'.[8] Thomas provokes the question of trauma and asks whether one's consciousness might also be purged from being sinned against. This is an important, albeit neglected nuance that provides further possible implications for the church today.

---

[8] Thomas, 'Perfecting', *Holiness*, 302.

Bibliography

Primary sources

Aland, Kurt, Barbara Aland, Johannes Karavidopoulos, Carlo M. Martini and Bruce M. Metzger, eds. *Novum Testamentum Graece*. 28th edn. Stuttgart: Deutsche Bibelgesellschaft, 2012.
The Apocryphal Old Testament, edited by H. F. D. Sparks. Oxford: Oxford University Press, 1984.
Aristophanes. Translated by J. Henderson. 5 vols. LCL. Cambridge: Harvard University Press, 1998–2008.
Biblia Hebraica Stuttgartensia. Stuttgart: Deutsche Bibelgesellschaft, 1997.
The Dead Sea Scrolls Study Edition, 2 vols, edited by Florentino García Martínez and Eibert J. C. Tigchelaar. 2nd edn. Leiden: Brill, 1997–8.
Euripides. *Helen, Phoenician Women, Orestes*. Translated by David Kovacs. Vol. 5. LCL. Cambridge: Harvard University Press, 2002.
The Hebrew-English Edition of the Babylonian Talmud, edited by Isidore Epstein. 30 vols. London: The Soncino Press, 1965–89.
Holmes, Michael W. *The Apostolic Fathers: Greek Texts and English Translations*. 3rd edn. Grand Rapids: Baker Academic, 2007.
Josephus. Translated by Henry St. J. Thackeray et al. 10 vols. LCL. Cambridge: Harvard University Press, 1926–65.
The Mishnah. Translated by Herbert Danby. Oxford: Oxford University Press, 1933.
The Old Testament Pseudepigrapha. 2 vols, edited by James H. Charlesworth. New Haven: Yale University Press, 1985.
Philo. Translated by F. H. Colson, G. H. Whitaker and Ralph Marcus. 12 vols. LCL. Cambridge: Harvard University Press, 1929–62.
Philostratus of Athens. *Apollonius of Tyana*. Translated by Christopher P. Jones. 3 vols. LCL. Cambridge: Harvard University Press, 2005–6.
Plato. Translated by H. N. Fowler et al. 12 vols. LCL. Cambridge: Harvard University Press, 1969.
Plutarch. *Moralia*. Translated by Frank Cole Babbitt et al. 15 vols. LCL. Cambridge: Harvard University Press, 1927–69.
Septuaginta: SESB Edition, edited by Alfred Rahlfs and Robert Hanhart. Stuttgart: Deutsche Bibelgesellschaft, 2006.
Xenophon. Translated by C. L. Brownson, O. J. Todd et al. 7 vols. LCL. Cambridge: Harvard University Press, 1914–40.

Secondary sources

Adams, Edward. 'The Cosmology of Hebrews'. In *The Epistle to the Hebrews and Christian Theology*, edited by Richard Bauckham, Daniel R. Driver, Trevor A. Hart and Nathan MacDonald, 122–39. Grand Rapids: Eerdmans, 2009.

Alexander, Philip S. *Mystical Texts: Songs of the Sabbath Sacrifice and Related Manuscripts.* Companion to the Qumran Scrolls 7. London: T&T Clark, 2006.
Alexander, Philip S. 'The Dualism of Heaven and Earth in Early Jewish Literature and its Implications'. In *Light Against Darkness: Dualism in Ancient Mediterranean Religion and the Contemporary World*, edited by Bennie H. Reynolds III, Armin Lange, Eric M. Meyers and Randall Styers, 169–85. Journal of Ancient Judaism Supplements 2. Göttingen: Vandenhoeck & Ruprecht, 2011.
Alexander, Philip S. and Loveday C. A. Alexander, 'Priesthood and Sacrifice in the Epistle to the Hebrews: The 2017 Didsbury Lectures'. Nazarene Theological College, 2017, unpublished.
Allen, David L. *Hebrews*. New American Commentary. Nashville: B&H, 2010.
Allen, David L. *Lukan Authorship of Hebrews*. Nashville: B&H, 2010.
Allen, David M. 'More Than Just Numbers: Deuteronomic Influence in Hebrews 3:7–4:11'. *Tyndale Bulletin* 58.1 (2007): 129–49.
Allen, David M. *Deuteronomy and Exhortation in Hebrews: A Study in Narrative Re-Presentation.* Wissenschaftliche Untersuchungen zum Neuen Testament 2.238. Tübingen: Mohr Siebeck, 2008.
Allen, David M. 'Why Bother Going Outside?: The Use of the Old Testament in Heb 13:10–16'. In *The Scriptures of Israel in Jewish and Christian Tradition: Essays in Honour of Maarten J. J. Menken*, edited by Bart J. Koet, Steve Moyise and Joseph Verheyden, 239–52. Supplements to Novum Testamentum 148. Leiden: Brill, 2013.
Allen, David M. 'Introduction: The Study of the Use of the Old Testament in the New'. *Journal for the Study of the New Testament* 38.1 (2015): 3–16.
Anderson, David R. *The King-Priest of Psalm 100 in Hebrews*. Studies in Biblical Literature 21. New York: Peter Lang, 2001.
Anderson, Gary A. *Sin: A History*. New Haven: Yale University Press, 2009.
Anderson, Kevin L. *Hebrews: A Commentary in the Wesleyan Tradition*. New Beacon Bible Commentary. Kansas City: Beacon Hill Press, 2013.
Anderson, Kevin L. 'Purity in the Epistle to the Hebrews'. In *Purity: Essays in Bible and Theology*, edited by Andrew Brower Latz and Arseny Ermakov, 153–76. Eugene, OR: Wipf & Stock, 2014.
Andriessen, Paul. 'Das grössere und vollkommenere Zelt (Hebr 9,11)'. *Biblische Zeitschrift* 15.1 (1971): 76–92.
Angers, Dominique. *L'Aujourd'hui en Luc-Actes, chez Paul et en Hébreux: Itinéraires et associations d'un motif deutéronomique*. Beihefte zur Zeitschrift für die neutestamentliche Wissenschaft 251. Berlin: de Gruyter, 2017.
Asumang, Annang. *Unlocking the Book of Hebrews: A Spatial Analysis of the Epistle to the Hebrews*. Eugene, OR: Wipf & Stock, 2008.
Attridge, Harold W. '"Let Us Strive to Enter That Rest": The Logic of Hebrews 4:1–11'. *The Harvard Theological Review* 73 (1980): 279–88.
Attridge, Harold W. 'The Uses of Antithesis in Hebrews 8–10'. *The Harvard Review* 79 (1986): 1–9.
Attridge, Harold W. *Hebrews: A Commentary on the Epistle to the Hebrews*. Hermeneia. Minneapolis: Fortress Press, 1989.
Attridge, Harold W. 'Giving Voice to Jesus'. In *Psalms in Community*, edited by Harold W. Attridge and Margot E. Fassler, 101–12. Leiden: Brill, 2004.
Attridge, Harold W. 'The Psalms in Hebrews'. In *The Psalms in the New Testament*, edited by Steve Moyise and Maarten J. J. Menken, 197–212. London: T&T Clark, 2004.

Attridge, Harold W. 'The Beginnings of Christian Theology'. In *The Origins of New Testament Theology*, edited by Rainer Hirsch-Luipold and Robert Matthew Calhoun, 157–78. Tübingen: Mohr Siebeck, 2020.

Auld, Graeme. 'Leviticus at the Heart of the Pentateuch?' In *Reading Leviticus: A Conversation with Mary Douglas*, edited by John F. A. Sawyer, 40–51. Journal for the Study of the Old Testament Supplement Series 227. Sheffield: JSOT Press, 1996.

Awabdy, Mark. *Leviticus: A Commentary on Leueitikon in Codex Vaticanus*. Septuagint Commentary Series. Leiden: Brill, 2019.

Backhaus, Knut. *Der Hebräerbrief*. Regensburger Neues Testament. Regensburg: Friedrich Pustet, 2009.

Backhaus, Knut. *Der Sprechende Gott: Gesammelte Studien zum Hebräerbrief*. Wissenschaftliche Untersuchungen zum Neuen Testament 240. Tübingen: Mohr Siebeck. 2009.

Backhaus, Knut. 'Zwei harte Knoten: Todes- und Gerichtsangst im Hebräerbrief'. *New Testament Studies* 55.2 (2009): 198–217.

Baigent, J. W. 'Jesus as Priest: An Examination of the Claim that the Concept of Jesus as Priest may be Found in The New Testament Outside the Epistle to the Hebrews'. *Vox Evangelica* 12 (1981): 34–44.

Balberg, Mira. *Blood for Thought: The Reinvention of Sacrifice in Early Rabbinic Literature*. Oakland, CA: University of California Press, 2017.

Balentine, Samuel E, ed. *The Oxford Handbook of Ritual and Worship in the Hebrew Bible*. Oxford: Oxford University Press, 2020.

Balz, Host and Gerhard Schneider, eds. *Exegetical Dictionary of the New Testament*. Translated by Geoffrey W. Bromiley. 3 vols. Grand Rapids: Eerdmans, 1990–3.

Barnard, Jody A. *The Mysticism of Hebrews: Exploring the Role of Jewish Apocalyptic Mysticism in the Epistle to the Hebrews*. Wissenschaftliche Untersuchungen zum Neuen Testament 2.331. Mohr Siebeck: Tübingen, 2012.

Barnard, Jody A. 'Ronald Williamson and the Background of Hebrews'. *Expository Times* 124.10 (2013): 469–79.

Barr, James. *The Semantics of Biblical Language*. Oxford: Oxford University Press, 1961.

Barrett, C. K. 'The Eschatology of the Epistle to the Hebrews'. In *The Background of the New Testament and its Eschatology*, edited by W. D. Davies and D. Daube, 363–93. Cambridge: Cambridge University Press, 1956.

Barrett, C. K. *On Paul: Aspects of His Life, Work and Influence in the Early Church*. London: T&T Clark, 2003.

Barry IV, Richard J. 'The Two Goats: A Christian Yom Kippur Soteriology'. PhD diss., Marquette University, 2017.

Barth, Gerhard. *Der Tod Jesu Christi im Verständnis des Neuen Testaments*. Neukirchen-Vluyn: Neukirchener Verlag, 1992.

Bateman IV, Herbert W. ed. *Four Views on the Warning Passages in Hebrews*. Grand Rapids: Kregel, 2007.

Bauckham, Richard. 'The Divinity of Jesus Christ in the Epistle to the Hebrews'. In *The Epistle to the Hebrews and Christian Theology*, edited by Richard Bauckham, Daniel R. Driver, Trevor A. Hart and Nathan MacDonald, 15–36. Grand Rapids: Eerdmans, 2009.

Baylor, M. G. *Action and Person: Conscience in the Late Scholasticism and the Young Luther*. Brill: Leiden, 1977.

Beale, G. K. *The Temple and the Church's Mission*. New Studies in Biblical Theology 17. Downers Grove, IL: InterVarsity Press, 2004.

Beale, G. K. *Handbook on the New Testament Use of the Old Testament: Exegesis and Interpretation*. Grand Rapids: Baker Academic, 2012.
Bell, Catherine M. *Ritual Theory, Ritual Practice*. Oxford: Oxford University Press, 1992.
Bénétreau, Samuel. *L'Épître aux Hébreux*. 2 vols. Vaux-sur-Seine: Édifac, 1989–90.
Bengel, Johann Albrecht. *Gnomon of the New Testament*. 5 vols, edited by Ernest Bengel, A. R. Fausset and J. C. F. Steudel. 2nd edn. 1759. Reprint, Edinburgh: T&T Clark, 1858–9.
Bergen, Wesley. *Reading Ritual: Leviticus in Postmodern Culture*. Journal for the Study of the Old Testament Supplement Series 417. London: T&T Clark, 2005.
Berkowitz, Luci and Karl A. Squitier, eds. *Thesaurus Linguae Graecae: Canon of Greek Authors and Works*. 3rd edn. New York: Oxford University Press, 1990.
Bird, C. 'Typological Interpretation Within the Old Testament: Melchizedekian Typology'. *Concordia Journal* 26 (2000): 36–52.
Blass, Friedrich, Albert Debrunner and Robert W. Funk. *A Greek Grammar of the New Testament and Other Early Christian Literature*. Chicago: University of Chicago Press, 1961.
Blidstein, Moshe. *Purity, Community, and Ritual in Early Christian Literature*. Oxford: Oxford University Press, 2017.
Blomberg, Craig L. '"But We See Jesus": The Relationship between the Son of Man in Hebrews 2.6 and 2.9 and the Implications for English Translations'. In *A Cloud of Witnesses: The Theology of Hebrews in its Ancient Contexts*, edited by Richard Bauckham, Daniel D. Driver, Trevor A. Hart and Nathan MacDonald, 88–99. The Library of New Testament Studies 387. London: T&T Clark, 2008.
Boccaccini, G. *Middle Judaism: Jewish Thought, 300 B.C.E.–200 C.E.* Minneapolis: Fortress, 1991.
Bockmuehl, Markus. 'The Dynamic Absence of Jesus in Hebrews'. *Journal of Theological Studies* 70.1 (2019): 141–62.
Boda, Mark J. *A Severe Mercy: Sin and Its Remedy in the Old Testament*. Winona Lake, IN: Eisenbrauns, 2009.
Bosman, Philip R. '"Why Conscience Makes Cowards of us all": A Classical Perspective'. *Acta Classica* 40 (1997): 63–75.
Bosman, Philip R. *Conscience in Philo and Paul: A Conceptual History of the Synoida Word Group*. Wissenschaftliche Untersuchungen zum Neuen Testament 2.166. Tübingen: Mohr Siebeck, 2003.
Botner, Max, Justin Harrison Duff and Simon Dürr, eds. *Atonement: Jewish and Christian Origins*. Grand Rapids: Eerdmans, 2020.
Bouquet, Alan C. 'Numinous Uneasiness'. *The Modern Churchman* 9 (1966): 203–9.
Brand, Miryam T. *Evil Within and Without: The Source of Sin and Its Nature as Portrayed in Second Temple Literature*. Journal of Ancient Judaism Supplements 9. Göttingen: Vandenhoeck & Ruprecht, 2013.
Braun, Herbert. *An die Hebräer*. Handbuch zum Neuen Testament 14. Tübingen: Mohr Siebeck, 1984.
Brawley, Robert L. 'Discursive Structure and the Unseen in Hebrews 2:8 and 11:1: a Neglected Aspect of the Context'. *Catholic Biblical Quarterly* 55.1 (1993): 81–98.
Brondos, David A. *Jesus' Death in New Testament Thought*. 2 vols. Mexico City: Comunidad Teológica de México, 2018.
Brooks, Walter E. 'The Perpetuity of Christ's Sacrifice in the Epistle to the Hebrews'. *Journal of Biblical Literature* 89.2 (1970): 205–14.
Brower, Kent E. and Andrew Johnson, eds. *Holiness and Ecclesiology in The New Testament*. Grand Rapids: Eerdmans, 2007.

Brown, Colin, ed. *New International Dictionary of New Testament Theology*. 4 vols. Grand Rapids: Zondervan, 1986.
Bruce, Frederick F. *The Epistle to the Hebrews*. Rev. edn. The New International Commentary on the New Testament. Grand Rapids: Eerdmans, 1990.
Büchler, Adolph. *Studies in Sin and Atonement in the Rabbinic Literature of the First Century*. New York: Ktav, 1928.
Büchner, Dirk. 'Ἐξιλάσασθαι: Appeasing God in the Septuagint Pentateuch'. *Journal of Biblical Literature* 129.2 (2010): 237–60.
Burkert, Walter. *Greek Religion: Archaic and Classical*. Translated by John Raffan. Oxford: Blackwell, 1985.
Burnet, Regis, Didier Luciani and Geert Van Oyen, eds. *The Epistle to the Hebrews: Writing at the Borders*. Contributions to Biblical Exegesis and Theology. Leuven: Peeters, 2016.
Byron, John. 'Abel's Blood and the Ongoing Cry for Vengeance'. *Catholic Biblical Quarterly* 73.4 (2011): 743–56.
Byrskog, Samuel. 'Baptism in the Letter to the Hebrews'. In *Ablution, Initiation, and Baptism: Late Antiquity, Early Judaism, and Early Christianity*, edited by David Hellholm, Tor Vegge, Øyvind Norderval and Christer Hellholm, 587–604. Beihefte zur Zeitschrift für die neutestamentliche Wissenschaft 176. Berlin: de Gruyter, 2011.
Caird, George B. 'The Exegetical Method of the Epistle to the Hebrews'. *Canadian Journal of Theology* 5.1 (1959): 44–51.
Caird, George B. 'Just Men Made Perfect'. *London Quarterly and Holborn Review* 191 (1966): 89–98.
Caird, George B. *The Language and Imagery of the Bible*. London: Duckworth, 1980.
Calaway, Jared C. *The Sabbath and the Sanctuary: Access to God in the Letter to the Hebrews and its Priestly Context*. Wissenschaftliche Untersuchungen zum Neuen Testament 2.349. Tübingen: Mohr Siebeck, 2013.
Campbell, Constantine R. *Basics of Verbal Aspect in Biblical Greek*. Grand Rapids: Zondervan, 2008.
Campbell, Constantine R. *Advances in the Study of Greek: New Insights for Reading the New Testament*. Grand Rapids: Zondervan, 2015.
Campbell, K. M. 'Covenant or Testament? Heb. 9:16, 17 Reconsidered'. *Evangelical Quarterly* 44 (1972): 107–11.
Chalmers, Stuart P. *Conscience in Content: Historical and Existential Perspectives*. Bern: Peter Lang: 2013.
Chan, Alan Kan-Yau. *Melchizedek Passages in the Bible: A Case Study for Inner-Biblical and Inter-Biblical Interpretation*. Berlin: de Gruyter, 2016.
Chester, Andrew N. 'Hebrews: The Final Sacrifice'. In *Sacrifice and Redemption: Durham Essays in Theology*, edited by S. W. Sykes, 52–72. Cambridge: Cambridge University Press, 1991.
Christopher, Dany. *The Appropriation of Passover in Luke-Acts*. Wissenschaftliche Untersuchungen zum Neuen Testament 2.476. Tübingen: Mohr Siebeck, 2018.
Church, Philip. 'Hebrews 1:10-12 and the renewal of the cosmos'. *Tyndale Bulletin* 67.2 (2016): 269–86.
Church, Philip. *Hebrews and the Temple: Attitudes to the Temple in Second Temple Judaism and in Hebrews*. Supplements to Novum Testamentum 171. Leiden: Brill, 2017.
Church, Philip. 'The Punctuation of Hebrews 10:2 and Its Significance for the Date of Hebrews'. *Tyndale Bulletin* 71.2 (2020): 281–92.
Clines, David J. A., ed. *Dictionary of Classical Hebrew*. 9 vols. Sheffield: Sheffield Phoenix Press, 1993–2014.

Cliva, Claire. 'The Angel and the Sweat like "Drops of Blood" (Lk 22:43-44): $\mathfrak{P}^{69}$ and f^{13}'. *The Harvard Theological Review* 98.4 (2005): 419–40.

Cliva, Claire. *L'ange et la sueur de sang (Lc 22, 43-44) ou comment on pourrait bien écrire l'histoire*. Biblical Tools and Studies 7. Leuven: Peeters, 2010.

Cockerill, Gareth L. 'Melchizedek or "King of Righteousness"'. *Evangelical Quarterly* 63.4 (1991): 305–12.

Cockerill, Gareth L. 'Structure and Interpretation in Hebrews 8:1–10:18: A Symphony in Three Movements'. *Bulletin for Biblical Research* 11 (2001): 179–201.

Cockerill, Gareth L. 'Melchizedek Without Speculation: Hebrews 7.1–25 and Genesis 14.17–24'. In *A Cloud of Witnesses: The Theology of Hebrews in its Ancient Contexts*, edited by Richard Bauckham, Daniel D. Driver, Trevor A. Hart and Nathan MacDonald, 128–44. The Library of New Testament Studies 387. London: T&T Clark, 2008.

Cockerill, Gareth L. *The Epistle to the Hebrews*. The New International Commentary on the New Testament. Grand Rapids: Eerdmans, 2012.

Cody, Aelred. *Heavenly Sanctuary and Liturgy in the Epistle to the Hebrews: The Achievement of Salvation in the Epistle's Perspectives*. St. Meinrad, IN: Grail, 1960.

Colijn, Brenda B. '"Let us Approach": Soteriology in the Epistle to the Hebrews'. *Journal of the Evangelical Theological Society* 34 (1996): 571–86.

Collins, John J. and Daniel C. Harlow, eds. *The Eerdmans Dictionary of Early Judaism*. Grand Rapids: Eerdmans, 2010.

Compton, Jared. *Psalm 110 and the Logic of Hebrews*. The Library of New Testament Studies 537. London: Bloomsbury T&T Clark, 2015.

Congdon, R. D. 'The Doctrine of Conscience'. *Bibliotheca Sacra* 102 (1945): 226–32.

Cooper, Mark. 'To Quote or Not to Quote? Categorizing Quotations in the Epistle to the Hebrews'. *Journal for the Study of the New Testament* 44.3 (2022): 452–68.

Cortez, Felix H. 'From the Holy to the Most Holy Place: The Period of Hebrews 9:6–10 and the Day of Atonement as a Metaphor of Transition'. *Journal of Biblical Literature* 125.3 (2006): 527–47.

Cortez, Felix H. 'The Anchor of the Soul that Enters Within the Veil: The Ascension of the "Son" in the Letter to the Hebrews'. PhD diss., Andrews University, 2008.

Costigane, Helen. 'A History of the Western Idea of Conscience'. In *Conscience in World Religions*, edited by Jayne Hoose, 3–20. Notre Dame: University of Notre Dame Press, 1999.

Costley, Angela. 'A New Look at Hebrews 4:12–13'. *Proceedings of the Irish Biblical Association* 40 (2019): 23–40.

Costley, Angela. *Creation and Christ: An Exploration of the Topic of Creation in the Epistle to the Hebrews*. Wissenschaftliche Untersuchungen zum Neuen Testament 2.527. Tübingen: Mohr Siebeck, 2020.

Coune, Michel. 'Le Problème des Idolothytes et l'Éducation de la Syneidêsis'. *Recherches de science religieuse* 51 (1963): 497–534.

Cranz, Isabel. 'Priests, Pollution and the Demonic: Evaluating Impurity in the Hebrew Bible in Light of Assyro–Babylonian Texts'. *Journal of Ancient Near Eastern Religions* 14 (2014): 68–86.

Cranz, Isabel. *Atonement and Purification: Priestly and Assyro-Babylonian Perspectives on Sin and its Consequences*. Forschungen zum Alten Testament 2.92. Tübingen: Mohr Siebeck, 2017.

Crawford, M. R. '"Confessing God from a Good Conscience": I Peter 3:21 and Early Christian Baptismal Theology'. *Journal of Theological Studies* 67.1 (2016): 23–37.

Crowther, D. C. 'The Rhetorical Function of Jesus' Session: The Exaltation of Christ as the Ground for Moral Exhortation in the Epistle to the Hebrews'. PhD diss., Southeastern Baptist Theological Seminary, 2017.
Croy, N. Clayton. *Endurance in Suffering: Hebrews 12:1–13 in its Rhetorical, Religious, and Philosophical Context*. Society for New Testament Studies Monograph Series 98. Cambridge: Cambridge University Press, 1998.
Cullman, Oscar. *The Christology of the New Testament*. 2nd edn. London: SCM Press, 1963.
Cuypers, Michel. *The Banquet: A Reading of the Fifth Sura of the Qur'an*. Miami: Convivium, 2009.
Dahl, N. A. 'A New and Living Way: The Approach to God According to Hebrews 10:19–25'. *Interpretation* 5.4 (1951): 401–12.
D'Angelo, M. R. *Moses in the Letter to the Hebrews*. Society of Biblical Literature Dissertation Series 42. Missoula, MT: Scholars Press, 1978.
Danker, Frederick W., Walter Bauer, William F. Arndt and F. Wilbur Gingrich. *Greek-English Lexicon of the New Testament and Other Early Christian Literature*. 3rd edn. Chicago: University of Chicago Press, 2000.
Davidson, R. M. *Typology in Scripture: A Study of Hermeneutical Typos Structures*. Berrien Springs, MI: Andrews University, 1981.
Davies, J. H. 'The Heavenly Work of Christ in Hebrews'. In *Studia Evangelica, Vol. IV: Papers presented to the Third International Congress on New Testament Studies held at Christ Church, Oxford, 1965. Part I: The New Testament Scriptures*, edited by F. L. Cross, 384–9. Berlin: Akademie-Verlag, 1968.
Davies, Philip A. Jr. *The Place of Paideia in Hebrews' Moral Thought*. Wissenschaftliche Untersuchungen zum Neuen Testament 2.475. Tübingen: Mohr Siebeck, 2018.
Delitzsch, Franz. *System der biblischen Psychologie*. Leipzig: Dörffling und Franke, 1855.
Delitzsch, Franz. *Commentary on the Epistle to the Hebrews*. 2 vols. Translated by Thomas L. Kingsbury. 3rd edn. Edinburgh: T&T Clark, 1886–7.
Dennis, John. 'The Function of the חטאת Sacrifice: An Evaluation of the View of Jacob Milgrom'. *Ephemerides Theologicae Lovanienses* 78.1 (2002): 108–29.
deSilva, David A. *Despising Shame: Honour Discourse and Community Maintenance in the Epistle to the Hebrews*. Society of Biblical Literature Dissertation Series 152. Atlanta: Scholars Press, 1995.
deSilva, David A. 'Entering God's Rest: Eschatology and the Socio-Rhetorical Strategy of Hebrews'. *Trinity Journal* 21.1 (2000): 25–43.
deSilva, David A. *Perseverance in Gratitude: A Socio-Rhetorical Commentary on the Epistle 'to the Hebrews'*. Grand Rapids: Eerdmans, 2000.
deSilva, David A. *The Letter to the Hebrews in Social-Scientific Perspective*. Cascade Companions 15. Eugene, OR: Cascade, 2012.
De Wet, Chris L. 'The Messianic Interpretation of Psalm 8:4–6 in Hebrews 2:6–9. Part II'. In *Psalms and Hebrews: Studies in Reception*, edited by Dirk J. Human and Gert J. Steyn, 113–25. The Library of Hebrew Bible/Old Testament Studies 527. London: T&T Clark, 2010.
Dey, Lala. K. K. *The Intermediary World and Patterns of Perfection in Philo and Hebrews*. Society of Biblical Literature Dissertation Series 25. Missoula: Scholars, 1975.
Diels, H. A. *Die Fragmente der Vorsokratiker: Griechisch und Deutsch von Hermann Diels*. 3 vols. 9th edn. Berlin: Weidmannsche Verlagsbuchhandlung, 1959–60.
DiFransico, Lesley R. *Washing Away Sin: An Analysis of the Metaphor in the Hebrew Bible and its Influence*. Biblical Tools and Studies 23. Leuven: Peeters, 2016.

Docherty, Susan E. 'The Text Form of the OT Citations in Hebrews Chapter 1 and the Implications for the Study of the Septuagint'. *New Testament Studies* 55.3 (2009): 355–65.
Docherty, Susan E. *The Use of the Old Testament in Hebrews. A Case Study in Early Jewish Bible Interpretation*. Wissenschaftliche Untersuchungen zum Neuen Testament 2.238. Tübingen: Mohr Siebeck, 2009.
Docherty, Susan E. 'Recent Interpretation of Hebrews Chapters 3–4: Critical Issues and Scholarly Trends'. *Irish Theological Quarterly* 81.4 (2016): 385–96.
Docherty, Susan E. 'Composite Citations and Conflation of Scriptural Narratives in Hebrews'. In *Composite Citations in Antiquity. Volume 2: New Testament Uses*, edited by S. A. Adams and S. M. Ehorn, 190–208. The Library of New Testament Studies 593. London: Bloomsbury T&T Clark, 2018.
Docherty, Susan E. 'Crossing Testamentary Borders: Methodological Insights for OT/NT Study from Contemporary Hebrew Bible Scholarship'. In *Methodology in the Use of the Old Testament in the New: Context and Criteria*, edited by David Allen and Steve Smith, 11–23. The Library of New Testament Studies 597. London: Bloomsbury T&T Clark, 2019.
Docherty, Susan E. 'The Use of the Old Testament in Hebrews Chapter 13 and Its Bearing on the Question of the Integrity of the Epistle'. In *Son, Sacrifice, and Great Shepherd Studies on the Epistle to the Hebrews*, edited by David M. Moffitt and Eric F. Mason, 207–18. Wissenschaftliche Untersuchungen zum Neuen Testament 2.510. Tubingen: Mohr Siebeck, 2020.
Dodd, C. H. 'ἹΛΑΣΚΕΚΘΑΙ, its Cognates, Derivatives, and Synonyms, in the Septuagint'. *Journal of Theological Studies* 32.128 (1931): 352–60.
Dodd, C. H. *According to The Scriptures: The Sub-Structure of New Testament Theology*. London: Nisbet, 1952.
Dodds, E. R. *The Greeks and the Irrational*. Berkeley: University of California Press, 1966.
Douglas, Mary. *Purity and Danger: An Analysis of Concept of Pollution and Taboo*. London: Routledge, 1966.
Douglas, Mary. *In the Active Voice*. London: Routledge, 1982.
Douglas, Mary. 'The Forbidden Animals in Leviticus'. *Journal for the Study of the Old Testament* 59 (1993): 3–23.
Douglas, Mary. 'Poetic Structure in Leviticus'. In *Pomegranates and Golden Bells: Studies in Biblical, Jewish, and Near Eastern Ritual, Law, and Literature in Honour of Jacob Milgrom*, edited by David P. Wright, David Noel Freedman and Avi Hurvitz, 239–56. Winona Lake, IN: Eisenbrauns, 1995.
Douglas, Mary. *Natural Symbols: Explorations in Cosmology*. London: Routledge, 1996.
Dozeman, T. B. *Exodus*. Eerdmans Critical Commentary. Grand Rapids: Eerdmans, 2008.
Duff, Justin H. 'The Blood of Goats and Calves . . . and Bulls? An Allusion to Isaiah 1:11 LXX in Hebrews 10:4'. *Journal of Biblical Literature* 138 (2018): 765–83.
Duff, Justin H. '"With Loud Cries and Tears": Sin and the Consecration of the Incarnate Son in the Epistle to the Hebrews'. PhD diss., University of St Andrews, 2019.
Dunn, James D. G. *Christology in the Making: A New Testament Inquiry into the Origins of the Doctrine of the Incarnation*. London: SCM, 1980.
Dunn, James D. G. *The Partings of the Ways between Christianity and Judaism and their Significance for the Character of Christianity*. 2nd edn. London: SCM, 2006.
Dunnill, John. *Covenant and Sacrifice in the Letter to the Hebrews*. Society for New Testament Studies Monograph Series 75. Cambridge: Cambridge University Press, 1992.

Dunnill, John. *Sacrifice and the Body: Biblical Anthropology and Christian Self-Understanding*. London & New York: Routledge, 2016.
Duschinsky, Robbie. 'Recognizing Secular Defilement: Douglas, Durkheim and Housework'. *History and Anthropology* 25.5 (2014): 553–70.
Duschinsky, Robbie, Simone Schnall and Daniel H. Weiss, eds. *Purity and Danger Now: New Perspectives*. London: Routledge, 2016.
Dyer, Bryan R. *Suffering in the Face of Death: The Epistle to the Hebrews and Its Context of Situation*. The Library of New Testament Studies 568. London: Bloomsbury T&T Clark, 2017.
Easter, Matthew C. *Faith and the Faithfulness of Jesus in Hebrews*. Society for New Testament Studies Monograph Series 160. Cambridge: Cambridge University Press, 2014.
Eberhart, Christian A. *Studien zur Bedeutung der Opfer im Alten Testament: Die Signifikanz von Blut- und Verbrennungsriten im kultischen Rahmen*. Wissenschaftliche Monographien zum Alten und Neuen Testament 94. Neukirchen-Vluyn: Neukirchner Verlag, 2002.
Eberhart, Christian A. 'Characteristics of Sacrificial Metaphors in Hebrews'. In *Hebrews: Contemporary Methods—New Insights*, edited by Gabriella Gelardini, 37–64. Biblical Interpretation Series 75. Leiden: Brill, 2005.
Eberhart, Christian A. *The Sacrifice of Jesus: Understanding Atonement Biblically*. Minneapolis: Fortress Press, 2011.
Eberhart, Christian A. *Kultmetaphorik und Christologie: Opfer- und Sühneterminologie im Neuen Testament*. Wissenschaftliche Untersuchungen zum Neuen Testament 306. Tübingen: Mohr Siebeck, 2013.
Eberhart, Christian A. 'Introduction: Constituents and Critique of Sacrifice, Cult, and Atonement in Early Judaism and Christianity'. In *Sacrifice, Cult, and Atonement in Early Judaism and Christianity: Constituents and Critique*, edited by Henrietta L. Wiley and Christian A. Eberhart, 1–29. Resources for Biblical Study 85. Atlanta: SBL, 2017.
Eberhart, Christian A. 'To Atone or Not to Atone: Remarks on the Day of Atonement Rituals According to Leviticus 16 and the Meaning of Atonement'. In *Sacrifice, Cult, and Atonement in Early Judaism and Christianity: Constituents and Critique*, edited by Henrietta L. Wiley and Christian A. Eberhart, 197–231. Resources for Biblical Study 85. Atlanta: SBL, 2017.
Eberhart, Christian A., ed. *Ritual and Metaphor: Sacrifice in the Bible*. Resources for Biblical Study 68. Atlanta: SBL, 2011.
Eckstein, H. J. *Der Begriff Syneidesis bei Paulus: eine neutestamentlich-exegetische Untersuchung zum 'Gewissensbegriff'*. Wissenschaftliche Untersuchungen zum Neuen Testament 2.10. Tübingen: Mohr Siebeck, 1983.
Ehrlich, C. S., Anders Runesson and Eileen Schuller, eds. *Purity, Holiness, and Identity in Judaism and Christianity: Essays in Memory of Susan Haber*. Wissenschaftliche Untersuchungen zum Neuen Testament 305. Tübingen: Mohr Siebeck, 2013.
Eisele, Wilfried. *Ein unerschütterliches Reich: Die mittelplatonische Umformung des Parusiegedankens im Hebräerbrief*. Beihefte zur Zeitschrift für die neutestamentliche Wissenschaft 116. Berlin: de Gruyter, 2003.
Eisenbaum, Pamela M. 'Locating Hebrews within the Literary Landscape of Christian Origins'. In *Hebrews: Contemporary Methods — New Insights*, edited by Gabriella Gelardini, 213–37. Biblical Interpretation Series 75. Leiden: Brill, 2005.
Elgvin, Torlief. 'From the Earthly to the Heavenly Temple: Lines from the Bible and Qumran to Hebrews and Revelation'. In *The World of Jesus and the Early Church: Identity and Interpretation in Early Communities of Faith*, edited by Craig A. Evans, 12–36. Peabody, MA: Hendrickson, 2011.

Ellingworth, Paul. *The Epistle to the Hebrews: A Commentary on the Greek Text*. New International Greek Testament Commentary. Grand Rapids: Eerdmans, 1993.

Enns, Peter E. 'Creation and Re-creation: Psalm 95 and Its Interpretation in Hebrews 3:1–4:13'. *Westminster Theological Journal* 55.2 (1993): 255–80.

Eskola, Timo. *Messiah and the Throne: Jewish Merkabah Mysticism and Early Christian Exaltation Discourse*. Wissenschaftliche Untersuchungen zum Neuen Testament 2.142. Tübingen: Mohr Siebeck, 2001.

Eskola, Timo. *A Narrative Theology of the New Testament: Exploring the Metanarrative of Exile and Restoration*. Wissenschaftliche Untersuchungen zum Neuen Testament 350. Tübingen: Mohr Siebeck, 2015.

Espy, M. 'Paul's "Robust Conscience" Reexamined'. *New Testament Studies* 31.2 (1985): 161–88.

Fanning, B. M. *Verbal Aspect in New Testament Greek*. Oxford Theological Monographs. Oxford: Oxford University Press, 1990.

Feder, Yitzhaq. 'On *kuppuru*, *kipper* and Etymological Sins that cannot be Wiped Away'. *Vetus Testamentum* 60 (2010): 535–45.

Feder, Yitzhaq. *Blood Expiation in Hittite and Biblical Ritual: Origins, Context, and Meaning*. Writings from the Ancient World Supplement Series 2. Atlanta: SBL, 2011.

Feder, Yitzhaq. 'Contagion and Cognition: Bodily Experience and the Conceptualization of Pollution (ṭum'ah) in the Hebrew Bible'. *Journal of Near Eastern Studies* 72 (2013): 151–67.

Feder, Yitzhaq. *Purity and Pollution in the Hebrew Bible: From Embodied Experience to Moral Metaphor*. Cambridge: Cambridge University Press, 2022.

Feld, Helmut. *Der Hebräerbrief*. Erträge der Forschung 228. Darmstadt: Wissenschaftliche Buchgesellschaft, 1985.

Feldman, Liane M. *The Story of Sacrifice: Ritual and Narrative in the Priestly Source*. Forschungen zum Alten Testament 141. Tübingen: Mohr Siebeck, 2020.

Feldmeier, Reinhard and Hermann Spieckermann. *God of the Living: A Biblical Theology*. Translated by Mark E. Biddle. Waco, TX: Baylor University Press, 2011.

Filtvedt, Ole Jakob. 'Creation and Salvation in Hebrews'. *Zeitschrift für die neutestamentliche Wissenschaft und die Kunde der älteren Kirche* 106 (2015): 280–303.

Filtvedt, Ole Jakob. *The Identity of God's People and the Paradox of Hebrews*. Wissenschaftliche Untersuchungen zum Neuen Testament 2.400. Tübingen: Mohr Siebeck, 2015.

Finlan, S. *Sacrifice and Atonement: Psychological Motives and Biblical Patterns*. Minneapolis: Fortress Press, 2016.

Flemington, W. F. *The New Testament Doctrine of Baptism*. London: SPCK, 1948.

Foster, P. 'Echoes without Resonance: Critiquing Certain Aspects of Recent Scholarly Trends in the Study of the Jewish Scriptures in the New Testament'. *Journal for the Study of the New Testament* 38 (2015): 96–111.

France, R. T. 'The Writer of Hebrews as Biblical Expositor'. *Tyndale Bulletin* 47.2 (1996): 245–76.

Freedman, David Noel, ed. *Anchor Bible Dictionary*. 6 vols. New York: Doubleday, 1992.

Frevel, Christian. 'σήμερον—Understanding Psalm 95 Within, and Without, Hebrews'. In *Psalms and Hebrews: Studies in Reception*, edited by Dirk J. Human and Gert J. Steyn, 165–93. Library of Hebrew Bible/Old Testament Studies 527. London: T&T Clark, 2010.

Frevel, Christian and Christophe Nihan. 'Introduction'. In *Purity and the Forming of Religious Traditions in the Ancient Mediterranean World and Ancient Judaism*, edited by Christian Frevel and Christophe Nihan, 1–46. Dynamics in the History of Religions 3. Leiden: Brill, 2013.

Frey, Jörg. 'Die alte und die neue διαθήκη nach dem Hebräerbrief'. In *Bund und Tora: Zur theologischen Begriffsgeschichte in alttestamentlicher, frühjüdischer und urchristlicher Tradition*, edited by F. Avemarie and H. Lichtenberger, 263–310. Wissenschaftliche Untersuchungen zum Neuen Testament 92. Tübingen: Mohr Siebeck, 1996.

Friedeman, Caleb T., ed. *Listen, Understand, Obey: Essays on Hebrews in Honor of Gareth Lee Cockerill*. Eugene, OR: Wipf & Stock, 2017.

Frymer-Kensky, Tikva. 'Pollution, Purification, and Purgation in Biblical Israel'. In *The Word of the Lord Shall Go Forth: Essays in Honour of David Noel Freedman in Celebration of his Sixtieth Birthday*, edited by Carol L. Meyers and M. O'Connor, 399–410. Winona Lake, IN: Eisenbrauns, 1983.

Fuhrmann, Sebastian. 'Failures Forgotten: The Soteriology in Hebrews revisited in the light of its quotation of Jeremiah 38:31–34 [LXX]'. *Neotestamentica* 41.2 (2007): 296–316.

Fuhrmann, Sebastian. *Vergeben und Vergessen: Christologie und Neuer Bund im Hebräerbrief*. Wissenschaftliche Monographien zum Alten und Neuen Testament 113. Neukirchen-Vluyn: Neukirchener Verlag, 2007.

Fuhrmann, Sebastian. 'The Son, the Angels, and the Odd: Psalm 8 in Hebrews 1 and 2'. In *Psalms and Hebrews: Studies in Reception*, edited by Dirk J. Human and Gert J. Steyn, 83–98. The Library of Hebrew Bible/Old Testament Studies 527. London: T&T Clark, 2010.

Gäbel, Georg. *Die Kulttheologie des Hebräerbriefes: Eine exegetisch-religionsgeschichtliche Studie*. Wissenschaftliche Untersuchungen zum Neuen Testament 2.212. Tübingen: Mohr Siebeck, 2006.

Gäbel, Georg. 'Rivals in Heaven: Angels in the Epistle to the Hebrews'. In *Angels: The Concept of Celestial Beings: Origins, Development and Reception*, edited by Friedrich V. Reiterer, Tobias Nicklas and Karin Schöpflin, 357–76. Deuterocanonical and Cognate Literature Yearbook 2007. Berlin: de Gruyter, 2007.

Gäbel, Georg. '"You Don't Have Permission to Access This Site": The Tabernacle Description in Hebrews 9:1–5 and Its Function in Context'. In *Son, Sacrifice, and Great Shepherd Studies on the Epistle to the Hebrews*, edited by David M. Moffitt and Eric F. Mason, 135–75. Wissenschaftliche Untersuchungen zum Neuen Testament 2.510. Tubingen: Mohr Siebeck, 2020.

Gane, Roy E. *Leviticus, Numbers*. NIV Application Commentary. Grand Rapids: Zondervan, 2004.

Gane, Roy E. *Cult and Character: Purification Offerings, Day of Atonement, and Theodicy*. Winona Lake, IN: Eisenbrauns, 2005.

Gane, Roy E., and Ada Tager-Cohen, eds. *Current Issues in Priestly and Related Literature: The Legacy of Jacob Milgrom*. Atlanta: SBL, 2015.

Gause, R. Hollis. *Hebrews*. Pentecostal Commentary Series 7. Leiden: Brill, 2022.

Gelardini, G. *Verhärtet eure Herzen nicht: der Hebräer, eine Synagogenhomilie zu Tischa be-Aw*. Leiden: Brill, 2007.

Gelardini, G. 'The Inauguration of Yom Kippur According to the LXX and its Cessation or Perpetuation According to the Book of Hebrews: A Systematic Comparison'. In *The Day of Atonement: Its Interpretations in Early Jewish and Christian Traditions*, edited by Thomas Hieke and Tobias Nicklas, 225–54. Themes in Biblical Narrative 15. Leiden: Brill, 2011.

Gelardini, G. *Deciphering the Worlds of Hebrews: Collected Essays*. Supplements to Novum Testamentum 184. Leiden: Brill, 2021.

Gelardini, G., and Harold Attridge, eds. *Hebrews in Contexts*. Arbeiten zur Geschichte des antiken Judentums und des Urchristentums 91. Leiden: Brill, 2016.

Geller, Stephen A. 'Blood Cult: Toward a Literary Theology of the Priestly Work of the Pentateuch'. *Prooftexts* 12 (1992): 97–124.
Gheorghita, Radu. *The Role of the Septuagint in Hebrews: An Investigation of its Influence with Special Consideration to the Use of Hab 2:3–4 in Heb 10:37–38*. Wissenschaftliche Untersuchungen zum Neuen Testament 2.160. Tübingen: Mohr Siebeck, 2003.
Gilders, William K. *Blood Ritual in the Hebrew Bible: Meaning and Power*. Baltimore: Johns Hopkins University Press, 2004.
Gilders, William K. 'Blood and Covenant: Interpretive Elaboration on Genesis 9.4–6 in the Book of Jubilees'. *Journal for the Study of the Pseudepigrapha* 15 (2006): 83–118.
Ginsburskaya, M. 'Purity and Impurity in the Hebrew Bible'. In *Purity: Essays in Bible and Theology*, edited by Andrew Brower Latz and Arseny Ermakov, 3–29. Eugene, OR: Wipf & Stock, 2014.
Girard, René. *Things Hidden Since the Foundation of the World*. Translated by Stephen Bann and Michael Mann. Stanford: Stanford University Press, 1987.
Girard, René. *Violence and the Sacred*. Translated by Patrick Gregory. London: Athlone, 1995.
Gooch, P. W. 'Conscience in 1 Corinthians 8 and 10'. *New Testament Studies* 33.2 (1987): 244–54.
Gordon, Robert P. 'Better Promises: Two Passages in Hebrews against the Background of the Old Testament Cultus'. In *Templum Amicitiae: Essays on the Second Temple Presented to Ernst Bammel*, edited by William Horbury, 439–49. Journal for the Study of the New Testament Supplement Series 48. Sheffield: JSOT Press, 1991.
Gordon, Robert P. *Hebrews*. Sheffield: Sheffield Academic Press, 2000.
Gorman, Frank H. *The Ideology of Ritual: Space, Time and Status in the Priestly Theology*. Journal for the Study of the Old Testament Supplement Series 91. Sheffield: JSOT Press, 1990.
Grässer, Erich. *Der Glaube im Hebräerbrief*. Marburger theologische Studien 2. Marburg: N. G. Elwert, 1965.
Grässer, Erich. 'Das Wandernde Gottesvolk: Zum Basismotiv des Hebräerbriefes'. *Zeitschrift für die neutestamentliche Wissenschaft und die Kunde der älteren Kirche* 77 (1986): 167–9.
Grässer, Erich. *An die Hebräer*. 3 vols. Evangelisch-katholischer Kommentar zum Neuen Testament 17. Zurich: Benziger, 1990–7.
Gray, Patrick. *Godly Fear: The Epistle to the Hebrews and Greco-Roman Critiques of Superstition*. Academia Biblica 16. Atlanta: SBL, 2003.
Gray, Patrick and Amy Peeler. *Hebrews: An Introduction and Study Guide*. London: Bloomsbury T&T Clark, 2020.
Greenberg, James A. *A New Look at Atonement in Leviticus: The Meaning and Purpose of Kipper Revisited*. Bulletin for Biblical Research Supplement 23. Winona Lake, IN: Eisenbrauns, 2019.
Griffiths, Jonathan I. *Hebrews and Divine Speech*. The Library of New Testament Studies 507. London: Bloomsbury T&T Clark, 2014.
Griffiths, Jonathan I., ed. *The Perfect Saviour: Key Themes in Hebrews*. Nottingham: Inter-Varsity Press, 2012.
Grogan, Geoffrey W. 'Christ and His People: An Exegetical and Theological Study of Hebrews 2.5–18'. *Vox Evangelica* 6 (1969): 54–71.
Gunton, Colin. *The Actuality of Atonement: A Study of Metaphor, Rationality and the Christian Tradition*. London: T&T Clark, 1988.
Guthrie, Donald. *Hebrews: An Introduction and Commentary*. Tyndale New Testament Commentaries 15. Downers Grove, IL: InterVarsity Press, 2008.

Guthrie, George H. *The Structure of Hebrews: A Text-Linguistic Analysis*. Supplements to Novum Testamentum 73. Leiden: Brill, 1994.
Guthrie, George H. *Hebrews*. NIV Application Commentary. Grand Rapids: Zondervan, 1998.
Guthrie, George H. 'Hebrews' Use of the Old Testament: Recent Trends in Research'. *Currents in Biblical Research* 1.2 (2003): 271–94.
Guthrie, George H. 'Hebrews'. In *Commentary on the New Testament Use of the Old Testament*, edited by G. K. Beale and D. A. Carson, 919–95. Grand Rapids: Baker Academic, 2007.
Guthrie, George H. 'Time and Atonement in Hebrews'. In *So Great a Salvation: A Dialogue on the Atonement in Hebrews*, edited by George H. Guthrie, Jon C. Laansma and Cynthia Long Westfall, 209–27. The Library of New Testament Studies 516. London: Bloomsbury T&T Clark, 2019.
Guthrie, George H., Cynthia L. Westfall and Jon C. Laansma, eds. *So Great a Salvation: A Dialogue on the Atonement in Hebrews*. The Library of New Testament Studies 516. London: Bloomsbury T&T Clark, 2019.
Guthrie, George H., and Russell D. Quinn. 'A Discourse Analysis of the Use of Psalm 8:4–6 in Hebrews 2:5–9'. *Journal of the Evangelical Theological Society* 49.2 (2006): 235–46.
Haber, Susan. 'From Priestly Torah to Christ Cultus: The Re-Vision of Covenant and Cult in Hebrews'. *Journal for the Study of the New Testament* 28.1 (2005): 105–24.
Haber, Susan. *'They Shall Purify Themselves': Essays on Purity in Early Judaism*, edited by Adele Reinhartz. Early Judaism and its Literature 24. Atlanta: SBL, 2008.
Hägglund, F. *Isaiah 53 in the Light of Homecoming After Exile*. Forschungen zum Alten Testament 2.31. Tübingen: Mohr Siebeck, 2008.
Hagner, Donald A. *Hebrews*. New International Bible Commentary 14. Peabody, MA: Hendrickson, 1990.
Hagner, Donald A. *Encountering the Book of Hebrews: An Exposition*. Grand Rapids: Baker Academic, 2002.
Hahn, Scott W. 'A Broken Covenant and the Curse of Death: A Study of Hebrews 9:15–22'. *Catholic Biblical Quarterly* 66.3 (2004): 416–36.
Hamm, Dennis. 'Praying "Regularly" (not "Constantly"): A Note on the Cultic Background of at Luke 24:53, Acts 10:2 and Hebrews 9:6, 13:15'. *Expository Times* 116 (2004): 50–2.
Harris, D. M. *Hebrews*. Exegetical Guide to the Greek New Testament. Nashville: B&H, 2019.
Harrington, Hannah K. *The Purity and Sanctuary of the Body in Second Temple Judaism*. Göttingen: Vandenhoeck & Ruprecht, 2019.
Hauck, Albert, ed. *Realencyklopädie für protestantische Theologie und Kirche*. 24 vols. Leipzig: J. C. Hinrichs'sche Buchhandlung, 1896–1913.
Hay, David M. *Glory at the Right Hand: Psalm 110 in Early Christianity*. Society of Biblical Literature Monograph Series 18. Nashville: Abingdon, 1973.
Hays, Richard B. *Echoes of Scripture in the Letters of Paul*. New Haven: Yale University Press, 1989.
Hays, Richard B. '"Here We Have No Lasting City": New Covenantalism in Hebrews'. In *The Epistle to the Hebrews and Christian Theology*, edited by Richard Bauckham, Daniel R. Driver, Trevor A. Hart and Nathan MacDonald, 151–73. Grand Rapids: Eerdmans, 2009.
Hays, Richard B. *Reading Backwards: Figural Christology and the Fourfold Gospel Witness*. London: SPCK, 2015.
Hays, Richard B. *Echoes of Scripture in the Gospels*. Waco: Baylor University, 2016.
Hays, Richard B. *Reading with the Grain of Scripture*. Grand Rapids: Eerdmans, 2020.

Heen, E. M., and Philip D. W. Krey, eds. *Hebrews*. Ancient Christian Commentary on Scripture 10. Downers Grove: InterVarsity Press, 2005.

Hegermann, Harald. *Der Brief an die Hebräer*. Theologischer Handkommentar zum Neuen Testament 16. Berlin: Evangelische Verlagsanstalt, 1988.

Heidel, Andreas-Christian. *Das glaubende Gottesvolk: Der Hebräerbrief in israeltheologischer Perspektive*. Wissenschaftliche Untersuchungen zum Neuen Testament 2.540. Tübingen: Mohr Siebeck, 2020.

Hermann, Markus-Liborius. *Die "hermeneutische Stunde" des Hebräerbriefes: Schriftauslegung in Spannungsfeldern*. Freiburg im Breisgau: Herder, 2013.

Hill, David. *Greek Words and Hebrew Meanings: Studies in the Semantics of Soteriological Terms*. Society for New Testament Studies Monograph Series 5. Cambridge: Cambridge University Press, 1967.

Hockey, Katherine M., Madison N. Pierce and Francis Watson, eds. *Muted Voices of the New Testament: Readings in the Catholic Epistles and Hebrews*. Library of New Testament Studies 565. London: Bloomsbury T&T Clark, 2017.

Hoffmann, David Zvi. *Das Buch Leviticus*. 2 vols. Berlin: M. Poppelauer, 1905–6.

Hofius, Otfried. 'Das "erste" und das "zweite" Zelt: Ein Beitrag zur Auslegung von Hbr 9 1–10'. *Zeitschrift für die neutestamentliche Wissenschaft und die Kunde der älteren Kirche* 61.3 (1970): 271–7.

Hofius, Otfried. 'Inkarnation und Opfertod Jesu nach Hebr 10,19f'. In *Der Ruf Jesu und die Antwort der Gemeinde: Exegetische Untersuchungen Joachim Jeremias zum 70. Geburtstag gewidmet von seinen* Schülern, edited by Eduard Lohse, Christoph Burchard and Berndt Schaller, 132–41. Göttingen: Vandenhoeck & Ruprecht, 1970.

Hofius, Otfried. *Katapausis: Die Vorstellung vom endzeitlichen Ruheort im Hebräerbrief*. Wissenschaftliche Untersuchungen zum Neuen Testament 11. Tübingen: Mohr Siebeck, 1970.

Hofius, Otfried. *Der Vorhang vor dem Thron Gottes: Eine exegetisch-religionsgeschichtliche Untersuchung zu Hebräer 6,19f und 10,19f*. Wissenschaftliche Untersuchungen zum Neuen Testament 14. Tübingen: Mohr Siebeck, 1972.

Hofius, Otfried. 'The Fourth Servant Song in the New Testament Letters'. In *The Suffering Servant: Isaiah 53 in Jewish and Christian Sources*, edited by Bernd Janowski and Peter Stuhlmacher, 163–88. Translated by Daniel P. Bailey. Grand Rapids: Eerdmans, 2004.

Hollinger, Zoe. 'Rethinking the translation of τρέχωμεν τὸν . . . ἀγῶνα in Heb. 12.1 in light of ancient Graeco-Roman literature'. *The Bible Translator* 70.1 (2019): 94–111.

Holmes, C. T. *The Function of Sublime Rhetoric in Hebrews A Study in Hebrews 12:18–29*. Wissenschaftliche Untersuchungen zum Neuen Testament 2.465. Tübingen: Mohr Siebeck, 2018.

Horbury, W. 'The Aaronic Priesthood in the Epistle to the Hebrews'. *Journal for the Study of the New Testament* 19 (1983): 43–71.

Horsley, R. A. 'Consciousness and Freedom among the Corinthians: 1 Corinthians 8–10'. *Catholic Biblical Quarterly* 40.4 (1978): 574–89.

Hubert, H., and M. Mauss. *Sacrifice: Its Nature and Function*. Translated by W. D. Halls. 1898. Reprint. Chicago: University of Chicago Press, 1964.

Hughes, Graham. *Hebrews and Hermeneutics: The Epistle to the Hebrews as a New Testament Example of Biblical Interpretation*. Society for New Testament Studies Monograph Series 36. Cambridge: Cambridge University Press, 1979.

Hughes, John J. 'Hebrews IX 15ff. and Galatians III 15ff.: A Study in Covenant Practice and Procedure'. *Novum Testamentum* 21 (1979): 27–96.

Hughes, Philip Edgcumbe. 'The Blood of Jesus and His Heavenly Priesthood in Hebrews: Part II: The High-Priestly Sacrifice of Christ'. *Bibliotheca Sacra* 130 (1973): 195–212.

Hughes, Philip Edgcumbe. *A Commentary on the Epistle to the Hebrews*. Grand Rapids: Eerdmans, 1977.

Human, Dirk J., and Gert J. Steyn, eds. *Psalms and Hebrews: Studies in Reception*. The Library of Hebrew Bible/Old Testament Studies 527. London: T&T Clark, 2010.

Hundley, Michael B. *Keeping Heaven on Earth: Safeguarding the Divine Presence in the Priestly Tabernacle*. Forschungen zum Alten Testament 2.50. Tübingen: Mohr Siebeck, 2011.

Hurst, Lincoln D. 'How Platonic are Heb. viii.5 and ix.23f?' *Journal of Theological Studies* 34.1 (1983): 156–68.

Hurst, Lincoln D. 'The Christology of Hebrews 1 and 2'. In *The Glory of Christ in the New Testament: Studies in Christology in Memory of George Bradford Caird*, edited by L. D. Hurst and N. T. Wright, 151–64. Oxford: Oxford University Press, 1987.

Isaacs, Marie. *Sacred Space: An Approach to the Theology of the Epistle to the Hebrews*. Journal for the Study of the New Testament Supplement Series 73. Sheffield: JSOT Press, 1992.

Isaacs, Marie. 'Why Bother with Hebrews?' *The Heythrop Journal* 43 (2002): 60–72.

Isaacs, Marie. *Reading Hebrews & James: A Literary and Theological Commentary*. Macon: Smyth & Helwys, 2013.

Jamieson, R. B. 'Hebrews 9.23: Cult Inauguration, Yom Kippur and the Cleansing of the Heavenly Tabernacle'. *New Testament Studies* 62.4 (2016): 569–87.

Jamieson, R. B. 'When and Where Did Jesus Offer Himself? A Taxonomy of Recent Scholarship on Hebrews'. *Currents in Biblical Research* 15.3 (2017): 338–68.

Jamieson, R. B. *Jesus' Death and Heavenly Offering in Hebrews*. Society for New Testament Studies Monograph Series 160. Cambridge: Cambridge University Press, 2019.

Jamieson, R. B. *The Paradox of Sonship: Christology in the Epistle to the Hebrews*. Studies in Christian Doctrine and Scripture. Downers Grove, IL: InterVarsity Press, 2021.

Janowski, Bernd. *Sühne als Heilsgeschehen: Traditions- und religionsgeschichtliche Studien zur Sühnetheologie der Priesterschrift*. 2nd edn. Wissenschaftliche Monographien zum Alten und Neuen Testament 55. Neukirchen-Vluyn: Neukirchener Verlag, 2000.

Jenson, Philip Peter. *Graded Holiness: A Key to the Priestly Conception of the World*. Journal for the Study of the Old Testament Supplement Series 106. Sheffield: JSOT Press, 1992.

Jenson, Philip Peter. *Leviticus: An Introduction and Study Guide*. London: Bloomsbury T&T Clark, 2021.

Jeremias, Joachim. 'Hebräer 10:20: τοῦτ' ἔστιν τῆς σαρκὸς αὐτοῦ'. *Zeitschrift für die neutestamentliche Wissenschaft und die Kunde der älteren Kirche* 62 (1971): 131.

Jewett, R. *Paul's Anthropological Terms: A Study of Their Use in Conflict Settings*. Arbeiten zur Geschichte des antiken Judentums und des Urchristentums 10. Leiden: Brill, 1971.

Jewett, R. *Letter to Pilgrims: A Commentary on the Epistle to the Hebrews*. New York: Pilgrim Press, 1981.

Jipp, Joshua W. 'The Son's Entrance into the Heavenly World: The Soteriological Necessity of the Scriptural Catena of Hebrews 1.5–14'. *New Testament Studies* 56.4 (2010): 557–75.

Jobes, Karen H. 'Rhetorical Achievement in the Hebrews 10 "Misquote" of Psalm 40'. *Biblica* 72.3 (1991): 387–96.

Jobes, Karen H. 'Putting Words in His Mouth: The Son Speaks in Hebrews'. In *So Great a Salvation: A Dialogue on the Atonement in Hebrews*, edited by George H. Guthrie, Jon C. Laansma and Cynthia Long Westfall, 40–50. The Library of New Testament Studies 516. London: Bloomsbury T&T Clark, 2019.

Johnson, Earl S. *Hebrews*. Interpretation Series. Louisville: Westminster John Knox Press, 2008.

Johnson, Luke Timothy. *Hebrews: A Commentary*. New Testament Library. Louisville: Westminster John Knox, 2006.

Johnson, Luke Timothy. 'The Scriptural World of Hebrews'. *Interpretation* 57.3 (2003): 237–50.

Johnson, Richard W. *Going Outside the Camp: The Sociological Function of the Levitical Critique in the Epistle to the Hebrews*. Journal for the Study of the New Testament Supplement Series 109. Sheffield: Sheffield Academic Press, 2001.

Johnsson, William G. 'Defilement and Purgation in the Book of Hebrews'. PhD diss., Vanderbilt University, 1973.

Johnsson, William G. 'The Cultus of Hebrews in Twentieth-Century Scholarship'. *Expository Times* 89 (1978): 104–8.

Johnsson, William G. 'The Pilgrimage Motif in the Book of Hebrews'. *Journal of Biblical Literature* 97.2 (1978): 239–51.

Johnsson, William G. 'The Heavenly Sanctuary–Figurative or Real?' In *Issues in the Book of Hebrews*, edited by Frank L. Holbrook, 35–51. Silver Spring, MD: Biblical Research Institute, 1989.

Joseph, Simon J. '"In the Days of His Flesh, He Offered Up Prayers": Reimagining the Sacrifice(s) of Jesus in the Letter to the Hebrews'. *Journal of Biblical Literature* 140.1 (2021): 207–27.

Joslin, Barry C. 'Christ Bore the Sins of Many: Substitution and the Atonement in Hebrews'. *The Southern Baptist Journal of Theology* 11.2 (2007): 74–103.

Jürgens, Benedikt. *Heiligkeit und Versöhnung: Levitikus 16 in seinem literarischen Kontext*. Herders Biblische Studien 28. Freiburg: Herder, 2001.

Jürgens, Benedikt. 'LXX Psalm 39:7–10 in Hebrews 10:5–7'. In *Psalms and Hebrews: Studies in Reception*, edited by Dirk J. Human and Gert J. Steyn, 126–46. The Library of Hebrew Bible/Old Testament Studies 527. London: T&T Clark, 2010.

Kaiser Walter C. Jr., 'The Promise Theme and the Theology of Rest'. *Bibliotheca Sacra* 130 (1973): 135–50.

Karrer, Martin. *Der Brief an die Hebräer*. 2 vols. Ökumenischer Taschenbuch-Kommentar 20. Gütersloh: Gütersloher Verlagshaus, 2002–8.

Karrer, Martin. 'LXX Psalm 39:7–10 in Hebrews 10:5–7'. In *Psalms and Hebrews: Studies in Reception*, edited by Dirk J. Human and Gert J. Steyn, 137–43. The Library of Hebrew Bible/Old Testament Studies 527. London: T&T Clark, 2010.

Käsemann, Ernst. *The Wandering People of God: An Investigation of the Letter to the Hebrews*. Translated by Roy A. Harrisville and Irving L. Sandberg. Minneapolis: Augsburg Publishing House, 1984.

Kazen, Thomas. 'Dirt and Disgust: Body and Morality in Biblical Purity Laws'. In *Perspectives on Purity and Purification in the Bible*, edited by Baruch J. Schwartz, David P. Wright, Jeffrey Stackert and Naphtali S. Meshel, 43–64. The Library of Hebrew Bible/Old Testament Studies 474. London: T&T Clark, 2008.

Kazen, Thomas. *Issues of Impurity in Early Judaism*. Coniectanea Biblica: New Testament Series 45. Winona Lake, IN: Eisenbrauns, 2010.

Kazen, Thomas. *Jesus and the Purity Halakhah: Was Jesus Indifferent to Impurity?* Coniectanea Biblica: New Testament Series 30. Winona Lake, IN: Eisenbrauns, 2010.

Kazen, Thomas. *Emotions in Biblical Law: A Cognitive Science Approach*. Hebrew Bible Monographs 36. Sheffield: Sheffield Phoenix, 2011.

Kazen, Thomas. 'The Role of Disgust in Priestly Purity Law: Insights from Conceptual Metaphor and Blending Theories'. *Journal of law, Religion and State* 3.1 (2014): 62–92.

Keene, Thomas. 'Heaven is a Tent: The Tabernacle as an Eschatological Metaphor in the Epistle to the Hebrews'. PhD diss., Westminster Theological Seminary, 2010.
Kibbe, Michael. 'Is It Finished? When Did It Start? Hebrews, Priesthood, and Atonement in Biblical, Systematic, and Historical Perspective'. *Journal of Theological Studies* 65.1 (2014): 25–61.
Kibbe, Michael. *Godly Fear or Ungodly Failure? Hebrews 12 and the Sinai Theophanies*. Beihefte zur Zeitschrift für die neutestamentliche Wissenschaft 216. Berlin: de Gruyter, 2016.
Kibbe, Michael. '"You are a Priest Forever!" Jesus' Indestructible Life in Hebrews 7:16'. *Horizons in Biblical Theology* 39 (2017): 134–55.
Kim, Daniel E. 'Jewish and Christian Theology from the Hebrew Bible: The Concept of Rest and Temple in the Targumim, Hebrews, and the Old Testament'. In *Hebrews in Contexts*, edited by Gabriella Gelardini and Harold W. Attridge, 31–46. Arbeiten zur Geschichte des antiken Judentums und des Urchristentums 91. Leiden: Brill, 2016.
Kim, Kyu S. 'Better Than the Blood of Abel? Some Remarks on Abel in Hebrews 12:24'. *Tyndale Bulletin* 67.1 (2016): 127–36.
Kim, Kyu S. 'The Concept of διαθήκη in Hebrews 9.16–17'. *Journal for the Study of the New Testament* 43.2 (2020): 248–65.
Kim, Lloyd. *Polemic in the Book of Hebrews: Anti-Judaism, Anti-Semitism, Supersessionism?* Princeton Theological Monograph Series 64. Eugene, OR: Wipf & Stock, 2006.
Kinzer, Mark Stephen. '"All Things Under His Feet": Psalm 8 in the New Testament and in Other Jewish Literature of Late Antiquity'. PhD diss., University of Michigan, 1995.
Kistemaker, Simon J. 'Atonement in Hebrews: "A Merciful and Faithful High Priest"'. In *The Glory of the Atonement: Biblical, Historical & Practical Perspectives: Essays in Honour of Roger Nicole*, edited by Charles E. Hill and Frank A. James III, 163–75. Downers Grove, IL: InterVarsity Press, 2004.
Kittel, G., and G. Friedrich, eds. *Theological Dictionary of the New Testament*. Translated by Geoffrey W. Bromiley. 10 vols. Grand Rapids: Eerdmans, 1964–76.
Kiuchi, Nobuyoshi. *The Purification Offering in the Priestly Literature: Its Meaning and Function*. Journal for the Study of the Old Testament Supplement Series 56. Sheffield: JSOT Press, 1987.
Kiuchi, Nobuyoshi. *A Study of Hata and Hatta't in Leviticus 4-5*. Forschungen zum Alten Testament 2.2. Tübingen: Mohr Siebeck, 2003.
Kiuchi, Nobuyoshi. *Leviticus*. Abingdon Old Testament Commentaries 3. Nottingham, UK: Apollos, 2007.
Klauck, H. J. 'Accuser, Judge and Paraclete – on Conscience in Philo of Alexandria'. *Skrif en kerk* 20.1 (1999): 107–18.
Klawans, Jonathan. *Impurity and Sin in Ancient Judaism*. Oxford: Oxford University Press, 2000.
Klawans, Jonathan. *Purity, Sacrifice, and the Temple: Symbolism and Supersessionism in the Study of Ancient Judaism*. Oxford: Oxford University Press, 2006.
Klawans, Jonathan. 'Methodology and Ideology in the Study of Priestly Ritual'. In *Perspectives on Purity and Purification in the Bible*, edited by Baruch J. Schwartz, David P. Wright, Jeffrey Stackert and Naphtali S. Meshel, 84–95. The Library of Hebrew Bible/Old Testament Studies 474. London: T&T Clark, 2008.
Knöppler, Thomas. *Sühne im Neuen Testament: Studien zum urchristlichen Verständnis der Heilsbedeutung des Todes Jesu*. Wissenschaftliche Monographien zum Alten und Neuen Testament 88. Neukirchen-Vluyn: Neukirchener Verlag, 2001.

Koehler, L., W. Baumgartner and J. J. Stamm. *The Hebrew and Aramaic Lexicon of the Old Testament*. Edited and translated under the supervision of M. E. J. Richardson. 2 vols. Leiden: Brill, 2001.

Koester, Craig R. *The Dwelling of God: The Tabernacle in the Old Testament, Intertestamental Literature, and the New Testament*. Catholic Biblical Quarterly Monograph Series 22. Washington, DC: Catholic Biblical Association of America, 1989.

Koester, Craig R. *Hebrews: A New Translation with Introduction and Commentary*. Anchor Bible 36. New York: Doubleday, 2001.

Kraus, Wolfgang. 'Die Bedeutung von διαθήκη im Hebräerbrief'. In *The Reception of Septuagint Words in Jewish-Hellenistic and Christian Literature*, edited by Eberhard Bons, Ralph Brucker and Jan Joosten, 67–83. Wissenschaftliche Untersuchungen zum Neuen Testament 2.367. Tübingen: Mohr Siebeck, 2014.

Kraus, Wolfgang. 'Psalm 40(39):7–9 in the Hebrew Bible and in the Septuagint, with its Reception in the New Testament (Heb 10:5–10)'. In *XVI Congress of the International Organization for Septuagint and Cognate Studies: Stellenbosch, 2016*, edited by Gideon R. Kotzé, Wolfgang Kraus and Michaël N. Van Der Meer, 119–31. Atlanta: SBL, 2019.

Kraus, Wolfgang. 'Jesus als "Mittler" im Hebräerbrief'. In *Vermittelte Gegenwart: Konzeptionen der Gottespräsenz von der Zeit des Zweiten Tempels bis Anfang des 2. Jahrhunderts n. Chr.*, edited by Andrea Taschl-Erber and Irmtraud Fischer, 293–315. Wissenschaftliche Untersuchungen zum Neuen Testament 367. Tübingen: Mohr Siebeck, 2016.

Kuma, Herman V. A. *The Centrality of Αἷμα (Blood) in the Theology of the Epistle to the Hebrews: An Exegetical and Philological Study*. Lewiston, NY: Edwin Mellen, 2012.

Laansma, Jon C. *'I Will Give You Rest': The 'Rest' Motif in the New Testament with Special Reference to Mt 11 and Heb 3–4*. Wissenschaftliche Untersuchungen zum Neuen Testament 2.98. Tübingen: Mohr Siebeck, 1997.

Laansma, Jon C. 'Hidden Stories in Hebrews: Cosmology and Theology'. In *A Cloud of Witnesses: The Theology of Hebrews in its Ancient Contexts*, edited by Richard Bauckham, Daniel D. Driver, Trevor A. Hart and Nathan MacDonald, 9–18. The Library of New Testament Studies 387. London: T&T Clark, 2008.

Laansma, Jon C. 'The Cosmology of Hebrews'. In *Cosmology and New Testament Theology*, edited by Sean M. McDonough and Jonathan T. Pennington, 125–43. The Library of New Testament Studies 355. London: T&T Clark, 2008.

Laansma, Jon C. *The Letter to the Hebrews: A Commentary for Preachers and Teachers*. Eugene, OR: Cascade Books, 2017.

Laansma, Jon C. and Daniel J. Treier, eds. *Christology, Hermeneutics, and Hebrews: Profiles from the History of Interpretation*. The Library of New Testament Studies 423. London: T&T Clark, 2012.

Lakoff, George and Mark Johnson. *Metaphors We Live By*. Chicago: University of Chicago Press, 2003.

Lam, Joseph C. P. 'The Metaphorical Patterning of the Sin-Concept in Biblical Hebrew'. PhD diss., University of Chicago, 2012.

Lam, Joseph C. P. *Patterns of Sin in the Hebrew Bible: Metaphor, Culture, and the Making of a Religious Concept*. New York: Oxford University Press, 2016.

Lam, Joseph C. P. 'The Concept of Sin in the Hebrew Bible'. *Religion Compass* 12 (2018): e12260.

Lamp, Jeffrey S. *Hebrews: An Earth Bible Commentary: A City That Cannot be Shaken*. Earth Bible Commentary. London: Bloomsbury T&T Clark, 2020.

Lane, William L. *Hebrews*. 2 vols. Word Biblical Commentary 47A–B. Dallas: Word, 1991.
Laub, Franz. *Bekenntnis und Auslegung: Die paränetische Funktion der Christologie im Hebraërbrief*. Biblische Untersuchungen 15. Regensburg: Pustet, 1980.
Laub, Franz. '"Ein für allemal hineingegangen in das Allerheiligste" (Hebr 9,12) – Zum Verständnis des Kreuzestodes im Hebraërbrief'. *Biblische Zeitschrift* 35.1 (1991): 65–85.
Lee, Aquila H. I. *From Messiah to Preexistent Son: Jesus' Self-Consciousness and Early Christian Exegesis of Messianic Psalms*. Wissenschaftliche Untersuchungen zum Neuen Testament 2.192. Tübingen: Mohr Siebeck, 2005.
Lee, G. *Today When you Hear his Voice: Scripture, the Covenants, and the People of God*. Grand Rapids: Eerdmans, 2016.
Lee, Jihye. *A Jewish Apocalyptic Framework of Eschatology in the Epistle to the Hebrews: Protology and Eschatology as Background*. The Library of New Testament Studies 662. London: Bloomsbury T&T Clark, 2021.
Lehne, Susanne. *The New Covenant in Hebrews*. Journal for the Study of the New Testament Supplement Series 44. Sheffield: JSOT Press, 1990.
Lemos, T. M. 'Where There Is Dirt, Is There System? Revisiting Biblical Purity Constructions'. *Journal for the Study of the Old Testament* 37.3 (2013): 265–94.
Leschert, Dale F. *Hermeneutical Foundations of Hebrews*. Lewiston: Edwin Mellen, 1994.
Levine, Baruch A. *In the Presence of the Lord: A Study of Cult and Some Cultic Terms in Ancient Israel*. Studies in Judaism in Late Antiquity 5. Leiden: Brill, 1974.
Levine, Baruch A. *Leviticus*. JPS Torah Commentary. Philadelphia: Jewish Publication Society, 1989.
Levinson, Bernard M. *Deuteronomy and the Hermeneutics of Legal Innovation*. Oxford: Oxford University Press, 1997.
Lewis, C. S. *Studies in Words*. 2nd edn. Cambridge: Cambridge University Press, 1967.
Liddell, Henry George, Robert Scott and Henry Stuart Jones. *A Greek–English Lexicon*. 9th rev. edn. Oxford: Clarendon, 1996.
Liethart, Peter J. 'Womb of the World: Baptism and the Priesthood of the New Covenant in Hebrews 10.9–22'. *Journal for the Study of the New Testament* 22.78 (2000): 49–65.
Lincoln, Andrew T. 'Sabbath, Rest, and Eschatology in the New Testament'. In *From Sabbath to Lord's Day: A Biblical, Historical and Theological Investigation*, edited by D. A. Carson, 197–220. Eugene, OR: Wipf & Stock, 1982.
Lincoln, Andrew T. *Hebrews: A Guide*. London: T&T Clark, 2006.
Lindars, Barnabas, SFF. 'The Rhetorical Structure of Hebrews'. *New Testament Studies* 35.3 (1989): 382–406.
Lindars, Barnabas, SFF. 'Hebrews and the Second Temple'. In *Templum Amicitiae: Essays on the Second Temple Presented to Ernst Bammel*, edited by William Horbury, 410–33. Journal for the Study of the New Testament Supplement Series 48. Sheffield: JSOT Press, 1991.
Lindars, Barnabas, SFF. *The Theology of The Letter to the Hebrews*. Cambridge: Cambridge University Press, 1991.
Loader, William R. G. *Sohn und Hoherpriester: Eine traditionsgeschichtliche Untersuchung zur Christologie des Hebräerbriefes*. Wissenschaftliche Monographien zum Alten und Neuen Testament 53. Neukirchen-Vluyn: Neukirchener Verlag, 1981.
Loader, William R. G. 'Revisiting High Priesthood Christology in Hebrews'. *Zeitschrift für die Neutestamentliche Wissenschaft und die Kunde der älteren Kirche* 109.2 (2018): 235–83.

Löhr, Hermut. 'Thronversammlung und preisender Tempel. Beobachtungen am himmlischen Heiligtum im Hebräerbrief und in den Sabbatopferliedern aus Qumran'. In *Königsherrschaft Gottes und himmlischer Kult: im Judentum, Urchristentum und in der hellenistischen Welt*, edited by Martin Hengel and Anna Maria Schwemer, 185–205. Wissenschaftliche Untersuchungen zum Neuen Testament 55. Tübingen: Mohr Siebeck, 1991.

Löhr, Hermut. '"Umriß" und "Schatten". Bemerkungen zur Zitierung von Ex 25,40 in Hebr. 8'. *Zeitschrift für die Neutestamentliche Wissenschaft und die Kunde der älteren Kirche* 84 (1993): 218–32.

Löhr, Hermut. *Umkehr und Sünde im Hebräerbrief*. Beihefte zur Zeitschrift für die neutestamentliche Wissenschaft 73. Berlin: de Gruyter, 1994.

Löhr, Hermut. 'Anthropologie und Eschatologie im Hebräerbrief: Bemerkungen zum theologischen Interesse einer frühchristlichen Schrift'. In *Eschatologie und Schöpfung: Festschrift für Erich Gräßer zum siebzigsten Geburtstag*, edited by Martin Evang, Helmut Merklein and Michael Wolter, 169–99. Beihefte zur Zeitschrift für die neutestamentliche Wissenschaft 89. Berlin: de Gruyter, 1997.

Löhr, Hermut. 'Wahrnehmung und Bedeutung des Todes Jesu nach dem Hebräerbrief: Ein Versuch'. In *Deutungen des Todes Jesu im Neuen Testament*, edited by Jörg Frey and Jens Schröter, 455–76. Wissenschaftliche Untersuchungen zum Neuen Testament 181. Tübingen: Mohr Siebeck, 2005.

Long, Thomas G. *Hebrews*. Interpretation Series. Louisville: Westminster John Knox Press, 1997.

Long, Thomas G. 'Bold in the Presence of God: Atonement in Hebrews'. *Interpretation* 52.1 (1998): 53–66.

Longenecker, Richard N. 'The Melchizedek Argument of Hebrews: A Study in the Development and Circumstantial Expression of New Testament Thought'. In *Unity and Diversity in New Testament Theology: Essays in Honor of George E. Ladd*, edited by Robert A. Guelich, 161–85. Grand Rapids: Eerdmans, 1978.

Longenecker, Richard N. *The Epistle to the Romans: A Commentary on the Greek Text*. New International Greek Testament Commentary. Grand Rapids: Eerdmans, 2016.

Louw, Johannes P., and Eugene A. Nida, eds. *Greek-English Lexicon of the New Testament: Based on Semantic Domains*. 2nd edn. New York: United Bible Societies, 1989.

Luck, Ulrich. 'Himmlisches und irdisches Geschehen im Hebräerbrief: Ein Beitrag zum Problem des "historischen Jesus" im Urchristentum'. *Novum Testamentum* 6 (1963): 192–215.

Lust, Johan, Erik Eynikel and Katrin Hauspie. *A Greek-English Lexicon of the Septuagint: Revised Edition*. Stuttgart: Deutsche Bibelgesellschaft, 2003.

Lyonnet, S., and L. Sabourin, *Sin, Redemption, and Sacrifice: A Biblical and Patristic Study*. Rome: Biblical Institute, 1970.

Macaskill, Grant. 'Hebrews 8–10 and Apocalyptic Theology in the New Testament'. In *Son, Sacrifice, and Great Shepherd Studies on the Epistle to the Hebrews*, edited by David M. Moffitt and Eric F. Mason, 79–93. Wissenschaftliche Untersuchungen zum Neuen Testament 2.510. Tubingen: Mohr Siebeck, 2020.

Maccoby, H. *Ritual and Morality: The Ritual Purity System and Its Place in Judaism*. Cambridge: Cambridge University Press, 1999.

Mackie, Scott D. *Eschatology and Exhortation in the Epistle of the Hebrews*. Wissenschaftliche Untersuchungen zum Neuen Testament 2.223. Tübingen: Mohr Siebeck, 2007.

Mackie, Scott D. 'Heavenly Sanctuary Mysticism in the Epistle to the Hebrews'. *Journal of Theological Studies* 62.1 (2011): 77–117.

Mackie, Scott D. 'Ancient Jewish Mystical Motifs in Hebrews' Theology of Access and Entry Exhortations'. *New Testament Studies* 58.1 (2012): 88–104.

Mackie, Scott D. '"Let us draw near ... But not too near". A Critique of the Attempted Distinction between "Drawing Near" and "Entering" in Hebrews' Entry Exhortations'. In *Listen, Understand, Obey: Essays on Hebrews in Honour of Gareth Lee Cockerill*, edited by Caleb T. Friedeman, 17–36. Eugene, OR: Wipf & Stock, 2017.

Mackie, Scott D. 'Visually Oriented Rhetoric and Visionary Experience in Hebrews 12:1–4'. *Catholic Biblical Quarterly* 79.3 (2017): 476–97.

Mackie, Scott D., ed. *The Letter to the Hebrews: Critical Readings*. T&T Clark Critical Readings in Biblical Studies. London: Bloomsbury T&T Clark, 2018.

MacLeod, D. J. 'The Cleansing of the True Tabernacle'. *Bibliotheca Sacra* 152.605 (1995): 60–71.

MacRae, George W. 'Heavenly Temple and Eschatology in the Letter to the Hebrews'. *Semeia* 12 (1978): 179–99.

Maloney, F. J. 'The Reinterpretation of Psalm VIII and the Son of Man Debate'. *New Testament Studies* 27.5 (1981): 656–72.

Marcos, N. F. *The Septuagint in Context: Introduction to the Greek Version of the Bible*. Leiden: Brill, 2000.

Maré, Leonard P. 'The Messianic Interpretation of Psalm 8:4–6 in Hebrews 2:6–9. Part I'. In *Psalms and Hebrews: Studies in Reception*, edited by Dirk J. Human and Gert J. Steyn, 99–112. The Library of Hebrew Bible/Old Testament Studies 527. London: T&T Clark, 2010.

Marietta, Don E. 'Conscience in Greek Stoicism'. *Numen* 17.3 (1970): 176–87.

Marohl, M. J. *Faithfulness and the Purpose of Hebrews: A Social Identity Approach*. Cambridge: James Clark, 2010.

Marshall, I. Howard. 'Soteriology in Hebrews'. In *The Epistle to the Hebrews and Christian Theology*, edited by Richard Bauckham, Daniel R. Driver, Trevor A. Hart and Nathan MacDonald, 253–77. Grand Rapids: Eerdmans, 2009.

Martin, Michael W., and Jason A. Whitlark, eds. *Inventing Hebrews: Design and Purpose in Ancient Rhetoric*. Society for New Testament Studies Monograph Series 171. Cambridge: Cambridge University Press, 2018.

Marx, Alfred. *Les systèmes sacrificiels de l'Ancien Testament: Formes et fonctions du culte sacrificial à YHWH*. Vetus Testamentum Supplement 105. Leiden: Brill, 2005.

Mason, Eric F. *'You Are a Priest Forever': Second Temple Jewish Messianism and the Priestly Christology of the Epistle to the Hebrews*. Studies on the Texts of the Desert of Judah 74. Leiden: Brill, 2008.

Mason, Eric F. '"Sit at My Right Hand": Enthronement and the Heavenly Sanctuary in Hebrews'. In *A Teacher for All Generations: Essays in Honour of James C. VanderKam*, edited by Eric F. Mason, Kelley Coblentz Bautch, Angela Kim Harkins and Daniel A. Machiela, 901–16. Supplements to the Journal for the Study of Judaism 2.153. Leiden: Brill, 2012.

Maston, Jason. '"What is Man?" An Argument for the Christological Reading of Psalm 8 in Hebrews 2'. *Zeitschrift für die Neutestamentliche Wissenschaft und die Kunde der älteren Kirche* 112.1 (2021): 89–104.

McClymond, Kathryn. *Beyond Sacred Violence: A Comparative Study of Sacrifice*. Baltimore: Johns Hopkins University Press, 2008.

McCown, Wayne G. 'Holiness in Hebrews'. *Wesleyan Theological Journal* 16.2 (1981): 58–78.

McCruden, Kevin B. *Solidarity Perfected: Beneficent Christology in the Epistle to the Hebrews*. Beihefte zur Zeitschrift für die neutestamentliche Wissenschaft 159. Berlin: de Gruyter, 2008.

McCruden, Kevin B. 'The Eloquent Blood of Jesus: The Neglected Theme of the Fidelity of Jesus in Hebrews'. *Catholic Biblical Quarterly* 75.3 (2013): 504–20.

McKay, J. M. '"If they Will Enter my Rest": The Impact of the Greek Translation Technique of Psalm 95 for the Argument of Hebrews 3 and 4'. *Journal for the Study of the New Testament* 44.3 (2022): 390–410.

McKelvey, R. J. *Pioneer and Priest: Jesus Christ in the Epistle to the Hebrews*. Eugene, OR: Wipf & Stock, 2013.

Meshel, Naphtali S. *The 'Grammar' of Sacrifice: A Generativist Study of the Israelite Sacrificial System in the Priestly Writings with A 'Grammar' of Σ*. Oxford: Oxford University Press, 2014.

Meszaros, Julia and Johannes Zachhuber, eds. *Sacrifice in Modern Thought*. Oxford: Oxford University Press, 2013.

Metzger, Bruce M. *A Textual Commentary on the Greek New Testament: A Companion Volume to the United Bible Societies' Greek New Testament*. 2nd edn. Stuttgart: Deutsche Bibelgesellschaft, 1994.

Michel, Otto. *Der Brief an die Hebräer*. 12th edn. Kritisch-exegetischer Kommentar über das Neue Testament (Meyer-Kommentar) 13. Göttingen: Vandenhoeck & Ruprecht, 1966.

Milgrom, Jacob. 'Sin-Offering or Purification-Offering?' *Vetus Testamentum* 21.2 (1971): 237–9.

Milgrom, Jacob. *Cult and Conscience: The ASHAM and the Priestly Doctrine of Repentance*. Studies in Judaism in Late Antiquity 18. Leiden: Brill, 1976.

Milgrom, Jacob. 'Israel's Sanctuary: The Priestly "Picture of Dorian Gray"'. *Revue biblique* 83.3 (1976): 390–9.

Milgrom, Jacob. *Studies in Cultic Theology and Terminology*. Studies in Judaism in Late Antiquity 36. Leiden: Brill, 1983.

Milgrom, Jacob. 'Rationale for Cultic Law: The Case of Impurity'. *Semeia* 45 (1989): 103–9.

Milgrom, Jacob. *Leviticus 1–16: A New Translation with Introduction and Commentary*. Anchor Bible 3. New York: Doubleday, 1991.

Milgrom, Jacob. *Leviticus 17–22: A New Translation with Introduction and Commentary*. Anchor Bible 3. New York: Doubleday, 2000.

Milgrom, Jacob. 'The Dynamics of Purity in the Priestly System'. In *Purity and Holiness: The Heritage of Leviticus*, edited by Marcel Poorthuis and Joshua J. Schwartz, 27–32. Leiden: Brill, 2000.

Milgrom, Jacob. 'Systemic Differences in the Priestly Corpus: A Response to Jonathan Klawans'. *Revue biblique* 112.3 (2005): 321–9.

Miller, Donald G. 'Why God Became Man: From Text to Sermon on Hebrews 2.5–18'. *Interpretation* 23.4 (1969): 408–24.

Miller, Neva F. *The Epistle to the Hebrews: An Analytical and Exegetical Handbook*. Dallas: Summer Institute of Linguistics, 1988.

Milligan, George. *The Theology of the Epistle to the Hebrews*. Edinburgh: T&T Clark, 1899.

Mitchell, A. C. 'Holding on to Confidence: παρρησία in Hebrews'. In *Friendship, Flattery, and Frankness of Speech*, edited by John T. Fitzgerald, 203–26. Supplements to Novum Testamentum 82. Leiden: Brill, 1996.

Mitchell, A. C. *Hebrews*. Sacra Pagina 13, edited by Daniel J. Harrington. Collegeville: Liturgical, 2009.

Moffatt, James. *A Critical and Exegetical Commentary on the Epistle to the Hebrews*. International Critical Commentary 40. Edinburgh: T&T Clark, 1924.

Moffitt, David M. 'Unveiling Jesus' Flesh: A Fresh Assessment of the Relationship Between the Veil and Jesus' Flesh in Hebrews 10:20'. *Perspectives in Religious Studies* 37.1 (2010): 71–84.

Moffitt, David M. *Atonement and the Logic of Resurrection in the Epistle to the Hebrews*. Supplements to Novum Testamentum 141. Leiden: Brill, 2011.

Moffitt, David M. 'Blood, Life, and Atonement: Reassessing Hebrews' Christological Appropriation of Yom Kippur'. In *The Day of Atonement: Its Interpretations in Early Jewish and Christian Traditions*, edited by Thomas Hieke and Tobias Nicklas, 211–24. Themes in Biblical Narrative 15. Leiden: Brill, 2012.

Moffitt, David M. 'Perseverance, Purity, and Identity: Exploring Hebrews' Eschatological Worldview, Ethics, and In-Group Bias'. In *Sensitivity to Outsiders: Exploring the Dynamic Relationship between Mission and Ethics in the New Testament and Early Christianity*, edited by Jacobus (Kobus) Kok, Tobias Nicklas, Dieter T. Roth and Christopher M. Hays, 357–81. Wissenschaftliche Untersuchungen zum Neuen Testament 364. Tübingen: Mohr Siebeck, 2014.

Moffitt, David M. 'Atonement at the Right Hand: The Sacrificial Significance of Jesus' Exaltation in Acts'. *New Testament Studies* 62.4 (2016): 549–68.

Moffitt, David M. 'Hebrews and the General Epistles'. In *T&T Clark Companion to the Doctrine of Sin*, edited by Keith L. Johnson and David Lauber, 111–25. London: Bloomsbury T&T Clark, 2016.

Moffitt, David M. 'The Role of Jesus' Resurrection in the Epistle to the Hebrews, Once Again: A Brief Response to Jean-René Moret'. *New Testament Studies* 62.2 (2016): 308–14.

Moffitt, David M. 'Serving in the Tabernacle in Heaven: Sacred Space, Jesus's High-Priestly Sacrifice, and Hebrews' Analogical Theology'. In *Hebrews in Contexts*, edited by Gabriella Gelardini and Harold W. Attridge, 259–79. Arbeiten zur Geschichte des antiken Judentums und des Urchristentums 91. Leiden: Brill, 2016.

Moffitt, David M. 'Hebrews'. In *T&T Clark Companion to Atonement*, edited by Adam J. Johnson, 533–6. London: Bloomsbury T&T Clark, 2017.

Moffitt, David M. 'Jesus' Heavenly Sacrifice in Early Christian Reception of Hebrews: A Survey'. *The Journal of Theological Studies* 68.1 (2017): 46–71.

Moffitt, David M. 'Modelled on Moses: Jesus' Death, Passover, and the Defeat of the Devil in the Epistle to the Hebrews'. In *Mosebilder: Gedanken zur Rezeption einer literarischen Figur im Frühjudentum, frühen Christentum und der römisch-hellenistischen Literatur*, edited by Michael Sommer, Erik Eynikel, Veronika Niederhofer and Elisabeth Hernitscheck, 279–97. Wissenschaftliche Untersuchungen zum Neuen Testament 390. Tübingen: Mohr Siebeck, 2017.

Moffitt, David M. 'Wilderness Identity and Pentateuchal Narrative: Distinguishing between Jesus' Inauguration and Maintenance of the New Covenant in Hebrews'. In *Muted Voices of the New Testament: Readings in the Catholic Epistles and Hebrews*, edited by Katherine M. Hockey, Madison N. Pierce and Francis Watson, 153–72. Library of New Testament Studies 565. London: Bloomsbury T&T Clark, 2017.

Moffitt, David M. 'It is Not Finished: Jesus' Perpetual Atoning Work as the Heavenly High Priest in Hebrews'. In *So Great a Salvation: A Dialogue on the Atonement in Hebrews*, edited by George H. Guthrie, Jon C. Laansma and Cynthia Long Westfall, 157–75. The Library of New Testament Studies 516. London: Bloomsbury T&T Clark, 2019.

Moffitt, David M. 'Weak and Useless? Purity, the Mosaic Law, and Perfection in Hebrews'. In *Law and Lawlessness in Early Judaism and Early Christianity*, edited by David Lincicum, Ruth Sheridan and Charles M. Stang, 89–103. Wissenschaftliche Untersuchungen zum Neuen Testament 420. Tübingen: Mohr Siebeck, 2019.

Moffitt, David M. 'Human Beings and Angels in Hebrews and Philo of Alexandria: Toward an Account of Hebrews' Cosmology'. In *Son, Sacrifice, and Great Shepherd Studies on the Epistle to the Hebrews*, edited by David M. Moffitt and Eric F. Mason, 13–30. Wissenschaftliche Untersuchungen zum Neuen Testament 2.510. Tubingen: Mohr Siebeck, 2020.

Moffitt, David M. 'Jesus as Interceding High Priest and Sacrifice in Hebrews: A Response to Nicholas Moore'. *Journal for the Study of the New Testament* 42.4 (2020): 545–52.

Moffitt, David M. '"Jesus' Sacrifice and the Mosaic Logic of Hebrews" New-Covenant Theology'. In *Understanding the Jewish Roots of Christianity: Biblical, Theological, and Historical Essays on the Relationship between Christianity and Judaism*, edited by G. R. McDermott, 51–68. Bellingham, WA: Lexham Press, 2021.

Moffitt, David M. 'Exodus in Hebrews'. In *Exodus in the New Testament*, edited by Seth M. Ehorn, 174–95. The Library of New Testament Studies 663. London: Bloomsbury T&T Clark, 2022.

Moffitt, David M. 'Boldly Approaching the Throne While Still Waiting for Salvation: The Dynamics of Heavenly Access and Jesus' Awaited Return in Hebrews' Soteriology'. In *The Letter to the Hebrews: Colloquium Biblicum Lovaniense, LXX, July 22-24, 2021*, edited by R. Burnet. Bibliotheca Ephemeridum Theologicarum Lovaniensium. Leuven: Peeters, forthcoming.

Moffitt, David M. and Eric F. Mason, eds. *Son, Sacrifice, and Great Shepherd Studies on the Epistle to the Hebrews*. Wissenschaftliche Untersuchungen zum Neuen Testament 2.510. Tubingen: Mohr Siebeck, 2020.

Montefiore, H. A. *Commentary on the Epistle to the Hebrews*. London: A&C Black, 1964.

Moore, Nicholas J. 'Review of Atonement and the Logic of Resurrection in the Epistle to the Hebrews, by David M. Moffitt'. *Journal of Theological Studies* 64 (2013): 673–5.

Moore, Nicholas J. 'Jesus as "The One who Entered his Rest": The Christological Reading of Hebrews 4.10'. *Journal for the Study of the New Testament* 36.4 (2014): 383–400.

Moore, Nicholas J. *Repetition in Hebrews: Plurality and Singularity in the Letter to the Hebrews, Its Ancient Context, and the Early Church*. Wissenschaftliche Untersuchungen zum Neuen Testament 2.388. Tübingen: Mohr Siebeck, 2015.

Moore, Nicholas J. '"In" or "Near"? Heavenly Access and Christian Identity in Hebrews'. In *Muted Voices of the New Testament: Readings in the Catholic Epistles and Hebrews*, edited by Katherine M. Hockey, Madison N. Pierce and Francis Watson, 185–98. Library of New Testament Studies 565. London: Bloomsbury T&T Clark, 2017.

Moore, Nicholas J. 'Heaven's Revolving Door? Cosmology, Entrance, and Approach in Hebrews'. *Bulletin for Biblical Research* 29.2 (2019): 187–207.

Moore, Nicholas J. 'Sacrifice, Session and Intercession: The End of Christ's Offering in Hebrews'. *Journal for the Study of the New Testament* 42.4 (2020): 521–41.

Moore, Nicholas J. '"Vaine Repeticions"? Re-evaluating Regular Levitical Sacrifices in Hebrews 9:1–14'. In *Son, Sacrifice, and Great Shepherd Studies on the Epistle to the Hebrews*, edited by David M. Moffitt and Eric F. Mason, 115–34. Wissenschaftliche Untersuchungen zum Neuen Testament 2.510. Tubingen: Mohr Siebeck, 2020.

Moore, Nicholas J. '"The True Tabernacle" of Hebrews 8:2 Future Dwelling with People or Heavenly Dwelling Place?' *Tyndale Bulletin* 72 (2021): 49–71.

Morales, L. Michael. 'Atonement in Ancient Israel: The Whole Burnt Offering as Central to Israel's Cult'. In *So Great a Salvation: A Dialogue on the Atonement in Hebrews*, edited by George H. Guthrie, Jon C. Laansma and Cynthia Long Westfall, 27–39. The Library of New Testament Studies 516. London: Bloomsbury T&T Clark, 2019.

Moret, Jean-René. 'Le rôle du concept de purification dans l'Épître aux Hébreux: une réaction à quelques propositions de David M. Moffitt'. *New Testament Studies* 62.2 (2016): 289–307.
Moret, Jean-René. *Christ, la Loi et les Alliances: Les lettres aux Hébreux et de Paul: regards croisés*. Théologie biblique 3. Berlin: LIT Verlag, 2017.
Morrison, Michael D. *Who Needs a New Covenant? Rhetorical Function of the Covenant Motif in the Argument of Hebrews*. Princeton Theological Monograph Series 85. Eugene, OR: Wipf & Stock, 2008.
Moscicke, Hans M. *The New Day of Atonement: A Matthean Typology*. Wissenschaftliche Untersuchungen zum Neuen Testament 2.517. Tübingen: Mohr Siebeck, 2020.
Mosser, Carl. 'No Lasting City: Rome, Jerusalem and the Place of Hebrews in the History of Earliest "Christianity"'. PhD thesis, University of St Andrews, 2004.
Motyer, Steve. 'The Temple in Hebrews: Is It There?' In *Heaven on Earth: The Temple in Biblical Theology*, edited by T. Desmond Alexander and Simon Gathercole, 177–89. Carlisle: Paternoster, 2004.
Moyise, Steve. 'Intertextuality and the Study of the Old Testament in the New Testament'. In *The Old Testament in the New Testament: Essays in Honour of J. L. North*, edited by Steve Moyise, 14–41. Journal for the Study of the New Testament Supplement Series 189. Sheffield: Sheffield Academic Press, 2000.
Moyise, Steve. *The Old Testament in the New: An Introduction*. London: Continuum, 2001.
Muir, Steven. 'Social Identity in the Epistle to the Hebrews'. In *T&T Clark Handbook of Social Identity in the New Testament*, edited by J. B. Tucker and C. A. Baker, 425–39. London: Bloomsbury T&T Clark, 2014.
Muraoka, Takamitsu. *A Greek-English Lexicon of the Septuagint*. Leuven: Peeters, 2009.
Nairne, Alexander. *The Epistle of Priesthood: Studies in the Epistle to the Hebrews*. Edinburgh: T&T Clark, 1913.
Nash, R. H. 'The Notion of Mediator in Alexandrian Judaism and The Epistle to The Hebrews'. *Westminster Theological Journal* 40.1 (1977): 89–115.
Nelson, Richard D. *Raising up a Faithful Priest*. Louisville: Westminster John Knox, 1993.
Nelson, Richard D. 'He Offered Himself: Sacrifice in Hebrews'. *Interpretation* 57.3 (2003): 251–65.
Neusner, J. *The Idea of Purity in Ancient Israel: The Haskell Lectures, 1972–1973*. Studies in Judaism in Late Antiquity 1. Leiden: Brill, 1973.
Newton, Michael. *The Concept of Purity at Qumran and in the Letters of Paul*. Society for New Testament Studies Monograph Series 53. Cambridge: Cambridge University Press, 2005.
Nihan, Christophe. *From Priestly Torah to Pentateuch: A Study in the Composition of the Book of Leviticus*. Forschungen zum Alten Testament 2.25. Tübingen: Mohr Siebeck, 2007.
Nihan, Christophe. 'Forms and Functions of Purity in Leviticus'. In *Purity and the Forming of Religious Traditions in the Ancient Mediterranean World and Ancient Judaism*, edited by Christian Frevel and Christophe Nihan, 311–67. Dynamics in the History of Religions 3. Leiden: Brill, 2013.
Nihan, Christophe. 'The Templization of Israel: Some Remarks on Blood Disposal and Kipper in Leviticus 4'. In *Text, Time, and Temple: Literary, Historical, and Ritual Studies in Leviticus*, edited by Francis Landy, Leigh M. Trevaskis and Bryan D. Bibb, 94–130. Hebrew Bible Monographs 64. Sheffield: Sheffield Phoenix, 2015.

Nissilä, K. *Das Hohepriestermotiv im Hebräerbrief: Eine exegetische Untersuchung*. Schriften der finnischen exegetischen Gesellschaft 33. Helsinki: Oy Liiton Kirjapaino, 1979.

Orr, Peter. *Exalted Above the Heavens: The Risen and Ascended Christ*. New Studies in Biblical Theology 47. Downers Grove, IL: InterVarsity Press, 2018.

Osborne, Grant R., and George H. Guthrie. *Hebrews: Verse by Verse*. Osborne New Testament Commentaries. Bellingham, WA: Lexham Press, 2021.

Osborne, H. 'Συνείδησις'. *Journal of Theological Studies* 32.126 (1931): 167–79.

Ounsworth, Richard. *Joshua Typology in the New Testament*. Wissenschaftliche Untersuchungen zum Neuen Testament 2.328. Tübingen: Mohr Siebeck, 2012.

Outler, Albert C., and Richard P. Heitzenrater, eds. *John Wesley's Sermons: An Anthology*. Nashville: Abingdon Press, 1991.

Peeler, Amy L. B. *You Are My Son: The Family of God in the Epistle to the Hebrews*. The Library of New Testament Studies 486. London: Bloomsbury T&T Clark, 2014.

Peeler, Amy L. B. 'The Eschatological Son: Christological Anthropology in Hebrews'. In *Anthropology and New Testament Theology*, edited by Jason Maston and Benjamin E. Reynolds, 161–76. The Library of New Testament Studies 529. London: Bloomsbury T&T Clark, 2018.

Pennington, Jonathan T. *Heaven and Earth in the Gospel of Matthew*. Supplements to Novum Testamentum 141. Leiden: Brill, 2007.

Peterson, David. *Hebrews and Perfection: An Examination of the Concept of Perfection in the 'Epistle to the Hebrews'*. Society for New Testament Studies Monograph Series 47. Cambridge: Cambridge University Press, 1982.

Peterson, David. *Possessed by God: A New Testament Theology of Sanctification and Holiness*. New Studies in Biblical Theology. Grand Rapids: Eerdmans, 1995.

Peterson, David. 'Perfection: Achieved and Experienced'. In *The Perfect Savior: Key Themes in Hebrews*, edited by Jonathan Griffiths, 125–45. Nottingham: InterVarsity, 2012.

Peterson, David. *Hebrews: An Introduction and Commentary*. Tyndale New Testament Commentaries 15. Downers Grove, IL: InterVarsity Press, 2020.

Pfitzner, Victor C. *Hebrews*. Abingdon New Testament Commentaries. Nashville, TN: Abingdon Press, 1997.

Philip, Mayjee. *Leviticus in Hebrews: A Transtextual Analysis of the Tabernacle Theme in the Letter to the Hebrews*. Oxford: Peter Lang, 2011.

Pierce, C. A. *Conscience in the New Testament: A Study of Syneidesis in the New Testament*. Studies in Biblical Theology 15. London: SCM, 1955.

Pierce, Madison N. 'Hebrews 3:7–4:11 and the Spirit's Speech to the Community'. In *Muted Voices of the New Testament: Readings in the Catholic Epistles and Hebrews*, edited by Katherine M. Hockey, Madison N. Pierce and Francis Watson, 173–84. Library of New Testament Studies 565. London: Bloomsbury T&T Clark, 2017.

Pierce, Madison N. *Divine Discourse in the Epistle to the Hebrews: The Recontextualization of Spoken Quotations of Scripture*. Society for New Testament Studies Monograph Series 178. Cambridge: Cambridge University Press, 2020.

Pierce, Madison N. 'Testing and Being Tested in the Epistle to the Hebrews'. In *Testing and Temptation in Second Temple Jewish and Early Christian Texts*, edited by Daniel L. Smith and Loren T. Stuckenbruck, 25–38. Wissenschaftliche Untersuchungen zum Neuen Testament 2.510. Tubingen: Mohr Siebeck, 2020.

Pinnock, Clark H. *Flame of Love: A Theology of the Holy Spirit*. Downers Grove, IL: InterVarsity Press, 1996.

Polen, Nehemia. 'Leviticus and Hebrews ... and Leviticus'. In *The Epistle to the Hebrews and Christian Theology*, edited by Richard Bauckham, Daniel R. Driver, Trevor A. Hart and Nathan MacDonald, 213–25. Grand Rapids: Eerdmans, 2009.

Porter, Stanley E. *Verbal Aspect in the Greek of the New Testament: With Reference to Tense and Mood*. Studies in Biblical Greek 1. New York: Peter Lang, 1989.

Porter, Stanley E. *Idioms of the Greek New Testament*. 2nd edn. Sheffield: JSOT Press, 1992.

Porter, Stanley E. 'The Use of the Old Testament in the New Testament: A Brief Comment on Method and Terminology'. In *Early Christian Interpretation of the Scriptures of Israel: Investigations and Proposals*, edited by Craig A. Evans and James A. Sanders, 79–96. Sheffield: Sheffield Academic Press, 1997.

Porter, Stanley E. *Linguistic Analysis of the Greek New Testament: Studies in Tools, Methods, and Practice*. Grand Rapids: Baker Academic, 2015.

Pursiful, Darrell J. *The Cultic Motif in the Spirituality of the Book of Hebrews*. Lewiston, NY: Edwin Mellen, 1993.

Radcliffe, T. 'Christ in Hebrews: Cultic Irony'. *New Blackfriars* 68 (1987): 494–504.

Rascher, Angela. *Schriftauslegung und Christologie im Hebräerbrief*. Beihefte zur Zeitschrift für die neutestamentliche Wissenschaft 153. Berlin: de Gruyter, 2007.

Rayburn II, Robert G. *'Yesterday, Today and Forever': The Narrative World of Ψ 94 [Ps 95] as a Hermeneutical Key to Hebrews*. Berlin: Peter Lang, 2019.

Regev, Eyal. *The Temple in Early Christianity: Experiencing the Sacred*. New Haven: Yale University Press, 2019.

Rendtorff, R. 'Another Prolegomenon to Leviticus 17:11'. In *Pomegranates and Golden Bells: Studies in Biblical, Jewish, and Near Eastern Ritual, Law, and Literature in Honour of Jacob Milgrom*, edited by David P. Wright, David Noel Freedman and Avi Hurvitz, 23–8. Winona Lake, IN: Eisenbrauns, 1995.

Retief, C. W. 'A Messianic Reading of Psalm 8'. *Old Testament Essays* 27.3 (2014): 992–1008.

Rhyder, Julia. *Centralizing the Cult: The Holiness Legislation in Leviticus 17–26*. Forschungen zum Alten Testament 134. Tübingen: Mohr Siebeck, 2019.

Ribbens, Benjamin J. 'Forensic-Retributive Justification in Romans 3:21–26: Paul's Doctrine of Justification in Dialogue with Hebrews'. *Catholic Biblical Quarterly* 74.3 (2012): 548–67.

Ribbens, Benjamin J. *Levitical Sacrifice and Heavenly Cult in Hebrews*. Beihefte zur Zeitschrift für die neutestamentliche Wissenschaft 222. Berlin: de Gruyter, 2016.

Ribbens, Benjamin J. 'Ascension and Atonement: The Significance of Post-Reformation, Reformed Responses to Socinians for Contemporary Atonement Debates in Hebrews'. *Westminster Theological Journal* 80.1 (2018): 1–23.

Ribbens, Benjamin J. 'The Positive Functions of Levitical Sacrifice in Hebrews'. In *Son, Sacrifice, and Great Shepherd Studies on the Epistle to the Hebrews*, edited by David M. Moffitt and Eric F. Mason, 95–113. Wissenschaftliche Untersuchungen zum Neuen Testament 2.510. Tubingen: Mohr Siebeck, 2020.

Ribbens, Benjamin J. 'The Sacrifice God Desired: Psalm 40.6–8 in Hebrews 10'. *New Testament Studies* 67.2 (2021): 284–304.

Richardson, Christopher A. *Pioneer and Perfecter of Faith: Jesus' Faith as the Climax of Israel's History in the Epistle to the Hebrews*. Wissenschaftliche Untersuchungen zum Neuen Testament 2.338. Tübingen: Mohr Siebeck, 2012.

Ricœur, Paul. *The Symbolism of Evil*. Translated by Emerson Buchanan. New York: Harper & Row Publishers, 1967.

Ricœur, Paul. *The Rule of Metaphor: Multi-disciplinary Studies of the Creation of Meaning in Language*. Translated by Robert Czerny. Toronto: University of Toronto Press, 1975.

Ricœur, Paul. *Hermeneutics and the Human Sciences: Essays on Language, Action, and Interpretation.* Edited and translated by John B. Thompson. Cambridge: Cambridge University Press, 1981.
Riggenbach, Eduard. *Der Brief an die Hebräer.* 3rd edn. Kommentar zum Neuen Testament 24. Wuppertal: Brockhaus, 1987.
Ringleben, Joachim. *Wort und Geschichte: Kleine Theologie des Hebräerbriefes.* Göttingen: Vandenhoeck & Ruprecht, 2019.
Rissi, Mathias. *Die Theologie des Hebräerbriefs: Ihre Verankerung in der Situation des Verfassers und seiner Leser.* Wissenschaftliche Untersuchungen zum Neuen Testament 41. Tübingen: Mohr Siebeck, 1987.
Robertson, A. T. *A Grammar of the Greek New Testament in the Light of Historical Research.* Nashville: Broadman Press, 1934.
Robinson, N. H. G. *Christ and Conscience.* London: James Nisbet, 1956.
Rodriques, Adriani M. *Toward a Priestly Christology: A Hermeneutical Study of Christ's Priesthood.* Lanham, MD: Lexington Books/Fortress Academic, 2018.
Rogan, Wil. 'Purity in Early Judaism: Current Issues and Questions'. *Currents in Biblical Research* 16.3 (2018): 309–39.
Rooke, Deborah W. 'Jesus as Royal Priest: Reflections on the Interpretation of the Melchizedek Tradition in Heb 7'. *Biblica* 81 (2000): 81–94.
Rose, Christian. *Der Hebräerbrief.* Die Botschaft des Neuen Testaments. Göttingen: Vandenhoeck & Ruprecht, 2019.
Rothschild, C. K. *Hebrews as Pseudepigraphon: The History and Significance of the Pauline Attribution of Hebrews.* Wissenschaftliche Untersuchungen zum Neuen Testament 235. Tübingen: Mohr Siebeck, 2009.
Runge, S. E., and C. J. Fresh, eds. *The Greek Verb Revisited: A Fresh Approach for Biblical Exegesis.* Bellingham, WA: Lexham Press, 2016.
Rutledge, Fleming. *The Crucifixion: Understanding the Death of Jesus Christ.* Grand Rapids: Eerdmans, 2015.
Sakenfeld, Katharine Doob, ed. *New Interpreter's Dictionary of the Bible.* 5 vols. Nashville: Abingdon, 2006–9.
Sandmel, S. 'Parallelomania'. *Journal of Biblical Literature* 81 (1962): 1–13.
Sargent, Benjamin. *David Being a Prophet: The Contingency of Scripture upon History in the New Testament.* Beihefte zur Zeitschrift für die neutestamentliche Wissenschaft 207. Berlin: de Gruyter, 2014.
Schenck, Kenneth L. 'Keeping His Appointment: Creation and Enthronement in Hebrews'. *Journal for the Study of the New Testament* 19.66 (1997): 91–117.
Schenck, Kenneth L. *Understanding the Book of Hebrews: The Story Behind the Sermon.* Louisville: Westminster John Knox Press, 2000.
Schenck, Kenneth L. 'A Celebration of the Enthroned Son: The Catena of Hebrews 1'. *Journal of Biblical Literature* 120.3 (2001): 469–85.
Schenck, Kenneth L. *Cosmology and Eschatology in Hebrews: The Settings of the Sacrifice.* Society for New Testament Studies Monograph Series 143. Cambridge: Cambridge University Press, 2007.
Schenck, Kenneth L. 'An Archaeology of Hebrews' Tabernacle Imagery'. In *Hebrews in Contexts*, edited by Gabriella Gelardini and Harold W. Attridge, 240–58. Arbeiten zur Geschichte des antiken Judentums und des Urchristentums 91. Leiden: Brill, 2016.
Schenck, Kenneth L. 'Shadows and Realities'. In *Exploring Intertextuality: Diverse Strategies for New Testament Interpretation of Texts*, edited by B. J. Oropeza and Steve Moyise, 81–92. Eugene, OR: Wipf & Stock, 2016.

Schenck, Kenneth L. *A New Perspective on Hebrews: Rethinking the Parting of the Ways.* Lanham: Fortress Academic, 2019.

Schierse, Franz-Joseph. *Verheissung und Heilsvollendung: Zur theologischen Grundfrage des Hebräerbriefes.* Müchener Theologische Studien 1. Historische Abteilung 9. Munich: Karl Zink, 1955.

Schinkel, A. *Conscience and Conscientious Objections.* Amsterdam: Pallas Publications, 2007.

Schlosser, J. 'La médiation du Christ d'après l'Épître aux Hébreux'. *Revue des sciences religieuses* 63 (1989): 169–81.

Scholer, John M. *Proleptic Priests: Priesthood in the Epistle to the Hebrews.* Journal for the Study of the New Testament: Supplement Series 49. Sheffield: JSOT Press, 1991.

Schönlein, P. 'Zur Entstehung eines Gewissensbegriffes bei Griechen und Römern'. *Rheinisches Museum für Philologie* 112.4 (1969): 289–305.

Schreiner, T. R. *Hebrews.* Biblical Theology for Christian Proclamation. Nashville: B&H, 2015.

Schunack, Gerd. *Der Hebräerbrief.* Zürcher Bibelkommentare 14. Zürich: Theologischer Verlag, 2002.

Schwartz, Baruch J. 'The Prohibitions Concerning the 'Eating' of Blood in Leviticus 17'. In *Priesthood and Cult in Ancient Israel*, edited by Gary A. Anderson and Saul M. Olyan, 34–66. Journal for the Study of the Old Testament Supplement Series 125. Sheffield: JSOT Press, 1991.

Schwartz, Baruch J. 'The Bearing of Sin in the Priestly Literature'. In *Pomegranates and Golden Bells: Studies in Biblical, Jewish, and Near Eastern Ritual, Law, and Literature in Honour of Jacob Milgrom*, edited by David P. Wright, David Noel Freedman and Avi Hurvitz, 3–21. Winona Lake, IN: Eisenbrauns, 1995.

Sedlacek, James E. *The Verbal Aspect Integral to the Perfect and Pluperfect Tense-Forms in the Pauline Corpus: A Semantic and Pragmatic Analysis.* Studies in Biblical Greek 22. New York: Peter Lang, 2022.

Seel, Otto. 'Zur Vorgeschichte des Gewissens-begriffes, im altgriechischen Denken'. In *Festschrift Franz Dornseiff zum 65. Geburtstag*, edited by H. Kusch, 291–319. Leipzig: VEB Bibliographisches Institut, 1953.

Selby, G. S. 'The Meaning and Function of Συνείδησις in Hebrews 9 and 10'. *Restoration Quarterly* 28.3 (1986): 145–54.

Sevenster, J. N. *Paul and Seneca.* Supplements to Novum Testamentum 4. Leiden: Brill, 1961.

She, King L. *The Use of Exodus in Hebrews.* Studies in Biblical Literature 142. New York: Peter Lang, 2011.

Siebenthal, Heinrich von. *Ancient Greek Grammar for the Study of the New Testament.* New York: Peter Lang, 2019.

Siker, Jeffrey S. *Sin in the New Testament.* Oxford: Oxford University Press, 2020.

Silva, Moisés. 'Perfection and Eschatology in Hebrews'. *Westminster Theological Journal* 39.1 (1976): 60–71.

Silva, Moisés, ed. *New International Dictionary of New Testament Theology and Exegesis.* 5 vols. 2nd edn. Grand Rapids: Zondervan, 2014.

Simisi, Seth M. *Pursuit of Perfection: Significance of the Perfection Motif in the Epistle to the Hebrews.* Eugene, OR: Wipf & Stock, 2016.

Sklar, Jay. *Sin, Impurity, Sacrifice, Atonement: The Priestly Conceptions.* Hebrew Bible Monographs 2. Sheffield: Sheffield Phoenix, 2005.

Sklar, Jay. 'Sin and Impurity: Atoned or Purified? Yes!' In *Perspectives on Purity and Purification in the Bible*, edited by Baruch J. Schwartz, David P. Wright, Jeffrey Stackert and Naphtali S. Meshel, 23–4. The Library of Hebrew Bible/Old Testament Studies 474. London: T&T Clark, 2008.

Sklar, Jay. 'Sin and Atonement: Lessons from the Pentateuch'. *Bulletin for Biblical Research* 22 (2012): 267–91.
Sklar, Jay. *Leviticus: An Introduction and Commentary*. Tyndale Old Testament Commentaries 3. Downers Grove, IL: InterVarsity Press, 2013.
Small, B. C. *The Characterization of Jesus in the Book of Hebrews*. Biblical Interpretation Series 128. Leiden: Brill, 2014.
Smillie, Gene. '"The One who is Speaking" in Hebrews 12:25'. *Tyndale Bulletin* 55.2 (2004): 275–94.
Smith, Barry D. *The Meaning of Jesus' Death: Reviewing the New Testament's Interpretations*. London: Bloomsbury T&T Clark, 2017.
Smith, William R. *Lectures on the Religion of the Semites*. Edinburgh: A&C Black, 1889.
Snell, Bruno. *The Discovery of the Mind: The Greek Origins of European Thought*. Translated by T. G. Rosenmeyer. Cambridge: Harvard University Press, 1953.
Sorabji, R. *Moral Conscience Through the Ages: Fifth Century BCE to the Present*. Oxford: Oxford University Press, 2014.
Soskice, Janet M. *Metaphor and Religious Language*. Oxford: Clarendon, 1985.
Sowers, Sidney G. *The Hermeneutics of Philo and Hebrews: A Comparison of the Interpretation of the Old Testament in Philo Judaeus and the Epistle to the Hebrews*. Basel Studies of Theology 1. Richmond, VA: John Knox, 1965.
Spicq, Ceslas. 'La conscience dans le NT'. *Revue biblique* 47 (1938): 50–80.
Spicq, Ceslas. 'Le philonisme de l'Épître aux Hébreux'. *Revue biblique* 56 (1949): 212–42.
Spicq, Ceslas. *L'Épître aux Hébreux*. 2 vols. Etudes Bibliques. Paris: Gabalda, 1952–3.
Spicq, Ceslas. *Notes de lexicographie néo-testamentaire*. 2 vols. Orbis Biblicus et Orientalis 22.2. Fribourg; Göttingen: Éditions Universitaires, Vandenhoeck & Ruprecht, 1978.
Spicq, Ceslas. *Theological Lexicon of the New Testament*. Edited and translated by James D. Ernest. Peabody: Hendrickson, 1994.
Stack, Judith V. *Metaphor and the Portrayal of the Cause(s) of Sin and Evil in the Gospel of Matthew*. Biblical Interpretation Series 182. Leiden: Brill, 2020.
Stanley, Steve. 'Hebrews 9:6–10: The 'Parable' of the Tabernacle'. *Novum Testamentum* 37.4 (1995): 385–99.
Starr, Z. A. *Toward a History of Jewish Thought: The Soul, Resurrection, and the Afterlife*. Eugene, OR: Wipf & Stock, 2020.
Steensgaard, P. 'Time in Judaism'. In *Religion and Time*, edited by N. Balslev and J. N. Mohanty, 63–108. Leiden: Brill, 1993.
Stegemann, Ekkehard W., and Wolfgang Stegemann. 'Does the Cultic Language in Hebrews Represent Sacrificial Metaphors? Reflections on Some Basic Problems'. In *Hebrews: Contemporary Methods—New Insights*, edited by Gabriella Gelardini, 12–23. Biblical Interpretation Series 75. Leiden: Brill, 2005.
Stelzenberger, J. *Syneidesis im Neuen Testament*. Paderborn: F. Schöningh, 1961.
Stelzenberger, J. *Syneidesis bei Origenes: Studie zur Geschichte der Moraltheologie*. Paderborn: F. Schöningh, 1963.
Stelzenberger, J. *Syneidesis, Conscientia, Gewissen: Studie zum Bedeutungswandel eines moraltheologischen Begriffes*. Abhandlungen zur Moraltheologie 5. Paderborn: F. Schöningh, 1963.
Stendahl, J. K. 'The Apostle Paul and the Introspective Conscience of the West'. *The Harvard Theological Review* 56.3 (1963): 118–25.
Sterling, Gregory E. 'Ontology versus Eschatology: Tensions between Author and Community in Hebrews'. *Studia Philonica* 13 (2001): 190–211.

Stewart, Alexander. 'Cosmology, Eschatology, and Soteriology in Hebrews: A Synthetic Analysis'. *Bulletin for Biblical Research* 20 (2010): 545-60.
Steyn, Gert J. *A Quest for the Assumed LXX Vorlage of the Explicit Quotations in Hebrews*. Forschungen zur Religion und Literatur des Alten und Neuen Testaments 234. Göttingen: Vandenhoeck & Ruprecht, 2001.
Steyn, Gert J. 'The Reception of Psalm 95(94):7-11 in Hebrews 3-4'. In *Psalms and Hebrews: Studies in Reception*, edited by Dirk J. Human and Gert J. Steyn, 194-228. The Library of Hebrew Bible/Old Testament Studies 527. London: T&T Clark, 2010.
Stökl ben Ezra, Daniel. *The Impact of Yom Kippur on Early Christianity: The Day of Atonement from Second Temple Judaism to the Fifth Century*. Wissenschaftliche Untersuchungen zum Neuen Testament 163. Tübingen: Mohr Siebeck, 2003.
Stolz, L. *Der Höhepunkt des Hebräerbriefs Hebräer 12,18-29 und seine Bedeutung für die Struktur und die Theologie des Hebräerbriefs*. Wissenschaftliche Untersuchungen zum Neuen Testament 2.263 Tübingen: Mohr Siebeck, 2018.
Stott, Wilfred. 'The Conception of "Offering" in the Epistle to the Hebrews'. *New Testament Studies* 9.1 (1962): 62-7.
Stuckenbruck, L. T. *The Myth of Rebellious Angels: Studies in Second Temple Judaism and New Testament Texts*. Grand Rapids: Eerdmans, 2017.
Stylianopoulos, T. G. 'Shadow and Reality: Reflections on Hebrews 10:1-18'. *Greek Orthodox Theological Review* 17.2 (1972): 215-30.
Svendsen, Stefan N. *Allegory Transformed: The Appropriation of Philonic Hermeneutics in the Letter to the Hebrews*. Wissenschaftliche Untersuchungen zum Neuen Testament 2.269. Tübingen: Mohr Siebeck, 2009.
Swanson, Dwight D. 'Leviticus and Purity'. In *Purity: Essays in Bible and Theology*, edited by Andrew Brower Latz and Arseny Ermakov, 30-48. Eugene, OR: Wipf & Stock, 2014.
Swetnam, James. 'A Suggested Interpretation of Hebrews 9,15-18'. *Catholic Biblical Quarterly* 27 (1965): 373-90.
Swetnam, James. 'Greater and More Perfect Tent: A Contribution to the Discussion of Hebrews 9:11'. *Biblica* 47 (1966): 91-106.
Swetnam, James. *Jesus and Isaac: A Study of the Epistle to the Hebrews in the Light of the Aqedah*. Rome: Biblical Institute Press, 1981.
Sykes, S. W., ed. *Sacrifice and Redemption, Durham Essays in Theology*. Cambridge: Cambridge University Press, 1991.
Szkredka, S. *Sinners and Sinfulness in Luke: A Study of Direct and Indirect References in the Initial Episodes of Jesus' Activity*. Wissenschaftliche Untersuchungen zum Neuen Testament 2.434. Tübingen: Mohr Siebeck, 2017.
Telscher, Guido. *Opfer aus Barmherzigkeit: Hebr 9,11-28 im Kontext biblischer Sühnetheologie*. Forschung zur Bibel 112. Würzburg: Echter, 2007.
Theissen, G. *Untersuchungen zum Hebräerbrief*. Studien zum Neuen Testament 2. Gütersloh: Gütersloher Verlagshaus Gerd Mohn, 1969.
Thiessen, Matthew. 'Hebrews and the End of the Exodus'. *Novum Testamentum* 49 (2007): 353-69.
Thiselton, Anthony C. *The First Epistle to the Corinthians: A Commentary on the Greek Text*. New International Greek Testament Commentary. Grand Rapids: Eerdmans, 2000.
Thomas, Gordon J. 'The Perfecting of Christ and the Perfecting of Believers in Hebrews'. In *Holiness and Ecclesiology in The New Testament*, edited by Kent E. Brower and Andy Johnson, 293-310. Grand Rapids: Eerdmans, 2007.

Thompson, James W. *The Beginnings of Christian Philosophy: The Epistle to the Hebrews*. Catholic Biblical Quarterly Monograph Series 13. Washington: The Catholic Biblical Association of America, 1982.
Thompson, James W. 'EPHAPAX: The One and the Many in Hebrews'. *New Testament Studies* 53.4 (2007): 566–81.
Thompson, James W. *Hebrews*. Paideia. Grand Rapids: Baker Academic, 2008.
Thompson, James W. 'Middle Platonism'. In *Reading the Epistle to the Hebrews: A Resource for Students*, edited by Eric F. Mason and Kevin B. McCruden, 31–52. Resources for Biblical Study 85. Atlanta: SBL, 2011.
Thompson, James W. *Strangers on the Earth: Philosophy and Rhetoric in Hebrews*. Eugene, OR: Wipf & Stock, 2020.
Thornton, T. C. G. 'The Meaning of αἱματεκχυσία in Heb. IX.22'. *Journal of Theological Studies* 15.1 (1964): 63–65.
Thrall, M. 'The Pauline use of συνείδησις'. *New Testament Studies* 14.1 (1967): 118–25.
Thüsing, Wilhelm. 'Lasst uns hinzutreten (Hebr 10:22): zur Frage nach dem Sinn der Kulttheologie im Hebräerbrief'. *Biblische Zeitschrift* 9.1 (1965): 1–17.
Thüsing, Wilhelm. *Studien zur neutestamentlichen Theologie*. Wissenschaftliche Untersuchungen zum Neuen Testament 82. Tübingen: Mohr Siebeck, 1997.
Toorn, Karel van der, Bob Becking and Pieter W. van der Horst, eds. *Dictionary of Deities and Demons in the Bible*. Leiden: Brill, 1995. 2nd Rev. edn. Grand Rapids: Eerdmans, 1999.
Übelacker, Walter. 'Die Alternative Leben oder Tod in der Konzeption des Hebräerbriefs'. In *Lebendige Hoffnung – ewiger Tod?!*, edited by Michael Labahn and Manfred Lang, 235–63. Arbeiten zur Bibel und ihrer Geschichte 24. Leipzig: Evangelische Verlagsanstalt, 2007.
Vanhoye, Albert. 'Longue marche ou accis tout proche? Le context biblique de Hébreux 3,7–4,11'. *Biblica* 49 (1968): 9–26.
Vanhoye, Albert. *Structure and Message of the Epistle to the Hebrews*. Subsidia Biblica 12. Rome: Editrice Pontificio Instituto Biblico, 1989.
Vanhoye, Albert. 'La "Teleiôsis" du Christ: Point capital de la Christologie sacerdotale d'Hébreux'. *New Testament Studies* 42.3 (1996): 321–38.
Vanhoye, Albert. *Old Testament Priests and the New Priest: According to the New Testament*. Translated by J.B. Orchard. Rev. edn. Leominster, Herefordshire: Gracewing 2009.
Vanhoye, Albert. *A Different Priest: The Epistle to the Hebrews*. Translated by Leo Arnold. Rhetorica Semitica. Miami, FL: Convivium, 2011.
Vanhoye, Albert. *The Letter to the Hebrews: A New Commentary*. Translated by Leo Arnold. Mahwah: Paulist Press, 2015.
Vanhoye, Albert. *A Perfect Priest: Studies in the Letter to the Hebrews*. Edited and translated by Nicholas J. Moore and Richard J. Ounsworth. Wissenschaftliche Untersuchungen zum Neuen Testament 2.477. Tübingen: Mohr Siebeck, 2018.
Vermes, Geza. *Scripture and Tradition in Judaism: Haggadic Studies*. Leiden: Brill, 1961.
Villiers, Gerda de. 'Reflections on Creation and Humankind in Psalm 8, the Septuagint and Hebrews'. In *Psalms and Hebrews: Studies in Reception*, edited by Dirk J. Human and Gert J. Steyn, 69–82. The Library of Hebrew Bible/Old Testament Studies 527. London: T&T Clark, 2010.
Vis, Joshua M. 'The Purification Offering of Leviticus and the Sacrificial Offering of Jesus'. PhD diss., Duke University, 2012.
Vis, Joshua M. 'The Purgation of Peoples Through the Purification Offering'. In *Sacrifice, Cult, and Atonement in Early Judaism and Christianity: Constituents and Critique*, edited by Henrietta L. Wiley and Christian A. Eberhart, 33–57. Resources for Biblical Study 85. Atlanta: SBL, 2017.

Walker, Peter. 'A Place for Hebrews? Contexts for a First-Century Sermon'. In *The Letter to the Hebrews: Critical Readings*, edited by Scott D. Mackie, 276–88. T&T Clark Critical Readings in Biblical Studies. London: Bloomsbury T&T Clark, 2018.

Wallace, Daniel B. *Greek Grammar Beyond the Basics: An Exegetical Syntax of the New Testament*. Grand Rapids: Zondervan, 1996.

Walser, Georg. *Old Testament Quotations in Hebrews*. Wissenschaftliche Untersuchungen zum Neuen Testament 2.356. Tübingen: Mohr Siebeck, 2013.

Walton, John H. 'Equilibrium and the Sacred Compass: The Structure of Leviticus'. *Bulletin for Biblical Research* 11 (2001): 293–304.

Warren, E. J. *Cleansing the Cosmos: A Biblical Model for Conceptualizing and Counteracting Evil*. Eugene, OR: Wipf & Stock, 2012.

Wedderburn, A. J. M. 'Sawing Off the Branches: Theologizing Dangerously *Ad Hebraeos*'. *Journal of Theological Studies* 56.2 (2005): 393–414.

Weiss, Hans-Friedrich. *Der Brief an die Hebräer*. 15th edn. Kritisch-exegetischer Kommentar uber das Neue Testament 13. Göttingen: Vandenhoeck & Ruprecht, 1991.

Weiss, Harold. 'Sabbatismos in the Epistle to the Hebrews'. *Catholic Biblical Quarterly* 58 (1996): 674–89.

Welbourne, D. *God-dimensional Man*. London: Epworth Press, 1972.

Wenham, Gordon J. *The Book of Leviticus*. New International Commentary on the Old Testament. Grand Rapids: Eerdmans, 1997.

Westcott, Brooke F. *The Epistle to the Hebrews. The Greek Text with Notes and Essays*. 3rd edn. London: Macmillan, 1920.

Westfall, Cynthia L. *A Discourse Analysis of the letter to the Hebrews: The Relationship between Form and Meaning*. The Library of New Testament Studies 297. London: T&T Clark, 2005.

Westfall, Cynthia L. 'Space and Atonement in Hebrews'. In *So Great a Salvation: A Dialogue on the Atonement in Hebrews*, edited by George H. Guthrie, Jon C. Laansma and Cynthia Long Westfall, 229–48. The Library of New Testament Studies 516. London: Bloomsbury T&T Clark, 2019.

Wevers, John William. *Notes on the Greek Text of Leviticus*. Septuagint and Cognate Studies 44. Atlanta: Scholars Press, 1997.

Whitfield, B. J. *Joshua Traditions and the Argument of Hebrews 3 and 4*. Beihefte zur Zeitschrift für die neutestamentliche Wissenschaft und die Kunde der älteren Kirche 194. Berlin: de Gruyter, 2013.

Whitlark, Jason A. *Resisting Empire: Rethinking the Purpose of the Letter to 'the Hebrews'*. The Library of New Testament Series 484. London: Bloomsbury T&T Clark, 2014.

Wikgren, Allen Paul. 'Patterns of Perdition in the Epistle to the Hebrews'. *New Testament Studies* 6 (1960): 159–67.

Wiley, Henrietta L., and Christian A. Eberhart, eds. *Sacrifice, Cult, and Atonement in Early Judaism and Christianity: Constituents and Critique*. Resources for Biblical Study 85. Atlanta: SBL, 2017.

Wiley, H. Orton. *The Epistle to the Hebrews*. Rev. edn. Kansas City: Beacon Day Press, 1984.

Williamson, Ronald. 'Platonism and Hebrews'. *Scottish Journal of Theology* 16.4 (1963): 415–24.

Williamson, Ronald. *Philo and the Epistle to the Hebrews*. Arbeiten zur Literatur und Geschichte des hellenistischen Judentums 4. Leiden: Brill, 1970.

Williamson, Ronald. 'Hebrews 4:15 and the Sinlessness of Jesus'. *Expository Times* 86 (1974): 4–8.

Willi-Plein, Ina. 'Some Remarks on Hebrews from the Viewpoint of Old Testament Exegesis'. In *Hebrews: Contemporary Methods—New Insights*, edited by Gabriella Gelardini, 25–36. Biblical Interpretation Series 75. Leiden: Brill, 2005.

Witherington III, Ben. *Letters and Homilies for Jewish Christians: A Socio-Rhetorical Commentary on Hebrews, James and Jude.* Downers Grove, IL: InterVarsity Press, 2007.

Wray, Judith H. *Rest as a Theological Metaphor in the Epistle to the Hebrews and the Gospel of Truth: Early Christian Homiletics of Rest.* Society of Biblical Literature Dissertation Series 166. Atlanta: Scholars Press, 1998.

Wright, David P. *The Disposal of Impurity: Elimination Rites in the Bible and in Hittite and Mesopotamian Literature.* Society of Biblical Literature Dissertation Series 101. Atlanta: Scholars Press, 1987.

Wright, David P. 'Two Types of Impurity in the Priestly Writings of the Bible'. *Koroth* 9 (1988): 180–93.

Wright, David P. 'The Spectrum of Priestly Impurity'. In *Priesthood and Cult in Ancient Israel,* edited by Gary A. Anderson and Saul M. Olyan, 150–81. Journal for the Study of the Old Testament Supplement Series 125. Sheffield, JSOT Press, 1991.

Wright, David P., David Noel Freedman and Avi Hurvitz, eds. *Pomegranates and Golden Bells: Studies in Biblical, Jewish, and Near Eastern Ritual, Law, and Literature in Honour of Jacob Milgrom.* Winona Lake, IN: Eisenbrauns, 1995.

Wright, N. T. 'Pictures, Stories, and the Cross: Where Do the Echoes Lead?' *Journal of Theological Interpretation* 11.1 (2017): 49–68.

Young, David. *The Concept of Canon in the Reception of the Epistle to the Hebrews.* The Library of New Testament Studies 658. London: Bloomsbury T&T Clark, 2021.

Young, Norman H. 'ΤΟΥΤ' ΕΣΤΙΝ ΤΗΣ ΣΑΡΚΟΣ ΑΥΤΟΥ (Heb. x. 20): Apposition, Dependent, or Explicative?' *New Testament Studies* 20.1 (1973): 100–4.

Young, Norman H. 'The Impact of the Jewish Day of Atonement Upon the Thought of the New Testament'. PhD diss., University of Manchester, 1973.

Young, Norman H. 'Αἱματεκχυσία: A Comment'. *Expository Times* 90.6 (1979): 180.

Young, Norman H. 'The Gospel According to Hebrews 9'. *New Testament Studies* 27.2 (1981): 198–210.

Ancient index

OLD TESTAMENT

Genesis (Gen.)
1.1	96
1.26-30	128
3.7-13	10, 13
4.7	133
4.10	149
6.5	10 n.66
8.21	10 n.66
14	131
14.17-24	131
42.21	10
43.12 LXX	52 n.157

Exodus (Exod.)
6.6 LXX	79
7.8	76
9.26	76
12	76–9
12.1-7	76
12.1-30	77
12.12	78
12.21-2	76
12.23	77, 80
12.23 LXX	77
13.5	76
13.15 LXX	79
15–40	105
15.13 LXX	79
15.15	76
16.35	57 n.189
19–24	105
24	71, 114
25	43 n.82
25.8 LXX	45 n.97
25.9 LXX	46 n.106, 47 n.117
25.40 LXX	45, 45 n.97, 46 n.106, 47 n.117
26.30 LXX	47 n.117
28.29-30	132 n.54
29.4	118
29.12 LXX	114
29.20-1	118
29.21	118
29.28-42	87 n.187
29.36 LXX	96 n.21
40.12	118 n.154

Leviticus (Lev.)
1–7	105
1.2	105
1.5 LXX	69 n.59
2.1-15	68 n.56
3	147
4	105, 105 n.78
4–5	52, 105 n.71, 105 n.78
4–5 LXX	116 n.138
4.1-2	52 n.161
4.1-35	105 n.76
4.1-5.26 MT	106 n.79
4.1–6.7	105, 147 n.167
4.1–6.18	106 n.79
4.2	51 n.151, 108
4.3	105 n.78
4.3-12	105 n.77
4.7 LXX	114
4.12	52 n.161
4.13	106, 108
4.13 LXX	52
4.13-21	105 n.77
4.14	51 n.151
4.18 LXX	114
4.20 LXX	116, 116 n.138
4.22	51 n.151, 52 n.161, 106, 108
4.22 LXX	106
4.22-3	106
4.22-6	105 n.77
4.23	105 n.78
4.25 LXX	114

4.26 LXX	116, 116 n.138	14.10-31	105 n.71
4.27	51 n.151, 52 n.161, 106, 108	14.12-28	105 n.76
		15.5-6	118 n.154
4.27-8	106, 108	15.14-15	105 n.71
4.27-35	105 n.77	15.29-30	105 n.71
4.30 LXX	114	16	67–8, 105, 105 n.78
4.31 LXX	116 n.138	16.1-28	148
4.34 LXX	114	16.1-34	35
4.35 LXX	116 n.138	16.3	105 n.78
5	105–6	16.3-4	67
5.1	11 n.70	16.4	118 n.154
5.1-13	106	16.5	105 n.78
5.2-3	105 n.76	16.8	68
5.2-5	106	16.10 LXX	116 n.138
5.6 LXX	116 n.138	16.11-14	68
5.10 LXX	116 n.138	16.16	35, 52, 54, 95, 97–8
5.13 LXX	116 n.138	16.19	35, 97, 116
5.14-15	52 n.161	16.21	52
5.14–6.7	106	16.23-8	68
5.16 LXX	116 n.138	16.24	118 n.154
5.17	106, 108	16.25	70
5.17-19	108	16.26	118 n.154
5.18	51 n.151	16.26 LXX	116 n.138
5.18 LXX	52, 116 n.138	16.29-34	148
5.19	106	16.30	68, 95, 98, 116, 147
5.20-5 MT	105 n.76	16.34	95
5.23-6 MT	12, 107	17.1-10	147
5.26 LXX	116 n.138	17.11	114 n.130, 146–8, 146 n.156, 147 n.171
6.1-6	105 n.76		
6.4	106		
6.4-7	12, 107	17.15	118 n.154
7.11-34	147	19.22 LXX	116 n.138
7.33 LXX	69 n.59	20.3	35, 54, 97
8	71	21.15	49 n.136
8.6	118	21.23	35, 54, 97
8.15 LXX	96 n.21, 114	22.6	118 n.154
8.23-30	118	23.26-32	67
8.30	118	24.15	38
9.9 LXX	114	25.29 LXX	74 n.99
10.1-2	35	25.48 LXX	74 n.99
10.2	35		
10.4-5	35	Numbers (Num.)	
10.10	33–4	5.11 LXX	52
11–15	36	13–14	57
11.40	118 n.154	14.33-4	57 n.189
12.6-7	105 n.71	15.22-31	51 n.151, 52, 53
12.7-8	147	16.46-50	68 n.56
13–14	12	18.16 LXX	74 n.99
14.8-9	118 n.154	19	36, 71, 119 n.161

19.1-21	111–12	Psalms (Ps./Pss.)	
19.7-8	118 n.154	1.2	85
19.13	54	2	128 n.21
19.20	35, 54, 97	2.7	128 n.21
19.22	116 n.138	8	127–30, 127 n.11, 128 n.19, 128 n.20, 128 n.21, 128 n.22
23.3-8	87 n.187		
29.7-11	67		
32.13	57 n.189	8.4	127 n.13
35.33	36	8.4a	127 n.13
		8.4b	127 n.13
Deuteronomy (Deut.)		8.4b LXX	127 n.13
2.7	57 n.189	8.5	127
4.17	46 n.104	8.6	127, 129
7.8 LXX	79	8.6b	127
9.26 LXX	79	8.6-8	127
12.11	140 n.112	8.7 LXX	129, 129 n.26
13.15 LXX	79	8.7a LXX	129 n.26
15.15 LXX	79	8.8-9 LXX	129
16.1-8	76	24.4	10
24.18 LXX	79	39.7-9 LXX	84–6
		39.7 LXX	85 n.172
1 Samuel (1 Sam.)		39.9 LXX	85 n.173
24.5	10	40	84–6, 89, 91, 131
25.31	10	40.8	85, 85 n.173
		45.6-7	128 n.21
2 Samuel (2 Sam.)		51.10	10
24.10	10	78.5-67	57 n.189
		78.69	41 n.69
2 Kings (2 Kgs)		94 LXX	52, 57
23.21-3	76	95	57, 57 n.195, 140
		95.10	52 n.154
1 Chronicles (1 Chron.)		105.27-45	57 n.189
6.31	140 n.112	106.6-33	57 n.189
28.12 LXX	47 n.117	110	91 n.205, 129
28.19 LXX	47 n.117	110.1	128 n.21, 129, 132, 143, 145, 155
2 Chronicles (2 Chron.)		110.4	131, 132
30.1-27	76	110.9 LXX	74 n.99
		131.8	140 n.112
Ezra		136.36	57 n.189
6.19-22	76		
		Proverbs (Prov.)	
Nehemiah (Neh.)		8	126 n.4
9.21	57 n.189	17.18 LXX	141 n.122
		22.26 LXX	141 n.122
Job			
15.15	97 n.27	Ecclesiastes (Eccl.)	
27.6 LXX	11	10.20 LXX	11

Isaiah (Isa.)
1.18-20   55
6.1-9   41 n.69
52.13–53.12   81
53.12 LXX   79, 81–2
57.17 LXX   130 n.39
66.1   140 n.112

Jeremiah (Jer.)
2.22   55
17.12   41 n.69
31   21, 117
31.31-4   85
31.33-4   116–17

Ezekiel (Ezek.)
5.11   34 n.16
8.6   34 n.16
8.10   46 n.104
10.3-5   34 n.16
10.18-19   34 n.16
11.22   34 n.16
20.1-31   57 n.189
23.38-9   34 n.16
24.21   34 n.16
36.25-6   119
36.25-7   18
40–8   47
44.7   34 n.16
44.7 LXX   69 n.59
44.15 LXX   69 n.59

Daniel (Dan.)
7.13   130 n.36

Hosea (Hos.)
2.10-23   57 n.189
9.7-8   78 n.129

APOCRYPHA

1 Maccabees (1 Macc.)
13.39   52 n.157

Judith (Jdt.)
5.20   52 n.157

Sirach (Sir.)
17.4   128 n.22

23.2   52 n.157
29.14-19   141 n.122
42.18   11 n.71
51.19   52 n.157

Tobit (Tob.)
3.3   52 n.157

Wisdom of Solomon (Wis.)
7.22   126 n.4
7.25-6   126 n.4
7.26   126 n.4
9.1-4   126 n.4
9.2   126 n.4, 128 n.22
15.17   50 n.141
17.10   11

NEW TESTAMENT

Matthew (Mt.)
21.16   128 n.23
26.17-29   79 n.132
26.28   116 n.137
26.36-46   134

Mark (Mk)
1.4   116 n.137
10.45   147
14.12-25   79 n.132
14.24   114 n.130
14.32-42   134

Luke (Lk.)
1.68   74 n.99
1.77   116 n.137
2.38   74 n.99
2.41   76 n.118
3.33   116 n.137
4.18   116 n.137, 116 n.139
9.31   79 n.132
10.18   96
18.13   95 n.10
21.28   75 n.110
22.15-20   79 n.132
22.40-6   134
24.47   116 n.137

John (Jn)

1.3	126
1.29	79 n.132
1.36	79 n.132
6	57 n.189
6.7	130 n.39
12.31	96
14.6	102 n.57
17.17	89
17.19	89

Acts

2.38	116 n.137
5.2	13 n.85
5.31	116 n.137
7	57 n.189
7.44	47 n.117
10.43	116 n.137
13.38	116 n.137
23.1	13
24.16	13
26.18	116 n.137

Romans (Rom.)

2.15	9, 13
3.24	75 n.110
3.25	147
8.23	75 n.110
8.26	137 n.86
8.34	139
9.1	9, 13
12.1	86
13.1-7	9
13.5	13
14	49

1 Corinthians (1 Cor.)

1.30	75 n.110
3.16-17	43 n.85
4.1–5	9
4.4	13 n.85
5.7	79 n.132
6.2-4	128 n.17
8	49
8.7	13, 13 n.86
8.7-13	13 n.86
8.10	13
8.12	13
10.1-13	57 n.189
10.25	13
10.27	13
10.28	13
10.29	13
15.3	4
15.25-8	129
15.27-8	128 n.23

2 Corinthians (2 Cor.)

1.12	13
4.2	13
5.11	13
5.21	147
12.2	41 n.73

Galatians (Gal.)

3.19-20	142 n.127

Ephesians (Eph.)

1.7	75 n.110
1.14	75 n.110
1.20-2	128 n.23, 129
4.30	75 n.110
5.1-2	86 n.178
6.12	96

Philippians (Phil.)

2.5-11	130
3.21	128 n.23
4.18	86 n.178

Colossians (Col.)

1.14	75 n.110, 116 n.137
1.16	126
1.20	96
2.16-23	49

1 Timothy (1 Tim.)

1.5	13
1.19	13
2.5	142 n.127
3.9	13
4.2	13

2 Timothy (2 Tim.)

1.3	13
2.12	128 n.17

Titus (Tit.)

1.15	13

Hebrews (Heb.)
1–2 130
1.1-3 33, 103
1.1-4 126, 132
1.2 18, 40, 126, 128, 130
1.2b 126
1.3 2, 39, 48 n.124, 49, 53, 69, 74, 75, 82, 89, 94–5, 96, 110, 116, 117, 121, 126, 126 n.4, 129, 136 n.79, 137, 143, 145, 155, 156
1.3-4 39
1.3-14 88
1.3c 126
1.4 148 n.180
1.4-5 130 n.41
1.5 128 n.21, 130
1.5-14 126, 127, 131
1.6 40
1.8 130, 144
1.8-9 128 n.21
1.10 41, 50
1.10-11 31, 44, 154
1.12-13 84 n.170
1.13 127, 128 n.21, 129, 145
1.13-14 129
1.14 76 n.111, 129
2.1 48, 61 n.3
2.1-4 56, 75, 127
2.2 48, 56, 76, 95 n.8
2.3 95 n.8
2.5 18, 40, 127, 129
2.5-6 129
2.5-9 127
2.5-11 88–9
2.5-18 88, 102
2.6-8 127, 128 n.21, 129, 130
2.6b-8 129, 130
2.7a 88, 130
2.7-8 130
2.8 116, 127, 129 n.31
2.9 82 n.154, 88, 130
2.10 82 n.154, 88, 109, 109 n.99, 110
2.10-11
2.11
2.14 77–8, 82 n.154, 88, 88 n.192, 96 n.17, 99, 100, 102, 130, 135–6
2.14-15 76–9, 135, 136 n.76
2.14-18 136
2.15 77, 78
2.16 136, 136 n.76
2.16-18 135–7, 139
2.17 39, 48 n.124, 53, 69, 82 n.154, 94–5, 136–7, 136 n.79, 137
2.17-18 88, 137
2.18 134, 135–6, 137, 138
3.1 40, 69, 133
3.3 148 n.180
3.4 61 n.3
3.6 130
3.7 128, 140
3.7-11 57
3.7-4.11 56, 140
3.8 48, 61 n.3
3.9 50
3.10 52, 57, 57 n.196
3.11 95 n.8, 139
3.12 48, 50, 52, 58
3.13 48, 48 n.124, 140
3.14 40, 109 n.99
3.15 48, 57, 140
3.16 48
3.17 48 n.125, 56, 57 n.196
3.18 48 n.127, 95 n.8, 139
3.19 48, 50
4.1 139
4.3 50, 57, 139
4.4 50, 139
4.5 57, 95 n.8, 139
4.6 48
4.7 48, 57, 140
4.8 140
4.8-9 44
4.10 50

4.11	46 n.109, 48, 57, 139	6.11	109 n.99
		6.12	48, 76 n.111
4.12	56 n.183, 61 n.3	6.17	141
4.13	56, 56 n.183	6.19	43, 69
4.14	39, 41, 130, 137	6.19-20	39, 40, 101
4.14-15	69	6.20	40, 69, 101, 131, 144
4.14-16	40, 118 n.147, 137, 138, 139, 140	7.1-2	131
4.15	40, 48 n.124, 87 n.183, 88, 110, 111 n.113, 134, 135, 137	7.1-28	130, 131
		7.3	109 n.99, 130, 131, 144, 145
		7.4-10	131
4.16	137–8, 139, 150	7.5	100, 100 n.46
5.1	48 n.124, 85, 87, 130, 136–7	7.11	33, 76, 105, 109, 109 n.99, 132, 132 n.50
5.1-4	87		
5.1-10	86–7, 130	7.13-14	132
5.2	52–3, 52 n.155, 87, 137	7.15	132 n.50
		7.15-16	132
5.3	48 n.124, 69, 85, 87, 130	7.16	141
		7.17	141, 144
5.5	69, 130, 130 n.41	7.19	33, 105, 109, 109 n.99, 141
5.5-6	141		
5.5-10	87	7.20	141
5.6	131, 144	7.20-8	69
5.7	75 n.108, 80, 83 n.158, 86, 87, 99, 102, 134–5, 138	7.21	141, 144
		7.22	141, 141 n.122
		7.23-4	131, 141
5.7-8	134–5	7.24	144
5.7-10	131	7.25	69, 109 n.99, 132 n.56, 133, 135, 138–9, 143, 150
5.8	130, 131, 135		
5.8-9	87		
5.9	109, 109 n.99, 110		
5.10	69, 131	7.26	39, 41, 41 n.74, 48 n.125, 74, 87, 88, 110
5.11	48		
5.11-6.12	56		
5.12-14	61 n.3	7.26-7	94, 141
5.14	109, 109 n.99, 110	7.26-8	86, 87–8
5.14-6.1	111	7.27	48 n.124, 52, 69, 71 n.71, 82, 85, 87–8, 89, 108, 144
6.1	48, 50, 51, 109, 109 n.99, 110, 116, 134, 156		
		7.28	109, 109 n.99, 110, 137, 144
6.1-2	118		
6.4-8	53	8.1	32 n.6, 41, 126, 132 n.52, 145
6.5	18, 40		
6.6	130	8.1-2	39, 132
6.7-9	61 n.3	8.1-3	69
6.8	95 n.8, 109 n.99	8.1-6	41 n.67, 44, 45, 47, 142
6.10	50		

8.2	32, 42, 43, 45, 69, 143	9.9	2, 14, 14 n.91, 15 n.99, 22, 32, 33, 49, 68, 85, 90, 97, 99, 103, 109, 109 n.99, 113, 154, 156
8.3	69, 85, 99		
8.4	85, 130 n.41		
8.5	42, 43 n.82, 45, 45 n.96, 46 n.109, 46 n.110, 109 n.99, 112		
		9.9-10	32, 33, 98, 103, 105, 109, 154
8.5a	45	9.9-14	49
8.5b	45	9.10	33, 99, 101, 102–3
8.6	76, 142	9.10-14	49
8.7	76	9.11	42, 69, 73, 73 n.96, 80, 100, 109, 109 n.99
8.8	76, 109 n.99, 142		
8.8-12	75, 85, 142		
8.8-13	21, 116	9.11-12	40, 73–5, 79, 79 n.134, 94, 97 n.30
8.9	136 n.76		
8.10	21, 116, 119		
8.12	48, 48 n.124, 95 n.12, 117	9.11-14	31, 73–5, 103, 154
		9.11-17	61
8.13	31, 44, 103, 142, 154	9.12	39, 43, 69, 73, 73 n.96, 74–5, 75 n.108, 75 n.110, 78–9, 82, 97, 144, 148
9.1	42, 42 n.76, 55, 103		
9.1-3	42 n.77		
9.1-5	43 n.84		
9.1-7	31	9.12-14	39, 73, 79 n.134
9.1-8	42	9.12-15	79
9.1-10	31, 32, 68	9.12-17	75–6
9.1-15	102	9.13	49 n.136, 68, 82, 97, 99, 102–3, 109, 111, 115, 118, 119 n.161, 120
9.1-28	41 n.67		
9.2	32 n.9, 42, 43		
9.2-3	68		
9.3	43, 43 n.82, 69, 101	9.13-14	17, 20, 21, 51, 69, 71, 98–9, 103, 109, 111, 113, 118 n.151
9.4	70		
9.5	43, 68, 71, 95 n.12		
9.5b	71	9.14	2, 14, 14 n.91, 15 n.99, 22, 48, 49, 50, 51, 55, 56 n.184, 58, 69, 74, 75, 82, 85, 88, 94, 95, 96, 97, 98, 101, 103, 104, 109, 110, 117, 121, 134, 148, 150, 154, 155, 156
9.6	32 n.9, 42, 42 n.77, 73 n.96, 109 n.99, 132 n.54		
9.7	32 n.3, 42, 42 n.77, 52–3, 55, 68–9, 69 n.59, 71 n.71, 74, 82, 83 n.158, 85, 87, 88, 94, 97, 108, 148		
		9.14-15	90
9.7-14	115	9.15	48, 75, 75 n.108, 75 n.110, 76, 79, 142
9.7-15	69		
9.8	32, 32 n.9, 42, 42 n.77, 43, 101		
		9.15-17	75–6, 82, 85, 142
9.8-9	32 n.8	9.15-19	73

9.15-20	115	9.27-8	80–3, 133 n.60
9.16-17	76	9.28	39, 40, 48 n.124, 49, 69, 79, 80–1, 83, 85, 143, 144, 145, 148
9.18	82 n.154, 114		
9.18-21	71		
9.18-22	96	9.28a	81
9.18-23	114	10.1	33, 46, 68, 85, 89, 90, 103, 105, 109, 109 n.99, 112, 112 n.120, 139, 144, 145, 150
9.19	115, 118, 119 n.161, 120		
9.19-20	114		
9.20	97		
9.21	71, 82, 114, 115, 118, 119 n.161, 120	10.1-2	90, 103
		10.1-3	69
9.21-2	95	10.1-4	32, 33, 49–50, 68, 83, 109, 111, 112–13, 151, 155
9.22	2, 82, 95 n.8, 96, 97, 113–16, 114 n.129, 117, 121, 148, 155, 156		
		10.1-18	83
		10.2	2, 14, 14 n.91, 15 n.99, 22, 48 n.124, 40–50, 55, 58, 82, 85, 95, 96, 98, 109, 112–13, 117, 121, 154, 155, 156
9.22-3	49, 54, 79, 95		
9.23	2, 39, 41, 45 n.96, 53–4, 69, 82, 94, 95–7, 96 n.16, 96 n.21, 101, 113 n.124, 114, 115, 116, 117, 121, 148, 148 n.180, 155, 156		
		10.2-3	51
		10.2-4	17, 50
		10.3	48 n.124, 49–50, 90, 112, 113, 117, 151, 156
9.23a	97, 116		
9.23-6	90, 97 n.30		
9.23b	97	10.4	2, 48 n.124, 50, 68, 82, 112, 112 n.119, 113, 117, 121, 155, 156
9.24	39, 40, 41, 42, 43, 47, 79, 80–1, 94, 138		
9.24a	81	10.5	40, 85, 86, 88, 90
9.24-5	69, 79, 97 n.30	10.5-10	84–6, 88–90
9.24-6	80, 94, 95, 97, 144	10.5-14	61, 83–90, 84 n.168, 89, 133 n.60
9.24-8	61, 80–3		
9.24b	81		
9.25	43, 68, 69, 74, 79, 82, 83, 85, 89, 94, 97	10.5b-7	84–5
		10.6	48 n.124, 85 n.172, 85 n.174
9.25-6	69, 79, 81, 83	10.6-10	88
9.25-6a	81	10.7	85
9.26	2, 39, 48 n.124, 49, 79–80, 82, 82 n.154, 83, 94, 109 n.99, 117, 121, 148, 155, 156	10.8	48 n.124, 83, 85–6
		10.9	85, 85 n.173
		10.9-10	88
		10.10	83, 83 n.158, 85, 86, 87, 88, 89, 101, 103, 133, 144
9.26b	81		
9.27	77, 80–1	10.10-14	84, 89

10.11	2, 48 n.124, 52, 71 n.71, 82, 85, 89, 108, 112 n.118, 112 n.119, 117, 121, 144–5, 155, 156	10.27	95 n.8
		10.28-9	56, 75
		10.29	49 n.136, 97, 130, 133
		10.30-1	95 n.8
		10.31	56
10.11-12	32	10.32	133 n.64
10.11-14	84, 89–90	10.34	137 n.85
10.12	48 n.124, 83, 85, 89, 90, 144–5	10.35	48
		10.39	48, 95 n.8
10.12-13	126, 145	11.1	11 n.75
10.12-14	39, 49, 69, 144, 148	11.1-40	140
10.14	83–4, 89, 89 n.198, 90, 97, 109, 109 n.99, 110, 133, 144, 145	11.4	85. 148–9, 148 n.180, 149, 149 n.184
		11.6	139, 150
10.15	128	11.9	44
10.16	21, 117, 119	11.9-10	140
10.16-17	21, 85, 116–17, 142	11.10	40, 46, 140
10.17	48 n.124, 117	11.12	41
10.17-18	117, 121, 155	11.13-16	140
10.18	48 n.124, 85, 115–17	11.16	100
		11.17	85
10.19	43, 56, 82, 97, 101, 119, 139, 148, 150	11.19	32 n.8
		11.22	109 n.99
10.19-21	39	11.25	48 n.124
10.19-22	13, 49, 55, 56 n.184, 140, 150	11.28	78, 114 n.133
		11.31	48 n.127
10.20	43, 69, 99, 100, 101, 101 n.51, 102	11.35	75 n.110, 76 n.116
10.20-1	40	11.38	52
10.21-2	101, 142	11.40	109, 109 n.99, 110
10.22	2, 14, 14 n.91, 15, 15 n.99, 15 n.104, 17, 22, 48 n.132, 49, 55, 58, 69, 71, 82, 86, 86 n.176, 90, 98, 101, 103, 104, 109, 115, 118–20, 118 n.151, 121, 139, 148, 150, 154, 156	12.1	48, 48 n.124, 133
		12.2	39, 109, 109 n.99, 126, 145
		12.3	48, 48 n.125
		12.3-4	134
		12.4	48 n.124, 82 n.154
		12.7	86
		12.9	99, 102
		12.10	133
		12.14	133
10.24	50	12.14-29	56
10.24-5	149	12.15	49 n.136
10.25	5, 5 n.17, 48, 58	12.15-16	48 n.129
10.26	48 n.124, 48 n.125, 53	12.18	139, 150
		12.18-21	150
10.26-7	53, 56	12.18-24	150
10.26-39	56	12.20	150

12.22	18, 40, 44, 139, 140, 150	5.2	53 n.162
12.22-3	150	1 John (1 Jn)	
12.23	41, 109, 109 n.99, 110	3.5	79 n.132
12.24	82, 94, 115, 118, 118 n.151, 119 n.161, 120, 141, 142, 148–50, 148 n.180, 149 n.184, 150	Revelation (Rev.) 2.9 5.6 20.6 21-2	96 79 n.132 128 n.17 47
12.25	41, 75, 95 n.8	**JEWISH SOURCES**	
12.25-9	150	**QUMRAN/DEAD SEA SCROLLS**	
12.26	41		
12.28	135	**1QM**	
12.29	61 n.3, 95 n.8	I, 1-17	77 n.126
13.3	86		
13.4	49 n.136	**1QS**	
13.4-5	48 n.129	IV, 20-2	18
13.8	132, 144	VIII, 4-10	43
13.9	138, 139		
13.10	32	**11Q13**	131 n.45
13.10-11	39		
13.11	43, 48 n.124, 69, 69 n.62	**4Q400** 1 I, 14-20	97
13.11-12	70 n.65, 82, 86, 94	1 I, 15-20	97
13.12	82 n.154, 133		
13.14	40, 44, 140	**4Q401**	131 n.45
13.15	82, 86, 100, 100 n.46, 132 n.54	**4Q402**	
13.18	11, 12 n.80, 14, 14 n.91, 15 n.99, 18, 49, 156	1, 3–10 **4Q403**	97
13.20	61 n.3, 82 n.154	1 I, 41-6	41 n.69
13.21	50		
13.24	133	**4Q504** 8 I, 4-5	128 n.22
James (Jas)			
2.17	50	**4QFlor**	
2.26	50	1, 1-19	128 n.21
1 Peter (1 Pet.)		**CD**	
1.18-19	79 n.132	3.7-9	57 n.189
2.19	13	3.12-13	57 n.189
2.24	79 n.132, 81		
3.16	13	**JOSEPHUS**	
3.20-2	118		
3.21	13	*Antiquities of the Jews (Ant.)*	
3.22	128 n.23	1.209	13

1.48	13, 56 n.185	*De decalogo* (*Dec.*)	
1.179-81	131 n.45	2–17	57 n.189
2.25-6	13	41	16 n.111
2.52	13	86–7	12
3.13	13	87	11
3.102-87	32 n.5		
3.123	68 n.58	*Quod deterius potiori insidiari soleat* (*Det. Pot. Ins.*)	
3.181-3	68 n.58		
3.224-57	32 n.5	20	16 n.111
3.320	13	21	16 n.111
4.285-6	13	21.107	43
6.2	141 n.122	107	16 n.111
11.109	76 n.118	146	11 n.72, 12
13.316	12 n.78, 13		
13.414	13	*Quod Deus sit immutabilis* (*Deus Imm.*)	
15.136	76 n.114	122–35	12
16.102-3	13 n.84	126	11
16.103	13	128	11
16.212	13	128–9	12, 107

Against Apion (*Apion.*)

		De ebrietate (*Ebr.*)	
2.77	32 n.5	125	11
2.193-8	32 n.5		
2.218	13	*Against Flaccus* (*Flacc.*)	
		7	11

Jewish War (*War*)

		Quis rerum divinarum heres sit (*Her.*)	
1.453	11, 13 n.83	6	11 n.73, 12
2.280	76 n.118	6–7	12, 12 n.78
2.582	11 n.68, 13 n.83	179	67 n.49
3.501	13		
4.189	13	*De Josepho* (*Jos.*)	
4.193-4	13 n.82	196-7	12
5.213-18	68 n.58		
6.438	131 n.45	*Legum allegoriae* (*Leg. All.*)	
		3.79-82	131 n.45

PHILO OF ALEXANDRIA

Legatio ad Gaium (*Leg. Gai.*)

De Abrahamo (*Abr.*)

		165	11
253	131 n.45	306	138
		341	11 n.73

De cherubim (*Cher.*)

		De opificio mundi (*Op. Mund.*)	
		52	128 n.22
45	141 n.122	84	128 n.22
		128	11, 16

De confusione linguarum (*Conf. Ling.*)

121	11 n.75		

De congressu eruditionis gratia (*Congr.*)

De posteritate Caini (*Poster. C.*)

89.107	67 n.49	48	67 n.49
99	131 n.45	59	11

De praemiis et poenis (Praem. Poen.)
84	11

Quod omnis probus liber sit (Prob.)
99	11
124	11 n.73
149	11

De specialibus legibus (Spec. Leg.)
1.203–4	11, 12
1.235	12, 107
1.257–8	12
1.259–60	12
1.269	12
1.294	16 n.111
2.49	11 n.72, 12
2.148	76 n.118
2.245	76 n.118
4.6	12, 107
4.40	12

De virtutibus (Virt.)
124	11 n.72

De vita Mosis (Vit. Mos.)
2.26	47 n.117
2.26–44	45 n.97
2.74–160	68 n.58
2.81	43
2.81–2	68 n.58
2.81–3	16 n.111
2.107	16 n.111
2.224	76 n.118

PSEUDEPIGRAPHA

1 (Ethiopic) Enoch (1 En.)
6–7	96 n.17
7.1-6	97
10.13	77 n.126
12.3-4	97
14	41 n.69
15.1-7	97
39	139 n.106
45	139 n.106
71.5	41 n.69

2 (Syriac) Baruch (2 Bar.)
4.3-7	47
6.7	70 n.66
73.1	139 n.106
85.9-11	139 n.106

2 (Slavonic) Enoch (2 En.)
22.1-10	41 n.72
31.1-5	128 n.22
58.2-3	128 n.22

3 (Greek) Baruch (3 Bar.)
11	41 n.69
14	41 n.69

3 (Hebrew) Enoch (3 En.)
1.7	41 n.69

4 Ezra
6.45-6	128 n.22
6.54	128 n.22
7.36-8	139 n.106
8.52	139 n.106
13.1	77 n.126
14.29-30	57 n.189

4 Maccabees (4 Macc.)
5.25	137 n.85

Joseph and Asenath (Josh. Asen.)
8.9	139 n.106

Jubilees (Jub.)
1.19-20	78 n.129
1.27	76 n.114
1.29	76 n.114
2.1	76 n.114
2.14	128 n.22
10.5-6	78 n.129
10.11	78
18.18-19	78 n.130
49.2-3	78
49.13-15	77 n.120
50.4	57 n.189

Psalms of Solomon (Pss. Sol.)
17.23-8	128 n.21

Testament of Dan (T. Dan)
5.10-13	139 n.106

Testament of Levi (*T. Levi*)
2.5-9   41 n.69, 41 n.72
3.1-8   41 n.69

Testaments of the Twelve Patriarchs (*Test. XII Patr.*)
4.3-4   7 n.30

RABBINIC SOURCES

Mishnah (=m.)
Qiddushin (*Qidd.*)
1.8   32 n.5

Pesahim (*Pesaḥ.*)
8.1   76 n.118

Yoma
8.9   52 n.157

Babylonian Talmud (=b.)
Pesahim (*Pesaḥ.*)
64b   76 n.118

Sanhedrin (*Sanh.*)
38b   128 n.22

Sukkah
52a   128 n.21

Midrash (=Midr.)
Genesis Rabbah (*Gen. Rab.*)
19.7   41 n.72
44.8   128 n.21

Psalms (*Ps.*)
2.9   128 n.21

EARLY JEWISH AND CHRISTIAN SOURCES

1 Clement (*1 Clem.*)
39.5   97 n.27
41.2   32 n.5

Ascension of Isaiah (*Asc. Isa.*)
7–10   41 n.74
11.12-3   41 n.74

Assumption of Moses (*Ass. Mos.*)
10.1   77 n.126

Barnabas (*Barn.*)
1.4   7 n.30
16.1-10   43
19.12   7 n.30

Confessions (*Conf.*)
11   150 n.191

Didache (*Did.*)
4.14   7 n.30

Hermas, *Vision* (Hermas, *Vis.*)
28.4   7 n.30

Liber Antiquitatum Biblicarum (*LAB*)
19.6-7   57 n.189

OTHER GRECO-ROMAN SOURCES

Aristophanes
Equites (*Eq.*)
184   10

Thesmophoriazusae (*Thesm.*)
476–7   10

Aristotle
Poetics (*Poet.*)
1457b   61 n.7

Rhetoric (*Rhet.*)
1411b   61 n.7

Euripides
Orestes (*Orest.*)
396   10
397   10 n.64
1524   10 n.64

Philostratus
Vita Apollonii (*Vit. Apoll.*)
7.14   10

Plato
Republic (*Rep.*)
2.368d–9a   9 n.59

Plutarch
De sera numinis vindicta (Sera)
554.10   10

Polybius
Historiae (Hist.)
4.86.5   10 n.63

Seneca (the Younger)
Epistulae morales (Ep.)
41.1   17 n.118

Xenophon
Anabasis (Anab.)
1.3.10   10

Author index

Alexander, Philip S. 41 n.69
Anderson, Gary A. 24, 38
Attridge, Harold W. 21, 99 n.39, 135

Backhaus, Knut 17 n.113, 17 n.118
Barnard, Jody A. 118 n.150, 140 n.118
Barr, James 6 n.26
Barrett, C. K. 39, 130
Barry IV, Richard J. 39
Beale, G. K. 23 n.162
Bengel, Johann Albrecht 143 n.144
Bergen, Wesley 108 n.92
Bird, C. 131
Blomberg, Craig L. 127 n.12
Boda, Mark J. 106 n.83, 107
Bosman, Philip R. 6 n.28, 7 n.31, 9, 9 n.58, 10 n.64
Bouquet, Alan C. 156
Bruce, Frederick F. 4 n.11, 57 n.196, 83, 85 n.171, 107, 126

Caird, George B. 62
Chalmers, Stuart P. 14 n.90
Church, Philip 21, 44, 45, 45 n.96, 46, 46 n.106, 47 n.116, 73 n.96, 99
Cockerill, Gareth L. 3 n.7, 43 n.80, 51, 57 n.190, 110 n.103, 126, 131, 132 n.50, 138 n.90, 138 n.94, 140, 142
Cody, Aelred 18 n.123, 19, 19 n.131
Cooper, Mark 23 n.167
Coune, Michel 14 n.90

Davidson, R. M. 47
Davies, J. H. 69 n.59, 69 n.60, 120
Davies Philip A. Jr. 49
Delitzsch, Franz 7, 14, 33 n.12, 42 n.77, 45 n.96, 80, 112 n.117, 142
deSilva, David A. 15 n.98, 56 n.184
Dodds, E. R. 56 n.184
Douglas, Mary 24–5, 25 n.175, 33, 37–8, 54

Dunn, James D. G. 4 n.11, 129
Dyer, Bryan R. 3 n.8

Easter, Matthew C. 86 n.181
Eberhart, Christian A. 68, 86
Eckstein, H. J. 7 n.31, 9
Ellingworth, Paul 85 n.171, 114 n.130, 116 n.139, 137 n.82, 139

Feld, Helmut 63
Feldman, Liane M. 34 n.14
Feldmeier, Reinhard 142 n.128
France, R. T. 129–30
Frevel, Christian 34
Frymer-Kensky, Tikva 35 n.27
Fuhrmann, Sebastian 75 n.108, 136 n.76

Gäbel, Georg 5, 18, 19, 19 n.132, 43 n.84, 44, 64, 64 n.21, 65, 70 n.67, 74 n.97, 84, 84 n.168, 89, 89 n.196, 89, n.198, 91, 96 n.20, 118, 119 n.161, 136 n.79, 141, 145, 156
Gane, Roy E. 51 n.150, 52, 53 n.167, 54 n.175
Gelardini, G. 67 n.48, 70 n.66
Gilders, William K. 72
Ginsburskaya, M. 36
Gorman, Frank H. 72 n.83
Grässer, Erich 12 n.80, 22 n.150, 137 n.84, 141 n.123
Greenberg, James A. 72 n.84, 98 n.32, 104, 105 n.78, 106 n.83, 107 n.86, 107 n.90
Guthrie, George H. 23 n.167, 80 n.138

Hägglund, F. 81 n.142
Hay, David M. 139
Hays, Richard B. 22–3
Hermann, Markus-Liborius 14
Hoffmann, David Zvi 36 n.27
Hofius, Otfried 43 n.82, 82

Hughes, Graham 18 n.120
Hughes, Philip Edgcumbe 19–20
Hundley, Michael B. 24, 34, 71, 104
Hurst, Lincoln D. 39, 45–6

Isaacs, Marie 15, 41, 85 n.171

Jamieson, R. B. 61 n.2, 64–6, 81–2, 89, 145 n.152, 145–6
Janowski, Bernd 79 n.133
Jenson, Philip Peter 55
Jewett, R. 7–8
Johnson, Luke Timothy 20, 22, 50 n.140,
Johnson, Mark 38, 62 n.9
Johnsson, William G. 15–16, 25, 53–4, 57, 83, 97, 114–15, 117

Kähler, Martin 7–8
Karrer, Martin 15, 82 n.154
Käsemann, Ernst 57, 101 n.49
Kazen, Thomas 36 n.33, 38
Kibbe, Michael 64 n.23, 65
Kim, Daniel E. 140 n.109
Kim, Kyu S. 76 n.112, 148 n.180, 149 n.184
Kistemaker, Simon J. 95
Kiuchi, Nobuyoshi 105 n.71, 106 n.83, 107–8
Klawans, Jonathan 35 n.27, 35–8, 48
Knöppler, Thomas 95 n.10
Koester, Craig R. 21, 41, 76–7, 98 n.33, 138
Kraus, Wolfgang 143 n.134

Laansma, Jon C. 139–40
Lakoff, George 38, 62 n.9
Lam, Joseph C. P. 38, 55
Lane, William L. 50–1, 53, 62, 113, 113 n.123, 131 n.42, 149 n.186
Lee, Jihye 40 n.64
Lemos, T. M. 37, 37 n.38
Levine, Baruch A. 108
Lincoln, Andrew T. 140
Lindars, Barnabas, SFF. 2 n.4, 4–6, 15, 62, 104, 153–4
Loader, William R. G. 63–6, 69–70, 97 n.30, 120
Löhr, Hermut 42, 137 n.83
Long, Thomas G. 157
Longenecker, Richard N. 86
Luck, Ulrich 102 n.56

Mackie, Scott D. 14, 40 n.62, 138
MacLeod, D. J. 96 n.16
Marietta, Don E. 7 n.31
Maurer, Christian 8–9
McClymond, Kathryn 68, 68 n.56
McCruden, Kevin B. 109 n.101, 110, 148 n.180
McKelvey, R. J. 39 n.55, 44
Metzger, Bruce M. 70 n.66, 112 n.116, 129 n.26
Michel, Otto 96 n.17, 110
Milgrom, Jacob 26, 34 n.16, 34–5, 35 n.24, 37, 54, 68 n.51, 72, 97, 105 n.71, 106, 106 n.83, 107–8, 116–17, 146 n.154, 147–8, 154–5
Miller, Donald G. 127
Moffatt, James 46 n.114, 94
Moffitt, David M. 63–6, 69–72, 73 n.96, 76 n.116, 78 n.128, 82, 84 n.167, 120 n.167, 129 n.34, 130, 132, 132 n.56, 132 n.59, 133, 133 n.60, 141, 143, 143 n.136, 143 n.143, 145, 146, 148, 151
Montefiore, H. A. 75 n.110
Moore, Nicholas J. 25 n.182, 46 n.105, 74, 132–3, 133 n.60, 141, 143, 145, 151
Morales, L. Michael 85 n.174
Motyer, Steve 44
Moyise, Steve 22–3

Nelson, Richard D. 25 n.184, 82, 104
Neusner, J. 37
Nihan, Christophe 34, 105 n.71

Quinn, Russell D. 129, 130 n.35

Peeler, Amy L. B. 126, 128, 129 n.27
Peterson, David 21, 33 n.13, 110–11
Pfitzner, Victor C. 118 n.149
Philip, Mayjee 45, 69 n.62
Pierce, C. A. 7–8, 8 n.43, 15 n.99
Pinnock, Clark H. 135
Porter, Stanley E. 22 n.155, 74 n.100, 133 n.65

Rascher, Angela 45
Rhyder, Julia 147
Ribbens, Benjamin J. 43, 65 n.35, 65 n.39, 65–6, 91 n.205, 94, 99, 99 n.39, 115 n.136, 147

Ricœur, Paul 38, 56
Rissi, Mathias 41 n.74
Rogan, Wil 36 n.33

Schenck, Kenneth L. 23, 44, 46 n.114, 96
Schinkel, A. 9
Schönlein, P. 7 n.31
Schreiner, T. R. 22, 119
Schwartz, Baruch J. 39, 72, 147 n.170
Selby, G. S. 14–16
Sevenster, J. N. 8 n.43
Simisi, Seth M. 109 n.101
Sklar, Jay 36, 72–3, 106 n.83
Sorabji, R. 9
Soskice, Janet M. 38 n.50, 62 n.3
Spicq, Ceslas 39, 141 n.122
Stegemann, Ekkehard W. 62
Stegemann, Wolfgang 62

Stelzenberger, J. 8
Stolz, L. 142
Stylianopoulos, T. G. 113 n.124

Thomas, Gordon J. 158
Thompson, James W. 17, 99 n.35, 99 n.40
Thornton, T. C. G. 114, 114 n.132

Villiers, Gerda de 127
Vis, Joshua M. 73, 147–8

Walker, Peter 44 n.92
Wallace, Daniel B. 58 n.198, 129 n.31
Wedderburn, A. J. M. 25 n.180
Westcott, Brooke F. 50, 88
Whitlark, Jason A. 77 n.125, 126 n.2
Williamson, Ronald 16 n.110, 40 n.61
Wright, David P. 35 n.27

Subject index

Abel 148–50, 155
Abraham 12, 40, 47, 128, 135–6
Adam 13, 47, 128–9
access
    into the heavenly tabernacle 101–2,
        114–15, 118–19, 123, 139–40
    restricted. *See* defilement, as restricted
        access
    to God 34, 51, 55, 104, 148, 150
    to Zion 150
addressees. *See* recipients
apocalyptic 39–41
apostasy. *See also* sin; temptation, of
    recipients
    in Hebrews 3–4, 53, 56–8, 133, 139, 154
ascension 63, 65, 66
assurance 4–5, 141–4, 148, 150–2, 155
atonement. *See also* blood; offering(s);
    purification; tabernacle; Yom
    Kippur
    Day of. *See* Yom Kippur
    Hebrews scholarship surrounding 5,
        61–5, 138, 143, 145, 151
    in Leviticus 146–8
    lexical terminology concerning 71–3,
        94–5, 146–8
    in relation to intercession. *See*
        intercession, atonement in relation to
    substitutionary 79, 81–2, 147. *See also*
        purification, as ransom; ransom

baptism 4, 48, 103, 118–19. *See also*
    immersion; washings
blood. *See also* atonement; offering(s);
    purification; tabernacle; Yom
    Kippur
    of Abel 148–50, 155
    of Jesus 54, 62, 69, 71–2, 73–5, 93–4,
        101, 106, 111–12, 120, 144–6,
        148–51, 155
    manipulation of 54, 63, 68, 69–70,
        76–7, 114–15, 145–6

as the medium of purgation 82, 93–4,
    96, 97, 114–15, 148, 155
perpetual nature of 143–5, 148–51, 155
as representative of death 62, 64–5, 82,
    146–7
as representative of life 64, 82, 146–7
shedding of 114–15
speaking 82, 148–50
sprinkling of 68, 77–8, 114–15, 118–20,
    145, 149

conscience. *See also* consciousness
    Hebrews scholarship regarding 4–5,
        14–22
    historical development and
        interpretation of 6–14
    Levitical cult in relation to 19–20,
        98–9, 106–9
consciousness. *See also* conscience
    defiled 14–20, 49–50, 53, 55–6
    perfection of 21–2
    purification of. *See* purification, of the
        consciousness
    of sin in Hebrews 4–6, 14–22, 49–50,
        55, 103–4, 133–4, 155–7
    of sin in Leviticus 105–9
covenant
    inauguration 71, 96–7, 114–15
    and Jesus' death 75–6, 82, 85, 114–15,
        117
    new 21, 31, 75–6, 99, 114–15, 117, 132,
        141–2, 149–50
    old 51, 75–6, 99, 105, 109, 114–15,
        149–50

date of Hebrews 4, 32, 32 n.5, 43–4, 103
Dead Sea Scrolls. *See* Qumran
death. *See also* Jesus, death of
    defeat of 77–8
    redemptive. *See* redemption, and Jesus'
        death
    and sacrificial metaphor 61–3

defilement. *See also* impurity; purification; sin; tabernacle; Yom Kippur
  as restricted access 55
  consciousness of 16, 49–51, 117, 154. *See also* consciousness, of sin
  effects of 33–9, 55–8, 150–1, 154
  in the Levitical cult 33–9, 97–8, 105, 147–8, 154
  metaphorical nature of 33–4, 37–9
  of the heavenly tabernacle 53–4, 97–8, 154
  reality of 24–5, 37–9, 53, 117, 154
  sin in relation to 37–9, 49–51, 82, 93, 105, 117, 154–8

enthronement. *See* Jesus, enthronement of

faith 50, 149
  of Jesus. *See* Jesus, faithfulness of
forgiveness
  lexical issues concerning 67, 72–3, 115–17, 155–6
  of sins 3, 4, 21–2, 84 n.168, 133, 134, 136, 137, 138, 149

guilt. *See also* consciousness, of sin in Hebrews
  in Hebrews 15, 21, 56, 56 n.184, 151, 155
  in the Levitical cult 12, 52, 104, 105–9, 120, 155
  offering. *See* offering(s), guilt-reparation
  and shame 9, 56 n.184, 157

holiness
  Christian 90, 133–4
  in Leviticus 33–5, 111
  positional 85, 88–9, 90, 97, 101, 103, 119, 133, 150
Holy of Holies. *See also* tabernacle
  defiled. *See* defilement, in the Levitical cult, of the heavenly tabernacle
  in the earthly tabernacle 42–3, 63, 68, 70, 71, 74, 94, 140
  in the heavenly tabernacle 43, 63, 65, 69, 73, 94, 99, 101, 120, 140, 144, 145, 148, 150
  purified. *See* purification, of the earthly tabernacle, of the heavenly tabernacle

immersion 37. *See also* baptism; washings
impurity 35–7, 48–9. *See also* defilement; sin
  ritual–moral
  types of 35–7, 35 n.27
intercession
  atonement in relation to 95, 132–3, 136, 138–9, 143

James 50
Jerome 7, 7 n.34
Jesus
  body of 40, 83–6, 89, 132
  death of 5–6, 61–6, 69–70, 75–9, 81–3, 90, 114, 116–17, 134, 142, 146–7
  enthronement of 88, 94, 125–7, 130, 137
  faithfulness of 86, 94, 136
  flesh of 40, 87, 99–102
  as guarantor 141–2
  as high priest 66, 69, 73, 87, 89, 90, 94, 95, 110, 125–6, 130–6, 141, 143–5
  incarnation of 88, 90, 101–2, 126–8, 130, 132, 134–5, 137, 142
  as intercessor 95, 132–3, 136, 138–9, 143
  as mediator 76, 142
  obedient life of 40, 67, 74, 83–91, 101–2, 110, 119, 125–6, 130–1, 134–5
  as offering. *See* offering(s)
  perfection of. *See* perfection, of Jesus in Hebrews
  resurrection of 132
  as Son 126–31
  suffering of 63, 70 n.65, 79, 84, 86, 87, 88–89, 101, 102, 110, 134–5
Josephus 11, 13, 153
judgement 56, 80, 148
justification 3, 22 n.150, 153, 156

Law(s) 21, 50, 52, 56, 76, 83, 85, 105, 106, 112, 114–15, 116–17, 119

Melchizedek 130–2
metaphor. *See also* defilement, metaphorical nature of
  sacrifice as 61–2, 64, 86

Middle Platonism 17, 39–40. *See also* Platonism
Moses 42–5, 47, 56, 57, 58, 76, 78, 128, 142, 150, 154
offering(s). *See also* atonement; blood; purification, Yom Kippur
  burnt 67, 85–6
  daily 52, 87, 108
  guilt-reparation 12, 105–7
  of Jesus 94
  of Jesus' blood 51, 61, 69, 73, 79, 93, 94, 108, 117, 119, 125, 143–6, 148, 149, 150, 151, 153, 154–5. *See also* blood, of Jesus
  of Jesus' body 85–6, 88, 89
  of Jesus' life 74, 83, 85–6, 88, 89, 101–2, 119, 126–7, 154
  Jesus' earthly 73, 81–3, 84, 88, 89, 90, 91, 94, 119
  Jesus' heavenly 3, 6, 18–20, 46, 61, 63, 64–5, 66, 69, 72, 73, 80, 81–3, 84, 89, 90, 91, 93, 94, 95, 104, 107–8, 109, 111, 113, 117, 119, 120–1, 125, 127, 136–7, 141, 143–6, 148, 150, 151, 153–6
  Jesus' personal 86–8
  Levitical 17, 18–20, 22, 26, 32, 68, 82, 85–6, 87, 99, 103, 105–9, 112–13, 117, 145, 146–8, 151
  once-for-all 80, 85, 125, 141, 143–5, 151
  perpetual 125, 132 n.59, 143, 144–5, 148, 150, 151, 155. *See also* blood, perpetual nature of
  sin-purification 67, 73, 85–6, 95, 105, 105 n.71, 107
  vegetal 68 n.56

Passover 76–9. *See also* redemption, and the paschal lamb
Paul 8–9, 13 n.86, 14, 49, 50, 66, 86
perfection
  of believers in Hebrews 109–12
  in Hebrews 33, 50, 103, 105, 109–13, 151
  of Jesus in Hebrews 87, 89, 109–11, 131
  Levitical cultic limitations of 49, 83, 105, 109, 112, 132
  and purification 21, 90, 103, 109–13, 151
Philo of Alexandria 11–13, 16–18, 39–40, 46–7, 107, 126, 138, 153, 156

Platonism. *See also* Middle Platonism
  within Hebrews 16–18, 39–40
  terminology 16
purgation. *See* purification
purification. *See also* atonement; blood; defilement; offering(s); sin; Yom Kippur
  of the consciousness 16–22, 50–1, 55–6, 101, 111–13, 117–20, 133–4, 148, 150–1, 155–7
  earthly–heavenly 17–21, 81, 98, 103, 111–13, 155
  of the earthly tabernacle 34, 97, 148
  of the heavenly tabernacle 54, 69, 79, 82, 89, 94–8, 114, 136–7, 142
  internal–external 18–21, 49, 98–9, 102–3, 104, 108–9, 111, 118, 120, 155
  in the Levitical cult 33, 68, 75, 105–9, 111–13, 115–16
  perfection in relation to 21–2, 103, 109, 111–13
  as ransom. *See also* atonement, substitutionary; ransom 72–3
  ritual–moral 48–9
  of sin 94, 116, 126, 130, 155
  as total purgation 90, 103, 109, 111–17, 120–1, 151, 156
purity 12, 25, 34, 37, 55, 96, 97

Qumran 39, 97, 131

ransom 72–3, 75, 77, 82, 146–8. *See also* atonement, substitutionary; purification, as ransom
recipients. *See also* apostasy; temptation, of recipients
  situation of 3–6, 31–3, 56, 58, 133–4, 150
red heifer 37, 70–1, 111–12
redemption. *See also* Passover
  eternal 73–5
  and Jesus' death 73–9
  and the paschal lamb 76–9
repentance 50–1
rest 139–41
ritual 2, 3, 5, 6, 24–5, 104–5, 107–9, 113, 150–1, 154–5

sanctification 72, 73, 89 n.195, 90, 99, 111, 119, 132, 154

sanctuary. *See* tabernacle
sin. *See also* atonement; apostasy; defilement; impurity; temptation
   consciousness of. *See* consciousness, of sin in Hebrews, of sin in Leviticus
   as dead works 50–1, 82
   in Hebrews 48–53
   intentional 12, 51–3, 105, 107, 133
   in Leviticus 33–9
   post-baptismal 4–5, 133
   purification of. *See* purification, of sins, of the consciousness
   remove 54, 73, 80, 82
   take away 82, 83, 89, 112–13, 121, 145
   unintentional 12, 51–3, 94, 105, 106, 107, 108, 133
Stoicism 8, 8 n.43, 16, 87 n.183
suffering
   of Jesus. *See* Jesus, suffering of
   servant 81–3

tabernacle. *See also* temple; Yom Kippur
   curtain 43, 69, 99–102
   defiled. *See* defilement, in the Levitical cult, of the heavenly tabernacle
   earthly 31–2, 34–5, 42–7, 58, 69, 71, 75, 79–80, 103, 105, 114, 148
   in heaven 2, 18–9, 39, 40, 41–7, 53–4, 58, 69, 73, 75, 79–80, 93–8, 101, 112, 114–6, 120, 132, 141–3
   pre-existent 47
   purified. *See* purification, of the earthly tabernacle, of the heavenly tabernacle
   terminology 41–6
   wilderness 45
temple. *See also* tabernacle
   second 32, 39, 41, 43–5
   terminology 43–5
temptation. *See also* apostasy
   and divine help 95, 134, 136, 137–8
   of Jesus 87, 88, 134–6
   of the recipients 5–6, 58, 133–4, 137–8, 150

washings 36. *See also* baptism; immersion

Yom Kippur. *See also* atonement; blood; offering(s); purification; tabernacle
   Hebrews' appropriation of 67, 68–73, 73–6, 79–80, 91, 94–5, 97
   in Leviticus 67–8, 97–8
   Levitical offerings in relation to 105–6, 116
   purpose of 116, 147–8
   sin with regards to 52–3, 108–9

www.ingramcontent.com/pod-product-compliance
Lightning Source LLC
Chambersburg PA
CBHW062218300426
44115CB00012BA/2117